The Cambridge Companion to the
History of Multinationals and Society

Geoffrey Jones and Sabine Pitteloud present the latest research on the global history of multinationals and their impact on society and the environment. Bringing together leading international scholars, these essays survey key themes in our relationship with multinationals, from taxation and corruption to gender and the climate. Though multinationalism is often associated with large corporations like Apple or Nestlé, the contributors highlight the remarkable diversity in multinational strategies and organizational structures. They challenge the idea of an inescapable rise of multinationals by looking beyond the experience of Western countries and considering the effects of dramatic political shifts. Multinationals have often acted opportunistically, with their resilience carrying social costs through the exploitation of weak regulations, corrupt governments, inequalities, poor human rights, and environmental harm. This is an essential introduction to the historical role of multinationals for scholars and students as well as for policymakers and stakeholders navigating today's economic landscape.

GEOFFREY JONES is Isidor Straus Professor of Business History at Harvard Business School. His latest books include *Deeply Responsible Business: A Global History of Values-Driven Leadership*. He is a fellow of the Academy of International Business.

SABINE PITTELOUD is an assistant professor of history at UniDistance Suisse. Her latest book (coedited with Sandra Bott and Janick Schaufelbuehl) is *Environmental Regulation and the History of Capitalism: The Role of Business from Stockholm 1972 to the Climate Crisis*.

Cambridge Companions to History

Cambridge Companions to History provide accessible and thought-provoking introductions to key topics, eras, places and figures, invaluable to both the student and scholar. Edited by leading academics, each volume contains specially commissioned essays by a team of expert contributors from around the world, presenting cutting-edge research and suggesting new paths of inquiry for the reader. Companions are designed not only to offer a comprehensive overview of their chosen topic, but also to provoke debate and discussion. Like the highly successful Cambridge Companions to Literature and Cambridge Companions to Philosophy series, these volumes are ideal for use by students, and will be of interest also to the curious general reader.

A full list of recent titles in the series can be found at the following address: www.cambridge.org/history-companions

The Cambridge Companion to the
History of Multinationals and Society

Edited by
GEOFFREY JONES
Harvard Business School

SABINE PITTELOUD
UniDistance Suisse

CAMBRIDGE
UNIVERSITY PRESS

Shaftesbury Road, Cambridge CB2 8EA, United Kingdom

One Liberty Plaza, 20th Floor, New York, NY 10006, USA

477 Williamstown Road, Port Melbourne, VIC 3207, Australia

314–321, 3rd Floor, Plot 3, Splendor Forum, Jasola District Centre,
New Delhi – 110025, India

103 Penang Road, #05–06/07, Visioncrest Commercial, Singapore 238467

Cambridge University Press is part of Cambridge University Press & Assessment, a department of the University of Cambridge.

We share the University's mission to contribute to society through the pursuit of education, learning and research at the highest international levels of excellence.

www.cambridge.org
Information on this title: www.cambridge.org/9781009679596

DOI: 10.1017/9781009679558

© Cambridge University Press & Assessment 2026

This publication is in copyright. Subject to statutory exception and to the provisions of relevant collective licensing agreements, no reproduction of any part may take place without the written permission of Cambridge University Press & Assessment.

When citing this work, please include a reference to the DOI 10.1017/9781009679558

First published 2026

A catalogue record for this publication is available from the British Library

A Cataloging-in-Publication data record for this book is available from the Library of Congress

ISBN 978-1-009-67959-6 Hardback
ISBN 978-1-009-67960-2 Paperback

Cambridge University Press & Assessment has no responsibility for the persistence or accuracy of URLs for external or third-party internet websites referred to in this publication and does not guarantee that any content on such websites is, or will remain, accurate or appropriate.

For EU product safety concerns, contact us at Calle de José Abascal, 56, 1°, 28003 Madrid, Spain, or email eugpsr@cambridge.org

Contents

List of Figures and Tables	page vii
List of Contributors	viii
Acknowledgments	xv

Introduction: The History of Multinationals and Society   1
GEOFFREY JONES AND SABINE PITTELOUD

Part I   Fashioning Global Worlds

1 Multinationals in Historical Perspective   11
  GEOFFREY JONES AND SABINE PITTELOUD

2 Multinationals and the Environment   38
  ANN-KRISTIN BERGQUIST AND GEOFFREY JONES

3 Multinationals and the Changing Face of Chinese Globalization   64
  ADAM FROST AND SHUANG FROST

4 Multinationals and Global Value Chains   89
  VALERIA GIACOMIN AND ANDREA COLLI

Part II   Governments and Institutions

5 Multinationals and Organized Business   117
  PIERRE EICHENBERGER AND SABINE PITTELOUD

6	Multinationals and Dictatorship MARCELO BUCHELI	144
7	Multinationals and Taxation BORIS GEHLEN AND CHRISTIAN MARX	167
8	Multinationals and Market Integration GRACE BALLOR	191

Part III Stakeholders

9	Multinationals and Labor THOMAS FETZER	217
10	Multinationals and Gender PAULA DE LA CRUZ-FERNÁNDEZ	240
11	Multinationals and Corruption GEOFFREY JONES	266

Part IV Geopolitics

12	Multinationals and Imperialism: The Indian Trajectory CHINMAY TUMBE	293
13	Multinationals and Nationality ALFRED RECKENDREES	313
14	Multinationals, Latin America, and Dependency Theories ANDREA LLUCH AND RORY M. MILLER	338

Index — 363

Figures and Tables

Figures

1.1 Globalization waves in history 1840–2026.   *page* 12
3.1 Chinese foreign direct investment outflows and inflows
     1979–2021 (in 2022 US $ billion).   72

Tables

1.1 World outward FDI stock as a percentage of world output
     1913–2024 (%)   12

Contributors

GRACE BALLOR is an assistant professor of history at Bocconi University. She is the author of *Enterprise and Integration: Big Business and the Making of the Single European Market* (Cambridge University Press, 2026). Her research focuses on the historical political economy of contemporary Europe, the intersections of global capitalism and global governance, and the economic history of climate change. Her work has been published in scholarly journals including *American Historical Review*, *Business History*, *Business & Politics*, *Business History Review*, and *Enterprise & Society*.

ANN-KRISTIN BERGQUIST is a professor of economic history and the director of the Uppsala Center for Business History, Uppsala University. Her research is focused on business history and the environment. She currently leads a research project on the role of transnational business associations in global climate governance, while she is also part of a research program that addresses the political economy of investments in low-carbon technologies. In 2019, she was the guest editor of a special issue on "Business History and the Environment Revisited" in *Business History Review*. Her recent publications include (with Thomas David) "Beyond Planetary Limits! The International Chamber of Commerce, the United Nations, and the Invention of Sustainable Development," *Business History Review* (2023) and (with Mattias Näsman) "Safe before Green! The Greening of Volvo Cars in the 1970s–1990s," *Enterprise & Society* (2023).

MARCELO BUCHELI is a professor at Gies College of Business, University of Illinois at Urbana-Champaign. He studies the political strategies of multinationals in a historical perspective and the integration between management studies and history. His awards include the *Global Strategy Journal* Best Article Prize in 2024, the Mira Wilkins Award of the Business History Conference in 2011, and the *Business History Review* Best Article Award in 2004. He is the author of *Bananas and Business: The United Fruit Company in Colombia, 1899–2000* (New York University Press, 2005), and has published in many scholarly journals including *Business History, Enterprise & Society, Journal of Economic History, Academy of Management Perspectives, Journal of International Business Studies, Journal of Management Studies,* and *Strategic Management Journal.* He is the president-elect of the Business History Conference in the United States for 2026–2027.

ANDREA COLLI is a professor of economic and global history at Bocconi University. His research interests include the history of Italian capitalism and its interactions with the political system, with a particular interest in the relationship between globalization and geopolitics from a historical and contemporary perspective. His most recent book (with Veronica Binda) is *Globalization: A Key Idea for Business and Society* (Routledge, 2024). He is currently teaching masters and executive education courses in the history of international relations, geopolitics, and the impact of geopolitical dynamics over the international economy and business activities.

PAULA DE LA CRUZ-FERNÁNDEZ is a historian of business specializing in multinationals and gender. Her publications include "Marketing the Hearth: Ornamental Embroidery and the Building of the Multinational Singer Sewing Machine Company," *Enterprise & Society* (2015) and *Gendered Capitalism: Sewing Machines and Multinational Business in Spain and Mexico, 1850–1940* (Routledge, 2021). She works as a consultant conducting oral histories and historical research, as well as writing and serving as a research communicator, including for the Business History Conference in the United States.

PIERRE EICHENBERGER is a senior lecturer in international history at the Institute of Political Studies, University of Lausanne. His research focuses on the history of capitalism, business and employers' associations, strikes, and social policy. He is writing, together with Thomas David, a book on the influence of business on global economic governance, entitled *Businesses of the World, Unite! The International Chamber of Commerce and Global Capitalism in the Twentieth Century*. His other publications include *Mainmise sur l'État social: Mobilisation patronale et caisses de compensation en Suisse (1908–1960)* (Alphil–Presses universitaires suisses, 2016) and "Swiss Capitalism, or The Significance of Small Things," *Capitalism: A Journal of History and Economics* (2022).

THOMAS FETZER is an associate professor in the Department of International Relations, Central European University. His research deals with the role of ideas in the international political economy, with a specific focus on economic nationalism, the relationship between economic globalization and labor, and the interconnection between international political economy and security studies. His publications include *Paradoxes of Internationalization: British and German Trade Unions at Ford and General Motors 1967–2000* (Manchester University Press, 2012) and (edited with Stefan Berger) *Nationalism and the Economy: Explorations into a Neglected Relationship* (Central European University Press, 2019).

ADAM FROST is a fellow of the Danish Institute of Advanced Studies and an assistant professor in the Department of Business and Sustainability at Southern Denmark University. He combines archival, ethnographic, and computational methods to explore entrepreneurship and informal organizing, with a focus on emerging market contexts. His recent publications include (with Shuang Frost) "Taxi Shanghai: Entrepreneurship and Semi-colonial Context," *Business History* (2024), "Markets under Mao," *China Quarterly* (2024), and "History from the Dustbins," *Enterprise & Society* (2023). His dissertation "Speculation and Profiteering: The Entrepreneurial Transformation of Socialist China" was awarded the 2023 Herman E. Krooss Prize for Best

Dissertation in Business History by the Business History Conference in the United States.

SHUANG FROST is an assistant professor of digital innovation and business transformation at Aarhus University. Her research adopts ethnographic approaches to explore community-based technological innovations and entrepreneurial actions. Her recent publications include "Creating 'Liminal Community': Communal Liminal Experience and Identity Transformation among Black Women Tech Founders in Detroit," *Academy of Management Learning and Education* (2024) and (with Adam Frost) "Taxi Shanghai: Entrepreneurship and Semi-colonial Context," *Business History* (2021). She is currently the principal investigator of a research project on "Cultivating Women Tech Founders" supported by the Independent Research Fund in Denmark.

BORIS GEHLEN is a professor of business history at the Institute of History, Stuttgart University. His research interests include business history, financial history, and the history of regulation. His publications include *Paul Silverberg (1876–1959): Ein Unternehmer* (Steiner, 2007), *Die Thyssen-Bornemisza-Gruppe: Eine Transnationale Business Group in Zeiten des Wirtschaftsnationalismus (1932–1955)* (Schöningh, 2021), and (edited with Christian Marx and Alfred Reckendrees) *International Business, Multi-nationals, and the Nationality of the Company* (Routledge, 2024). He is a member of the scientific advisory board of the Gesellschaft für Unternehmensgeschichte and chairman of the scientific advisory board of the Institut für Bank- und Finanzgeschichte.

VALERIA GIACOMIN is an assistant professor in the Department of Social and Political Sciences, Bocconi University. Before joining Bocconi, she held postdoctoral positions at Harvard Business School and the University of Southern California. Her research focuses on the plantation economy in Southeast Asia, global value chains, clustering and historical geography, and entrepreneurial history. She is currently writing a book on the impact of agribusiness on the environment since the late nineteenth century. She has published in multiple scholarly journals including *Business History*, *Business History Review*, *Enterprise*

& *Society*, *Management and Organizational History*, *Journal of Global History*, and *Journal of Business Ethics*. Her research on the history of the palm oil industry in late colonial and postcolonial Southeast Asia was awarded the European Business History Association's Best Dissertation Prize in 2018 and the Mira Wilkins Prize at the Business History Conference in 2019.

GEOFFREY JONES is Isidor Straus Professor of Business History at Harvard Business School. He researches the history, social and ecological impact, and responsibility of global business. His books include *Multinationals and Global Capitalism: From the Nineteenth to the Twenty First Century* (Oxford University Press, 2005), *Profits and Sustainability: A History of Green Entrepreneurship* (Oxford University Press, 2017), and *Deeply Responsible Business: A Global History of Values-Driven Leadership* (Harvard University Press, 2023). He is a coeditor of the journal *Business History Review*, a fellow of the Academy of International Business, and an international fellow of the British Academy.

ANDREA LLUCH is a researcher at the National Council of Scientific and Technical Research of Argentina. She is also an associate professor and a member of the Business History Research Group at the School of Management, University of Los Andes. Andrea has been president of the Business History Conference and the Argentine Economic History Association. Additionally, she is a correspondent member of the Academy of History of Argentina. Her latest book (edited with Martín Monsalve Zanatti and Marcelo Bucheli) is *A Business History of Latin America* (Routledge, 2025).

CHRISTIAN MARX is a researcher at the Leibniz Institute for Contemporary History and a lecturer at the University of Trier. His research focuses on the history of National Socialism, corporate networks, central banking, and multinationals in the chemical industry. His publications include "Between National Governance and the Internationalization of Business: The Case of Four Major West German Producers of Chemicals, Pharmaceuticals and Fibres, 1945–2000," *Business History* (2019), "Reorganization of Multinational Companies in the Western European Chemical Industry: Transformations in Industrial Management and Labor, 1960s to 1990s," *Enterprise & Society* (2020), and *Wegbereiter der Globalisierung: Multinationale Unternehmen der westeuropäischen Chemieindustrie in der Zeit nach dem Boom (1960er–2000er Jahre)* (Vandenhoeck & Ruprecht, 2023).

RORY M. MILLER was a reader in international business history at the University of Liverpool Management School. His research interests are in Latin American business history, in particular the strategies of foreign investors in the region since the mid nineteenth century. He is the author of *Britain and Latin America in the Nineteenth and Twentieth Centuries* (Longman, 1993) and *Empresas británicas, economía y política en el Perú, 1850–1934* (Instituto de Estudios Peruanos, 2010). He has also coedited volumes on Peruvian and Chilean economic and business history.

SABINE PITTELOUD is an assistant professor of contemporary history at UniDistance Suisse. Her publications include *Les multinationales suisses dans l'arène politique (1942–1993)* (Droz, 2022), the coedited volume (with Sandra Bott and Janick Schaufelbuehl) *Environmental Regulation and the History of Capitalism: The Role of Business from Stockholm 1972 to the Climate Crisis* (Routledge, 2025), and "Have Faith in Business: Nestlé, Religious Shareholders, and the Politicization of the Church in the Long 1970s," *Enterprise & Society* (2024), which was the winner of the Philip Scranton Best Article prize in 2025 awarded by the Business History Conference in the United States. She is a principal investigator in a research project on "Organized Business and Environmental Governance in Western Europe [1945–1995]" funded by the Swiss National Science Foundation, and serves as coeditor in chief of the journal *Entreprises et histoire*.

ALFRED RECKENDREES is an associate professor of business history at Copenhagen Business School. His research focuses on economic and institutional change in the nineteenth and twentieth centuries, and on entrepreneurship and innovation. His publications include *Die "Deutschland AG": Historische Annäherungen an den bundesdeutschen Kapitalismus* (Klartext, 2013), *Beiersdorf: The Company behind the Brands Nivea, tesa, Hansaplast & Co* (C. H. Beck, 2018), "Economic Nationalism and the Nationality of the Company," *Journal of Modern European History* (2020), and "International Business, Multinationals, and the Nationality of the Company," *Business History* (2022).

CHINMAY TUMBE is an associate professor in economics at the Indian Institute of Management Ahmedabad (IIMA). His research interests are business and economic history and migration studies. He is the author of *India Moving: A History of Migration* (Penguin, 2018) and *The Age of Pandemics, 1817–1920: How They Shaped India and the World* (Harper Collins, 2020). His research articles have been published in scholarly journals including *Science, Business History Review*, and *Business History*. He helped establish the IIMA Archives.

Acknowledgments

This volume is the culmination of years of dedication by business historians to documenting the emergence and evolution of multinational companies, building upon the seminal work of Mira Wilkins in this field. It is also a collective endeavor, shaped through collaboration rather than in isolation.

We extend our deepest gratitude to all participants of the online workshop held on June 20–21, 2024. Despite navigating different time zones, they diligently presented early drafts of their chapters and provided thoughtful feedback on each other's work in progress.

We also wish to highlight the invaluable role of Harvard Business School, a long-standing hub for business history research since the 1920s. It was at Harvard that we first began collaborating in 2021, engaging in discussions over lunches about the societal impact of multinationals. Much has changed since then, making this book all the more timely and relevant.

Finally, we are grateful to UniDistance Suisse for its financial support in bringing this volume to publication.

GEOFFREY JONES AND
SABINE PITTELOUD

Introduction
The History of Multinationals and Society

This Companion volume presents the latest research on the history of multinational enterprises (MNEs) and their impact on society and the environment. Multinational enterprises are often associated with large and powerful corporations like Ford or Coca-Cola. Their products are deeply embedded in our daily lives: waking up in an IKEA bed, being awakened by the alarm on an iPhone, putting on Levi's jeans, drinking a Nescafé before commuting in a Tesla or BYD electric vehicle, reading emails at work on a Lenovo laptop, and ending the day by watching a Metro-Goldwyn-Mayer classic on Netflix. However, these products and services represent just the tip of the iceberg. Behind them lies a complex global production network that integrates capital, labor, and diverse resources from around the world.

It is not necessary to be big to be called an MNE. Indeed, for at least two centuries not only have big businesses crossed national borders but so have many thousands of small and medium-sized firms. A working definition of an MNE is not size, but whether a firm owns and controls assets in more than one country. Simply exporting goods or services usually does not qualify. Owning and controlling assets in foreign countries is called foreign direct investment (FDI) to distinguish it from portfolio investment, which consists of capital flows across borders with no managerial control. It is the difference between an individual buying a few shares on a foreign stock exchange versus US-based software MNE Nvidia acquiring full control of Arm Holdings, a leading British technology company, for US $40 billion in 2020. Often MNEs like Nvidia wholly control their foreign affiliates, but they may also collaborate with other foreign or local firms in joint ventures or engage in cartels. One of the major contributions of business history research has been to show the remarkable heterogeneity of MNE strategies and organization over time.

Equally diverse and far-reaching are the societal impacts of MNEs. By exploiting natural resources worldwide, generating pollution through their production processes or standardizing technical standards, they have profoundly altered the environment and climate. Their products and branding both reflect social values and reshape lifestyles. As major taxpayers and active participants in politics, philanthropy, and public discourse, MNEs have played a significant role in coproducing governance and influencing institutions. Over time, they have interacted with a wide range of political regimes, including colonial administrations, dictatorships, socialist states, and weak governments vulnerable to corruption.

Overall, there is little doubt that MNEs have been and remain major shapers of the global economy and our modern world. The revenues of a handful of MNEs are higher than the GDPs of some nation-states. In 2025 the market capitalization of Tesla was almost as large as the GDPs of Switzerland and Sweden. A form of business organization once dominated by US, European, and Japanese firms has now become far more heterogeneous as Chinese, Indian, and other firms from the Global South have invested internationally. With the expansion of the internet and related technologies, a new cohort of MNEs such as Google and Alibaba have become key players of the world economy. At the same time, the persistence and worsening of major global challenges since the 2000s – particularly climate change and other ecological crises, rising inequality and fiscal deficits, the erosion of democratic legitimacy, and the spread of autocratic alternatives – have sparked growing scrutiny of globalization and of the role MNEs may have played in exacerbating, rather than alleviating, some of these issues.

It has been half a century since Mira Wilkins, the pioneer in studying the history of MNEs, published her two seminal books on the emergence of US-based MNEs before 1914[1] and their subsequent growth between World War I and the 1970s.[2] Their publication was a milestone not only in business history, but for the many other disciplines studying

MNEs. The very concept of a "multinational" had only been belatedly developed by economists in the early 1960s, and there was a widespread assumption at that time that they were primarily a post–World War II phenomenon, and an US one. Since the pathbreaking books by Wilkins were published, there have been decades of research in business history (and other disciplines) on the topic, including by Wilkins herself, which has explored the rich, diverse, and global history of MNEs back to the nineteenth century and earlier.[3]

Multinational enterprises have been variously described as the "global goliaths of the 21st Century"[4] and the "new Leviathans."[5] Much of the formidable body of research on multinationals has had the implicit assumption that MNEs had a linear upward trajectory, even if their growth was sometimes interrupted by world events including wars, revolutions, sudden changes of government, and economic shocks and downturns. Reflecting the assumption of linearity, the discipline of international business, which specializes in studying MNEs, has notoriously focused its attention more on "entry strategies" than exits and divestments. It has also largely implicitly assumed that MNEs had a positive impact on the world.[6]

However, in the words of business historian Alfred D. Chandler and historian of ideas Bruce Mazlish twenty years ago, MNEs have multiple intentional and unintentional impacts on the environment and society, and "we need better knowledge before we pass judgement on our new Leviathans."[7] More recently, international business scholars have also called for a clearer understanding of the societal impact of MNEs, recognizing that studying their long-term effects requires close engagement with the business history literature.[8]

This Companion therefore answers the calls for engaging with the historical evidence to examine the long-term impact of MNEs. History matters in explaining recent grand challenges. It is indeed evident that ecological and social impacts often take time to become visible and therefore need to be examined in a long-term perspective.[9] Moreover, impacts are highly context dependent and new activities do not take place in a vacuum but are heavily influenced by past trajectories. An accumulating body of research has also made it possible for the study of impact to move beyond economic metrics, and to consider a variety of stakeholders.[10] Aggregate cost-benefit analyses often struggle to account for public discontent and tend to overlook the social groups and regions negatively affected by the international strategies of MNEs. Lastly, the growing number of business history case studies across different time periods and geographies has provided nuanced insights into the ongoing and often polarized debates regarding the impacts of MNEs.

The book is organized in four parts. Part I considers the impact of MNEs in fashioning our global world. In Chapter 1, Geoffrey Jones and Sabine Pitteloud draw on the rich business history literature to provide a framework for understanding the emergence and growth of MNEs over time. Chapter 2 by Ann-Kristin Bergquist and Geoffrey Jones examines the environmental impact of MNEs over the long term, highlighting in particular the malign role of natural resource MNEs in the developing world. In Chapter 3, Adam Frost and Shuang Frost emphasize the discontinuities seen in Chinese MNE investment over time, contrasting the remarkable difference between the first global economy before 1929 and the contemporary global era. Their suggestion that the impact of strategies of Chinese MNEs in Africa in recent decades is more positive than that of their predecessors from Europe and the United States demonstrates how historical evidence can be used to challenge excessively broad generalizations about MNEs. In Chapter 4, Valeria Giacomin and Andrea Colli highlight that the global value chains of MNEs created employment in emerging markets, but sometimes at the cost of human rights violations, while technology transfer was limited.

Part II studies the interactions between MNEs, governments, and institutions. Chapter 5 by Pierre Eichenberger and Sabine Pitteloud shows how MNEs organized politically to promote their interests and opportunistically adapted the form of their collective action to changing political circumstances. Chapter 6 by Marcelo Bucheli underscores how MNEs often accommodated authoritarian governments and even actively supported regime change toward dictatorships when facing labor unrest and socialist redistributive policies. In Chapter 7, Boris Gehlen and Christian Marx discuss to what extent the goal of MNEs to maximize profits conflicted with the aim of states to collect fiscal revenue and explore MNE tax avoidance strategies. Chapter 8 by Grace Ballor looks at how MNEs contributed to shape market integration and progressively seized the business opportunities it offered, which led to uneven societal outcomes and public discontent.

Part III deals with how MNEs interacted with and impacted a variety of stakeholders over time. In Chapter 9, Thomas Fetzer discusses the extent to which MNEs transferred labor practices across borders and impacted industrial relations and the power of labor unions. Chapter 10 by Paula de la Cruz-Fernández explores how MNEs contributed to reproduce and globalize gender stereotypes through their products, their hiring practices, and their organization of production, for instance in company towns. Chapter 11 by Geoffrey Jones demonstrates that while the use of corruption by MNEs is intrinsically difficult to document, historical evidence suggests that its use by MNEs, including blue chip ones, has been quite extensive, notably in countries with weaker institutions.

Part IV analyzes how MNEs were impacted by and coped with geopolitical evolutions, including a variety of regime changes. In Chapter 11, Chinmay Tumbe explains why India, despite its large market, only attracted a small portion of world FDI and how the roots of this trajectory are found in the impacts of imperialism and the way subsequent Indian governments regulated FDI after the country's independence. Chapter 12 by Alfred Reckendrees discusses the meaning of nationality for multinationals and illustrates how MNEs proved resilient in a variety of political contexts such as wars, social unrest, and authoritarian regimes thanks to the strategic use of this notion. Chapter 13 by Andrea Lluch and Rory M. Miller revisits from a business history perspective the dependency theories debate in Latin America and shows that market-seeking companies had an overall better developmental track record than resource-seeking ones.

Collectively the chapters in this Companion have three broad conclusions. First, the book emphasizes that the history of MNEs has seen much discontinuity. There have often been assumptions of linearity about the growth of MNEs. Earlier business history contributions have long stressed that growth patterns have been far from linear. There have been exogenous shocks – wars, revolutions, expropriations; dramatic shifts in geographical location – most FDI was located in the non-Western world prior to 1929, then for next fifty years became largely a matter of cross-investment between developed countries. The chapters in this volume challenge even further the idea of teleological development by looking beyond the experience of Western countries.

The historical evidence in this Companion also confirms that MNEs are diverse – organizationally, strategically, and in terms of ethics – and shaped by contexts. While research in international business typically aspires to develop universalist theories, this volume shows how important geographic, institutional, and political contexts are in influencing the nature of MNEs' impact. For example, the chapters show that MNEs were more willing to engage in corruption in countries with weaker institutions. It is also clear that resource-seeking MNEs operating under colonial rules had no interest in aligning their economic goals with the well-being of populations.

Finally, the chapters in this Companion demonstrate that MNEs are a resilient organizational form of business that has survived shocks and changing policy regimes. It has long been accepted that MNEs diffused technologies and employed large amounts of labor, but the historical evidence points to the darker side of things. Resilience had social costs – arbitrage of weak regulations, bribery and corrupt governments, poor human rights records, poor environmental records, and inequality. Overall, MNEs have often behaved in a very opportunistic fashion. Their CEOs and business associations supported political regimes (democratic or not) and regulations that favored their economic operations.

Notes

1. Wilkins, M. *The Emergence of Multinational Enterprise*, Cambridge, MA, Harvard University Press, 1970.
2. Wilkins, M. *The Maturing of Multinational Enterprise*, Cambridge, MA, Harvard University Press, 1974.
3. Wilkins, M. "The History of Multinationals: A 2015 View," *Business History Review* 89, 3 (2015), 405–414.
4. Foley, C. F., Hines, J., and Wessel, D. (eds.) *Global Goliaths: Multinational Corporations in the 21st Century Economy*, Washington, DC, Brookings Institution Press, 2021.
5. Chandler, A. D. and Mazlish, B. (eds.) *Leviathans: Multinational Corporations and the New Global History*, Cambridge, Cambridge University Press, 2005.

6. Jones, G. "Renewing the Relevance of IB: Can Some History Help?" in Verbeke, A., Van Tulder, R., Rose, E. L., and Wei, Y. (eds.) *The Multiple Dimensions of Institutional Complexity in International Business Research.* Bingley, Emerald, 2021, 77–92.
7. Chandler and Mazlish, *Leviathans*, 4.
8. Wiessner, Y. T., Giuliani, E., Wijen, F., and Doh, J. "Towards a More Comprehensive Assessment of FDI's Societal Impact," *Journal of International Business Studies* 55, 1 (2024), 62–63.
9. Fridenson, P. and Scranton, P. *Reimagining Business History*, Baltimore, MD, Johns Hopkins University Press, 2013.
10. Wiessner et al. "Towards a More Comprehensive Assessment," 51, 63.

Part I

Fashioning Global Worlds

GEOFFREY JONES AND
SABINE PITTELOUD

1

Multinationals in Historical Perspective

Business historians have demonstrated that there is nothing new about multinational enterprises (MNEs) and globalization. Their antecedents stretch back centuries. From the nineteenth century MNEs played central roles in the waves of globalization and deglobalization shown in Figure 1.1, which provides a visual – and subjective – representation to highlight trends regarding cross-border integration (especially capital, trade, and migration flows) and the political climate for investors since the nineteenth century.

Multinational enterprises were the immediate drivers of these globalization waves, even though public policies and available technologies shaped the overall context. Table 1.1 provides estimates of the world stock of foreign direct investment (FDI) compared to world output between 1913 and 2024.

Table 1.1 suggests that by 1914 FDI had reached a considerable importance in the world economy. This fell away for much of the twentieth century during the Great Reversal, before MNE investment regained its importance by 1990. It then grew rapidly, although, as will be discussed later, there is evidence of this growth plateauing from the 2010s, or at least taking different forms. This chapter will proceed chronologically looking at the role of MNEs in driving globalization and deglobalization.

1.1 Antecedents to MNEs before the Nineteenth Century

Trade across geographical boundaries dates back for centuries, and actors loosely called merchants were its principal drivers. This has led some

Table 1.1 *World outward FDI stock as a percentage of world output 1913–2024 (%)*

1913	1960	1980	1990	2010	2024
9.0	4.4	4.8	9.6	30.3	30.0

Source: Jones, G. "Origins and Development of Global Business," in da Silva Lopes, T., Lubinski, C., and Tworek, H. J. S. (eds.) *The Routledge Companion to the Makers of Global Business*, New York, Routledge, 2020, 17–34; United Nations Conference on Trade and Development, *World Investment Report 2024*

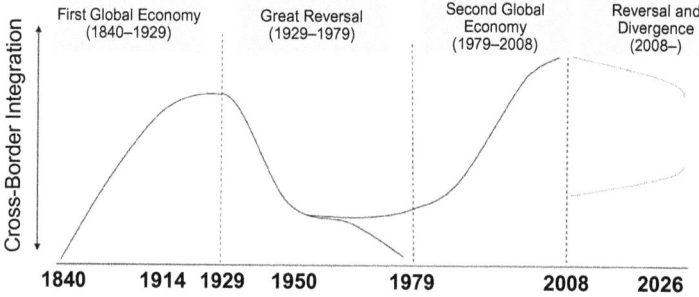

Figure 1.1 Globalization waves in history 1840–2026.
Source: the authors

scholars to define such figures as MNEs. One study identifies the first MNEs existing in the Old Assyrian Kingdom just after 2000 BCE.[1] While most writers are uncomfortable about using the term "multinational enterprises" to describe fluid groups of traders operating in the political contexts of empires rather than nation-states, it is clear that merchants and bankers were active across political boundaries for millennia across China, South Asia, Europe, the Middle East, and Africa and formed key components of diaspora communities.[2] The fifteenth-century Florence-based Medici have been described as the "first multinational bank."[3]

Between the sixteenth and nineteenth centuries European shippers and traders also built international networks centered around shipping captured West Africans across the Atlantic to work as slaves in plantations and mines in the Americas and the Caribbean. European governments "chartered" or gave monopoly powers to groups of merchants who formed quasi-governmental proto-MNEs.[4] An example was the Royal African Company, chartered in Britain in 1672, which was launched to engage in the transatlantic trade in slaves and by the early eighteenth century controlled the British forts in West Africa, which also enabled private slave trading. However, logistical constraints – it could take months or even years for letters containing key information to reach their destinations – were very different than in the nineteenth century and later.[5]

Perhaps the largest of these proto-MNE chartered trading companies was the English East India Company (EIC), chartered in 1600 with a monopoly of trade with Asia, or the "East Indies" as it was called at the time. Alongside its Dutch counterpart and rival, the EIC dominated trade between Europe and Asia in the seventeenth and eighteenth centuries. By the middle of the eighteenth century the EIC had a London head office of 350 administrators, and it functioned as a vertically integrated business that operated along the value chain from the procurement of Asian commodities like spices and tea to their wholesaling in Europe. It also established silk-spinning factories in South Asia. It industrialized the growing of opium in South Asia, which it exported to China in return for tea and other commodities. After 1765 the EIC began collecting revenue in one Indian province after another, supported by its private army.[6] It can be seen as a particularly lawless form of global capitalism at a time when warship diplomacy ruled international relations. Chapter 12 will look in detail at the impact of the EIC on India and the legacy it left.

1.2 Global Business and the First Wave of Globalization 1840–1929

From the mid nineteenth century thousands of firms, largely based in Western countries that had experienced the Industrial Revolution, established operations in foreign countries. Multinational enterprises as organizational forms are generally dated from this period, despite the earlier and lengthy history of business operating across borders. Merchant houses and banks were particularly prominent expanding abroad. The search for raw materials and food led firms to engage in foreign operations too. Meanwhile the first instances of MNEs manufacturing abroad included small Swiss cotton textile firms in the 1830s.[7] This type of MNE expansion was stimulated by the spread of protectionism from the late nineteenth century as manufacturing firms jumped over the tariff barriers that blocked their exports by establishing local production.[8] This strategy was especially evident in chemicals, machinery, and branded consumer products. However, at least one-half of world FDI was invested in natural resources by 1914, and a further one-third in related services, especially financing, insuring, and transporting commodities and foodstuffs.[9]

The firms of different countries varied in their propensity to invest abroad. Britain alone was the home of nearly one-half of world FDI in 1914, and the United States and Germany accounted for a further 14 percent each. Firms from several small European countries, especially the Netherlands, Sweden, and Switzerland, were very active internationally.[10] While Canada, the United States, and Britain occupied the first, second, and eighth places in a listing of the ten largest host economies in 1929, the other countries were (in order) India, Cuba, Mexico, Argentina, Chile, Malaya, and Venezuela. This indicated the importance of resource-seeking FDI.[11]

Both public policy and technology were key to the expansion of MNEs in the first wave of globalization. Regarding the former, the expansion of Western imperialism over much of Asia and Africa, the spread of an international legal system that enforced contracts and private property rights, numerous trade treaties, and the international gold standard reduced the risks of doing business abroad, primarily for firms from the West. Access to capital was facilitated by the growth of large globally oriented capital markets in specialized cities such as London and Paris.[12] Technology had also sharply reduced the cost of distance compared to earlier periods. The advent of steam-driven railroads from the 1830s, and faster sailing ships and then steamships, shrank geographical distance. There was a revolution in communication costs caused by the invention of the electric telegraph. The impact of the telegraph was not immediate, as submarine technology was so expensive it was mainly used by governments and large firms, but over time it became fundamental in enabling the boundaries of firms to expand inside countries and then over borders. It made formal managerial control over distant operations much easier.[13]

The growth of MNEs was enabled by innovation in organizational structures that reduced the risks of operating internationally. There was constant experimentation with organizational design, and the organizational forms employed were heterogeneous.[14] Some MNEs, such as US-based Singer Sewing Machine Company, which accounted for 90 percent of the world's sewing machines by 1914, developed complex organizational structures and managerial hierarchies. It followed what became a classic pattern of growth for MNEs – beginning with building a business in its home market and then expanding internationally.[15] However Singer, and other large MNEs such as J & P Coats and Lever Brothers, coexisted with many small and family-owned firms. There were also thousands of "freestanding" firms – the equivalent to the much discussed "born global" firms of today – which were established with tiny head offices in Britain and the Netherlands to operate internationally and conducted little or no business in their home economies.[16] These freestanding firms often proved robust, employing socialization methods of control in place of formal bureaucracy and formed parts of clusters of businesses, or business groups organized around trading companies.[17]

In the decades before World War I MNEs drove globalization by creating trade flows, constructing marketing channels, building infrastructure, and establishing markets. By 1914 the production and marketing of most of the world's mineral and renewable resources including rubber, tropical fruits, and tea were controlled by US and European MNEs. The commodity chains created by these firms were at the core of world economic integration. Much of the infrastructure of the global economy – the telegraph, ports, railroads, and electricity and gas utilities – was also put in place by international business enterprises. Multinational trading companies both facilitated and created trade flows between developed and developing countries, often investing in creating plantations and opening mines, and the processing of minerals and commodities.[18] European overseas banks built extensive branch networks throughout the Southern Hemisphere and Asia and financed the exchange of manufactured goods for commodities.[19]

World War I was a major exogenous shock for MNEs. The expropriation of German-owned affiliates by US, British, and other Allied governments not only virtually reduced the stock of German FDI to zero, but also signaled the end of the era when MNEs could operate in most countries on the same terms as domestic ones. The Russian Revolution in 1917 resulted in France and Belgium losing two-thirds of their total foreign investment.[20]

Yet MNEs proved resilient in managing some political risks, if not the abolition of the entire capitalist system as in Russia.[21] During the 1920s MNE investments resumed, even if short-term and speculative capital flows became much more prominent in the world economy. There were large foreign investments by US automobile companies Ford and General Motors and many other US-based MNEs.[22] Switzerland-based company Nestlé, which had invested massively in Australia and in the United States during World War I to supply Allied armies, possessed eight factories and a dense commercial network to distribute its dairy products across the globe by 1920.[23] German MNEs reentered foreign markets, sometimes – as has been shown in the case of personal care company Beiersdorf – developing complex organizational structures to "cloak" their German ownership in case of further expropriations in the future.[24]

While MNEs' economic impact in the first global economy was formidable, so were their environmental and social impacts, as chapters in this volume will explore further. Manufacturing MNEs transferred technologies, products, and brands across borders. Companies also transferred the values behind brands. For example, the multinational growth of the beauty industry drove a worldwide homogenization of beauty ideals and practices. The features and habits of White people became established as the benchmarks of global beauty.[25]

Given the absence of appropriate infrastructure in many developing countries, MNEs frequently introduced not only technologies specific to their activities, but also social infrastructures such as police, postal, and education systems. In some cases, they created entire towns: an example was Ford Motor Company's ultimately unsuccessful Fordlândia started in Brazil in 1928.[26] A number of these ventures were noticeably exploitative. William Lever, the founder of the pioneering British soap manufacturer Lever Brothers (which merged with its Dutch equivalent to become Unilever in 1929), acquired a giant concession to grow oil palms in the Belgian Congo in 1911. Lever established a paternalistic model village around his factory at Port Sunlight in

Britain, but Leverville, the equivalent in the Belgian Congo, was characterized by violence, hunger, and sickness, with the inhabitants being virtual slaves.[27]

The impact of this first wave of MNE investment was multifaceted and not always positive. As Chapter 2 explores, the extensive MNE investment in natural resources often had negative environmental consequences. Meanwhile knowledge spillovers from MNE investment to the non-Western world were limited. Most natural resources FDI was highly enclavist. Multinational enterprises were large employers of labor, but expatriates were typically employed in the higher-skilled jobs. Technological diffusion worked best when MNEs went to a country with the institutional arrangements, human capital, and entrepreneurial values to absorb transferred knowledge, much of which was tacit and not readily codified. Multinational enterprises may have been more impactful, as one study of the impact on late colonial western India has shown, in diffusing Western consumer capitalism and "brand-name capitalism."[28]

Many of the gains from the first global economy were unevenly shared. This was most clearly seen in the cases of the huge natural resources concessions that colonial regimes and assorted dictators had granted to Western firms, such as the United Fruit banana plantations in Central America discussed in Chapter 6. To entice firms to make investments in mines, railroads, and so on, foreign firms were often given large, long-term, and tax-free concessions by governments in Latin America and elsewhere. These concessions turned Western companies into supporters of repressive governments and associated Western capitalism with dictatorships and colonial regimes.

Multinational enterprises were significant drivers of this global inequality. As commodity exports surged in Latin America, income inequality soared as the owners of land became wealthy. Meanwhile mining and other extractive Western MNEs employed thousands of local people, typically paid low wages and offered few avenues for improvement. The creators and owners of large global corporations in the United States and Europe also became wealthy. This contributed to the huge rise in income inequality evident by the early 1900s. Inequality and unfairness prompted the growth of unionized labor, labor internationalism, and socialist parties.

1.3 MNEs and the Great Reversal 1929–1979

Multinational enterprises encountered numerous challenges after 1929 as liberal policy regimes gave way to a variety of government restrictions on cross-border integration. If the management of geographical distance had been a major managerial challenge before the 1920s, the management of governments and their policies rose sharply up corporate agendas subsequently. Between 1929 and 1938 the real value of world exports declined by 9.4 percent. By the end of the 1930s half of world trade was affected by tariffs. There was no recovery to 1929 levels until after World War II. The integration of world markets went into reverse.

This globalization reversal happened even though transport and communication innovations continued to reduce the costs of geographical distance. Telephones and automobiles progressively became items of mass consumption, especially in the United States. Air travel became quite widespread, if costly. While new technologies like radio and cinema allowed human beings to discover the world and observe one another as never before, cultural distance and fragmentation remained pervasive, if not exacerbated by these new communication channels. Populism, nationalism, and racism proliferated across countries. Governments sought to block foreign MNEs alongside imports and capital flows and immigrants. Simultaneously, in the context of rising unemployment, investments abroad were also increasingly debated during the interwar period, especially in small outward-oriented economies in Western Europe. For instance, the main watchmakers' business associations and the Swiss government cooperated to establish an official cartel and introduced regulation aimed at preventing relocations by requesting permits to open new factories and by prohibiting the export of watchmaking machines.[29]

The nationality of firms rose rapidly up political agendas after World War I, and receptivity to MNEs did not recover after the end of the war. Although the United States shifted from being the world's largest debtor nation to being a net creditor over the course of World War I, this was accompanied by a growing nationalism that resulted in major restrictions on foreign ownership in shipping, telecommunications, resources, and other industries.[30] However, in some cases foreign nationality could be an asset, as exemplified in Chapter 13. For instance, German

MNEs benefited from not being British in interwar India as nationalists challenged British colonial rule.[31]

After the end of World War II the spread of communism, decolonization, and the subsequent growth of restrictions on foreign MNEs and widespread nationalization of foreign-owned natural resource investments in the developing world combined to dramatically reduce foreign investments beyond the West. By 1980 the six largest hosts for FDI were the United States, Britain, Canada, Germany, France, and the Netherlands. Brazil, the first developing economy, was in seventh place. Australia, Indonesia, and Italy followed.[32]

Although capital and trade flows all fell sharply, MNEs did not disappear during these decades. Several rabidly nationalistic regimes, such as Japan in the 1930s, blocked new foreign investment and squeezed existing foreign-owned businesses. However, Nazi Germany, while it used exchange controls to block profit remittances, exercised few restrictions on foreign businesses beyond requiring that they excluded Jews and others considered undesirable from the management of affiliates in Germany. As a result, US and other foreign firms such as General Motors and IBM were able to sustain growing businesses, albeit ones whose profits they needed to plow back into their German operations, and as a result contributed to strengthening the Nazi state.[33] The ability of MNEs to finance their subsidiaries by plowing back profits, or lending from local banks, meant that their businesses were much less impacted by the interwar collapse of capital flows than might have been expected.

Multinational enterprises were more robust than an aggregate view of markets would suggest. In interwar Britain, as elsewhere, there were significant divestments as manufacturing MNEs closed their affiliates, but there were at least as many new entrants. United States and other firms in fast-growing consumer products such as automobiles – and component industries such as tires – invested heavily in manufacturing in British and foreign markets.[34] There were strong continuities rather than massive disruption in the global maritime world of shipping, trading, and ports.[35]

Numerous international cartels strove to regulate prices and output on a global scale. By the 1930s a high percentage of world trade was controlled by such international cartels. In manufacturing, the world electric lamp cartel controlled three-fourths of world output of electric lamps between the mid 1920s and World War II. Commodities such as oil, tin, aluminum, and tea saw wide-ranging and quite long-lasting international cartels. While they may be seen as part of the story of growth-retarding institutions during this era, it is evident that most cartels were rarely able to control prices and production outputs for too long before new competitors appeared, unless they were strongly supported by governments. More importantly, however, they were often not agents of deglobalization. They rather represented competition by another means and helped perpetuate trade flows by reducing uncertainty. They were sometimes powerful actors in the transfer of knowledge and intellectual property across borders.[36]

Multinational enterprises increasingly cooperated politically during such turbulent times. In the early 1920s the International Chamber of Commerce and the International Organization of Industrial Employers were established to foster international cooperation among businesses about international economic negotiations and the rise of the labor movement. These associations paralleled the creation of the League of Nations in 1920 and of the International Labor Organization in 1919 and ushered in a new era of collective business diplomacy.[37] Multinational enterprises also established various national associations of foreign investors to seek the diplomatic assistance of their home government in case of nationalization or the freeze of their assets abroad, as shown in Chapter 5.

Multinational enterprises faced much greater restrictions after World War II. This explains why the period ranging from 1945 to 1979 can be equally interpreted as the continuation of the Great Reversal and the origins of the second global economy. The Communist states of the Soviet Union, Eastern Europe, and China excluded capitalist firms from their borders. The Communist world resembled an alternative global economy, but one without capitalist firms, at least until the deterioration of political relations between China and the Soviet Union halted attempts at economic integration.[38]

Even beyond the Communist world, much of the world restricted or banned foreign companies in some industries. In European and other developed countries, tight exchange controls enabled governments to vet or sometimes prohibit investments from other firms. In major European economies, including Britain, France, and Italy, large swathes of industry were nationalized and taken out of capitalist control, domestic or foreign. The United States was broadly more open to foreign firms, although they were blocked from sectors considered strategic, including defense, airlines, and broadcast media.[39]

In the postcolonial world the restrictions on global capitalism were much greater. In both Africa and Asia there was widespread restriction and expropriation of foreign firms. The Suez Crisis in 1956 epitomized the twilight of European imperial control over trade flows and economic development. Multinational enterprises and their dedicated business associations, such as the Geneva-based International Association for the Promotion and Protection of Private Foreign Investments, which regrouped US and European businessmen from oil majors, large banks, and multinational companies, promoted the establishment of investment treaties between host and home states to protect foreign operations in this new context.[40] Entrepôts and colonial outposts that remained open to MNEs, such as Singapore and Hong Kong, experienced rapid economic growth, although their equally successful and larger "newly industrializing countries" counterparts South Korea and Taiwan adopted Japanese-style restrictions on MNEs. During the 1970s Western MNEs lost ownership of much of the world's natural resources as Middle Eastern and other governments expropriated assets.

There was optimism among many governments in the Global South, who were asking for a new international economic order that would break past dependencies and enable a path toward successful economic development under local control. The overthrow of the democratically elected socialist government in Chile in 1973 and the infamous involvement of the US-based International Telephone and Telegraph Corporation (ITT) in this coup orchestrated by the Central Intelligence Agency soon broke such hopes. Simultaneously, international organizations, including the Organisation for Economic Co-operation and Development and the International Labour Organization, established the first international guidelines to regulate MNEs, although with little effect due to their nonbinding nature. Political hostility to MNEs kept FDI flows to most of Africa and Asia low. In Asia there was no FDI in China before 1979, and little in Japan and India.[41] As Chapter 12 shows, the Indian government's selective attitude after independence – welcoming FDI only in particular strategic industrial sectors, and the enactment of the Patent Act and the Foreign Exchange Regulation Act in the early 1970s – made the country an unattractive host for MNEs. Fifty-four already established foreign companies had applied to exit India by 1977–1978.[42]

1.4 MNEs and the Origins of the Second Global Economy 1945–1979

After World War II ended MNEs made substantial contributions to the rebuilding of the global economy. Service firms such as management consultancies, advertising agencies, hotels, and film distributors served as significant conduits for the international diffusion of US management practices, values, and lifestyles. Their activities involved limited capital investment compared to manufacturing or mining, which meant that their growing importance could not be captured by FDI data.

As US management consultancies such as McKinsey globalized from the late 1950s, they both created and served markets for consultancy services. They diffused managerial best practice from the United States, initially primarily to Western Europe, where they opened branches.[43] Trading companies developed global networks exploiting information asymmetries. Japan's general trading companies (*sogo shosha*) survived their dismantling by the Allied occupation after World War II to become the central drivers of Japan's foreign trade and FDI.[44] Shipping bulk companies were especially important actors in the postwar boom. A new generation of Greek shipowners headed by Aristotle Onassis and Stavros Niarchos took advantage of regulatory arbitrage opportunities by, for example, registering ships using flags of convenience and basing themselves in tax havens such as Monaco.[45]

Multinational banking also assumed a new importance. As British and US banks took advantage of the Bank of England's liberal policies toward foreign exchange markets during the late 1950s, the development of the Eurodollar markets in London provided a dynamic new source of funding for global capitalism. In the interests of financial stability, governments had sought to tightly regulate their financial markets since the Great Depression and had separated them from each other by exchange controls. The new unregulated Eurocurrency and Eurobond markets soon began to capture a rising share of financial intermediation from regulated domestic markets.[46] The new financial markets were global in scope, but physically located in a small number of financial centers, of which London stood at the apex, with Paris as a second smaller center.[47] Also important were offshore centers in the Caribbean and elsewhere whose primary attraction was not the size of domestic markets, but a combination of light regulation, little taxation, and political stability.[48]

The physical location of international financial markets in a few geographies formed part of a wider pattern of the concentration of business activity in certain cities and regions during the postwar decades. The advantages of proximity and agglomeration drove such patterns. The Silicon Valley computer technology cluster emerged during the 1950s and 1960s, where an unusual convergence of technological skills, educational institutions, and venture capital led to the creation of multiple entrepreneurial firms that grew as global MNEs that dominated innovation in many parts of the information technology industry. In the computer industry it proved impossible for Western European firms, let alone those from emerging markets, to build competitive businesses. Such evolutions did not go unnoticed in some European countries, especially France, initiating a hot public debate about the "American Challenge," even if concrete restrictions on US FDI remained overall limited.[49]

During the 1950s most of the international cartels of the interwar years were dismantled, while US MNEs invested on a large scale in Western Europe, initially in response to a "dollar shortage," which encouraged US firms to establish factories to supply customers in countries that lacked the dollars to buy US products. United States MNEs often located their European headquarters in countries with low taxation, especially Luxembourg, Belgium, and Switzerland.[50] There was initially little rationalized production, and intra-firm trade was low. However, from the 1960s, firms began to seek geographical and functional integration across borders, as examined in Chapter 8. The process of building integrated production systems was difficult. While a European MNE such as Unilever was a prominent proponent of European economic integration from the 1950s, it struggled to achieve regional integration of its own production and marketing facilities.⁵¹ Since full employment prevailed in Western booming economies, the Swiss and German governments introduced policies fostering relocations and outsourcing, especially for the textile sector.⁵²

Global business also often changed its form, rather than disappearing, and resilience remained a prominent feature. Whilst foreign ownership of natural resources vastly declined, especially during the 1970s, foreign orchestration of commodity trade flows and dominance of higher value-added activities did not. World trade in commodities was increasingly handled by giant commodity trading firms such as the grain trader Cargill, the largest private company in the United States. While large integrated oil companies lost control of their oil fields in many countries, they kept control of refineries, tankers, and distribution facilities. New forms of independent trading companies emerged as key players in the global economy. Several of the most important, including André and Philipp Brothers, were either based in Switzerland or used Switzerland-based affiliates to book most of their transactions. Switzerland offered a low-tax environment and corporate secrecy, with the added benefit of not belonging to the United Nations. This enabled the companies to trade with governments, such as that of apartheid-era South Africa, that were subject to trade embargoes. The most noteworthy example was the trading house of Marc Rich, founded in 1974 by disgruntled former employees of Philipp Brothers, which had revenues of US $15 billion by 1980. It flourished as the world's largest independent oil trader by clandestinely selling Iranian oil to Israel and South Africa.⁵³ Renamed Glencore in 1993, the company became a poster child for Western MNE corruption in developing countries, especially Africa, as discussed in Chapter 11.

Multinational enterprises continued to prove adept at pursuing strategies to respond to anti-foreign sentiments or critical governmental policies. They assumed local identities. Unilever retained its large consumer goods business in India and other emerging markets such as Turkey by means of employing local nationals in senior management positions, selling equity shares to local investors, and investing in industries deemed desirable by governments, such as chemicals in India.⁵⁴ Nestlé was also very successful at overcoming government restrictions and at spreading Nescafé instant coffee consumption around the world during the postwar years. Nestlé's lack of adaptation of its commercial practices to sell its baby formula in poor countries would nevertheless lead to one of the most iconic corporate scandals of the twentieth century and to an international boycott of its products.[55]

Many MNEs used development assistance programs to penetrate new markets. For instance, Coca Cola benefited from the United States Agency for International Development to build bottling plants in various parts of the developing world, leading to a surge of consumption of sugary drinks and littering issues.[56] Multinational enterprises also learned that interventionist government policies could work in their favor. In Latin America postwar governments imposed high tariffs to achieve import substitution manufacturing, but they did not prohibit ownership of industries by foreign MNEs. The Brazilian and other Latin American governments offered incentives to attract MNEs to build manufacturing facilities in automobiles and other industries.

1.5 MNEs and the Second Global Economy 1979–2008

As the world spectacularly reglobalized from the 1980s, among the most dramatic policy changes was the worldwide embrace of global capitalism. State planning, exchange controls and other instruments of interventionist policies were abandoned. The most striking change came in China which, after 1978, opened its economy once more to global firms. In 2001 China's joined the World Trade Organization, resulting in significant cuts in Chinese tariffs. A decade earlier the fall of the Berlin Wall and the collapse of the Soviet Union had reopened Eastern Europe to global business. The World Bank and the International Monetary Fund (IMF) advocated developing countries to further attract FDI and to agree to investment treaties and arbitration procedures, which would allow multinational companies to sue governments in case of conflicts over national policies.[57]

As Chapter 8 shows, economic integration in Europe also accelerated with the launch of the Single Market in 1992, which opened new possibilities for economies of scale and standardization. The European Roundtable of Industrialists, a vocal group of CEOs from large European MNEs, were strong supporters of the European single market's four freedoms – that is, the free flows of goods, services, labor, and capital – while strongly opposing social and fiscal harmonization.

On the other side of the Atlantic, Argentina, Brazil, Paraguay, and Uruguay formed the Mercosur free trade area in 1991, which saw a tenfold increase in trade between the participating countries during its first decade. Subsequent tensions between Argentina and Brazil, however, handicapped economic integration. In 1994 the North American Free Trade Agreement (NAFTA) established a free trade zone between the United States, Canada, and Mexico, reinforcing trends toward a regional division of labor. For instance, after a long history of relocations within the United States when facing labor demands and unionism and the opening of the first TV manufacturing plant in Ciudad Juárez under the Mexican government's *maquiladora* plan in 1969, the Radio Company of America (RCA) – which had been acquired by the French-owned company Thomson in 1987 – closed its historical plant in Bloomingdales in 1998.[58] At that time, eight thousand workers were employed by the former RCA in Mexico and more than half of the TVs sold in the United States were assembled in the country.

The role of MNEs in the growth and dynamics of the second global economy was considerable. The ratio of inward FDI stock to GDP rose in the world from 9.6 percent to 30.3 percent between 1990 and 2010. The same increase applied on average to the developed world, but there were outliers. In Britain, inward FDI stock rose from 20.1 percent of GDP to 48.4 percent between 1990 and 2010. The scale of acquisitions of British firms by US MNEs led one author to describe Britain as a "vassal state."[59] In the developing world the ratio of inward FDI stock to GDP increased from 13.4 percent to 29.1 percent.[60]

As during the fast globalization wave during the late nineteenth century, MNEs were drivers of economic integration. There was a striking globalization of many services. These included insurance and reinsurance, where firms such as AIG, Allianz, and Swiss Re expanded globally. In leisure and retailing, the coffee chain Starbucks, which made its first investment outside the United States in Japan in 1996, and retail companies such as Wal-Mart, Zara, and Uniqlo became symbolic of the new global era.

The global significance of MNEs based beyond North America, Western Europe, and Japan also rose. During the 1960s and 1970s, manufacturers based in South Korea and Taiwan began to invest abroad, typically first in other emerging markets. They were usually small-scale and used labor-intensive technology. A second wave of MNEs, based in both East Asia and Latin America, began to expand globally from the 1980s, often after they had built scale and corporate competences in their protected domestic markets. They were prominent in assembly-based and knowledge-based industries including electronics, automobiles, and telecommunications. These investments often originated from firms embedded in the business groups that characterized emerging markets, including the *multilatinas* in Latin America.[61] This was followed by the growth of Chinese MNEs in international markets, as shown in Chapter 3.

The ability of firms from emerging markets to become significant actors in global capitalism rested on several factors. They were sometimes able to leverage incumbent MNEs as customers through subcontracting and other linkages. The spread of management education, as well as the growing number of international students at US business schools, provided firms outside the developed core with well-trained and globally minded managers. Finally, there was a new generation of state-owned or partly state-owned firms, which could invest in building global businesses without the constraint of having to deliver private shareholder returns. In China, state support facilitated the emergence of highly competitive local firms even in high-technology sectors.[62]

The dynamic growth of MNEs, drawn from a widening range of home countries, was apparent. Little or no aggregate evidence remained of spillovers from MNE affiliates to local firms in the same sector, especially in developing countries. Multinational enterprises continued to have no incentive to encourage knowledge leakages to competitors. In many developing countries local firms still lacked the capabilities to compete with large MNEs. Governments sought to attract foreign firms by designating free-trade areas or export-processing zones, most of which failed to attract more than the low value-added, low-skilled segments of industry value chains.

As MNEs moved resources across borders in pursuit of profitability opportunities, they also continued to reinforce trends more than counter them. Despite the availability of technologies that permitted the dispersal of economic activities, global firms served as major actors in the clustering of higher value-added activities in "global cities" and regions such as Silicon Valley and Bangalore. A significant difference with earlier eras was the outsourcing of domestic jobs to foreign countries. Apple, for example, outsourced manufacturing of its iconic iPhones to Taiwan-based Foxconn, which manufactured them in a plant in Zhengzhou, China, where the venture received massive subsidies from the local and provincial governments. In 2017, in response to geopolitical risks, Foxconn and India's Tata Electronics also began assembling the iconic smartphone in India, which by 2025 accounted for 15 percent of world iPhone production.

The aggregate evidence on domestic employment loss and hollowing out in the United States and other developed home economies was not straightforward. However, it is likely that global firms played a significant role in the widening wealth gaps that became a feature of the second global economy. Enabled by the rise of theories of shareholder value and the rapid expansion of stock options, chief executives awarded themselves very large remuneration even as real incomes remained highly subdued, especially in the United States. The second global economy was also characterized by extensive gaming and outright corporate fraud among large global corporations, facilitated by the ability to transfer funds through offshore financial centers that had opaque reporting requirements. They formed part of a patchwork of free ports, loopholes, and legal fictions, all operating outside the borders of nation-states, through which corporate earnings flowed and were magnified.[63]

1.6 MNEs and the Era of Reversal and Divergence since 2008

As in the previous era of globalization, a financial crisis provided a massive exogenous shock to the global economy. The world financial crisis of 2008–2009 was itself the result in part of three decades of the financialization of capitalism, enabled by the deregulation of the financial services industry, which had been tightly regulated by most governments between the 1930s and the 1970s. Global financial assets rose from US $56 trillion in 1990 to US $206 trillion in 2007. Financialization was accompanied by several financial crises – including currency and stock market collapses in Asia in 1997 and the collapse of the US and other stock markets in 2000 – before the collapse of Lehman Brothers, which developed into a full-scale global financial crisis.

The global financial crisis resulted in a severe economic downturn. It was within the context of economic stagnation and rising inequality in many countries that several populist governments came to power that looked upon liberal and cosmopolitan capitalism with disfavor and pursued nationalistic agendas. This trend was first evident in emerging markets such as Turkey, Thailand, and the Philippines, as well as Russia, but subsequently spread to some Western economies characterized by extreme inequality and/or high levels of immigration. Britain's decision in 2016 to leave the European Union (EU) – the so-called Brexit – was motivated by a surge of right-wing populism focused on increasing economic and political sovereignty and expelling unwanted migrants from the EU. The election of Donald Trump as the US president in that year and his reelection eight years later likewise reflected widespread alarm about the scale of illegal immigration into the United States, as well as alienation from an establishment blamed for inequality and lack of opportunity.

The administration of President Donald Trump between 2017 and 2021 saw a surge of trade protectionist and anti-immigrant rhetoric in the United States, as well as the United States' withdrawal from many international agreements such as the Paris climate change agreement signed in 2015. The successor administration of Joe Biden rejoined the Paris agreement, but retained most of the Trump administration's anti-globalization measures and introduced new ones. The idiosyncratically named Inflation Reduction Act in 2022, which introduced large financial initiatives to promote clean energy, contained strong protectionist provisions. For example, the large subsidies designed to promote the manufacture and use of electric vehicles (EVs) stipulated that EVs manufactured and assembled in Europe were ineligible, while US automobile manufacturers were required to develop supply chains that did not depend on China. The subsequent second Trump administration after 2025 intensified the trade protectionism pursued by the Biden administration, while undermining or withdrawing from international institutions and norms.

Finally, human rights and safety standards violation scandals, such as the Rana Plaza garment factory collapse in Bangladesh in 2005, which resulted in the deaths of more than a thousand workers, triggered further regulatory efforts on global value chains by some

European government, including France, Germany, and Norway, as well as international organizations. Despite strong lobbying by MNEs, the EU Corporate Sustainability Due Diligence Directive was ultimately accepted by the European Parliament in 2024. This new directive compelled headquarters to monitor their subsidiaries and subcontractors to make sure they mitigated their impacts on human rights and the environment. However, as China, India, Japan, the United States, and other major economies were not party to the EU directive, the legislation had no more than token significance.

There were some years of declining trade flows and FDI in this period, which led some scholars to pronounce a new era of deglobalization[64] whilst others were skeptical that the available data supported such a conclusion.[65] A study of global connectedness in 2024 found no evidence that globalization had gone into reverse, although economic flows between the United States and China did fall sharply after 2016.[66] Although there was considerable noise in existing data – caused, for example, by the impact of the COVID-19 epidemic between 2020 and 2023 and by the large sums flowing through offshore financial centers that were largely disconnected from the real economy – the primary evidence for another reversal was to be found in shifting sentiments and policies rather than economic data. The surge in anti-globalization policy statements among political and other leaders in both developed and emerging markets was striking. The policies of the second Trump administration were radical and accelerated a reconfiguration of global value chains, yet they formed part of a trend rather than a sudden aberration.[67]

A growth of industrial policies containing anti-foreign provisions seemed indicative of the direction of travel of policymakers in many countries. After 2008 micro-protectionist measures multiplied with the widespread adoption of local content rules, public procurement discrimination against foreign firms, export taxes and quotas, and trade-distorting subsidies. An IMF report identified more than twenty-five hundred industrial policy interventions worldwide in 2023 alone, of which more than two-thirds were trade distorting as they discriminated against foreign business interests. The world's three major economies, China, the EU, and the United States, accounted for nearly half of these new policies.[68]

Still it can be argued that, just as in the period between 1950 and 1979, there might be simultaneous waves of both deglobalization and globalization. At the core of the new wave was digitalization. The "Magnificent Seven" US-based technology companies – Apple, Microsoft, Alphabet, Amazon, Meta, Nvidia, and Tesla – used the World Wide Web and cloud computing to build dominance in their sectors. Their Chinese counterparts – Baidu, Alibaba, Tencent, Xiaomi, ByteDance, Meituan, and JD.com – have done the same. A McKinsey Global Institute report in 2016 demonstrated that cross-border flows of data and information generated more economic value than global goods trade. For several reasons, the extent of digitalization is not captured in conventional FDI data, which primarily measure tangible assets rather than intangibles such as intellectual property, data, and software. Digitalization also facilitates cross-border data flows, enabling companies to control operations remotely and without requiring traditional physical presence, making it difficult to accurately measure FDI based on location.[69]

Although the United States and the EU retained their positions as the leading homes of MNEs, China's (including Hong Kong) share of world FDI stock reached 12 percent in 2010 and stood at 16 percent in 2023.[70] As shown in Chapter 3, Chinese-based firms were preeminent in the green industries, including renewable energy, EVs, and batteries. The global role of Chinese MNEs formed part of a wider pattern in which North American and European MNEs faced growing competition from MNEs based in Asia, the Arab Gulf, Latin America, and elsewhere. In other words, globalization was being reshaped rather than entirely upended.

1.7 Conclusion

Multinational enterprises were powerful actors in the spread of global capitalism after 1840. Emerging out of the industrialized Western economies, they created and cocreated markets and ecosystems through their ability to transfer a package of financial, organizational, and cultural assets, skills, and ideologies across national borders. They became major drivers of trade growth, which they often organized within their own boundaries. They have been shapers of as well as responders to globalization waves over the past two centuries. There was a great deal of heterogeneity in the organizational forms employed in global business. Multinational enterprises were a highly resilient form of business enterprise able to withstand exogenous shocks and shifts in policy regimes, unless they involved – as with the spread of Communism – the elimination of capitalism in its entirety.

Multinational enterprises were also actors in periodic deglobalization waves because they functioned as reinforcers of gaps in wealth and income rather than disrupters of them. Existing research suggests that they were often disappointing institutions for knowledge and technology transfer. During the first global economy, MNE resources and related investments were highly enclavist and embedded in the institutional arrangements of Western imperialism and autocratic dictators. Western MNEs reinforced rather disrupted institutional and societal norms, which restricted growth in many countries outside the West. It was striking that the most successful non-Western economies since the 1960s – Japan, South Korea, Taiwan, and (from the 1980s) China either excluded foreign MNEs or, more importantly, obliged them to transfer technologies to local firms. The historical evidence does not support a general argument that foreign MNEs are positive for economic development, although excluding them has had its own problems. For instance, India's shifting restrictive policies toward foreign MNEs and subdued level of FDI discussed in Chapter 12 probably deterred the development of certain industries, especially in manufacturing.

Multinational enterprises often functioned as part of the problem, rather than part of the solution, to the grand challenges faced by the world. In the more recent globalization era since the 1980s, the strategies of Western MNEs moved beyond the practices of the colonial past, but linkages and spillovers to local economies have often remained disappointingly low. Their ability and motivation to locate value-added activities in the most attractive locations means that they strengthen clustering rather than encourage dispersion of knowledge. Still the impact of MNEs was a complex mixture of positive and negative factors. History provides a valuable lens to understand these impacts to better inform policymakers and others now and in the future.

Notes

1. Moore, K. *Birth of the Multinational: 2000 Years of Ancient Business History from Ashur to Augustus*, Copenhagen, Copenhagen Business School, 1999.
2. Jones, G. *Multinationals and Global Capitalism*, Oxford, Oxford University Press, 2005, 36–37.
3. Dinesen, C. "The Medici and Renaissance Complexity: How the Challenges of Renaissance Banking Finally Defeated the First Multinational Bank," in Dinesen, C. (ed.) *Absent Management in Banking: How Banks Fail and Cause Financial Crisis*, Cham, Springer International, 2020, 15–32.
4. Carlos, A. M. and Nicholas, S. "Giants of an Earlier Capitalism: The Chartered Trading Companies as Modern Multinationals," *Business History Review*, 62, 3 (1988), 398–419.
5. Rönnbäck, K. "Transactions Costs of Early Modern Multinational Enterprise: Measuring the Transatlantic Information Lag of the British Royal African Company and Its Successor, 1680–1818," *Business History*, 58, 8 (2016), 1147–1163.
6. Bowen, H. V. *The Business of Empire: The East India Company and Imperial Britain, 1756–1833*, Cambridge, Cambridge University Press, 2006.
7. Jones, G. and Schröter, H. (eds.) *The Rise of Multinationals in Continental Europe*, Aldershot, Edward Elgar, 1993.
8. Wilkins, M. *The Emergence of Multinational Enterprise*, Cambridge, MA, Harvard University Press, 1970.
9. Jones, *Multinationals*, 21.
10. Schröter, H. G. *Aufstieg der kleinen: Multinationale Unternehmen aus fünf kleinen Staaten vor 1914*, Berlin, Duncker & Humblot, 1993.
11. Wilkins, M. "Comparative Hosts," *Business History*, 36, 1 (1994), 18–50.
12. Cassis, Y. *Capitals of Capital: A History of International Financial Centres 1780–2005*, Cambridge, Cambridge University Press, 2006.
13. Jones, G. "Origins and Development of Global Business," in da Silva Lopes, T., Lubinski, C., and Tworek, H. J. S. (eds.) *The Routledge Companion to the Makers of Global Business*, New York, Routledge, 2020, 17–34, at 19.
14. Da Silva Lopes, T., Casson, M., and Jones, G. "Organizational Innovation in the Multinational Enterprise: Internalization Theory and Business History," *Journal of International Business Studies*, 50, 8 (2019), 1338–1358.
15. Carstensen, F. V. *American Enterprise in Foreign Markets: Singer and International Harvester in Imperial Russia*, Chapel Hill, University of North Carolina Press, 1984.
16. Wilkins, M. and Schröter, H. (eds.) *The Free-Standing Company in the World Economy, 1836–1996*, Oxford, Oxford University Press, 1998.
17. Jones, G. *Merchants to Multinationals*, Oxford, Oxford University Press, 2000.
18. Jones, G. (ed.) *The Multinational Traders*, London, Routledge, 1998.

19. Jones, G. *British Multinational Banking 1830-1990*, Oxford, Clarendon Press, 1998.
20. Jones, *Multinationals*, 203.
21. Moazzin, G. "Investing in the New Republic: Multinational Banks, Political Risk, and the Chinese Revolution of 1911," *Business History Review*, 94, 3 (2020), 507–534.
22. Wilkins, M. *The Maturing of Multinational Enterprise*, Cambridge, MA, Harvard University Press, 1974.
23. Donzé, P.-Y. "The Advantage of Being Swiss: Nestlé and Political Risk in Asia during the Early Cold War, 1945–1970," *Business History Review*, 94, 2 (2020), 373–396, at 380.
24. Jones, G. and Lubinski, C. "Managing Political Risk in Global Business: Beiersdorf 1914–1990," *Enterprise & Society*, 13, 1 (2012), 85–119.
25. Jones, G. *Beauty Imagined: A History of the Global Beauty Industry*, Oxford, Oxford University Press, 2010, 15–93.
26. Wilkins, M. and Hill, F. E. *American Business Abroad: Ford on Six Continents*, Detroit, MI: Wayne State University Press, 1964, 169–170, 176–178, 184.
27. Marchal, J. *Lord Leverhulme's Ghosts: Colonial Exploitation in the Congo*, London, Verso, 2008.
28. Hayes, D. E. *The Emergence of Brand-Name Capitalism in Late Colonial India: Advertising and the Making of Modern Conjugality*, London, Bloomsbury Academic, 2023.
29. Boillat, J. *Les véritables maîtres du temps: Le cartel horloger suisse (1919–1941)*, Neuchatel, Alphil, 2013.
30. Wilkins, M. *The History of Foreign Investment in the United States 1914–1945*, Cambridge, MA, Harvard University Press, 2004.
31. Lubinski, C. *Navigating Nationalism in Global Enterprise: A Century of Indo-German Business Relations*, Cambridge, Cambridge University Press, 2022.
32. Jones, "Origins," 23.
33. Turner, H. A. *General Motors and the Nazis: The Struggle for Control of Opel, Europe's Biggest Carmaker*, New Haven, CT, Yale University Press, 2005.
34. Jones, G. and Bostock, F. "U.S. Multinationals in British Manufacturing before 1962," *Business History Review*, 70, 1 (1996), 207–256.
35. Miller, M. *Europe and the Maritime World*, Cambridge, Cambridge University Press, 2011.
36. Jones, *Multinationals*, 90–92.
37. David, T. and Eichenberger, P. "'A World Parliament of Business'? The International Chamber of Commerce and Its Presidents in the Twentieth Century," *Business History*, 65, 2 (2023), 260–283.
38. Kirby, W. C. "China's Internationalization in the Early People's Republic: Dreams of a Socialist World Economy," *China Quarterly*, 188 (2006), 870–890.

39. Wilkins, M. "An Overview of Foreign Companies in the United States, 1945–2000," in Jones, G. and Gálvez-Muñoz, L. (eds.) *Foreign Multinationals in the United States*, London, Routledge, 2002, 18–49.
40. Batselé, F. "Foreign Investors of the World, Unite! The International Association for the Promotion and Protection of Private Foreign Investments (APPI) 1958–1968," *European Journal of International Law*, 34, 2 (2023), 424–425.
41. Jones, *Multinationals*, 257–258.
42. Choudhury, P. and Khanna, T. "Charting Dynamic Trajectories: Multinational Enterprises in India," *Business History Review*, 88, 1 (2014), 133–169, at 139.
43. Kipping, M. "American Management Consulting Companies in Western Europe, 1920–1990: Products, Reputation and Relationships," *Business History Review*, 84, 10 (1999), 60–69.
44. Yonekawa, S. *General Trading Companies: A Comparative and Historical Study*, Tokyo, United Nations University Press, 1990.
45. Harlaftis, G. *Creating Global Shipping: Aristotle Onassis, the Vagliano Brothers, and the Business of Shipping*, Cambridge, Cambridge University Press, 2019, 172–262.
46. Schenk, C. "The Origins of the Eurodollar Market in London: 1955–1963," *Explorations in Economic History*, 35, 2 (1998), 221–238.
47. Balaban, I. A. "The Establishment of the Eurodollar Market in Paris and the Failure of Regulation and Reform, 1959–1964," *Business History*, 66, 7 (2024), 1735–1757.
48. Ogle, V. "Archipelago Capitalism: Tax Havens, Offshore Money, and the State, 1940s–1970s," *American Historical Review*, 122, 5 (2017), 1431–1458.
49. Schaufelbuehl, J. M. "The Transatlantic Business Community Faced with US Direct Investment in Western Europe, 1958–1968," *Business History*, 58, 6 (2016), 880–902.
50. Leimgruber, M. "'Kansas City on Lake Geneva' Business Hubs, Tax Evasion, and International Connections around 1960," *Zeitschrift Für Unternehmensgeschichte*, 60, 2 (2015), 123–140.
51. Jones, G. and Miskell, P. "European Integration and Corporate Restructuring: The Strategy of Unilever c1957–c1990," *Economic History Review*, 57 (2005), 113–139.
52. Hesse, J.-O. "The German Textile Puzzle: Selective Protectionism and the Silent Globalization of an Industry," *Business History Review*, 93, 2 (2019), 221–246.
53. Ammann, D. *The Secret Lives of Marc Rich*, New York, St. Martin's Press, 2009.
54. Jones, G. *Renewing Unilever: Transformation and Tradition*, Oxford, Oxford University Press, 2005.
55. Donzé, "The Advantage," 390–391.

56. Elmore, B. J. *Citizen Coke: The Making of Coca-Cola Capitalism*, New York, W. W. Norton, 2015.
57. Perrone, N. M. *Investment Treaties and the Legal Imagination: How Foreign Investors Play by Their Own Rules*, Oxford, Oxford University Press, 2021.
58. Cowie, J. R. *Capital Moves: RCA's Seventy-Year Quest for Cheap Labor*, New York, The New Press, 2001.
59. Hanton, A. *Vassal State: How America Runs Britain*, Swift Press, London, 2024.
60. Jones, "Origins," 27.
61. Aguilera, R. V., Ciravegna, L., Cuervo-Cazurra, A., and Gonzalez-Perez, M. A., "*Multilatinas* and the Internationalization of Latin American Firms," *Journal of World Business*, 52 (2017), 447–460.
62. Cuervo-Cazurra, A., Inkpen, A., Musacchio, A., and Ramaswamy, K. "Governments as Owners: State-Owned Multinational Companies," *Journal of International Business Studies*, 45 (2014), 919–942.
63. Abrahamian, A. A. *The Hidden Globe: How Wealth Hacks the World*, New York, Riverhead Books, 2024.
64. Witt, M. A. "De-globalization: Theories, Predictions, and Opportunities for International Business Research," *Journal of International Business Studies* 50, 7 (2019), 1053–1077.
65. Linsi, L. and Gristwood, E. "The Myth of Deglobalization: Multinational Corporations in an Era of Growing Geopolitical Rivalries," *Politics and Governance*, 12 (2024), 1–19.
66. Altman, S. A. and Bastian, C. R. *DHL Global Connectedness Report 2024*, NYU Stern, March 2024.
67. Jones, G. and Giacomin, V. "Deglobalization and Alternative Futures," *Harvard Business School Technical Note*, No.322-089, revised March 10, 2022.
68. Ilyina, A., Pazarbasioglu, C., and Ruta, M. "Industrial Policy Is Back But the Bar to Get It Right Is High," *IMF Blog*, April 12, 2024. www.imf.org/en/Blogs/Articles/2024/04/12/industrial-policy-is-back-but-the-bar-to-get-it-right-is-high.
69. McKinsey Global Institute, "Digital Globalization: The New Era of Global Flows" (February 24, 2016).
70. UNCTAD, *World Investment Report*, 2024.

Further Reading

Abrahamian, A. A. *The Hidden Globe: How Wealth Hacks the World*, New York, Riverhead Books, 2024.

Jones, G. *Multinationals and Global Capitalism: From the Nineteenth to the Twenty-First Century*, Oxford, Oxford University Press, 2005.

Petitjean, O. and Du Roy, I. (eds.) *Multinationales: Une histoire du monde contemporain*, Paris, La Découverte, 2025.

Wilkins, M. *The Emergence of Multinational Enterprise*, Cambridge, MA, Harvard University Press, 1970.

Wilkins, M. *The Maturing of Multinational Enterprise*, Cambridge, MA, Harvard University Press, 1974.

ANN-KRISTIN BERGQUIST AND
GEOFFREY JONES

2

Multinationals and the Environment

2.1 Multinationals and the Environment

Since the nineteenth century, multinational enterprises (MNEs) have been among the primary contributors to global environmental degradation. Their impact was initially most evident through large-scale investments in mining and agriculture that altered landscapes and ecosystems, particularly in the Global South. As consumer companies expanded from national to international markets from the late nineteenth century, MNEs also perpetuated wasteful consumption patterns and excessive packing waste in their home countries. After World War II, there was an unprecedented surge in industrial production and energy consumption. Multinational enterprises played a crucial role by spreading technologies, mass consumption patterns, and production practices worldwide.

It was only in the 1960s that growing environmental awareness began to seriously challenge the practices of MNEs. But especially in developing countries, environmental regulations and governance structures remained weak. Prominent MNEs, especially those in fossil fuels, became purveyors of misleading information concerning scientific evidence on climate change and other critical environmental challenges. In the past three decades, some MNEs have asserted their roles as advocates for sustainability, but their efforts have frequently involved persuasive marketing initiatives that projected a green image rather than genuine sustainability.

The question is why MNEs have not taken a more positive role in responding to environmental challenges. The existing literature has to be trawled carefully to find convincing answers. Business historians have often concentrated on the environmental strategies of firms within their national boundaries rather than across borders.[1] Meanwhile the international business literature has been surprisingly narrow in addressing the environmental impact of MNEs. It has heavily focused on the "pollution haven hypothesis" that suggests that stricter environmental regulations in developed countries led polluting industries to relocate to countries with more lenient regulation, which will be discussed later in this chapter. This may reflect that the discipline has tended to focus on positive aspects of MNE activity.[2]

This chapter looks at the relationship between MNEs and the environment over time. An important methodological point is that the evidence has to be carefully contextualized. In particular, knowledge of environmental impacts has changed substantially over time. It would be absurd, for example, to be critical of a company for not combating climate change before World War I when it was more than half a century later before convincing scientific evidence on the subject became available. The chapter proceeds chronologically. Section 2.2 examines the period before 1960. Section 2.3 focuses on the decades between 1960 and 2000. Section 2.4 addresses the past twenty-five years.

2.2 MNEs and the Environment before 1960

Multinational enterprises are frequently seen as primary agents of resource extraction and environmental degradation, not only because of their transnational reach, but also due to their significant economic power, which still is evident as of the mid-2020s. The environmental impact of MNEs began to gain momentum in the late nineteenth century and the first global economy. During this period, the expansion of resource-extractive industries such as oil, mining, rubber, and chemicals – facilitated by innovations from the Second Industrial Revolution – enabled MNEs to exploit vast amounts of natural resources globally. Steam-powered railroads and ships, along with advances in electricity, the combustion engine, and chemical industries, allowed these corporations to operate across borders with greater efficiency while also increasing their environmental footprint. By 1914, as

Chapter 1 observes, many of the world's resources were being produced, traded, and distributed by these MNEs.

A first wave of environmentalism emerged in the late nineteenth century, which developed gradually alongside industrialization and the first global economy before petering out in the interwar years. It was characterized by antipollution movements in the United States and Western Europe and a nature conservation movement, which, among other things, led to the establishment of national parks. Yellowstone National Park in the Rocky Mountains in the United States was the first national park in the world, created in 1872. The first MNEs with significant environmental impact were engaged in resource-extractive industries such as oil, mining, rubber, chemicals, and tropical food plantations, while they operated at the time with minimal or no environmental regulation. While there were some instances of conflicts around polluting firms being pressured to reduce their environmental impact in the late nineteenth and early twentieth centuries – such as those involved in metal smelting, oil drilling, and pulp and paper manufacturing – these efforts were largely limited to specific regions in the United States and Europe. In general, governments accepted the negative effects of industrial pollution, viewing it as an inevitable trade-off for job creation and economic growth.

The negative impact of mining in particular was evident. From the late nineteenth century Western mining corporations were equipped with powerful technologies that enabled them to reshape natural landscapes and ecosystems over vast distances.[3] Even much earlier in the era of the Industrial Revolution, the copper industry stood out for the profoundly toxic nature of smelter emissions, which contained high concentrations of sulfur dioxide and heavy metals such as arsenic.[4] A hundred years later, the industry became increasingly capital-intensive as technological development allowed it to mine and smelt low-grade ores from large individual deposits. Thus, when the operations of large copper companies expanded to countries in the Global South, the environmental effects became immense.

Chile provides an example of the impact of MNE investment in copper. Already during the 1860s, a few foreign companies, mainly British, were active in Chile, but the industry soon exhausted its high-grade ores and lagged in developing new technologies, and by 1900, the country only accounted for 5 percent of world copper production. United States mining entrepreneurs became interested in the country as new American technologies became available to exploit low-grade ores. In 1912, Guggenheim Brothers, a large US mining company that already owned the largest privately held business in Mexico because of its huge investments in silver, created the Chile Exploration Company with the purpose to put in operation the largest open-pit copper mine in the world – the Chuquicamata mine. This giant mine was sold to Anaconda Copper Company, based in the United States, in 1923 after Guggenheim Brothers made the decision to invest in nitrate operations in Chile, which did not prove profitable in the end.[5]

Guggenheim Brothers' nitrate activities had a significant negative environmental impact on the Atacama Desert, but their copper mining operations, particularly at the Chuquicamata mine, were even more damaging and increased vastly when Anaconda scaled the production. The smelting processes involved in copper extraction released large quantities of sulfur dioxide and other pollutants, causing respiratory issues and health problems for nearby communities. Additionally, local water sources were contaminated with heavy metals and toxic chemicals, while extensive open-pit mining led to massive pits and waste heaps, permanently altering the region's topography and destroying habitats.[6]

Oil companies such as Standard Oil (whose successors include ExxonMobil) and Royal Dutch Shell (Shell) also expanded their operations globally, with little or no regard for environmental consequences, most of which were unknown at the time. In Mexico, the oil was initially located under the rainforests near the Gulf of Mexico (known as the Gulf of America in the United States since 2025). The capital investments in Mexican oil came from both American and British companies that from 1906 began to drill over large areas, causing saltwater to penetrate the lands.[7] Standard Oil and Shell entered Mexico in 1910 and 1919 respectively – the latter by acquiring S. Pearson & Son's Mexican Eagle Company, which had discovered massive oil deposits in 1910.[8] During the explorations, drilling, and transportation, frequent oil spills caused contamination of rivers, lakes, and groundwater, while the establishment of oil fields and associated infrastructures led to extensive deforestation, habitat destruction, and much else. Similar cases were found wherever oil extraction spread. The only place where the ecological costs were less immediate was in the Gulf after World War II, since the extraction took place in an environment almost without people and little life of any kind. However, oil pumped out from the Gulf was as bad for climate change as elsewhere.[9]

It is important to note that most of the world's oil outside the United States and the Soviet Union was produced by a small number of large MNEs. In 1928 in Latin America, more than 40 percent of the oil was produced by Shell and Standard Oil. In 1937, the same two companies produced 88 percent of the oil in the Netherlands East Indies.[10] One study has observed that twenty MNEs have been historically responsible for the world's accumulated carbon dioxide emissions resulting from oil and natural gas between 1889 and 2014. The list includes ExxonMobil, Chevron, British Petroleum, and Shell, alongside more recent entrants to the industry, including state-owned oil companies such as Saudi Aramco, National Iranian, and Pemex.[11]

The use of oil as a product also had a tremendous impact on the environment. Petrochemicals derived from oil created new materials such as plastics, which added to the tonnage of durable waste. Oil also permitted the development of the automobile industry with its far-reaching negative environmental impact. The global expansion of the US corporations – General Motors and Chrysler – took the automobile around the world. The production of cars required large quantities of raw materials, including steel, rubber, glass, and various metals, while the manufacturing process generated significant industrial waste, including hazardous chemicals, metal scraps, and wastewater.

In Latin America, Ford launched a notable venture in the Brazilian Amazon in 1927 – Fordlândia. This ambitious project aimed to establish a self-sufficient rubber plantation in the Amazon rainforest to supply Ford's automobile manufacturing needs, leading to the purchase of approximately 2.5 million acres of land along the Tapajós River. The clearing of the rainforest for rubber cultivation severely reduced biodiversity, displacing many plant and animal species. After years of struggle and significant financial losses, the Ford Motor Company abandoned Fordlândia, eventually selling the land back to the Brazilian government in 1945.[12]

Deforestation was a significant consequence of MNE activities, particularly in tropical forests. European colonialists showed interest in the

Caribbean's tropical forests as early as the eighteenth century, but the introduction of motor-driven chainsaws and tractors in the twentieth century enabled access to previously remote areas. In Latin America, advanced sawmill technology from the United States and Europe overshadowed local efforts to produce mahogany furniture for export, as locals could neither afford nor compete with modern sawmills. By the 1940s, logging activities in Latin America intensified. Degraded lands were replaced by softwood monocultures – a trend that accelerated in the 1950s and became widespread throughout the tropics in the 1960s.[13]

In the tropics, the spread of plantations run by MNEs such as the US-based United Fruit Company (United Fruit) discussed in Chapter 6, caused particularly negative environmental disruptions. United Fruit controlled large swathes of agricultural land and banana production in Central America. Vast areas of tropical rainforests were cleared, leading to habitat loss for innumerable species and a significant reduction in biodiversity. The lack of crop rotation and diversification led to soil erosion and nutrient depletion.[14] To increase banana yields and combat pests and diseases, the company used large amounts of chemical pesticides and fertilizers from the 1940s, including a widespread use of toxic chemicals, such as DDT, which leached into the soil and waterways. The impacts on plantation workers and local populations also became more apparent during this time, as chronic exposure to these chemicals led to long-term health issues. Only from the 1970s did the environmental degradation caused by United Fruit's practices become more widely recognized.[15]

Environmental destruction caused by MNEs in the textile industry began with colonial-era textile production. During British colonial rule, India became a major supplier of raw cotton for British textile mills. This cotton monoculture led to severe environmental consequences, including soil depletion, deforestation, and water scarcity due to intensive farming practices. Following World War II, Western MNEs relocated labor-intensive industries such as textiles to the Global South, driven by cheaper labor and weaker regulations. The US companies Levi Strauss and J.C. Penney are often cited as early adopters of such outsourcing from the 1960s, particularly to countries like Mexico and the Philippines. Consequently, river pollution from textile dyeing and finishing processes in countries like Bangladesh and India became widespread, while pesticide-intensive cotton cultivation further degraded the soil. The environmental crisis worsened with the emergence of synthetic fabrics like polyester, outsourcing to developing countries, and eventually the rise of fast fashion.[16]

The beauty industry was also pernicious. From the start, marketing depended on extensive and wasteful packaging. From the 1950s, the favored packaging for many beauty products became plastic, which replaced glass and ceramic containers. Plastic was preferred because of its flexibility and light weight, yet this plastic waste could not be recycled. Plastic is not biodegradable, and instead goes through photo-degradation that breaks it down into microscopic sizes over a period extending from one hundred to five hundred years. The accumulating plastic in oceans, much of it from the MNE beauty and food industries, has had devastating impacts on marine life.[17]

The negative environmental impact of consumer goods MNEs such as Lever Brothers (later Unilever) and Nestlé was also significant. They expanded across borders selling soap, baby food, and a growing range of other products. Their business model involved advertising and extensive and environmentally wasteful packaging. They and their successors forged an international consumer society in which consumers were encouraged to buy products they often did not need regardless – as economist J. K. Galbraith observed in *The Affluent Society*, published in 1958 – of their environmental consequences.[18] By the middle of the century, Coca-Cola had developed into one of the most conspicuous companies in the world, with overseas retailers and bottlers representing a third of its business. To save costs, the company introduced one-way steel cans in the 1960s, and a decade later, plastic bottles.[19] Eventually, the extensive use of single-use containers contributed to widespread littering and plastic pollution of rivers and oceans in Asia, Africa, and Latin America, due to nonexistent or poor waste management systems.

The growth of MNE activities, both in the first global economy and in the subsequent Great Reversal, had broadly negative environmental impacts across issues ranging from biodiversity loss to climate change and environmental injustice. The global oil industry was at the center of many of the problems. Cheap oil reduced transportation costs, facilitated the creation of petrochemical products such as plastics for packaging, and enabled the growth of the automobile industry, along with the development of efficient machinery for logging, plantation, and mining. The critique of corporate actions is necessarily retrospective given the limited environmental knowledge and the absence of significant regulation, particularly in the Global South. When environmental concerns subsequently became more prominent, however, a major problem was that the global economy had been built on the unchecked and unpriced exploitation of the environment.

2.3   MNEs and the Environment 1960–2000

In the 1960s, there was finally a sudden rise of environmental concerns by scientists that spread to the public and political agendas. There was not one cause but several contributing factors. First there were major water and air pollution episodes, including American rivers catching fire from toxic waste and smog events causing the deaths of thousands like in London in 1952. The use of nonbiodegradable surfactants in the synthetic detergents industry led to polluted rivers and lakes across Europe and the United States. In 1969, a major oil blowout spilled around 4 million gallons of oil onto the Californian coastline. The incident led to the National Environmental Policy Act, which mandated federal agencies to prepare environmental assessments and environmental impact assessments. Second, a new generation of writers raised environmental issues to a wider public audience. In the United States, the most noteworthy was Rachel Carson, whose *Silent Spring*, published in 1962, denounced the pesticide DDT for poisoning wildlife and birds and in effect acting as a human carcinogen. In 1966, Kenneth Boulding published *The Economics of the Coming Spaceship Earth* and presented the idea that the Earth should be viewed as a closed, finite system with limited resources. Third, these growing concerns coincided with new social movements, including anti-Vietnam War protests, women's liberation, and the civil rights movement in the United States, which questioned existing societal and political assumptions. Finally, on December 24, 1969, the astronauts on the Apollo 8 spaceship, which was the first to orbit the moon, photographed the planet against the darkness of space. The photograph, which became known as "Earthrise," was widely adopted by the growing environmental movement.[20]

A number of institutional innovations signaled the rising importance of the environmental movement. New environmental nongovernmental organizations (NGOs) were created, including Friends of the Earth in 1969. On April 22, 1970, the first Earth Day was held in the United States involving 20 million people marching for a healthier environment. In 1972, the first United Nations (UN) conference on international issues was held in Stockholm. In the United States and, after a delay, Western Europe, a raft of new consumer safety and environmental regulations was introduced in the 1970s. In 1970, the United States formed the Environmental Protection Agency, which enforced new environmental regulations over the chemical and other industries.[21]

Studies of the initial reaction of big business to this second wave of environmentalism have largely looked at the national level and highlighted variations between countries. Andrew J. Hoffman's study of the chemical and petroleum industries in the United States emphasized the evolution of corporate strategies. Many corporations in the 1960s simply believed that environmental concerns were exaggerated. After 1970, there was rather annoyed commitment to compliance with the new environmental laws in the context of growing numbers of lawsuits against chemical firms from environmentalist activists.[22] Their German counterparts responded quite similarly during the 1960s, but during the 1970s, MNEs such as Henkel and Bayer began to invest more in environmentally sustainable products and strategies, even beginning to promote themselves as "green giants." A study by business historians Geoffrey Jones and Christina Lubinski argued the key influence in the German case was that these two firms were headquartered in the state of North Rhine–Westphalia and were particularly exposed to the complaints of local citizens and politicians about polluted rivers and bad smells.[23]

Geoffrey Jones's study of the history of Unilever provided a more specific example of changing MNE strategies toward the environment. Initial concerns involved food additives and ingredients. Alarm was raised at the start of the 1960s when a new emulsifying agent used in margarine gave large numbers of Dutch consumers a skin rash. The brand was withdrawn, compensation was paid, and a corporation-wide scheme was put into practice whereby local companies introducing new additives to foods, detergents, or personal products had to consult the corporate division of research. However, Unilever's highly decentralized organization meant that there was a great diversity of practices, which was to become characteristic of the firm's environmental strategies.[24]

During the 1970s, Unilever's engagement with environmental issues rose. It provided facilities for the International Chamber of Commerce staff preparing for the UN conference in Stockholm in 1972. The corporate Annual Report in 1972 for the first time included a section on "Conservation of the Environment." One of the firm's main board directors returned from a visit to the United States in 1972 convinced that environmental concerns would be a major issue for the future, and also expressing optimism that MNEs were part of the solution as they could facilitate "the spread of new environmental technology from one country to another."[25] However Unilever struggled to develop a coherent environmental policy as it found that environmental concerns and regulations – and the response of Unilever companies to them – were much higher in some countries (like Germany and Switzerland) than others (like Britain and the nations of Southern Europe). Nor were environmental strategies linear. In the 1970s, the momentum waned as governments and the public turned their attention to the impact of rising oil prices.[26] The company lagged behind its competitors Henkel and Procter & Gamble in researching alternatives to the phosphates used in synthetic detergents, which were blamed for the eutrophication of lakes. Not until 1986 did Unilever launch a zero-phosphate brand for its Swiss subsidiary.[27]

In the 1980s, Unilever's environmental policies came under increasing scrutiny. While Henkel and Procter & Gamble increasingly highlighted their green credentials in advertising their brands, Unilever continued to lack corporation-wide policies. It took isolated initiatives to reduce packaging in environmentally conscious countries like Germany but did very little elsewhere. Environmental practices were particularly weak in many of its factories in emerging markets. Unilever argued that it followed the environmental standards set by each national government and that it would lose competitiveness if it introduced more environmentally friendly technologies. This stance began to shift only in the 1990s.[28]

It would appear some MNEs were more adept than Unilever in transferring green technologies across borders. A case study of the Dutch brewing company Heineken showed both an initial reluctance to address environmental issues – the word was not mentioned in its annual reports in the 1960s – but also an eventual willingness to transfer cleaner technologies across borders. During the 1990s, having developed more sustainable ways of purifying wastewater in the Netherlands in the previous decade, Heineken rolled out water purification plants across its businesses in Europe, followed by Asia, and in 1999, it began to build installations in Africa. The company also became embroiled in environmentalist campaigns against its bright yellow beer crates, which contained cadmium pigments. After a threatened consumer boycott in 1995, Heineken began switching to green crates, as well as green bottles. The first green crate was introduced in Germany in 1993, and six years later the yellow crate disappeared in the Netherlands.[29]

The MNEs involved in natural resources remained among the most exposed to environmental criticisms. During the postwar decades, the British trading companies in Southeast Asia, including Guthries and Harrisons & Crosfield, as well as the Unilever-owned United Africa Company, were dominant in expanding Malaysia's palm oil production, turning the country into one of the world's largest producers, alongside Indonesia. During the 1970s and 1980s, all of these investments were localized, meaning that local companies rather than MNEs dominated the production of palm oil.[30] However the leading MNEs, including Unilever and Nestlé, were huge consumers of palm oil for their food and other products. The industry brought some prosperity to the region at the cost of enormous environmental damage. Large areas of rainforest were cleared to make way for palm oil plantations, which drove up greenhouse gas emissions and destroyed critical habitat for endangered species. The similarities with the consequences of United Fruit's plantations in Central America and the Caribbean during the first half of the twentieth century are striking.

As noted earlier, the oil companies were major drivers of climate change, but in this period, they added insult to injury through notorious episodes of climate change denial. Exxon has been shown to be both internally aware of the drivers of climate change since the 1970s and active in discrediting the scientific evidence.[31] During the 1990s, Exxon and other oil companies were leading members of the Global Climate Coalition, a business advocacy group dedicated to blocking policies against climate change, although following the Kyoto Agreement in 1997 there was some divergence between the American and the European oil MNEs, with BP and Shell leaving the Coalition. Their preferred strategy became greenwashing to avert criticism. In 2000, BP rebranded itself as "Beyond Petroleum," a campaign that ran for eight years before BP was overtaken by a massive environmental scandal associated with an explosion on the Deepwater Horizon oil rig in the Gulf of America.[32]

A case study of Shell enables a more nuanced look at one of the oil MNEs. As in the case of Unilever, policy developments in the United States – where Shell had a large business – were an important catalyst. New legislation – the Clean Air Act in 1963 and the Air Quality Act in 1967 – brought environmental issues to the attention of Shell's management that leaded gasoline was likely to be the target of governments.[33] The exhaust emissions from automobiles was the major environmental concern, with California a hotbed of environmental activism. In 1970, the US Congress thus passed the Clean Air Act (CAA), mandated a staggering 90 percent reduction in hydrocarbon (HC) and carbon monoxide (CO) emissions by 1975, based on the emission levels of 1970 car models. By 1976, a comparable 90 percent reduction in nitrogen oxide (NO_x) emissions was also required. The key technology that made it possible for automobile manufacturers to comply with the CAA was the three-way catalytic converters introduced by the Swedish car MNE Volvo, which could operate only on unleaded fuel.[34]

Shell introduced its lead-free gasoline to the American market, though after failing to find many customers, withdrew it again, and then in 1974 relaunched it after US legislation required that unleaded gasoline be made available at service stations. Elsewhere Shell adopted a policy of acting when regulations mandated the removal of lead, which happened sooner than it expected as political pressure against "acid rain" in the 1980s rose. Again, it was the NO_x emissions from cars that caused acid rain, and unleaded petrol was needed to implement the three-way catalytic converters. Subsequently Shell's policies became an environmentalist cause célèbre with the proposed sinking in the North Sea of the decommissioned Brent Spar oil rig in the mid 1990s. This became the target of a major Greenpeace campaign. The British government supported the proposal, as did Shell's British affiliate, but other European governments and the Shell subsidiaries in those countries opposed it. In 1995, Shell's corporate leadership ordered the British subsidiary to abandon the plan.[35]

The Shell case demonstrates a couple of important issues. First, MNEs consist of a coalition of different national (or regional) companies that can take different views on environmental matters, partly influenced by their home governments. Great caution is required to avoid treating MNEs as simple black boxes rather than a coalition of interests. Second, MNEs strategies are impacted by the policies of important host governments, and more especially in this period the United States.

The oil industry can also serve as an example that the impact of MNEs is multidimensional. The core activities of the oil companies, let alone numerous pollution incidents, make their environmental impact appear negative. Yet in the 1970s and 1980s, oil companies such as Exxon, Mobil, Amoco, and ARCO played a crucial role in the emergent solar cell industry, investing in small start-ups that could not raise funds. By 1980, US-based oil MNEs accounted for 85 percent of world sales of solar modules, driving technological innovation. However, the low profits made on solar energy compared to oil led to wholesale divestment by the oil MNEs from the solar industry during the second half of the 1980s and the 1990s.[36] This established a pattern whereby the big oil MNEs entered renewable energy and with their capital resources were able to improve technologies, but they then divested again as the money made from oil was simply the rational decision with respect to profitability – too tempting. While MNEs developed technologies that could potentially reduce environmental impacts, these innovations were often overshadowed by their continuous engagement in other environmentally harmful activities, in this case drilling for oil.

The international business literature on MNEs and the environment in this period has focused on the "pollution haven hypothesis," which suggested that MNEs relocated polluting activities to countries with weaker environmental regulations to avoid the compliance costs of their home economies. Despite a great deal of research on the topic, however, little empirical evidence remained to support the hypothesis, not least because it only concerned a small part of MNE activity. Yet there is considerable evidence – if anecdotal – of extensive ecological damage by MNEs active especially in the developing world. The environmental damage done by oil companies in the Niger Delta from the 1950s has been well documented.[37]

There was also plenty of evidence of poor environmental practices in countries lacking strong environmental regulations or enforcement. The disaster that befell the Indian operations of the US chemical MNE Union Carbide was the single most dramatic incident. On the night of December 2–3, 1984, in Bhopal, a large amount of methyl isocyanate, a highly toxic gas used in pesticide production, leaked from a tank at a plant owned by Union Carbide in India. The leak was caused by a series of failures, including poorly maintained equipment, inadequate safety procedures, and a lack of emergency planning. Thousands of people were immediately exposed to the gas, leading to respiratory failure and death. Estimates vary on the death toll, with official numbers ranging from 2,259 to more than 20,000. Many more suffered long-term health problems from exposure. Although Union Carbide settled with the Indian government by offering US $470 million in compensation in 1989, this was widely seen as insufficient given the scale of the suffering and damage.

The extent to which MNEs could damage the environment was constrained (at least partially) by governmental regulation. The general trend during the last decades of the twentieth century was for countries to introduce and tighten environmental regulations, but there were large national differences, especially across the Global South. A new Chilean constitution in 1980, for example, included a clause that Chilean nationals had "the right to live in an unpolluted environment" although this declaration was considered vague and less prioritized than economic rights.

During the so-called Chilean copper boom in the 1990s, more than thirty MNEs entered Chilean mining. Some observers have argued that the presence of foreign companies functioned as a driver for the greening of the Chilean copper industry, as MNEs strived to keep up with international environmental standards. On the other hand, the environmental and public health problems associated with this rapid expansion were increasingly evident, with copper mining and smelting generating extensive air and water pollution in the northern and central portions of the country. In the 1990s, Chile saw increased activism from environmental organizations while Chilean environmental policymaking was driven primarily by external forces linked to economic globalization.[38] In contrast, the Peruvian government sold the highly polluting La Oroya smelter to the US MNE Doe Run Company in 1997, and then proceeded to exercise little control over it. Doe Run was pursued for multiple environmental violations in the United States. In 2007, an American NGO identified La Oroya as one of the ten most polluted places on earth.[39]

Multinational enterprises also acted collectively to lobby on environmental regulations, both within their home economies and internationally. The previously mentioned Global Climate Coalition actively lobbied against an inclusion of binding commitments by states to the UN Framework Convention on Climate Change in 1992 and the Kyoto Protocol in 1997, but collective lobbying on environmental regulations started earlier. The United Nations Environment Programme (UNEP), which emerged after the Stockholm Conference in 1972 as the anchor organization in global environmental governance, did not interact directly with individual MNEs. The International Chamber of Commerce (ICC) functioned as the first primary link between the interests of MNEs and UNEP.

The policies of the UN were important to MNEs at the time. In 1974, the UN General Assembly had adopted the New International Economic Order (NIEO), which called for measures such as increased regulation of foreign investment, nationalization of resources, and greater control by host countries over their natural resources. There were therefore good reasons for MNEs to work closely with the UN to influence its environmental policy recommendations to governments. Major MNEs, including Shell and Exxon, Unilever, and others, were distinguished members of the ICC, and when UNEP hosted its first conference on industry and the environment in 1984, it was attended and sponsored by these companies and by a wide range of other MNEs. The ICC played a major role in the "neoliberal turn" of the UN's environmental policies from the mid 1980s, which stressed free trade, the market mechanism, clean technology transfers, and business self-regulation, rather than binding rules and legislation, as a promising way forward. The concept of sustainable development, defined and launched by the Brundtland Commission in 1987, was impregnated with market-friendly ideas. When the ICC in 1991 published the

"Business Charter for Sustainable Development," a new self-regulation program for the world industry, it was partly drafted by Shell and endorsed by the UN.[40]

At the UN's Conference on Environment and Development in Rio in 1992 (also known as the Earth Summit or the Rio Conference), the ICC was accompanied by the Business Council for Sustainable Development (BCSD) formed with forty-eight business leaders from around the world, representing MNEs such as 3M, ALCOA, Dow Chemical, ENI, Shell, Chevron, ABB, Volkswagen, and Nippon Steel.[41] External observers at the time noted that the Rio Conference was a landmark success for the MNEs. The final documents not only treated MNEs with a gentle hand but also praised them as key actors in the "battle to save the planet."[42] In contrast to the 1970s and the UN's early attempts to regulate MNEs, the institutional environment that developed during the run-up to the Rio Conference and in the 1990s placed MNEs in the driver's seat of environmentalism.

2.4 MNEs and the Environment since 2000

Perhaps the most visible change in the relationship between MNEs and the environment after 2000 was rhetorical, which already had taken ground in the 1990s. This was the era of corporate environmentalism, when large MNEs became self-declared champions of sustainability and asserted their leading role in solving the world's environmental challenges. The top twenty-five firms in the 2024 rankings of the world's most sustainable companies by the magazine *Corporate Knights* included wind-energy MNEs like Denmark's Vestas and Germany's Nordex, the French machinery MNEs Schneider and Alstom, the Swedish telecom MNE Ericsson, and the Finnish petrochemical and refining company Neste.[43] Barron's list of the one hundred most sustainable corporations in 2023 had the bleach MNE Clorox in first place, the health and hygiene manufacturer Kimberly Clark in second place, and the consumer goods company Procter & Gamble in tenth place.[44] Evidently the concept of sustainability had grown to be a very broad church in the corporate world, which was why to a greater or lesser extent every MNE on the planet claimed to be on the journey to sustainability by the third decade of the twentieth century.

There was no single factor behind this sudden, apparent greening of MNEs. As concerns about the environment grew, new government policies mandated or provided incentives to invest in sustainability. Nongovernmental organizations both pressured corporations and formed alliances with them. In some industries, a new cohort of green consumers emerged willing to support firms that cared about the environment. The concept of sustainability was progressively broadened after the Brundtland Commission in 1987 joined social issues and economic growth with protecting the environment. As new metrics were introduced, the reliance on self-reporting incentivized the selective reporting of environment performance – also known as greenwashing – enabling managers to develop greener images to please consumers and investors while avoiding deep investments in true environmental sustainability.[45]

In the early 2000s, the concept of environmental, social, and governance (ESG) began to develop, building on earlier ideas of corporate social responsibility (CSR) and socially responsible investing (SRI) from the 1960s and 1970s. The term "ESG" gained prominence in 2004 after a landmark report titled "Who Cares Wins," which was initiated by the United Nations Global Compact in collaboration with major financial institutions. A very large international pool of capital was soon available for corporations meeting approved ESG metrics. By 2020, the total assets under management that included some ESG component had reached US $11 trillion in the United States and $17 trillion in Europe. However, by then the problems of the whole category were also apparent, including a lack of transparency in ratings and the challenges of bundling diffuse components into a single concept. Close examination showed that the portfolios of ESG funds were often like conventional funds.[46] Despite much discussion about global firms, the country of registration of MNEs also appeared to significantly influence its environmental performance. A study of two thousand institutional investors who signed the Principles for Responsible Investment between 2003 and 2017 demonstrated that the US-based companies in their portfolios showed no improved ESG performance. Europe-based companies did show a much-improved ESG performance.[47]

Many other strategies designed to let market disciplines prompt more corporate sustainability also delivered discouraging results. In 2021, dozens of leading MNE banks, including Citibank, Deutsche

Bank, and Lloyds Bank, formed the UN-led Net Zero Banking Alliance. It represented 40 percent of global banking assets, but a study published three years later showed no impact at all on lending practices.[48]

Despite the near-universal spread of the language of sustainability, there continued to be plentiful anecdotal evidence of MNEs' poor behavior – or incompetence – in environmental matters. There were certainly exceptions, although rarely of large MNEs based in the developed world. The Brazilian beauty MNEs Natura and O Boticáro, for example, have displayed over the past four decades strong commitments to sustainability in their sourcing and marketing strategies. Natura achieved carbon neutrality in 2007.[49] However, these role models were exceptions, and their impact was by definition far less than the giant commodity and resource MNEs that paid lip service to sustainability while energetically downgrading the natural environment. The commodity trading companies active in emerging markets were some of the worst offenders. Glencore, whose corporate website proclaimed in 2024 that the corporation sought to "minimize and mitigate harm to the environment, through environmental stewardship and responsible resource management across our global operations," has been accused of environmental damage across Africa, and especially in the Congo.[50] The spill from BP's Deepwater Horizon oil rig in 2010, caused by lax safety standards, was a major environmental disaster in the Gulf of Mexico (Gulf of America).

Nor were all the environmental scandals confined to resources and trading MNEs. Volkswagen (VW), which won the Green Car of the Year award for its Jetta TDI model launched in 2009, installed software on its diesel cars that allowed them to cheat emissions tests in the United States. Volkswagen's strategy, which was discovered in 2015, involved a systematic commitment to defraud governments and cheat consumers. The company was anxious to expand its (low) sales of diesel engines in the United States, but finding that its engines could not meet new US emission test standards, the decision was made in 2006 to apply software that would cheat on the emission tests. Dozens of engineers and managers became involved in the decades-long scandal. This reflected in part VW's centralized decision-making, which discouraged dissent while showing tolerance for breaking rules in order to achieve results.[51]

The VW emissions scandal was, however, indirectly related to the European Union's strict limits on CO_2 emission. In Europe, diesel engines were popular because they generally produce lower CO_2 emissions compared to gasoline engines, while the problem was that diesel engines tend to produce higher levels of nitrogen oxide (NO_x). In order to support their broader goal of maintaining compliance with CO_2 regulations in Europe and avoiding the costs and technical challenges associated with genuinely reducing NO_x emissions, VW turned to deceptive practices. In 2015, VW's Green Car of the Year award was taken away.[52] The case of VW demonstrates the broader challenge of MNEs. They operate across different markets with different standards that may, as in the case of the car industry, increase transaction costs and generate diseconomies of scale.[53]

In response to the growing attention paid to environmental issues, in this period many MNEs began to develop global environmental standards and more globally uniform environmental policies, even as environmental regulations continued to vary a lot between countries. Pressure from NGOs and the reputational impact of disasters like Bhopal and Deepwater Horizon were among the early drivers. Transferring more advanced technologies to poorer and less regulated countries can also be less costly than applying less advanced technologies in some countries and can lower coordination costs.[54]

A particular problem was that MNEs were known to have transferred environmentally damaging activities to associated companies whose activities were not reported in their annual reports. A 2013 study that used data on 269 subsidiaries in twenty-seven countries belonging to 110 MNEs from twenty-two countries concluded that "typically, MNEs' response to mounting pressure from their home country stakeholders has been to exit the fields within which the pressure is strong by moving their corporate social irresponsibility practices to alternative locations in their subsidiaries."[55] The borders of MNEs are porous, and bad practices can be found and indeed encouraged in parts of the value chain for which the parent corporation can deny responsibility.

Insofar as MNEs transfer advanced environmental practices to developing countries, it might be assumed that their superior managerial and technological capabilities would permit a superior environmental impact than locally owned firms. Yet the evidence is particularly fragmentary on this subject, and it is not clear-cut. A study of foreign-owned versus locally owned firms in Mexico found their environmental performance broadly similar.[56] A particular challenge since the 2000s has been rather the role of global value chains in MNE business. Organizationally fragmented and spatially dispersed international business activity has emerged. Offshore production sites are in low-cost developing countries that were closely linked with lead firm buyers and MNEs from major consumer markets in Europe and North America.[57] Multinational enterprises rarely included the activities of the nominally independent firms in their value chains in sustainability reports, making a proper assessment of their environmental impact impossible.

In some cases, MNE affiliates had a more negative environmental effect than traditional arrangements. Waste was an example. The huge urban populations found in mega cities of Latin America, Africa, and Asia generated mountains of waste, which overwhelmingly ended up in dumps – not even landfills – which resulted in big emissions of greenhouse gases. As the problems mounted, the response of many larger cities was to contract with Western MNE waste companies such as Waste Management and Veolia. They had far better environmental technologies, but recycling rates often fell when they were employed. The reason was that in many countries, hundreds of thousands of waste pickers (or scavengers) working in the informal sector collected waste and worked in the dumps, recovering and recycling everything they could find. An estimate in 2007 was that Brazilian waste pickers recovered 90 percent of the postconsumer materials recycled by industry in that country in the 2000s.[58]

A more recent development has been the growth of Chinese-owned MNEs, discussed in Chapter 3. There is nothing specifically "anti-environment" about Chinese MNEs; indeed, China is a leader in many "green" industries, including electric vehicles (EVs) and renewable energy. Yet China as a home country to MNEs has comparatively weak environmental regulation – or rather, the execution of the regulation is highly fragmented. One estimate is that only 10 percent of China's environmental laws are enforced.[59] Moreover, Chinese investment in resource extraction carried with it serious environmental consequences in countries with limited environmental regulation.

During the 2010s, China became the second most important destination for Latin American exports, and two-thirds of these exports were in iron, oilseeds, copper, and crude petroleum. A 2016 study estimated that Latin American exports to China generated 15 percent more net greenhouse gas emissions and used twice as much water as other Latin American exports. Chinese MNE investment was also heavily concentrated in metals, coal, oil, and natural gas, alongside food and tobacco, automobile original equipment manufacturing, and communications. The China National Petroleum Corporation, the world's second largest oil company after Saudi Aramco, controlled China's investments in the oil industry throughout the region.[60]

While it is understandable to focus attention on large petroleum and metals MNEs, negative environmental consequences can arise from much smaller companies. Over the past two decades, for example, two Chinese MNEs invested heavily in the export of seaweed from Peru through their affiliates Algas Sudamérica and Globe Seaweed International. China has a booming demand for seaweed, particularly for its alginate content. Alginate finds uses in various industries, such as additives in the food industry, thickeners in cosmetics, and even in textile manufacture. Peru grew as Latin America's second largest exporter of seaweed, with 98 percent of its seaweed exports going to China. The activities of these companies have badly damaged marine life as algal meadows also produce 50–85 percent of the oxygen released into the atmosphere and help remove carbon dioxide. Globe Seaweed has been particularly involved in questionable practices. Between 2005 and 2023, it shipped more than 191,000 tons of seaweed to China and has been subject to seven sanctions imposed by the Peruvian Ministry of Production. The sanctions were for reporting false or incomplete information about its operations, obstructing the work of inspectors, carrying out fishing activities without authorization, and processing seaweed without certificates of origin.[61] Chapter 3 discusses the debates concerning the negative environmental impact of Chinese natural resource MNEs in Africa.

China emerged as the center of the global expansion of the EV industry. In the past decade, global EV sales, including both battery cars and plug-in hybrids, grew exponentially, partly with support from government subsidies.[62] The leading MNEs in this segment were

China-based BYD and US-based Tesla. Electric vehicles contributed to lower carbon emissions compared to traditional gasoline cars only if they were recharged with electricity produced by carbon-free energy. Another issue was the production of batteries for EVs, which required significant amounts of electricity and raw materials such as lithium, copper, cobalt, and nickel. There were major concerns about the future environmental impacts of such increased mining, while many of these minerals were concentrated in specific regions with weak environmental institutions, including cobalt in the Democratic Republic of Congo and lithium in Latin America. Despite significant progress in understanding the relationship between resource-based industrialization and environmental impact, it appears that the contemporary actions of MNEs under the banner of "green industrialization" may repeat the same harmful practices as in the past.

2.5 Conclusion

As a broad generalization, it is apparent that MNEs were one of the more significant contributors to environmental challenges before 1960. Multinational enterprises were heavily clustered in natural resources and in developing countries at least before World War II, and they made a significant contribution to deforestation, the creation of monocultures, and much else. Petroleum MNEs were by definition a driver of climate change because of the industry's role in greenhouse gas emissions. Meanwhile, the spread of consumer goods MNEs encouraged conspicuous consumption and wasteful packaging.

The situation after 1960 was more complex. The second wave of environmentalism and the emergence of environmental regulation raised the issue of the environment on corporate agendas. Multinational enterprises such as Unilever and Henkel began formulating environmental policies. Execution was another matter partly because many MNEs had governance structures fragmented on national or regional lines. This was a period when critics accused MNEs of transferring polluting activities to less regulated countries, a charge that was hard to prove in aggregate despite obvious examples such as the outsourcing of clothing manufacture, in part because companies reorganized their reporting structures so that affiliated companies did not need to report environmental impact.

What has been better documented is that oil MNEs, and Exxon in particular, knew about the risks of climate change and chose to obscure the scientific evidence in order to delay policy changes.

The period after 2000 introduced new complexities. Sustainability reports abounded, and large MNEs in unlikely industries were hailed as environmental champions. The reality was blatant greenwashing, including silence about the environmental performance of global value chains. Meanwhile, environmental damage committed by MNEs continued, especially in countries where regulation and enforcement were weak.

Notes

1. Bergquist, A. K. "Renewing Business History in the Era of the Anthropocene," *Business History Review*, 93, 1 (2019), 3–24.
2. Christmann, P. and Taylor, G. "International Business and the Environment," in Bansal, P. and Hoffman, A. J. (eds.) *Business and the Natural Environment*, Oxford, Oxford University Press, 2012, 50–69.
3. McNeill, J. R. *Something New under the Sun: An Environmental History of the Twentieth-Century World*, New York, W. W. Norton & Company, 2001.
4. Newell, E. "Atmospheric Pollution and the British Copper Industry, 1690–1920," *Technology and Culture*, 38, 3 (1997), 655–698.
5. Jones, G. and Fernandes, F. T. "The Guggenheims and Chilean Nitrates," Harvard Business School Case No. 819-141, revised January 3, 2019.
6. Damir, G.-M. and Rivera, F. "Copper Sulfide Mining at Chuquicamata and the Spread of Arsenic in Drinking Water in Chile, 1952–1971: A Derivation of Extractivism," *The Extractive Industries and Society*, 11 (2022), 101135, 1–10.
7. McNeill, *Something New*, 298–301.
8. Jones, G. *The State and the Emergence of the British Oil Industry*, London, MacMillan, 1981, 64–76, 217.
9. McNeill, *Something New*, 298–301.
10. Wilkins, M. "Comparative Hosts," *Business History*, 36, 1 (1994), 18–50, 37.
11. Heede, R. "Carbon Majors," *Accounting for Carbon and Methane Emissions: Methods & Results Report. Climate Mitigation Services* (2014), 25, table 5.
12. Grandin, G. *Fordlandia: The Rise and Fall of Henry Ford's Forgotten Jungle City*, New York, Metropolitan Books, 2010.
13. Tucker, R. P. *Insatiable Appetite: The United States and the Ecological Degradation of the Tropical World*, Berkeley, University of California Press, 2000, chapter 7.

14. Sedrez, L. "Environmental History of Modern Latin America," in Holloway, T. H. (ed.) *A Companion to Latin American History*, London, Blackwell, 2010, 443–450.
15. Tucker, *Insatiable Appetite*.
16. Niinimäki, K., Peters, G., Dahlbo, H., Perry, P., Rissanen, T., and Gwilt, A. "The Environmental Price of Fast Fashion," *Nature Reviews Earth & Environment*, 1, 4 (2020), 189–200.
17. Jones, G. "Deep Responsibility and Irresponsibility in the Beauty Industry," *Entreprises et Histoire*, 111, 2 (2023), 113–125.
18. Galbraith, J. K. *The Affluent Society*, Boston, MA, Houghton Mifflin, 1958.
19. Elmore, B. J. *Citizen Coke: The Making of Coca-Cola Capitalism*, New York, W. W. Norton & Company, 2015, chapter 8.
20. Jones, G. *Profits and Sustainability: A History of Green Entrepreneurship*, Oxford, Oxford University Press, 2017, 86–88.
21. Jones, *Profits*, 88–90.
22. Hoffman, A. J. *From Heresy to Dogma: An Institutional History of Corporate Environmentalism*, Stanford, CA, Stanford Business Books, 2001.
23. Jones, G. and Lubinski, C. "Making 'Green Giants': Environment Sustainability in the German Chemical Industry, 1950s–1980s," *Business History*, 54, 4 (2014), 621–649.
24. Jones, G. *Renewing Unilever: Transformation and Tradition*, Oxford, Oxford University Press, 2005, 340.
25. Jones, *Renewing*, 341.
26. Jones, *Renewing*, 342.
27. Jones, *Renewing*, 342–343.
28. Jones, *Renewing*, 344–347.
29. Sluyterman, K. "Green is More than the Colour of the Bottle: Environmental Issues at Heineken Breweries over the Long Term," *Low Countries Historical Review*, 137, 4 (2022), 43–64.
30. Jones, G. *Merchants to Multinationals*, Oxford, Oxford University Press, 2000, 263–265.
31. Oreskes, N. and Conway, E. M. *Merchants of Doubt*, New York, Bloomsbury, 2010, 169–215.
32. Boon, M. "A Climate of Change? The Oil Industry and Decarbonization in Historical Perspective," *Business History Review*, 93, 1 (2019), 101–125.
33. Sluyterman, K. "Royal Dutch Shell: Company Strategies for Dealing with Environmental Issues," *Business History Review*, 84, 2 (2010), 203–226.
34. Bergquist, A. K. and Näsman, M. "Safe before Green! The Greening of Volvo Cars in the 1970s–1990s," *Enterprise & Society*, 24, 1 (2023), 59–89.
35. Sluyterman, "Royal Dutch Shell."
36. Jones, *Profits*, 119–121, 331–332.

37. Eweje, G. "Environmental Costs and Responsibilities from Oil Exploitation in Developing Countries: The Case of the Nigeria Delta of Nigeria," *Journal of Business Ethics*, 69, 1 (2006), 27–56.
38. Lagos, G. "Developing National Mining Policies in Chile: 1974–1996," *Resources Policy*, 23, 1/2, (1997), 51–69.
39. Orihuela, J. C. "The Environmental Rules of Economic Development: Governing Air Pollution from Smelters in Chuquicamata and La Oroya," *Journal of Latin American Studies*, 46, 1 (2014), 151–183.
40. Bergquist, A. K. and David, T. "Beyond Planetary Limits! The International Chamber of Commerce, the United Nations, and the Invention of Sustainable Development," *Business History Review*, 97, 3 (2023), 481–511.
41. Bergquist, A. K. and Jones, G. "Institutional Entrepreneurship and Climate Change," in da Silva Lopes, T., Duguid, P., and Fredona, R. (eds.) *Climate Change and Business: Historical Perspectives*, New York, Routledge, 2025.
42. Hildyard, N. "Foxes in Charge of the Chickens," in Sachs, W. (ed.) *Global Ecology: A New Area of Political Conflict*, London, Zed Books, 1993, 22–33.
43. "2024 Global 100," www.corporateknights.com/rankings/global-100-rankings/2024-global-100-rankings/the-20th-annual-global-100, accessed May 20, 2024.
44. "Barron's Top 100 Sustainable Companies 2023." www.barrons.com/lists-rankings/top-sustainable-companies?page=1&, accessed May 14, 2024.
45. Dauvergne, P. and Lister, J. *Eco-Business: A Big Brand Takeover of Sustainability*, Cambridge, MA, MIT Press, 2013.
46. Jones, G. *Deeply Responsible Business: A Global History of Values-Driven Leadership*, Cambridge, MA, Harvard University Press, 2023, 309–323.
47. Brandon, R. G., Glassner, S., Krueger, Matos, P. P., and Steffen, T. "Do Responsibility Investors Invest Responsibly?" *Journal of Finance*, 26, 6 (2022), 1389–1432.
48. Sastry, P. R, Verner, E., and Ibanez, D. M. "Business as Usual: Bank Net Zero Commitments, Lending, and Engagements," *NBER Working Paper* 32402 (May 2024).
49. Jones, G. "Sustainability and Green Business in Latin America," in Lluch, A., Zanatti, M. M., and Bucheli, M. (eds.) *A Business History of Latin America*, New York, Routledge, 2025, 167–168.
50. www.glencore.com/sustainability/esg-a-z/environment#:~:text=We%20seek%20to%20minimise%20and,%2C%20energy%2C%20water%20and%20waste, accessed May 26, 2024.
51. Spinello, R. A. *Business Ethics: Contemporary Issues and Cases*, Los Angeles, CA, Sage, 2020, 253–261.
52. Fleming, C. "VW and Audi Give Back Green Car of the Tear Awards," *Los Angeles Times*, September 30, 2015.

53. Näsman, M. "The Political Economy of Emission Standards: Politics, Business and the Making of Vehicle Emissions Regulations in Sweden and Europe, 1960s–1980s." PhD Dissertation, Umeå University, 2021.
54. Christmann and Taylor, "International Business," 51–56.
55. Surroca, J., Tribó, J. A., and Zahra, S. A. "Stakeholder Pressure on MNEs and the Transfer of Socially Responsible Practices to Subsidiaries," *Academy of Management Journal*, 56 (2013), 549–572.
56. Muller, A. and Kolk, A. "Extrinsic and Intrinsic Drivers of Corporate Social Performance: Evidence from Foreign and Domestic Firms in Mexico," *Journal of Management Studies*, 47, 1 (2010), 1–26.
57. Kano, L., Tsang, E. W. K., and Henry Yeung, H. W.-C. "Global Value Chains: A Review of the Multi-disciplinary Literature," *Journal of International Business Studies*, 51, 4 (2020), 572–562.
58. Medina, M. *The World's Scavengers: Salvaging for Sustainable Consumption and Production*, Lanham, MD, AltaMiram, 2007.
59. Marsh, J. "Supplying the World's Factory: Environmental Impacts of Chinese Resource Extraction in Africa," *Tulane Environmental Law Journal*, 28 (2015), 393–407.
60. Ray, R. and Gallagher, K. P. "China in Latin America: Environment and Development Dimensions," *Revista Tempo do Mundo*, 2, 2 (2016), 131–154.
61. Pelcastre, J. "China Clears Chilean and Peruvian Marine Forests," *Dialogo Américas*, July 21, 2023, https://dialogo-americas.com/articles/china-clears-chilean-and-peruvian-marine-forests, accessed May 19, 2024.
62. Näsman, M. and Ballor, G. "The Car Industry and Climate Change: A Historical Review," GREEN, Centre for Geography, Resources, Environment, Energy and Networks, 2024, 1-62, 22-23.

Further Reading

Berghoff, H. and Rome, A. (eds.) *Green Capitalism? Business and the Environment in the Twentieth Century*, Philadelphia, University of Pennsylvania Press, 2017.

Bergquist, A. K. "Renewing Business History in the Era of the Anthropocene," *Business History Review*, 93, 1 (2019), 3–24.

Da Silva Lopes, T., Duguid, P., and Fredona, R. (eds.) *Climate Change and Business: Historical Perspectives*, New York, Routledge, 2025.

Jones, G. *Profits and Sustainability: A History of Green Entrepreneurship*, Oxford, Oxford University Press, 2017.

Oreskes, N. and Conway, E. M. *Merchants of Doubt*, New York, Bloomsbury, 2010.

ADAM FROST AND
SHUANG FROST

3

Multinationals and the Changing Face of Chinese Globalization

3.1 Introduction: Discontinuous Globalization

The history of multinational enterprises (MNEs), as told in Chapter 1, is characterized by strong continuities and discontinuities that map on to waves of globalization and deglobalization. To this story, we can add another layer of complexity: regional dynamics that were, at times, countercyclical to global trends. This chapter explores the history of Chinese MNEs and the changing face of China's globalization. As we will see, in this history, globalization processes were shaped as much by the contingencies of power and politics as by competitive market forces.

Chinese globalization twice rose, crested, and receded once again against the backdrop of an evolving global economy. In the first modern global economy, in the wake of the Opium Wars (1839–1860) and the signing of treaties between China and Western imperial powers, Chinese firms were forced to compete against foreign MNEs on unequal terms. While a number of enterprises did manage to successfully outcompete rivals both at home and abroad, their growth was ultimately curtailed by geopolitical forces and the rise of the Chinese Communist Party. It was only decades later in the 1980s, after China initiated global reintegration on its own terms, that Chinese firms once again invested overseas and rebuilt the capacity to compete against foreign MNEs. Since the turn of the twenty-first century, in the face of rising geopolitical tensions, China has begun electively disengaging with some regions while deepening its engagement with others. In this new emerging global order, Chinese

MNEs are reorienting investment away from developed economies and toward emerging markets.

The impact of China's globalization, both on China and the rest of the world, has been as multifaceted as the varieties of actors involved. Foreign MNEs have aided China's development by facilitating the transfer of new ideas and technologies from abroad. They have also acted as agents of imperialism and the traffickers of addictive substances. Chinese MNEs have emerged as leaders in the global green transition and have played a central role in building physical and digital infrastructure across the developing world. Some have been accused of acting in collusion with the Chinese state and of failing to uphold basic human and environmental rights. It is only by retracing the long history of Chinese globalization that we can begin to unpack this complexity.

3.2 The First Wave of Chinese MNEs (1800s–1949): Globalization at Gunpoint

China's participation in the first global economy was settled down the barrel of a gun. For centuries, late imperial China had been at the center of the premodern global economy and boasted a staggeringly large export sector. Strong demand in Western Europe and the Americas for Chinese exports (e.g., tea, silk, and porcelain), coupled with the lack of reciprocal demand in China for foreign manufactured products, created enduring trade imbalances. These stimulated massive outflows of silver bullion from Latin America – where some 80 percent of the world's silver was then being mined – into China.[1] Western powers, viewing trade through a mercantilist lens, grew increasingly reluctant to continue exporting so much silver; eventually they attempted to ameliorate the deficit by substituting silver with another valuable and lightweight commodity: opium. It was China's resistance to the opium trade that precipitated the First Opium War (1839–1842). And it was China's ignominious defeat in that and subsequent conflicts that resulted in the creation of "unequal treaties," which dictated unequal terms for China's participation in the first modern global economy.

Multinational enterprises featured centrally in this story of coercive globalization. Trading companies such as Britain's East India Company, Jardine Matheson, and John Swire & Sons, and US-based Russell &

Company served as the agents of imperial powers that furthered the economic and political interests of their home governments.[2] It was these firms that brokered the trade in opium in direct contravention of imperial edicts banning the narcotic. And it was they that instigated military intervention when their unlawful commercial claims were challenged by the Chinese government. Although this early generation of foreign MNEs had limited reach into China's vast and populous markets – they were largely confined to "treaty ports" where they operated through the aid of local intermediaries – the sociopolitical impact of their business activities was felt powerfully across China.

In addition to the deleterious impact on public health and social stability, the opium trade devastated China's domestic economy. Rising opium imports rapidly drained Chinese silver reserves, which inadvertently increased the tax burden on ordinary citizens and generated widespread popular discontent.[3] Beginning in the 1880s, Chinese authorities responded by permitting the domestic production of opium. While the strategy was successful insofar as it curbed the demand for imports and stymied the outflow of silver, it exacerbated the growing opium crisis. According to some estimates, by 1906, some 40 million Chinese – 10 percent of China's total population and nearly one-quarter of the male adult population – were opium users.[4] The unchecked spread of addiction severely undermined the perceived legitimacy of the imperial state and, arguably, hastened its demise.[5]

By the early twentieth century, the center of gravity in Sino-foreign competition had shifted away from narcotics and toward modern industry. A new generation of foreign MNEs, including Standard Oil, Singer, and Sherwin-Williams, introduced into China new technologies, managerial practices, and organizational forms.[6] By 1913, about seven hundred modern factories and mining enterprises had been established across the country.[7] Foreign firms also invested heavily in infrastructure and resource extraction. Foreign capital directly or indirectly controlled more than 90 percent of railways, 80 percent of modern shipping, 80 percent of modern coal mining, 100 percent of iron ore mining, and almost all export-import business.[8] While most MNEs activity was still limited to the areas immediately surrounding treaty ports, the impact of technological diffusion and knowledge spillovers was felt across a much larger space; the spatial dimensions of this can even be observed in differences in regional developmental outcomes a century later.⁹

Domestic Chinese businesses were quick to adapt to the influx of foreign technologies and ideas, particularly in China's textile industry. In the late eighteenth century, Chinese enterprises, many of which were "government-supervised, merchant-managed," began importing large numbers of spinning machines and set up mechanized production facilities in emulation of Western factories. Between 1890 and 1911, twenty-nine cotton mills were established across China, of which twenty-one were wholly undertaken by Chinese investors.¹⁰ To raise the necessary capital for continued expansion, some firms adopted new organizational forms. For example, Dasheng Cotton Mills, founded as an "official-supervised, merchant-managed" firm in 1895, was reorganized as a private joint stock company in 1904. This structure enabled it to attract greater private investment.¹¹ Between 1911 and 1922, Chinese investment in spinning machinery experienced a further one hundred-fold increase.¹² Through such aggressive expansion, domestic firms captured market share from their foreign rivals, kick-started Chinese industrialization, and contributed to a national project of "self-strengthening." However, the rapid expansion of industrial capacity also led to massive technological displacement; the spinning and looming of cotton – once the purview of women and key source of income for rural households – was increasingly done by machines on urban factory floors.

Across industries, new firms emerged to successfully compete against foreign MNEs in domestic markets, and some even took their competition abroad. Butterfly Brand, a cosmetics firm launched in 1918 by writer-entrepreneur Chen Diexian, produced popular varieties of tooth powder and vanishing cream; by 1923, the Butterfly Brand products were not only being sold to customers across China, but had reached markets in Southeast Asia.¹³ China Egg Produce Company, founded in Shanghai in 1923, adopted Western managerial structures to vertically integrate its businesses and engage in fierce price competition with British and American rivals such as Jardine Matheson and Union Cold Storage Company. By the 1930s, China Egg had risen to command a 30 percent market share of egg exports and had established overseas subsidiaries in London and Osaka.¹⁴ In the 1920s, Mayar Silk Mills, Limited pursued an aggressive acquisition strategy, imported advanced manufacturing technologies, and reorganized its operations for overseas expansion; by 1933, the year of the company's incorporation, Mayar had grown to become China's largest silk producer, with nearly two hundred varieties of natural silk and rayon products marketed across China, Southeast Asia, and the United States.[15]

Other Chinese firms were born global. Take for example Nanyang Brothers' Tobacco Company, a Hong Kong-based enterprise founded in 1905 by brothers Jian Zhaonan and Jian Yujie. The company achieved early success by establishing overseas sales offices targeting Chinese diaspora communities across Southeast Asia, including Thailand, Malaya, Indonesia, and Borneo.[16] Using the profits accumulated therefrom, Nanyang Brothers' entered mainland Chinese markets in 1915. There it engaged in intense commercial rivalry against British American Tobacco, a foreign MNE that had already developed an extensive Chinese distribution network and maintained a virtual monopoly over machine-rolled cigarettes.[17] Between 1912 and 1931, the company went from having more than 80 percent of its total sales in Southeast Asia to nearly 70 percent of its total sales in mainland China.[18]

These firms were part of the first wave of Chinese MNEs. Prior to the founding of the People's Republic of China in 1949, no fewer than forty-eight domestic commercial, financial, and industrial enterprises established overseas organizational capabilities, principally in Southeast Asia, but also in Japan, Western Europe, and the United States.[19] The motives that drove the internationalization of these firms varied. Some Chinese merchant families adopted multiple nationalities and spread their businesses overseas to reduce commercial and political risk. For example, Fujian native Guo Chunyuan, who came to hold Japanese nationality, founded a sprawling network of businesses in the sugar, rubber, and tea industries, with head offices spread across China, Taiwan, and Indonesia.[20] Others sought new markets for their products and services after saturating domestic ones. For example, matchmaking industrialist Liu Hongsheng built and remotely managed a business empire that stretched across Japan, the United States, and Britain.[21] Even in the face of competition against foreign MNEs that were often better capitalized, more technologically advanced, and legally privileged, a few Chinese firms thus succeeded in going global.

While this first wave of Chinese MNEs was ultimately curtailed, its end was brought about by geopolitical rather than competitive market forces. The full-scale invasion of China by Japan in 1937 marked a critical turning point during which firms were forced to suspend their mainland operations and explore alternative opportunities overseas, particularly in Southeast Asia. The outbreak of the Pacific War in 1941 dealt another blow, as oceanic shipping routes were blocked by Japanese occupation. Finally, the beginning of the true end came with the victory of the Chinese Communist Party (CCP) over its Nationalist rivals and the gradual nationalization of private industry. The lasting impact of this first wave of Chinese MNEs would be felt only through the continued spread of entrepreneurial Chinese diaspora networks and the activities of firms that were reborn as state-owned enterprises (SOEs).[22]

After the CCP's rise to national power in 1949, China experienced a sudden and protracted retreat from the global economy. The Chinese state, under the leadership of Mao Zedong, pursued an atavistic developmental strategy that emphasized self-sufficiency and the enhancement of domestic productive capabilities.[23] In the three decades following the founding of the People's Republic of China, China's foreign direct investment (FDI) remained minimal and the limited overseas business activity that did occur was politically motivated and tightly controlled by the state. A notable example was the construction of the Tanzania–Zambia Railway, part of the CCP's broader effort to promote socialist solidarity and strengthen ties with African nations by combining foreign aid with FDI.[24] Beyond a handful of state-directed projects, China's linkages with the global economy were limited to the exchange of basic goods, such as textiles and foodstuffs, for machinery and technologies underpinning China's domestic industrialization efforts.[25] While such coordinated flows enabled the continued development of strategic sectors, such as chemical fertilizer production and mining, they ultimately failed to stimulate broad-based economic development.[26]

3.3 The Second Wave (1980s–Present): China's Reentry into the Global Economy

China's participation in the second global economy occurred under a very different set of circumstances – ones largely dictated by China.

Even before the death of Mao Zedong in 1976, the CCP had already begun taking tentative steps toward reopening the economy to foreign capital. Mao himself supported increasing international trade to import advanced technologies and upgrade domestic production, and his successor, Hua Guofeng, approved the establishment of special economic zones for much the same reason.[27] For example, after the Sino-Soviet split led to a cessation of technical assistance, machinery, and advisory services from the Soviet Union, China began importing vehicles from abroad and signed licensing agreements with foreign automotive manufacturers, including French truck producer Berliet, to acquire new technologies and designs.[28] These early international collaboration agreements laid the foundations for subsequent Sino-foreign joint ventures (JVs), which drove the metamorphosis of China's nascent automotive industry.

Beginning in 1978, under the leadership of Deng Xiaoping, China's reglobalization accelerated: new laws were passed to allow for the creation of Sino-foreign JVs, special economic zones were established to attract foreign investment and reduce the administrative burden of contracting business, and state institutions mobilized to create incentives for local officials to engage with FDI.[29] The overt aim of such policies was to facilitate technological transfer and stimulate the expansion of domestic industrial capacity; policies dictated, for example, that in the formation of JVs, the domestic partner owned at least a 51 percent share of the company and the foreign partner guaranteed the transfer of technologies and technical knowledge. The CCP thus defined a limited framework within which foreign MNEs could begin to reengage with China, but in ways that aligned with the CCP's developmental priorities. As Deng Xiaoping put it, "we open our doors, but remain selective; we do not introduce anything without a purpose and a plan."[30]

While China's reopening attracted foreign MNEs eager to break into the world's most populous consumer market, pioneering firms soon confronted the complexities of doing business in a transitional economy. Beijing Jeep Corporation, founded in 1984 as a JV between American Motor Company (AMC) and Beijing Automotive Works, was one of the first Sino-American business ventures in the reform period. Although initially hailed as a breakthrough for the American automobile industry, the venture soon soured, as it became increasingly clear that the domestic and foreign partners held divergent goals. The Americans viewed the venture as a beachhead for expanding production into underdeveloped markets, and thus wanted to produce a model similar to AMC's existing line to market to Chinese consumers; the Chinese saw it as an opportunity to import advanced technologies and production techniques, and thus wanted to design a military Jeep to sell to the People's Liberation Army.[31] Such strategic misalignments plagued the JV throughout its inglorious two-decade existence.[32] While Beijing Jeep earned special notoriety, it was emblematic of an early generation of Sino-foreign collaborations that served as important vehicles of technological transfer, but often failed to live up to the lofty expectations of foreign investors.

Despite these early challenges, FDI inflows began to accelerate in the mid 1980s before surging after Deng Xiaoping's famous "Southern Tour" in 1992 – a pivotal event that marked the CCP's recommitment to continued economic reforms. According to World Bank data, the ratio of FDI inflows to GDP remained lower than 1 percent through 1990, but rose to a staggering peak of 6.2 percent of GDP in 1993. A combination of liberalizing policies, relative political stability, and the growing global demand for new investment opportunities contributed to a volume of foreign investment far greater than what could have been predicted even just a few years earlier.[33] By the mid 1990s, China had, according to calculations by the World Bank and the International Monetary Fund, become one of the largest trading nations and the recipient of more FDI than any other country in the world, with net inflows approaching nearly US $50 billion annually (see Figure 3.1). Thereafter, inward-flowing FDI continued to accelerate, reaching a peak of nearly US $350 billion in 2021. However, it must be noted that, while indicative of general trends, such data are also highly problematic. Because these data regard Hong Kong as a separate polity, counting capital flows between Hong Kong and mainland China as FDI, they are heavily distorted by "round tripping," wherein mainland firms channeled funds through Hong Kong for tax purposes.

China's outward FDI was much slower to take off. State policies that continued to prioritize domestic development permitted only SOEs and local government corporations to invest overseas.[34] Until 1985, a mere 189 investment projects with a total investment of US $197 million were

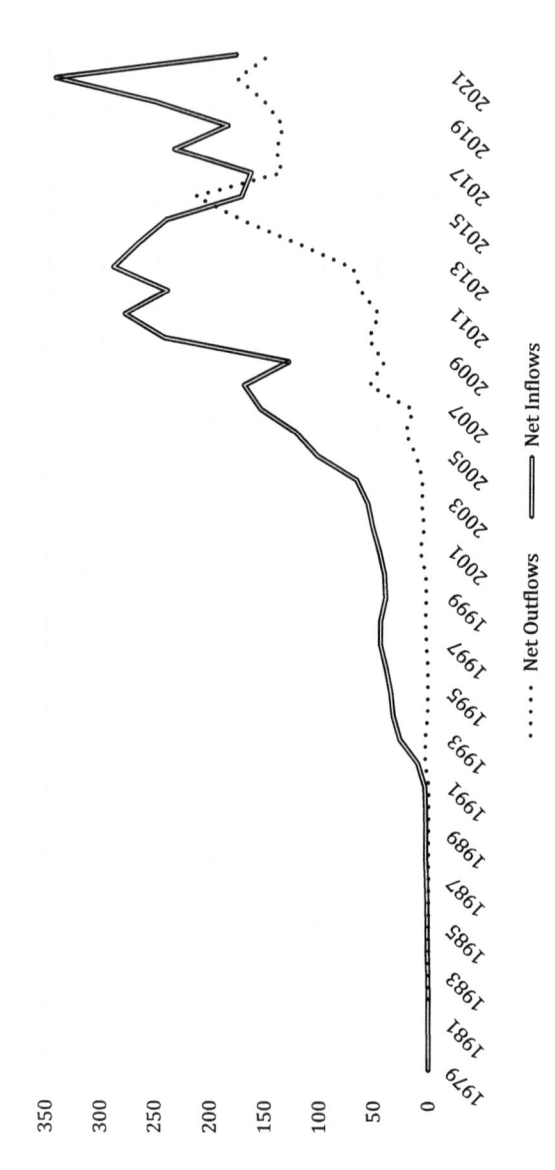

Figure 3.1 Chinese foreign direct investment outflows and inflows 1979–2021 (in 2022 US $ billion). Source: World Bank, Foreign Direct Investment, net inflows, and net outflows (BoP, current US$) [dataset], 2025

approved.[35] Much of this early investment activity was centrally directed natural resource-seeking, motivated primarily by domestic economic imperatives.[36] It was also poorly organized and managed: SOEs tended to rely on personal and ethnic ties when making overseas investments, and once investments had been made, they failed to adequately oversee them.[37]

Only after the turn of the twenty-first century did China's outward globalization accelerate. In anticipation of China's accession to the World Trade Organization (WTO) in 2001, the CCP launched its "going global" strategy, a major policy initiative that laid the groundwork for the expansions of overseas Chinese investment in target areas, such as resource exploration, technological exports, and R&D. As part of the broad initiative, the State Council granted export tax rebates, foreign exchange assistance, and other incentives to encourage Chinese enterprises to invest abroad. Such policy liberalization contributed to an average annual growth rate of 31.2 percent in outward FDI (OFDI) between 2002 and 2017.[38] By 2020, China had, according to data from the Statistical Bulletin of China, become the leading country in OFDI flows, with more than twenty-seven thousand Chinese MNEs operating in 188 countries and regions around the world.

Much of this activity continued to be driven by SOEs seeking access to new markets. For example, the electronics giant TCL, founded in 1981 as an audio cassette manufacturer, acquired the established German brand Schneider Rundfunkwerke and formed a JV with French telecommunications company Alcatel to break into the European smartphone and consumer electronics markets. By 2015, nearly half of TCL's revenues were being generated overseas. Other firms pursued a strategy of "going out to bring in," acquiring strategic assets abroad to increase their competitiveness at home. After a series of public scandals in China's food and dairy industry severely undermined consumer confidence in domestic brands, Bright Food Group, a food and beverage manufacturer wholly owned by the Shanghai municipal government, made a series of high-profile overseas acquisitions. Bright purchased controlling stakes of Synlait (a major dairy producer in New Zealand) in 2010, Manassen Foods (an Australian food producer) in 2011, and Weetabix (a British cereal company) in 2014. By leveraging the reputation of these foreign brands, the firm was able to regain the trust of Chinese consumers and consolidate its lead in domestic markets.

These SOEs could be viewed as partners in globalization with the Chinese state. State-run banks provided SOEs with preferential access to capital, and policies incentivized them to expand the size and complexity of their operations through overseas acquisitions.[39] In turn, SOEs tended to pursue strategies and investments preferred by the Chinese government.[40] Foreign direct investment channeled through SOEs served as an important instrument of China's foreign policy, which raised concerns about Chinese SOEs placing political objectives above human rights.[41] As late as 2014, centrally controlled SOEs continued to account for some 75 percent of China's foreign investment volume, much of which involved state-guided and heavily subsidized investments in strategically important regions.[42] Through such partnership, hundreds of Chinese state-owned MNEs grew to be the largest firms of their kind – according to *Fortune* magazine's global 500 list, nearly one-fifth of the world's largest state-owned MNEs were from China.

Beginning in 2003, with the lifting of prohibitions on private firms investing abroad, private MNEs became participants in China's globalization. Driven by domestic competitive pressure and stimulated by favorable government policies, many firms used overseas mergers and acquisitions (M&A) as a vehicle for internationalization.[43] Lenovo, which launched in 1984 as a spin-off of the Chinese Academy of Sciences, catapulted into global markets with its 2005 acquisition of IBM's personal computing division. Over the preceding two decades, the firm had grown from a domestic distributor of foreign-manufactured computers (AST, and later Hewlett-Packard and IBM) to China's best-selling personal computer producer. The IBM acquisition not only provided Lenovo with the ThinkPad brand, thus compensating for weak international branding, but also advanced PC manufacturing technologies that provided competitive advantages in both domestic and global markets.

Following Lenovo, a wave of private MNEs pursued high-profile acquisitions as a cornerstone of their globalization strategies. For example, in 2010, Hangzhou-based automotive manufacturer Zhejiang

Geely Holding Group Company acquired Swedish automaker Volvo from Ford Motor Company (with the aid of a subsidized €20 billion loan from the China Development Bank). In 2011, Tencent acquired a majority stake in American videogame developer Riot Games, creator of the popular multiplayer online game *League of Legends*. In 2016, home appliance and consumer electronics firm Haier acquired General Electric's appliance division. And in 2019, sports equipment company Anta Sports acquired a majority interest in Finland-based Amer Sports, thus adding to its portfolio well-known brands such as Wilson, Salomon, and Arc'teryx.

In attempting to carry out these M&A activities, Chinese firms faced powerful political headwinds. The 2019 Netflix original documentary *American Factory* provided a glimpse of this new face of globalization – one in which private Chinese MNEs were setting the terms for their host countries. Set in Moraine, Ohio, a town that experienced economic decline following the closure of a Ford plant in 2008, the film documents the events following the acquisition of the factory by Chinese investor Cao Dewang in 2014. Reopened and rebranded as Fuyao, the auto-glass manufacturing plant restored hundreds of jobs. However, tensions mounted as members of the American workforce struggled to adapt to the stringent demands of their Chinese employer and the Chinese management grappled with workers' desire to unionize.

Wanxiang, another pioneering Chinese MNE and the third largest automotive parts supplier in the United States, faced similar challenges in its mission to "earn foreigners' money, use foreigners' resources, and be foreigners' bosses in a foreigners' land."[44] After successfully acquiring prominent US part manufacturers Zeller and Fisker Automotive (renamed Karma) and reorganizing their operations to achieve greater efficiency and competitiveness, Wanxiang faced increasing resistance from local labor unions. Union leaders claimed that the company lacked sufficient local representation in its ranks of managers and refused to provide competitive wages and benefits. When Wanxiang later attempted to acquire Guidion Manufacturing, a financially distressed engine parts maker in Michigan, the deal was ultimately scuttled as a result of union opposition. The successes and failures of such investment activities thus shaped the perception of Chinese firms in the United States and had a powerful impact on the shifting landscape of Sino-US relations.

As M&A activity sharply contracted, greenfield investments emerged as the principal vehicle of Chinese OFDI, a trend driven in large part by the burgeoning electric vehicle (EV) industry. Fueled by state subsidies and nonfinancial incentives, China's domestic EV sector experienced explosive growth, first in the manufacturing of plug-in hybrids and later in the development of advanced, fully electric vehicles. By 2021, the penetration rate of EVs in China approached 20 percent, and the Chinese market for EVs had grown to constitute roughly 50 percent of the global market share.[45] As the number of Chinese EV firms proliferated in domestic markets to near saturation, the superabundance of capital, products, and talent sought new investments and markets overseas. The impact of such investment was felt most strongly in Europe, where a series of multibillion-euro projects pushed the share of greenfield investment (as a percentage of total OFDI) from a mere 2 percent in 2017 up to 78 percent in 2023.[46] For example, EV battery producer Contemporary Amperex Technology Company, Limited (CATL) established new lithium battery plants across Hungary, Germany, and France. Through such investments, CATL positioned itself as the key local supplier of leading European automakers, including BMW and Mercedes, preemptively sidestepping new import tariffs. Thus, even in the face of geopolitical headwinds and domestic economic doldrums, private Chinese MNEs have maintained a foothold in developed economies and continued to play a prominent role in facilitating the green transition.

3.4 A Third Wave: China's Turn toward Emerging Markets

After a precipitous decade-long rise, Chinese OFDI began to plateau around 2015. A confluence of factors ranging from growing geopolitical tensions with the United States, to trade disputes with Australia and Europe, to a global pandemic that originated in China contributed to this slowdown in Chinese overseas investment. State-owned MNEs were buffeted particularly hard by these headwinds. By 2022, the state-owned share of Chinese OFDI in Europe and the United States had fallen to a historic low – 12 percent and 10 percent respectively.[47] Some foreign analysts proclaimed the end of the golden age of China's overseas investment.

However, a closer look at the shifting patterns of Chinese OFDI suggests that this was perhaps just the beginning of a new era. At the same time as Chinese OFDI in developed markets was cresting, the CCP, under the leadership of Xi Jinping, made clear its ambition to become the economic leader of the developing world. The cornerstone of this strategic shift was the Belt & Road Initiative (BRI), a development strategy launched in 2013 that provided a framework for linking Central Asia, the Middle East, Southeast Asia, and Sub-Saharan Africa with China through unprecedented levels of trade and investment. Incentivized by preferential policies and seeking to align themselves with the state, many MNEs, both public and private, began to explore investments in BRI member states. By 2022, some sixteen thousand new BRI enterprises had been established, accounting for 34 percent of the total number of overseas enterprises set up by Chinese investors.[48] By 2023, cumulative BRI engagement exceeded US $1 trillion, of which nonfinancial investments comprised about US $419 billion.[49]

State-led investments were concentrated in resource extraction and infrastructure building. After the launch of the BRI, oil and gas SOEs such as China National Petroleum Corporation (CNPC), China National Offshore Oil Corporation (CNOOC), and China Petroleum & Chemical Corporation (Sinopec) accelerated investment in projects across Africa, Latin America, Central Asia, and Southeast Asia. Mineral extraction companies focused on Africa, setting up large-scale mining projects for copper in Zambia and the Democratic Republic of Congo, gold in Eritrea and Ghana, and uranium in Namibia. The extraction of resources bound for China was directly supported by infrastructural investments in roads, bridges, railways, and ports, which were financed through a combination of grants, aid, and loans (often at low interest rates and with generous schedules of return) and executed by Chinese SOEs. At the launch of the BRI, these state-owned MNEs with close ties to the CCP accounted for 69 percent of Chinese FDI in Africa.[50]

While this state-directed dual-investment strategy was crucial to absorbing overcapacity in China's construction industry and to securing resources for China's continued growth, it had a more mixed impact on host economies.[51] There is vigorous debate about the environmental impact of Chinese investment in Africa, with MNEs in extractive industries singled out for their poor record of environmental and human rights abuses.[52] For example, investigations into Chinese mining investments in the Democratic Republic of Congo found that workers in Chinese-owned mines were subjected not only to low wages and delayed payments, but also "colonial era levels" of discrimination and physical violence.[53] Other firms have been implicated in documented cases of severe environmental damage, including water pollution, deforestation, and habitat destruction (see Chapter 2 for the negative impact of Chinese MNEs on seaweed collection in Peru). While much of the criticism leveled at Chinese MNEs has been earned, many environmental and human rights issues are reflective of enduring structural problems that predate the arrival of Chinese firms. Western MNEs in extractive industries, including Swiss commodity trading and mining company Glencore, discussed in Chapter 11, have been mired in similar controversies for decades. Although this in no way absolves Chinese MNEs of responsibility for their actions, it suggests the extreme complexity of doing business in weak institutional contexts.

Such high levels of state-led investment have also raised international concerns about potential Chinese "debt traps" – the practice of a powerful nation extending excessive credit with the intent of leveraging the debt to extract political or economic concessions. However, there is growing consensus that such concerns have misrepresented the realities of Chinese OFDI. Take, for example, the controversial case of the Sri Lankan Hambantota port. After receiving two positive feasibility reports by Canadian and Danish companies, the Sri Lankan government first approached the United States and India to collaborate on a port construction project. Only after being rejected by both did it enter into an agreement with China. Later, when the economic situation in the country faltered, the government chose to lease the Hambantota port to a Chinese company for a period of ninety-nine years, using the cash it accrued therefrom to bolster its foreign reserves. Indeed, studies of this and other BRI projects have found that Chinese state-run banks have been willing to restructure loans, and that China has yet to seize an asset from any country.[54] One may well fault Chinese MNEs for willingly working with and enabling political strongmen. But "debt trap" narratives fail to capture the dynamics of these international partnerships where developing country partners are active agents, rather than credulous victims.

Private MNEs operating in emerging markets have often been painted with the same broad brush as their state-owned counterparts in a "widespread portrait of China's state-business relations [as that of] state-directed, collusive behavior."[55] Part of the reason for this overly reductive narrative is that some private firms, such as Huawei, have deep ties with the Chinese state, while other publicly listed companies are partially state-owned through state-run capital funds or investment corporations. Nevertheless, the distinction remains an important one, as (mostly) private MNEs represent a greater diversity of sectors and business models. Inter-sectoral differences in capital intensity and resource allocation have spelled very different outcomes in terms of job creation, the cultivation of human capital, and business ecosystem development. For example, whereas Chinese SOEs' investment in Africa was heavily concentrated in infrastructure building (42 percent) and resource extractions (22 percent), private investment focused more on manufacturing (31 percent) and trade and logistics (24 percent).[56] In this regard, Chinese private MNEs compared favorably to their North American and European counterparts, whose activities were concentrated in oil extraction and mining.[57]

There is strong evidence to suggest that whereas FDI in extractive industries is vulnerable to being captured by small and corrupt groups of elites, more diffuse Chinese investments in African manufacturing have had a positive impact on local income growth and firm productivity.[58] Take for example Chinese garment and footwear manufacturers in Ethiopia, a country whose tariff treaties with the United States and Europe attracted much overseas investment. Guangdong-based Huajian Group, one of the largest producers of women's footwear in China and maker of well-known brands such as Guess and Clarkes, established a shoe factory in Ethiopia in 2011. In response to the launch of the BRI in 2013, the company announced its plan to invest US $2 billion in a larger manufacturing zone, the Ethiopia China Huajian International Light Industry City, that was projected to create one hundred thousand local jobs.[59] The Jiangsu Sunshine Group, founded as a garment manufacturing collective in 1986, established the Sunshine Ethiopia Wool Textile plant in 2018; as part of the project, the Sunshine Group recruited three cohorts of 145 Ethiopian undergraduates for a one-year management training project in China, with the intention of drawing from this pool to replace 70–80 percent of its Chinese personnel.[60] While it is unclear the degree to which such investments facilitated technological transfer, they had a demonstrably positive impact on local job creation, income growth, and the development of human capital.

Chinese telecommunication MNEs have also played a pivotal role in the digitization of African economies. As early as the late 1990s, Chinese telecommunications giant Huawei, founded in 1987 by a retired officer of the People's Liberation Army, began building communications networks in Sub-Saharan Africa and the Middle East.[61] Beginning in the 2000s, Huawei set up technical training centers, first in Nigeria and Egypt and later in six other African countries, to train customers and contractors in the installation, usage, and servicing of Huawei equipment. By 2016, Huawei operated across forty African countries, and by 2018, the company and its subsidiaries owned approximately 70 percent of the 4G networks across the continent.[62] Over time, such private Chinese investments became increasingly capital intensive, technologically advanced, and oriented toward domestic (rather than third-country) consumption. Chinese MNEs, including Xiaomi, OPPO, and Realme, transitioned from marketing China-made products through overseas branches to direct manufacturing in host countries. Transsion, a mobile and smartphone manufacturer with virtually no presence in China, made an even bigger bet on African markets, investing heavily in manufacturing and R&D facilities in Nigeria, Ethiopia, and other countries; the firm grew to become Africa's top smartphone seller, commanding, by 2022, nearly 50 percent of the African smartphone market.[63] By laying critical infrastructure and supplying affordable and technologically sophisticated consumer telecommunications products, these firms played a crucial role in helping bridge the digital divide.

Taking advantage of expanding smartphone access, a new generation of Chinese platform MNEs sprang up to offer digitally enabled services in emerging markets. While many had ties with China's domestic tech giants, most were established not as corporate offshoots, but as "born global" start-ups with an explicit focus on developing regions. Take for example, Mico World, a Beijing-headquartered social media company that developed popular live-streaming services in the Middle

East, North Africa, and Southeast Asia. The firm achieved tremendous success through its strategy of recruiting influencers from liberal Muslim-majority countries such as Egypt to produce content for consumption in more conservative ones such as Saudi Arabia. By 2024, Mico World operated more than a dozen subsidiaries and had more than 100 million users worldwide. Another example is Kilimall, one of East Africa's leading e-commerce platforms. Kilimall was founded in 2014 by Yang Tao, a former Huawei employee who, after being sent to Africa, was shocked by the high prices and limited selection of goods. This experience inspired Yang to launch a digital marketplace that, by leveraging Chinese technologies and venture capital, would connect low-cost suppliers (based mostly in China) to local African merchants. Such platform companies thus had a powerful impact on their host contexts, creating new economic opportunities (though mostly in the form of gig work) and expanding the array of products and services available to consumers.

The aggregate impact of Chinese private investment is difficult to access given that only a minority of projects were captured in official statistics. While large-scale state-backed projects were registered with the Ministry of Commerce and widely publicized, the majority of smaller-scale investments – typically defined as projects worth less than US $10 million – occurred under the radar (often channeled through tax havens such as the Cayman Islands and British Virgin Islands).[64] According to a recent survey, the actual number of Chinese investment projects was somewhere in the region of three to seven times that captured in the Chinese Ministry of Commerce data.[65] Such investments sometimes aligned with and at other times diverged from Chinese state interests. For example, in seeking to exploit natural resources and access local markets, private Chinese businesses readily align themselves with China's geopolitical rivals, taking advantage of certain African countries' preferential trade deals with Western Europe and the United States.[66] Other firms engaged in informal (or overtly illegal) behaviors, directly undermining Chinese state efforts to promote a positive national image in host country contexts. For example, in the context of Nigeria, the activities of Chinese smugglers who illegally imported and sold textiles produced in Asia not only presented an intractable challenge to the protectionist policies of the host country government, but also exacerbated popular anti-Chinese sentiments.[67] While scholars highlight different sides of the complex face of Chinese globalization in Africa, with some emphasizing positive impacts and others negative ones, most agree on one thing: there are "many Chinas" and "many Africas."[68]

3.5 Conclusion

The history of Chinese MNEs is a story of discontinuous globalization. The first wave began in the late nineteenth and early twentieth centuries, when domestic Chinese firms successfully adopted new technologies and combined different organizational forms to compete against foreign MNEs in both domestic and overseas markets. This early experiment with globalization was ultimately aborted, though not as a result of market competition. Instead, the growth of Chinese MNEs was curtailed by geopolitical conflict, the outbreak of World War II, and the rise of the CCP. After the founding of the People's Republic of China in 1949, the Chinese economy was mostly closed off from global trade, and what little overseas activity did occur was politically motivated and state-controlled. Though China did continue to import foreign technologies in specific sectors, it was not enough to stimulate broad-based development. Only after the launch of Reform and Opening Up in 1978 did Chinese state-owned businesses begin reestablishing links with the global economy and accelerating technological transfer; it would be another two decades still before private enterprises were permitted to openly invest overseas. Finally, in the twenty-first century, in the face of rising geopolitical challenges, private Chinese MNEs gradually rose to the fore, and Chinese OFDI shifted away from the United States and Europe and toward emerging markets.

This story shows that the history of MNEs cannot be disentangled from considerations of power and politics. The conditions under which Chinese enterprises participated in the global economy have always been intrinsically linked to China's relative position in the world. In the late nineteenth century, when the global balance of power was decidedly in favor of industrializing European nations, Chinese firms were placed at a disadvantage relative to their foreign counterparts. Yet, through the adoption of new technologies and organizational forms, they played a critical role in strengthening the nation by driving nascent industrialization. In the early twenty-first century, as China consolidated its position as an emerging power, the state crafted targeted policies that shaped the activities of MNEs; these enabled and incentivized firms to develop new capabilities in certain sectors (such as telecommunications and green energy), invest in certain markets (such as BRI member states), and promote certain values (such as emphasizing economic rights over human ones). Under such conditions, Chinese MNEs came to wield disproportionate influence in both developed and emerging market contexts.

Though powerful, these political forces were nondeterministic. In opposition to narratives that portray the actions of Chinese MNEs as reflexive responses to the evolving agenda of the Chinese state, Chinese enterprises (both private and even state-owned ones) have represented varied interests that sometimes aligned with and at other times opposed those of their sovereign government. On the one hand, MNEs have served as critical vehicles for introducing advanced technologies into China and diffusing excess domestic capacity. On the other hand, the activities of less scrupulous or less politically savvy actors have marred China's reputation abroad and contributed to growing geopolitical tensions. In assessing the impact of Chinese globalization, both the influence of political forces and the varied responses of MNEs must thus be taken into account.

Notes

1. Flynn, D. O. and Giráldez, A. "Born with a 'Silver Spoon': The Origin of World Trade in 1571," in Flynn, D. O. and Giráldez, A. (eds.) *Metals and Monies in an Emerging Global Economy*, New York, Routledge, 1997.
2. Bickers, R. *China Bound: John Swire & Sons and Its World, 1816–1980*, London, Bloomsbury, 2020.
3. Brook, T. and Wakabayashi, B. T. (eds.) *Regimes: China, Britain, and Japan, 1839–1952*, Berkeley, University of California Press, 2000.
4. International Opium Commission. "Report of the International Opium Commission," in *Minutes of the Proceeding*, Shanghai, February 1–26, 1909, 1:120.
5. Nolan, P. *State and Market in the Chinese Economy: Essays on Controversial Issues*, London, Palgrave Macmillan, 1993.

6. Wilkins, M. "The Impacts of American Multinational Enterprise," in Fairbank, J. K. and May, E. R. (eds.) *America's China Trade in Historical Perspective: The Chinese and American Performance*, Cambridge, MA, Council on East Asian Studies, 1986.
7. Perkins, D. (ed.) *China's Modern Economy in Historical Perspective*, Stanford, CA, Stanford University Press, 1975, 118.
8. Hou, C. *Foreign Investment and Economic Development in China, 1840-1937*, Cambridge, MA, Harvard University Press, 1965, 127, 28.
9. Keller, W. and Shiue, C. H. "The Economic Consequences of the Opium War," CEPR Discussion Paper No. 16242, 2021.
10. Feuerwerker, A. "Handicraft and Manufactured Cotton Textiles in China, 1871-1910," *Journal of Economic History*, 30, 2 (1970), 338-378.
11. Köll, E. *From Cotton Mill to Business Empire: The Emergence of Regional Enterprises in Modern China*, Cambridge, MA, Harvard East Asian Monographs, 2003, 284.
12. Arnold, J. H. *China, a Commercial and Industrial Handbook*, Washington, DC, US Government Printing Office, 1926.
13. Lean, E. *Vernacular Industrialism in China: Local Innovation and Translated Technologies in the Making of a Cosmetics Empire, 1900-1940*, New York, Columbia University Press, 2020.
14. Chang, N. J. "Vertical Integration, Business Diversification, and Firm Architecture: The Case of the China Egg Produce Company in Shanghai, 1923-1950," *Enterprise & Society*, 6, 3 (2005), 419-451.
15. Xu, X. *Jindai jiangnan sizhi gongye shi*, Shanghai, Shanghai People's Press, 1991, 295-420.
16. Köll, E. "Nanyang Brothers Tobacco," in McCusker, J. J. (ed.) *History of World Trade since 1450*, Farmington Hills, MI: Macmillan Reference USA, 2005, 517-519.
17. Cox, H. "Learning to Do Business in China: The Evolution of BAT's Cigarette Distribution Network, 1902-41," *Business History*, 39, 3 (1997), 30-64.
18. Cochran, S. *Big Business in China: Sino-Foreign Rivalry in the Cigarette Industry, 1890-1930*, Cambridge, MA, Harvard University Press, 1980, 33.
19. Wu, S. "Organizational Capability, Entrepreneurship, and Environment Chinese Multinationals, 1912-1949" (MA thesis), Ohio State University, 2008.
20. Lin, M. "Overseas Chinese Merchants and Multiple Nationality: A Means for Reducing Commercial Risk (1895-1935)," *Modern Asian Studies*, 35 (2001), 985-1009.
21. Chan, K. Y. *Business Expansion and Structural Change in Pre-war China: Liu Hongsheng and His Enterprises, 1920-1937*, Hong Kong, Hong Kong University Press, 2006.
22. Frost, S. and Frost, A. "Taxi Shanghai: Entrepreneurship and Semi-colonial Context," *Business History*, 66, 2 (2024), 407-436.

23. Frost A. K. and Li Z. "Markets under Mao: Measuring Underground Activity in the Early PRC," *China Quarterly*, 258 (2024), 309–328.
24. Yu, G. T. "Working on the Railroad: China and the Tanzania–Zambia Railway," *Asian Survey*, 11 (1971), 1101–1117.
25. Kelly, J. M. *Market Maoists: The Communist Origins of China's Capitalist Ascent*, Cambridge, MA, Harvard University Press, 2021.
26. Meisner, M. *Mao's China and After*, New York, Free Press, 1999, 413–425.
27. Teiwes, F. C. and Sun, W. "China's New Economic Policy under Hua Guofeng: Party Consensus and Party Myths," *China Journal*, 66, 6 (2011), 1–23.
28. Jia-Zheng, Y. and Broggi, C. B. "The Metamorphosis of China's Automotive Industry (1953–2001): Inward Internationalisation, Technological Transfers and the Making of a Post-socialist Market," *Business History*, 67, 1 (2025), 211–238.
29. Zweig, D. *Internationalizing China: Domestic Interests and Global Linkages*, Ithaca, NY, Cornell University Press, 2002, 158–160.
30. Deng, X. *Selected Works of Deng Xiaoping*, Beijing, Renmin Chubanshe, 1993.
31. Young, M. N. and Tan, J. "Beijing Jeep at a Crossroads: Facing the Challenge of China's Entry into the WTO," *Asian Case Research Journal*, 5, 1 (2001), 1–26.
32. Mann, J. *Beijing Jeep: A Case Study of Western Business in China*, Oxford, Routledge, 2018.
33. Lardy, N. R. "The Role of Foreign Trade and Investment in China's Economic Transformation," *China Quarterly*, 144 (1995), 1065–1069.
34. Tian, W. and Yu, M. "China's Opening-Up Policies: Achievements and Prospects," in Tian, W. and Yu, M. (eds.) *Outward Foreign Direct Investment of Chinese Enterprises*, Singapore, Springer, 2022.
35. Wong, J. and Chan, S. "China's Outward Direct Investment: Expanding Worldwide," *China: An International Journal*, 1, 2 (2003), 273–301.
36. Buckley, P. J., Clegg, L. J., Cross, A. R., Liu, X., Voss, H., and Zheng, P. "The Determinants of Chinese Outward Foreign Direct Investment," *Journal of International Business Studies*, 38, 4 (2007), 499–518.
37. Tseng, C. S. "Foreign Direct Investment by PRC First-time Investors" (PhD Thesis), Bradford University, 1997.
38. Alon, I., Wang, H., Shen, J., and Zhang, W. "Chinese State-Owned Enterprises Go Global," *Journal of Business Strategy*, 35, 6 (2014), 3–18.
39. Peng, M. W. "The Global Strategy of Emerging Multinationals from China," *Global Strategy Journal*, 2 (2012), 97–107.
40. Luo, Y., Xue, Q., and Han, B. "How Emerging Market Governments Promote Outward FDI: Experience from China," *Journal of World Business*, 45, 1 (2010), 68–79.

41. Whelan, G. and Muthuri, J. N. "Chinese State-Owned Enterprises and Human Rights: The Importance of National and Intra-organizational Pressures," *Business & Society*, 56, 5 (2017), 738–781.
42. Chen, C. "Determinants and Motives of Outward Foreign Direct Investment from China's Provincial Firms," *Transnational Corporations*, 23, 1 (2015), 1–28.
43. Child, J. and Rodrigues, S. B. "The Internationalization of Chinese firms: A Case for Theoretical Extension?" *Management and Organization Review*, 1, 3 (2005), 381–410.
44. Abrami, R. M., Kirby, W. C., McFarlan, F. W., Wong, K. C., and Manty, T. "Wanxiang Group: A Chinese Company's Global Strategy," *Harvard Business School Case* 308-058, revised July 9, 2008.
45. He, H., Sun, F., Wang, Z., et al. "China's Battery Electric Vehicles Lead the World: Achievements in Technology System Architecture and Technological Breakthroughs," *Green Energy and Intelligent Transportation*, 1, 1 (2022), 1–24.
46. Kratz, A., Zenglein, M. J., Brown, A, Sebastian, G., and Meyer, A. "Dwindling Investments Become More Concentrated–Chinese FDI in Europe: 2023 Update," *MERICS Report*, 6 (2024).
47. China's Ministry of Commerce, the National Bureau of Statistics, and the State Administration of Foreign Exchange, "China's Outbound Direct Investment (ODI) 2022," Beijing, Shangwu Press, 2023.
48. Liao, R. "China's Outbound Investment Ranks among Highest Globally," *People's Daily*, October 12, 2023, retrieved from http://en.qstheory.cn/2023-10/12/c_929880.htm.
49. Nedopil, C. "China Belt and Road Initiative (BRI) Investment Report 2023," Griffith Asia Institute and Green Finance & Development Center at FISF Fudan University, 2024, retrieved from https://greenfdc.org/china-belt-and-road-initiative-bri-investment-report-2023.
50. Compagnon, D. and Alejandro, A. "China's External Environmental Policy: Understanding China's Environmental Impact in Africa and How It Is Addressed," *Environmental Practice*, 15, 3 (2013), 220–227.
51. Arikan, I., Arikan, A. M., and Shenkar, O. "Revisiting Emerging Market Multinational Enterprise Views: The Goldilocks Story Restated," *Journal of International Business Studies*, 53 (2022), 781–802.
52. Shinn, D. H. "The Environmental Impact of China's Investment in Africa," *Cornell International Law Journal*, 49, 1 (2016), 25–67.
53. Rights and Accountability in Development. "The Road to Ruin: Electric Vehicles and the Cobalt Workers," *RAID Report*, 2021, retrieved from https://raid-uk.org/wp-content/uploads/2023/03/report_road_to_ruin_evs_cobalt_workers_nov_2021.pdf.

54. Brautigam, D. and Rithmire, M. "The Chinese Debt Trap Is a Myth: The Narrative Wrongfully Portrays Both Beijing and the Developing Countries It Deals With," *The Atlantic*, February 6, 2021.
55. Gu, J., Zhang, C., Vaz, A., and Mukwereza, L. "The Road to Ruin: Electric Vehicles and the Cobalt Workers Chinese State Capitalism? Rethinking the Role of the State and Business in Chinese Development Cooperation in Africa," *World Development*, 81 (2016), 24–34.
56. Shen, X. "Private Chinese Investment in Africa: Myths and Realities," *Development Policy Review*, 33, 1 (2015), 83–106.
57. Brautigam, D. *The Dragon's Gift: The Real Story of China in Africa*, Oxford, Oxford University Press, 2009.
58. Darko, C., Occhiali, G., and Vanino, E. "The Chinese Are Here: Import Penetration and Firm Productivity in Sub-Saharan Africa," *Journal of Development Studies*, 57, 12 (2021), 2112–2135.
59. "Huajian Group Puts Its Best Foot Forward," *China Daily*, June 27, 2019, retrieved from www.chinadaily.com.cn/cndy/2019-06/27/con tent_37485271.htm.
60. "Chinese Textile Manufacturer's Investment Thrives in Ethiopia," *CGTN*, September 24, 2019, retrieved from https://news.cgtn.com/news/2019-09-24/Chinese-textile-manufacturer-s-investment-thrives-in-Ethiopia-KfxyL R6oGQ/index.html.
61. Murphy, D. C. *China's Rise in the Global South: The Middle East, Africa, and Beijing's Alternative World Order*, Stanford, CA, Stanford University Press, 2022.
62. Mackinnon, A. "For Africa, Chinese-Built Internet Is Better Than No Internet at All," *Foreign Policy*, Mar. 19, 2019, retrieved from https://for eignpolicy.com/2019/03/19/for-africa-chinese-built-internet-is-better-tha n-no-internet-at-all.
63. Voncujovi, S. "What Transsion Tells Us about Chinese Investment in Africa," *African Business*, August 21, 2024, retrieved from https://african .business/2024/08/technology-information/what-transsion-tells-us-about-chinese-investment-in-africa.
64. Sutherland, D. and Anderson, J. "The Pitfalls of Using Foreign Direct Investment Data to Measure Chinese Multinational Enterprise Activity," *China Quarterly*, 221 (2015), 21–48.
65. Shen, "Private Chinese Investment."
66. Klaver, M. and Trebilcock, M. "Chinese Investment in Africa," *Law and Development Review*, 4, 1 (2011), 168–217.
67. Akinrinade, S. and Olukoya, O. "Globalization and Deindustrialization: South-South Neo-Liberalism and the Collapse of the Nigerian Textile Industry," *The Global South*, 2, 2 (2008), 159–170.
68. Brautigam, *The Dragon's Gift*.

Further Reading

Cochran, S. *Encountering Chinese Networks: Western, Japanese, and Chinese Corporations in China, 1880–1937*, Los Angeles, CA, University of California Press, 2000.

Lee, C. K. *The Specter of Global China: Politics, Labor, and Foreign Investment in Africa*, Chicago, University of Chicago Press, 2017.

Murphy, D. C. *China's Rise in the Global South: The Middle East, Africa, and Beijing's Alternative World Order*, Stanford, CA, Stanford University Press, 2022.

Ramamurti, R. and Hillemann, J. "What Is 'Chinese' about Chinese Multinationals?" *Journal of International Business Studies*, 49 (2018), 34–48.

Zweig, D. *Internationalizing China: Domestic Interests and Global Linkages*, Ithaca, NY, Cornell University Press, 2002.

VALERIA GIACOMIN AND
ANDREA COLLI

4

Multinationals and Global Value Chains

4.1 Introduction

This chapter provides a historical overview of the relationship between multinational enterprises (MNEs) and global value chains (GVCs), how it evolved, and how it impacted business globalization. Global value chains are a multidisciplinary concept used to explain how production activities are organized globally. In his seminal work on GVCs, economic sociologist Gary Gereffi defined them as "sets of inter-organizational networks clustered around one commodity or product, linking households, enterprises, and states to one another within the world economy."[1] This chapter treats GVCs as a production-sharing model based on an international division of labor and coordination among specialized units operating in different geographies across the world. Global value chains are situationally specific networks, socially constructed and embedded, and locally integrated. They create a spiky system where activities cluster in specific locations, hyperconnected through service centers (global cities) and advanced transport infrastructure. This system works best when these locations are economically integrated, with minimal political friction among the nations involved. Thus, GVCs provide insights into the diffusion of capitalism and global development, particularly during intense globalization phases.

Business historians have shown that, in their international expansion, MNEs have clustered different phases of the production process or the product value chain in locations that offer the most efficiency, whether in terms of profitability, regulation, quality, or availability of labor. Multinational enterprises could connect these clusters thanks to declining transport costs and advancements in information and communication technology (ICT) since the middle of the nineteenth century. This strategy has promoted economic specialization in host countries that theoretically at least had the potential to facilitate technology transfer and local growth. As a result, and given their structure, GVCs are intrinsically connected to phases of expansion and integration of the world's economy, fueled by technological progress and favorable political and institutional conditions.

Since the Second Industrial Revolution of the late nineteenth century, MNEs have organized their investments and operations through GVCs. Embryonic GVC forms emerged through regional labor divisions in North–North and North–South contexts, with the former driven by market expansion in industrial regions and the latter focused on resource extraction in colonies. These networks, based on exploiting local resources and cheap labor, fueled Western industrialization, but deepened social and spatial inequalities in the developing world. By the end of the first global economy in the 1920s, many companies had developed complex value chains linking developing regions to industrial centers through direct ownership, vertical integration, and strategic partnerships.

After the world wars and the deglobalization of the interwar period, MNEs reorganized GVCs. This trend intensified after World War II with the process of decolonization and renewed business ties in newly independent countries. The end of the Cold War in the late 1980s accelerated global integration, fueled by liberalization in China, India, and the Global South. Technological advances and cheaper labor led MNEs to relocate labor-intensive GVC segments, driving specialization but worsening social inequalities. Since the late 2010s, the various trends discussed in Chapter 1, including deglobalization, the COVID-19 pandemic, and geopolitical tensions, have triggered a regionalization and decoupling of GVCs.

This chapter reviews the mutual impact of MNEs and GVCs, highlighting benefits like local development, infrastructure improvements, and technology sharing while addressing the darker aspects of this global structure. It demonstrates that GVCs reinforced inequalities intrinsic to global capitalism. While specialization increased interdependence and knowledge sharing, countries often failed to upgrade to advanced technologies due to institutional gaps and unethical practices, deepening income and tech disparities. Global value chains also created power imbalances within MNEs, leaving some units with less control, and made economies vulnerable to trade disruptions. Additionally, MNEs exploited GVCs to minimize taxes, shift liabilities through subcontractors, and avoid accountability for human rights violations in host economies.

Section 4.2 reviews the historical foundation of the GVC concept and the role of GVCs in the first global economy. Section 4.3 explores how MNEs and GVCs have shaped the global economy after World War II. Sections 4.4 and 4.5 examine the geographical, social, and political impacts of GVCs. Section 4.6 concludes.

4.2 The Antecedents of GVCs

The theorization of production networks began in 1930s Japan and gained prominence with Kaname Akamatsu's 1960s flying geese paradigm (FGP), which explored how advanced economies outsourced labor-intensive activities to lower-income countries, fostering industrialization.[2] However, the FGP overlooked factors like local institutions and the "middle-income trap." Conversely, other research, such as Immanuel Wallerstein's world systems theory focused on how "core" nations exploited "peripheral" ones, perpetuating global inequality.[3] In the 1980s, Gereffi and colleagues expanded this approach through the GVC framework, examining governance and power in production chains.

Extensive research in international business history has documented the role of MNEs and transnational entrepreneurs in spreading global capitalism,[4] providing insights into the long-term evolution and impact of GVCs.[5] Studies have examined how embryonic commodity chains, like nineteenth-century exports from New Zealand to Britain,[6] and sectors such as fur trading[7] and diamond cutting,[8] were shaped by these networks. Research on the Global South, particularly Southeast Asia,[9] highlights the influence of colonial legacies and market competition on GVCs, as well as the significant role of MNEs from emerging economies like Thailand[10] and South Korea.[11] Chapter 6 shows that in Central America, GVC development often intertwined with changes in institutional and political environments. Business history offers a deeper understanding of GVC development, showing how GVCs adapted to changes in institutional and political environments over time. The historical perspective reveals the long-term impact, complexity, and contradictions of GVCs, in contrast to the more static view offered by traditional management and international business (IB) approaches.[12]

As global integration unfolded alongside the expansion of colonial empires from the late nineteenth century to the interwar period, rudimentary versions of GVCs began to form. Unlike modern GVCs, which involve ownership and coordination across production processes, these early chains emerged from formalizing cross-border market relationships within and between imperial economies. Merchants, entrepreneurs, and companies coordinated dispersed production activities across locations, leading to two basic systems: one focused on commodity extraction for industrial processes, and the other on producing semifinished goods for global export, such as textiles and automotive products.

The most common system involved commodity trade and extraction in colonies and developed regions, with relatively short and unsophisticated chains. Early MNEs managed extraction, logistics, and sometimes manufacturing, supplying the industrializing Global North. An increasingly integrated financial system, centered in cities like London, New York, and Paris, supported long-distance trade, investments in transport and communication, and vertical integration in foreign locations.[13]

In many cases, MNEs quickly established monopolistic or oligopolistic positions by vertically integrating along the chain or horizontally within production segments. For instance, British companies Rio Tinto and Tharsis had a vast network of mining and processing operations in the Huelva region in southern Spain, later expanding to the Americas and Africa.[14] The British Indian Copper Corporation orchestrated a network of underground copper mines in India and the Spanish region of Cerro Muriano, concentrator plants, and a smelter and refinery.[15] Since the 1870s, John Rockefeller's Standard Oil established integrated operations in four continents, controlling refining and distribution operations through shipping terminals and storage facilities in major ports in Britain and Germany and established infrastructure and distribution networks in Russia (where it also had access to the Baku oil fields), China, Japan, Mexico, and Brazil.[16]

Multinational enterprises established production chains for several agricultural commodities sourced in bulk in different locations of the Global South. They were then transported to be processed in dedicated facilities in the Global North, where they had long-standing relationships or equity investments. This is the case for many well-researched agricultural commodities such as sugar, tobacco, coffee, cocoa, tea, and cinchona. Unlike simple international sourcing or export relations, trading companies and Western MNEs often controlled parts or the entire supply chain from extraction to processing and distribution across various locations. They achieved this through direct (usually partial) ownership or formal and informal agreements ensuring coordinated operations.

A prime example is Southeast Asia's rubber and later palm oil production. In the 1870s, the British introduced the highly productive *Hevea brasiliensis* rubber variety growing wild in the Amazon forests to Southeast Asia, a climatically similar area under British political control.[17] Colonial institutions and foreign scientists adapted the crop to the local environment, facilitating large-scale cultivation. Western "agency houses," such as the British Harrison and Crosfield, Barlows, and Guthrie, organized production and transportation to the West, where latex was processed into tires and other goods, quickly vertically integrating into plantation and processing facilities. Within two decades, the industry became pivotal for global automotive manufacturing and a strategic asset for the British Empire.[18]

By the early twentieth century, a few trading houses vertically integrated into large-scale plantations dominated rubber production. Not until the mid 1910s did tire manufacturers like Goodyear, Dunlop, and Firestone acquire their regional estates, controlling production along the whole supply chain. This plantation industry profoundly shaped the region's long-term development, fostering extensive trade and infrastructure growth. By the 1920s, Southeast Asia had overcome South

America in rubber exports and quickly came to account for the lion's share of global production. The emergence of this plantation cluster had positive spillovers in the regional economy, fostering rubber manufacturing by local ethnic Chinese entrepreneurs.[19] However, this global operation also resulted in uneven spatial development in the region, with infrastructure concentrated along coastal areas to connect estates with major ports and urban service centers like Singapore, Penang, Batavia, Medan, and Kuala Lumpur.

Furthermore, the colonial exploitation of the region traced a path of environmental degradation still evident today. By the early 1890s, extensive deforestation and soil erosion plagued several areas of Malaya, Borneo, and the Dutch East Indies (modern Indonesia), spurred by decades of tin mining and the demand for timber to support urbanization.[20] In the same period, the surge in demand for gutta-percha, vital for transoceanic cables, led to an environmental disaster involving the felling of more than 80 million trees in Southeast Asian rainforests, nearly driving the crop to extinction.[21] The destruction of the local forests and ecosystems continued steadily during the twentieth century with the expansion of the plantation system and the emergence of agribusiness in the region.

A similar example of a rudimentary commodity chain revolved around the production of animal and vegetable oils for making margarine, soap, and machinery lubricants. In the postwar period, palm oil emerged as a primary diversification from rubber in Southeast Asia, exacerbating deforestation and environmental crises in the region.[22] However, since the nineteenth century, palm oil, primarily sourced from Western Africa, had been used interchangeably with other vegetable oils such as copra, cottonseed, sunflower, and marine oils, the most critical being whale oil. Following an extraction phase close to the sourcing locations, these different types of oils underwent further refinement and bleaching processes in Europe and the United States. These activities tended to be primarily concentrated in the hands of a few companies, leading to oligopolistic structures controlling the most value-added activities along the chains, as patented research and technology were utilized for various purposes, including food production (such as margarine), soap manufacturing, lubrication, illumination, and even medicinal applications. For instance, in the case of whale oil in

Norway, the Anglo-Dutch company Unilever, which already dominated large portions of the production and sale of margarine and was a major player in edible fats, extended its presence to Norway and other competitive niche markets. This expansion was facilitated by its control over crucial stages of the commodity chain, mainly manufacturing and bleaching.[23]

A final example of early commodity chain involved the cultivation and processing of bananas. The US-owned United Fruit (UFC) and its competitor fruit producer Dole emerged as dominant players in the industry. They developed a highly integrated GVC in the late nineteenth century, focusing on asset-specific investments in Central America. As described in Chapter 6, UFC's strategy involved vertical integration across multiple countries, controlling plantations, transportation (the Great White Fleet), and marketing. The integrated production of bananas and other tropical fruits such as pineapple triggered several innovations in refrigerated sea transport and mechanization of canning and preservation, but destroyed ecosystems, violated workers' human rights, and led to political instability in the region.[24]

The second type of chain, though less common, involved exporting semifinished goods for final assembly or manufacturing in foreign markets. This approach was especially typical in textile production. In preindustrial times, the putting-out system – where raw materials were distributed to workers who processed them at home – operated through relatively short, regional chains for producing common textiles. However, the production of more valuable fibers like silk and premium wool relied on longer international networks. For example, in the eighteenth century, German merchants built a complex production system by importing high-quality wool from Spain and partnering with local dyers who sourced pigments like indigo from India and cochineal red from Mexico.[25] This collaboration allowed them to produce dyed textiles, which were then sold through an extensive distribution network across Europe, the Mediterranean, and Asia. Similarly, since the nineteenth century, silk produced in north Italy was processed into premium fabrics in Lyon (France) and Krefeld (Germany) and sold all over Europe.[26]

Another insightful example is the automotive giant Ford, which expanded its operations in Europe in the early twentieth century.

According to business historian Steve Tolliday, the initial phase involved shipping fully assembled cars to Europe. A second phase followed, lasting until the early 1930s when Ford established branch plants in various European countries to source parts and components locally and assemble "knocked down" parts produced in and shipped from the United States. The case of the American automaker illustrates how even embryonic forms of GVCs were sensitive to international trade costs and could be exposed to deglobalizing trends. When trade costs increased due to protectionist measures affecting both final and intermediate goods in the interwar period, it became advantageous for Ford to significantly alter its foreign investment strategy. The company gave up the fragmentation of production stages and instead established full-fledged manufacturing plants to serve the European market directly.[27]

Finally, the Swiss production of precision watches exemplifies the adaptation of GVCs over time. In the nineteenth century, Swiss watchmakers, primarily from the Jura region, became central to the European market for mechanical components through simple contractual agreements independent of major companies, fostering trade within the industry. After World War I, as watchmaking spread globally, Switzerland responded with protectionist measures. In the 1930s, concerned about unemployment and labor unrest, the Swiss government supported cartels like Allgemeine Schweizerische Uhrenindustrie AG (ASUAG) to centralize watch part distribution, standardize production, and regulate machine tool exports. This aimed to protect Swiss jobs and industry from global competition. Swiss components also supplied French and German producers, and Swiss machine tools were exported to emerging watch industries in Japan and the Soviet Union during the interwar period.[28]

In summary, while historical value chains differed from modern GVCs in terms of sectors, coordination, and technology, they shared similarities such as asymmetric power dynamics and vulnerability to geopolitical risks. Colonial infrastructure supported these chains, linking advanced economies in the Global North and deepening exploitation in the Global South. Multinational enterprises controlled these embryonic GVCs through monopolies and cartels, contributing to uneven development between well-connected ports and extraction sites in contrast to disconnected interiors and rural areas. While the partial disruption of these chains during the interwar years highlighted their dependence on industrialized countries and imperial powers, the ability of MNEs to readapt and restore these chains in the postwar period showed the resilience of these organizational structures through times of turbulence.

4.3 GVCs in the Postwar Period and the Second Global Economy

Since the postwar period, a convergence of factors significantly reduced the "cost of trade" for MNEs, leading to an acceleration of trade particularly from the 1970s onward. Advancements in information and communication technologies, stemming from scientific research during World War II and the Cold War, were major drivers of this second wave of globalization. Travel time shrank thanks to faster and more affordable land and air transport, while the introduction of containerization standardized and streamlined shipping processes in the 1970s.[29]

While technology was a crucial catalyst for growing integration, institutional arrangements in the form of international agreements and regulations played an equally significant role. As shown in Chapter 8, during the Cold War, the United States spearheaded bilateral agreements to bolster trade within the Western Bloc and endorsed the formation of the European Common Market, which began in the 1950s and accelerated in the 1990s. Meanwhile, the United States increasingly supported and in some cases (as in Guatemala and Indonesia) influenced the liberalization and regime changes in allied partner economies of the Global South. In 1979, China took the historical decision to initiate reforms to gradually open its market to international trade. Vietnam followed suit in 1986, while India and Turkey embarked on economic liberalization in the early 1990s.

In the postwar period, trade flows gradually increased, with Japan emerging as a major exporter of consumer electronics, notably transistor radios and semiconductors. Japanese companies rapidly expanded their domestic electronics production, benefiting from access to advanced technology through open licensing policies from US firms such as AT&T and RCA. Firms like Sony and Sanyo pioneered offshoring in the electronics industry by moving production to Hong Kong to lower costs and avoid trade barriers. In the 1960s, in regions like Okinawa and Taiwan, companies such as Toyo Radio and Tokai Wireless began exporting radios with Japanese support. American firms like Trans-Aire Electronics, Philco, and RCA soon followed, establishing offshore facilities in these areas.[30]

By the 1960s, these efforts had created a global production network across East Asian countries like Japan, South Korea, Hong Kong, Taiwan, and Singapore, driven by the need for lower labor costs and greater competitiveness. Manufacturing companies from the United States and Western Europe, particularly in industries with high labor costs, simple mechanization, and low margins, started moving segments of production and assembly, a phenomenon known as "global hopping."[31] Major US toy manufacturers like Louis Marx and Mattel established their first production subsidiaries in Japan in 1958 and Hong Kong in 1961.[32] In Switzerland, employers, authorities, and labor unions widely agreed that offshoring was beneficial to address labor shortages. This consensus that lasted until the 1970 crisis allowed Swiss MNEs to move low-skill tasks abroad while concentrating on higher-value production at home, backed by supportive government policies.[33] Even sophisticated productions like watch manufacturing moved to Asia after World War II due to rising demand and mass-production techniques. By the 1960s and 1970s, Hong Kong became a key hub for assembling watch parts for Swiss, American, and Japanese companies, anticipating a broader shift of the watch industry's value chain to Asia in the 1980s with the advent of quartz technology.[34]

In textile and apparel manufacturing, paradoxically, protectionist tendencies contributed to the reemergence of GVCs as the industry shifted production to countries without restrictive export quotas to the United States and the European Economic Community (EEC). This dynamic was prominent in the 1960s and 1970s. Hong Kong, as a British territory, became a major textile producer due to Japanese companies relocating to bypass quota restrictions on Japan and taking advantage of cheaper labor costs.[35] As a result, rather than vanishing, the German textile and apparel industry adapted, shifting to higher-value activities like design and branding while outsourcing labor-intensive production to lower-cost countries. Supported by selective protectionism and outward processing, where components were produced abroad and reimported, the industry remained competitive within the GVCs. Major German brands like Adidas, Puma, and Hugo Boss were among the first to expand their GVCs into Asia, while keeping their headquarters in Germany.[36]

The contextual emergence of export processing zones (EPZs) and special economic zones (SEZs) further favored the fragmentation of value chains and relocation of production in the Caribbean and East Asia, offering favorable fiscal, contractual, and infrastructural conditions for global businesses. Puerto Rico pioneered EPZ-style incentives in the late 1940s, followed by the Philippines, Mexico, Hong Kong, Taiwan, and, in the 1990s, several coastal cities in China. Despite opposition from trade unions in the United States and Europe, tax waivers and state subsidies drew corporations to these zones. This trend extended to various sectors, including car manufacturing, steel, pharmaceuticals, IT, and agriculture.[37] These EPZ incentives also spurred the emergence of regional chains and industrialization. For instance, in China, domestic companies engaged in so-called round-tripping, sending capital offshore and reinvesting it back as foreign direct investment (FDI) to gain tax benefits and incentives reserved for foreign investors.[38]

In the 1980s and 1990s, breakthroughs in telecommunications and data transfer technologies, including the internet, mobile networks, and improved subsea cables, accelerated global trade. This period saw a resurgence of GVCs driven by political, institutional, and technological convergence. Multinational enterprises shifted production to lower-cost offshore locations while keeping high-tech activities in advanced economies, leading to more complex and technologically advanced global production networks. Although development gains were uneven, GVCs integrated developing countries into the global economy, providing new markets for MNEs.

American semiconductor, computer peripherals, and home appliance manufacturers increasingly outsourced production to independent original equipment manufacturers (OEMs) in East Asia's EPZs and SEZs. This change reduced the need for equity control across the value chain. Over time, these OEMs gained expertise and diverse capabilities, attracting foreign MNEs for reasons beyond just cost-effective labor.[39] As OEMs evolved, the electronics GVCs also grew more complex with the emergence of electronics manufacturing services (EMS) providers. These companies operated on a contract basis, offering a range of services to OEMs, including design, engineering, assembly, testing, and distribution, all based on the OEMs' specifications (i.e., manufacturing of electronics components such as circuit boards and finished products). For instance, Foxconn, known initially as Hon Hai Precision Industry, was established in 1974 by Taiwanese entrepreneur Terry Gou but began as an OEM and eventually expanded over time into EMS. By the 1990s, it had become one of the world's largest contract subcontractors for major global brands like Apple, Dell, HP, and Sony.

After the fall of the Berlin Wall and the collapse of the Soviet Union, global trading tariffs dropped from 9 percent in the early 1990s to 2.5 percent by 2020, thanks to the General Agreement on Tariffs and Trade (GATT) and the World Trade Organization (WTO). This "hyper-globalization" era was supported by the Washington Consensus, which promoted fiscal discipline, deregulation, privatization, and trade liberalization, coinciding with the expansion of US hegemony, the North Atlantic Treaty Organization (NATO), and European Union (EU) growth.

From 1990 until the global financial crisis in 2008, global economic integration indicators surged. The ratio of global trade to world GDP nearly doubled, from 34 percent to more than 60 percent, while global FDI inflows grew from 0.5 percent to 5.3 percent of global GDP, and cross-border capital flows rose from 2 percent to 12 percent.[40] This period also saw the rise of non-equity, contract-based GVC arrangements with regional and local producers, which, though challenging to quantify, significantly advanced integration.[41] The share of international trade involving intermediate goods grew significantly between the early 1990s and 2008, rising from less than 50 percent to more than 60 percent. During the same period, global participation in value-added activities within GVCs also increased, with the participation rate climbing from around 44 percent in 1995 to 48 percent by 2008 and from 36 percent to 46 percent in developing countries.[42]

4.4 The Geographic and Sectorial Dimensions of GVCs

As global integration surged from the early 1990s to the 2008 global financial crisis, GVCs proliferated, exhibiting three distinct features.

First was the degree of external coordination, which varied from complete to absent coordination. Outsourcing historically served as a strategic alternative to vertical cross-border integration for companies operating internationally. As mentioned, MNEs traditionally decentralized the production of intermediate goods to local subsidiaries.[43] The extent of control over these subsidiaries typically corresponded to their role within the production process orchestrated by the headquarters, ranging from tight (wholly owned and vertically integrated) to medium (joint venture or partnership) and to loose (contractual agreement with third-party OEM or EMS). Firms within GVCs could add value to semifinished or finished products without direct oversight from a coordinating entity. However, MNE subsidiaries often still accounted for a significant share of that value up to the 1990s. Alongside equity-based ties to partially or fully owned subsidiaries, non-equity agreements eventually became more common, playing an important role in GVCs despite being harder to track in FDI-focused statistics.

Second, as for the "length" and geographical scope of GVC, research has focused on the strategies that MNEs used to shape their controlled chains by leveraging various locational factors, including different tax and duty regimes across countries. In a theoretically frictionless global economy, tax differences would not influence investment location decisions. However, in reality, tax avoidance and evasion strategies significantly shaped the geographic structure of GVCs coordinated by MNEs, given the considerable asymmetry in fiscal policies among countries.[44]

International agreements and efficient institutions streamlined GVCs, reducing trade costs and fueling expansion, particularly in high-tech sectors like semiconductors. Despite rising US–China tensions, these supply chains have grown in reach, following the growing ubiquity of the microchip. Since the early 2000s, global microchip production has exceeded the total number of all objects ever made by humanity, with an estimated 13 sextillion microchips manufactured in just over fifty years.[45] Once a specialized product, microchips have become so essential that their market now resembles that of a raw material rather than a conventional commodity.

The contemporary microchip GVC is highly specialized and geographically dispersed. The United States dominates semiconductor design, with Intel, NVIDIA, and Qualcomm holding a dominant market share. NVIDIA, for instance, has become a near-monopoly in advanced semiconductor chips for gaming and artificial intelligence. Founded in 1993 and based in Santa Clara, California, the company designs its chips in the United States, but outsources manufacturing (wafer fabrication, assembly, testing, and packaging) to leading third-party firms in East Asia. The "foundry" TSMC in Taiwan accounts for more than 60 percent of global production, while South Korea-based Samsung controls 20 percent. China plays a key role in assembly, testing, and packaging, handling 38 percent of global semiconductor packaging. The Netherlands-based ASML monopolizes extreme ultraviolet (EUV) lithography, essential for cutting-edge chips, while Japan supplies nearly 50 percent of semiconductor materials, including silicon wafers and photoresists.[46]

Third, the fragmentation of production into distinct stages significantly impacted the "technological depth" of GVCs, reflecting a reduction in trade costs. Since the end of the Cold War, GVCs have grown in both length and complexity, with variations across industries. Sectors like microelectronics, rare-earth mineral refining, tool manufacturing, precision instruments, and textiles feature the most extended and intricate chains, while financial services and real estate have shorter chains. This expansion has been driven by the diffusion of modularity in design and production, where processes are divided into standardized components made by independent global suppliers.[47]

Multinational enterprises with "long" or "deep" GVCs relied on numerous independent partners. For example, Apple's supply chain for iPhones and iPads in 2015 involved nearly two hundred companies, including major companies like TSMC and Foxconn, based either in China or with significant Chinese operations. Additionally, GVCs are interconnected; the smartphone chain, for instance, integrates the semiconductor sector. The number of stages within a chain and its technological depth do, however, carry inherent implications regarding economic specialization and the ability to craft comparative advantages, which, in turn, impact geopolitical equilibria among countries.

In recent years, geopolitical tensions have reshaped the geography of GVCs and globalization. Since 2008, globalization has slowed but not reversed, as seen in three key trends: the trade-to-GDP ratio has stabilized, net FDI/GDP has fallen to near zero, and migration growth has halved. Rather than a full retreat, these shifts signal a transition toward "slow-balization" and, especially, regionalization.[48] South–South trade relations have been increasingly strengthened by the geo-economic agendas of developing economies, particularly the BRICS countries.[49] China has solidified its role as Asia's leading assembly hub for tech-related GVCs, aggressively expanding its presence through FDI and partnerships across emerging markets in Asia, the Middle East, and Sub-Saharan Africa. While these investments initially focused on securing natural resources, they increasingly serve to establish China's own manufacturing networks and capture local markets as detailed in Chapter 3. Meanwhile, some countries in the Global South are working to reduce their reliance on China by integrating into specialized value chain segments that cater to markets seeking to decouple from Chinese production. Research indicates that while the United States has reduced the gross value of Chinese imports since 2016, the value-added produced in China within US imports has remained stable. This suggests that products partially assembled in China are being rerouted through third countries for final production.[50]

4.5 The Social and Political Dimensions of GVCs

While during the first wave of globalization, inequality rose both within and between countries, the postwar period saw a decline in domestic inequality as decolonizing nations began to catch up. Recent research on inequality and globalization has widely agreed that, while income gaps between countries narrowed during periods of global integration, inequality within countries tended to increase, particularly since the end of the Cold War.[51] The most recent phase of globalization has had indeed a significant positive impact on inequality at a global scale. Since the 1980s, approximately 3 billion people (around 40 percent of the world's population in 2020) have been lifted from poverty thresholds.

This remarkable achievement stemmed from rapid economic convergence, which has progressively narrowed the income gap across countries.[52] However, the effects of global integration on developed economies have been more contentious. Scholars widely agree that income inequality within individual countries, specifically within advanced nations, has steadily increased alongside integration. Data from the International Monetary Fund (IMF) demonstrate the upward trajectory of income inequality almost universally between 1985 and 2015, with some exceptions observed primarily in the Global South.[53]

Extensive evidence suggests that increased integration through international trade fosters income convergence, particularly in developing countries with substantial GVC participation, yielding a net positive effect. The GVC involvement correlates with various beneficial outcomes such as value-added producing activities, GDP growth, job creation, knowledge transfer, and skill development at a local level.[54] However, these outcomes are often unevenly distributed across local geography and social classes. Advanced infrastructure tends to be concentrated in selected locations, supporting industrial clusters or service hubs (global cities). Still, the benefits may not trickle down to the local population due to institutional shortcomings such as limited access to quality education, institutional voids, lack of affordable housing, inadequate fiscal oversight, and widespread corruption, among other factors.[55]

At the aggregate level, increasing participation in GVCs may theoretically enable countries to surpass the poverty threshold. However, without additional supporting factors such as working institutions, joining GVCs alone seems insufficient to positively impact human capital formation and break free from the low-income trap. This led to skepticism about the ability of low- and middle-income economies to advance into higher value-added stages of GVC due to the limited opportunities for further technological advancement.[56] Vietnam, for example, significantly boosted its GVC participation rate after 1995. However, without appropriate policies to transfer knowledge and technology into the economy, this growth has predominantly favored only labor-intensive, low-value-added activities, hampering the country's development trajectory.[57] In other words, GVC participation appears insufficient to lift underdeveloped and developing countries from low-income or poverty traps.

Other studies detailed the adverse social and developmental consequences of GVCs in developing economies, including environmental degradation, precarious employment conditions, and unequal opportunities for local suppliers.[58] When operating internationally, MNEs navigate a complex patchwork of contractual and treaty obligations governing cross-border investments. These often lack comprehensive rules addressing the social responsibilities of these enterprises, particularly concerning human rights. Non-equity modes of control, such as contractual relationships, further weaken the effective monitoring of human rights practices.[59] Chapter 2 in this volume demonstrates how MNEs exploited their porous borders to shift environmentally damaging activities to associated companies whose actions go undisclosed in annual reports or whose practices are audited by external partners. These practices illustrate how companies can leverage their GVCs and non-equity relationships with foreign subsidiaries to evade responsibility for harmful activities through "regulatory arbitrage," choosing profitability over ethics. This includes not only environmentally damaging operations but also practices unacceptable in MNEs' home countries, such as child labor, forced labor, and unsafe working conditions.[60]

Weak international oversight has allowed these practices to persist, with MNEs often outsourcing the most hazardous and labor-intensive tasks to regions with lax regulations. For instance, in April 2013, the collapse of the Rana Plaza building in Dhaka, Bangladesh, killed more than 1,100 people and injured more than 2,500. Despite visible cracks on the walls, workers were forced to continue working in the building, which housed several garment factories (and sweatshops), subcontracting for global brands such as Benetton, Zara, Mango, Primark, and Walmart. Rana Plaza was just the tip of the iceberg. Since 2005, multiple factory collapses have claimed lives in Bangladesh: 79 workers in 2005, 18 in 2006, 25 in 2010, and 124 in the Tazreen Fashion Factory fire in 2012. These disasters exposed the still present poor working conditions and inadequate safety standards in the worldwide garment industry. In the past decade, following the Rana Plaza tragedy, at least 109 more buildings in the same area have collapsed, killing at least 27 workers.

In 2024, a *New York Times* investigation exposed the limitations of social auditing in GVCs, where certifications can mask ongoing exploitation.[61] This was the case with sugar production, where suppliers to major food and beverage producers like Coca-Cola, PepsiCo, and Unilever are certified by auditing companies like Bonsucro to ensure humane labor practices. Despite these certifications, mills such as Dalmia Bharat Sugar in India and others engaged in severe abuses, including debt bondage, child labor, and pressuring women into unnecessary hysterectomies. Bonsucro's flawed audits, often controlled by the mills, frequently failed to uncover these issues, allowing major global brands to falsely claim ethical production.

A further issue involved the use of GVCs to disguise MNEs' relationships with authoritarian regimes, as in the case of Cisco in China. The company played a significant role in the Golden Shield Project, providing networking technology to the Chinese government, which used it to enhance its surveillance, censorship, and control over the internet. This involvement made Cisco complicit in human rights violations and the government's repressive activities, using the technology to suppress dissent and restrict freedom of expression.[62]

Existing literature on GVC, international trade, and development has primarily focused on the effects of offshoring on developing economies, often neglecting its impact on developed countries. However, specialized research as well as heated public debates have shown that GVC participation has also led to concerning political consequences in advanced economies. The concentration of most technologically advanced and high-value-added stages of production in developed economies has widened the gap between developed and developing countries, and also exacerbated geographical and social disparities within advanced economies. Offshoring through GVCs has increased wage inequality in the West, disproportionately benefiting highly skilled and educated individuals and capital owners in high-value-added sectors, while marginalizing medium and low-skilled workers in low-tech industries, such as textiles and electronics.[63]

This dynamic generated two distinct yet partially interconnected political outcomes. First, a recent surge in studies links trade, investment, GVC participation, and increased income inequality in developed nations to the mounting success of nationalist parties and populist governments, supported primarily by the impoverished low- and medium-income classes. Populist administrations started directing economic policies toward increased protectionism, promoting reshoring practices to safeguard their electoral base from globalization.[64] This supports the idea that growth in GVC participation during the second global economy contributed to the expansion of populist consensus – a phenomenon referred to as "globalization backlash."[65]

Second, following the end of the Cold War, GVCs were seen as facilitating a positive sum-game effect through a seamless international division of labor. However, external shocks have revealed vulnerabilities of excessive specialization. For example, during the 2008 global financial crisis, GVCs acted as a central conduit for the spread of economic downturn.[66] In the early 2020s, the COVID-19 crisis exposed the fragility of a system reliant on production fragmentation, prompting unexpected supply shortages, particularly for strategic or critical items like advanced technology or medical products.[67] For instance, during the pandemic, the US government struggled to source face masks for hospitals and healthcare workers. Meanwhile, Chinese manufacturers, who produced most of the global supplies, ramped up production but stockpiled it for their domestic market as technical limitations hindered the acceleration of production of most advanced models like the N95 mask.[68]

In other cases, governments leveraged their control over crucial stages of the value chain through trade barriers (tariff and nontariff) to delay or impede the technological advancement of other countries, resulting in a specific form of "weaponization" of trade relationships. For example, since 2017, the US government has promoted bipartisan actions to increase trade protectionism in the advanced semiconductor industry, aiming to restrict Chinese access to technologies deemed risky for national security.[69] Within the same GVCs, China maintained significant control over the extraction, processing, and refining of rare minerals (such as gallium and germanium) used in chip production. This control, in turn, enables key players in the industry to retaliate against US firms through export bans.[70]

Finally, COVID-19 showed that geopolitical shock can seriously disrupt the efficiency of GVCs and lead to structural outcomes such as the shortening or regionalization of value chains.[71] In certain industries, particularly those with technology- and knowledge-intensive stages, some chain segments can act as crucial bottlenecks for implementing strategic moves to deter geopolitical competitors. This was the case of the Chinese telecommunication company Huawei, which had to restructure its GVC since 2020, shifting the procurement of semiconductors for mobile phones from Taiwan to mainland China as a response to the semiconductor bans issued by the US administrations on the People's Republic of China.

4.6 Conclusion

This chapter traced the evolution of GVCs and their connection to the activity of MNEs in the global capitalist system. It explored how MNEs have impacted the development of GVCs from a long-term perspective and how GVCs, in turn, have shaped the global economy across different cycles of globalization. An international business history approach emphasizes how MNEs developed these production systems to access resources and manage global operations efficiently. It focuses on the broader context and historical factors, rather than just the mechanisms themselves. While these chains thrived during periods of globalization and peaceful international relations, this chapter demonstrated the resilience of these structures as deglobalization cycles only partially dismantled them. Following the demise of the first global economy during the interwar period, these production systems resurged and became more sophisticated after World War II, accelerating the industrialization of many Asian countries. However, this fast development led to unequal spatial and societal outcomes and the persistence of unethical and abusive practices by MNEs in the Global South. It exacerbated income inequality and political polarization in the Global North, ultimately threatening Western democracy and reinforcing authoritative tendencies elsewhere.

The historical evidence in this chapter suggested that the twenty-first century brought a noticeable slowdown in globalization across various metrics, from trade to capital flows and information exchange in the first decades of the new century. Traditionally, GVCs served as a precise barometer of the state of global capitalism, reflecting the global economy's well-being and offering insights into future trajectories. Terms like "decoupling," "de-risking," "friend-shoring," and "reshoring" have gained prominence since the mid 2010s, signaling the reorientation of GVCs toward regional systems of production and hence their transformation into shorter and less fragmented production chains. In sum, the future of GVCs remains uncertain amidst regionalization trends, geopolitical tensions among emerging and declining global powers, and the potential for new global integration frameworks.

Notes

1. Gereffi, G. and Korzeniewicz, M. *Commodity Chains and Global Capitalism*, Westport, CT, Praeger, 1994, 2.
2. Akamatsu, K. "A Historical Pattern of Economic Growth in Developing Countries," *Developing Economies*, 1 (1962), 3–25.
3. Wallerstein, I. *World-Systems Analysis: An Introduction*, Durham, NC, Duke University Press, 2004.
4. Jones, G. *Entrepreneurship and Multinationals: Global Business and the Making of the Modern World*, Cheltenham, Edward Elgar, 2013.
5. Hesse, J. O. and Neveling, P. "Global Value Chains," in da Silva Lopes, T., Lubinski, C., and Tworek, H. (eds.) *The Routledge Companion to the Makers of Global Business*, Abingdon, Routledge, 2017, 279–293.
6. Hunter, I. "Commodity Chains and Networks in Emerging Markets: New Zealand, 1880–1910," *Business History Review*, 79, 2 (2005), 275–304.
7. Declercq, R. "Transnational Entrepreneurs? German Entrepreneurs in the Belgian Fur Industry (1880 to 1913)," *Zeitschrift für Unternehmensgeschichte*, 60, 1 (2015), 52–74.
8. Henn, S. "Transnational Entrepreneurs and the Emergence of Clusters in Peripheral Regions: The Case of the Diamond Cutting Cluster in Gujarat (India)," *European Planning Studies*, 21, 11 (2013), 1779–1795.
9. Giacomin, V. "The Emergence of an Export Cluster: Traders and Palm Oil in Early-20th-Century Southeast Asia," *Enterprise & Society*, 19, 2 (2018), 272–308.
10. Pananond, P. "Breakout Multinationals: Emerging Market Multinationals in Global Value Chains," in Demirbag, M. and Yaprak, A. (eds.) *Handbook of Emerging Market Multinational Corporations*, Cheltenham, Edward Elgar, 2015, 91–111.
11. Jun, I. W. and Rowley, C. "Competitive Advantage and the Transformation of Value Chains over Time: The Example of a South Korean Diversified Business Group, 1953-2013," *Business History*, 61, 2 (2019), 343–370.
12. Jones, G. and Khanna, T. "Bringing History (Back) into International Business," *Journal of International Business Studies*, 37, 4 (2006), 453–468.

13. Cassis, Y. *Capitals of Capital: The Rise and Fall of International Financial Centres, 1780–2009*, New York, Cambridge University Press, 2010.
14. Harvey, C. E. *The Rio Tinto Company: An Economic History of a Leading International Mining Concern, 1873–1954*, Penzance, Alison Hodge, 1981.
15. Vernon, R. W. "Beyond Huelva: Other British Mining Legacies in Andalucia, Spain," Paper presented at the Proceedings of the 6th International Mining History Congress (2003).
16. Tarbell, I. M. *The History of the Standard Oil Company*, New York, McClure, Phillips and Company, 1904.
17. Giacomin, "The Emergence."
18. Bauer, P. T. *The Rubber Industry: A Study in Competition and Monopoly*, London, Longmans Green, 1948.
19. Yong, C. F., Gonzalo, J. A., and Carreira, M. M. *Tan Kah-Kee: The Making of an Overseas Chinese Legend*, Singapore, World Scientific, 1987.
20. Kathirithamby-Wells, J. *Nature and Nation: Forests and Development in Peninsular Malaysia*, Honolulu, University of Hawaii Press, 2005.
21. Tully, J. "A Victorian Ecological Disaster: Imperialism, the Telegraph, and Gutta-Percha," *Journal of World History*, 20, 4 (2009), 559–579.
22. Giacomin, V. "The Transformation of the Global Palm Oil Cluster: Dynamics of Cluster Competition between Africa and Southeast Asia (c. 1900–1970)," *Journal of Global History*, 13, 3 (2018), 374–398.
23. Sandvik, P. T. and Storli, E. "Big Business and Small States: Unilever and Norway in the Interwar Years," *Economic History Review*, 66, 1 (2013), 109–131.
24. Bucheli, M. *Bananas and Business*, New York, New York University Press, 2005.
25. Engel, A. *Farben der Globalisierung: Die Entstehung moderner Märkte für Farbstoffe 1500–1900*, Frankfurt, Campus, 2009.
26. Federico, G. and Cafagna, L. *Il filo d'oro: L'industria mondiale della seta dalla restaurazione alla grande crisi*, Venice, Marsilio Editore, 1994.
27. Tolliday, S. "The Origins of Ford of Europe: From Multidomestic to Transnational Corporation, 1903–1976," in Bonin, H., Lung, Y., and Tolliday, S. (eds.) *Ford: The European History*, Paris, Plage, 2003, 153–242.
28. Donzé, P -Y. *Business of Time: A Global History of the Watch Industry*, Manchester, Manchester University Press, 2022.
29. Binda, V. and Colli, A. *Globalization: A Key Idea for Business and Society*, Abingdon, Routledge, 2024, 60–64.
30. Koistinen, D. and Lipartito, K. "Offshoring, Outsourcing and Global Production Networks in Historical Context," *Entreprises et Histoire*, 1 (2019), 62–88.
31. Rivoli, P. *The Travels of a T-Shirt in the Global Economy: An Economist Examines the Markets, Power, and Politics of World Trade*, Hoboken, NJ, Wiley, 2009.

32. Westenhouser, K. B. *The Story of Barbie*, Paducah, KY, Collector Books, 1994, 8–9.
33. Pitteloud, S. "The Social Desirability of Offshoring: A Swiss Consensus (1945–1975)," *Zeitschrift für Unternehmensgeschichte*, 64, 2 (2019), 255–273.
34. Donzé, *Business of Time*.
35. Hesse and Neveling, "Global Value Chains."
36. Hesse, J. O. "The German Textile Puzzle: Selective Protectionism and the Silent Globalization of an Industry," *Business History Review*, 93, 2 (2019), 221–246.
37. Hesse and Neveling, "Global Value Chains."
38. Xiao, G. "People's Republic of China's Round-Tripping FDI: Scale, Causes and Implications," ADBI Discussion Paper, 2004.
39. Ernst, D. and Guerrieri, P. "International Production Networks and Changing Trade Patterns in East Asia: The Case of the Electronics Industry," *Oxford Development Studies*, 26, 2 (1998), 191–212.
40. The World Bank Open Data, available at https://data.worldbank.org; https://data.worldbank.org/indicator/BX.KLT.DINV.WD.GD.ZS
41. Milberg, W. *Outsourcing Economics: Global Value Chains in Capitalist Development*, New York, Cambridge University Press, 2013.
42. Carpa, N. and Martínez-Zarzoso, I. "The Impact of Global Value Chain Participation on Income Inequality," *International Economics*, 169 (2022), 269–290.
43. UNCTAD, "Global Value Chains: Investment for Trade and Development," World Investment Report, 2013, 141.
44. Zachariadis, I. "Multinational Enterprises, Value Creation and Taxation: Key Issues and Policy Developments," European Parliamentary Research Service Briefing, 2019.
45. Alemanni, C. *Il re invisibile: Storia, economia e sconfinato potere del microchip* (Italian Edition), Rome, LUISS University Press, 2024, 9.
46. Wai-chung Yeung, H., Huang, S., and Xing, Y. "From Fabless to Fabs Everywhere? Semiconductor Global Value Chains in Transition," Global Value Chain Report, WTO, 2023.
47. Sturgeon, T. J. "Modular Production Networks: A New American Model of Industrial Organization," *Industrial and Corporate Change*, 11, 3 (2002), 451–496.
48. Antràs, P. "De-globalisation? Global Value Chains in the Post-Covid-19 Age." ECB Forum, Central Banks in a Shifting World Conference Proceedings, 2021.
49. Duursma, A. and Masuhr, N. "Russia's Return to Africa in a Historical and Global Context: Anti-imperialism, Patronage, and Opportunism," *South African Journal of International Affairs*, 29, 4 (2022), 407–423.

50. Seong, J., White, O., Birshan, Smit, M., S. Lamanna, C., and Devesa, T. "Geopolitics and the Geometry of Global Trade: 2025 Update," McKinsey Global Institute, January 17, 2025
51. Milanovic, B. "The Three Eras of Global Inequality, 1820–2020 with the Focus on the Past Thirty Years," *World Development*, 177 (2024), figure 2.
52. Milanovic, B. "The Great Convergence," *Foreign Affairs*, 14 June 2023.
53. International Monetary Fund, "Fiscal Monitor: Tackling Inequality," October 2017.
54. Hollweg, C. H. "Global Value Chains and Employment in Developing Economies," Global Value Chain Development Report, 2019.
55. Draper, P. and Freytag, A. "Who Captures the Value in the Global Value Chain? High Level Implications for the World Trade Organization," E15 Initiative Report, International Centre for Trade and Sustainable Development (ICTSD) and World Economic Forum, Geneva, 2014.
56. Engel, J. and Taglioni, D. "The Middle-Income Trap and Upgrading along Global Value Chains," Global Value Chain Report, WTO, 2017.
57. Truong, H. Q. "Vietnam's Global Value Chains Participation and Policy Implications for South Korea–Vietnam Economic Cooperation," KIEP Research Paper, *World Economy Brief*, 2022, 22–37.
58. UNCTAD, "Global Value Chains: Investment for Trade and Development," 148.
59. Lundan, S. M. "Human Rights Issues in Multinational Value Chains," in Linarelli, J. (ed.) *Research Handbook on Global Justice and International Economic Law*, Cheltenham, Edward Elgar, 2013, 146–167.
60. Wuttke, T., Smit, L., Parshotam, A., Ancheita, A., and Meridian, A., "Human Rights and Environmental Due Diligence in Global Value Chains: Perspectives from the Global South," Working paper 02, Research Division Africa and Middle East Research Network Sustainable Supply Chains, German Institute for International and Security Affairs, 2022.
61. Rajagopalan, M. "How a Sugar Industry Stamp of Approval Hid Coerced Hysterectomies," *The New York Times*, July 30, 2024.
62. Jones, G. and Grandjean, E. "John Chambers, Cisco, and China: Upgrading a Golden Shield." *Harvard Business School Case* 318-158, revised July 20, 2023.
63. Lewandowski, P., Madoń, K., and Winkler, D. E. "The Role of Global Value Chains for Worker Tasks and Wage Inequality," Policy Research Working Paper, World Bank, 2023.
64. Jones, K. *Populism and Trade: The Challenge to the Global Trading System*, Oxford, Oxford University Press, 2021.
65. Colantone, I. and Stanig, P. "The Trade Origins of Economic Nationalism: Import Competition and Voting Behavior in Western Europe," *American Journal of Political Science*, 62, 4 (2018), 936–953.

66. Cattaneo, O., Gereffi, G., and Staritz, C. *Global Value Chains in a Postcrisis World: A Development Perspective*, Washington, DC, World Bank, 2010.
67. Raza, W., Grumiller, J. Grohs, H., Essletzbichler, J., and Pintar N. "Post Covid-19 Value Chains: Options for Reshoring Production back to Europe in a Globalised Economy," in *Policy Department*, Brussels, European Parliament, 2021.
68. Bradsher, K. and Alderman, L. "The World Needs Masks: China Makes Them, but Has Been Hoarding Them," *The New York Times*, March 13, 2020.
69. Fuller, D. B. "Weaponizing Interdependence & Global Value Chains: US Export Controls on Huawei," American Political Science Association (2022).
70. Lu, C. "Beijing Tightens Its Grip on the Critical Minerals Sector: The West Has Taken Steps to Slash Its Dependence on China, but It Still Commands Supply Chains – for Now." *Foreign Policy*, November 7, 2023.
71. Zhan, J. X. "GVC Transformation and a New Investment Landscape in the 2020s: Driving Forces, Directions, and a Forward-Looking Research and Policy Agenda," *Journal of International Business Policy*, 4, 2 (2021), 206–220.

Further Reading

Agarwal, R., Bajada, C., Green, R., and Skellern, K. *The Routledge Companion to Global Value Chains: Reinterpreting and Reimagining Megatrends in the World Economy*, New York, Routledge, 2021.

Casanova, L., Miroux, A., and Salum, F. C. *Innovation from Emerging Markets: From Copycats to Leaders*, Cambridge, Cambridge University Press, 2021.

Colli, A. *Dynamics of International Business: Comparative Perspectives of Firms, Markets and Entrepreneurship*, New York, Routledge, 2016.

Gereffi, G. *Global Value Chains and Development: Redefining the Contours of 21st Century Capitalism*, New York, Cambridge University Press, 2018.

Giacomin, V. "Clusters as Spaces for Global Integration," in da Silva Lopes, T., Lubinski, C., and Tworek, H. J. S. (eds.) *The Routledge Companion to the Makers of Global Business*, New York, Routledge, 2017, 264–278.

Part II

Governments and Institutions

PIERRE EICHENBERGER AND
SABINE PITTELOUD

5

Multinationals and Organized Business

5.1 Introduction: MNEs and Political Power

During the twenty-first century there has been both an increase in societal expectations for multinational enterprises (MNEs) and growing criticism of their failure to live up to these expectations. On the one hand, managers have been urged to act as "corporate citizens," and for their companies to pay their fair share in taxes and play a more active role in providing private governance in domains such as sustainability and human rights.[1] On the other hand, MNEs have been accused of challenging the sovereignty of nation-states, escaping the reach of democratic decisions, and blatant lobbying to shape the rules of the game for their own private benefit.

This chapter investigates how MNEs have defended their interests collectively through the creation of associations and clubs, and assesses the impact of these political activities. Their political involvement to secure and expand their foreign operations has had important societal impacts in host and home countries. First, when successful, MNEs have influenced states and international organizations to implement specific treaties and rules of law that favored their operations and impacted the political leeway and economic gains of other actors. Second, when executives of MNEs refused compromises with other social groups and other sectors of the business community, and embraced a self-serving agenda using secretive clubs and privileged connections, it negatively impacted the level of trust in government officials and public policies.

The political activities and influence of MNEs are inherently difficult to document because of the lack of transparency regulation as well as the elusive nature of power.[2] Indeed, since the economic activities of MNEs are often crucial to local, regional, and central governments in terms of jobs and fiscal revenues, policymakers are de facto inclined to be concerned about their corporate interests even in the absence of lobbying. In addition, when it comes to technical topics that do not attract much media coverage, such as negotiations about trade, investment, and tax treaties, companies' expertise is unlikely to be challenged.[3] Despite such pitfalls, business historians, using the archives of companies and business interest associations, have been able to assemble valuable empirical evidence on the defense by MNEs of their political agenda.[4]

A business history perspective on the collective political actions of MNEs and their impact on societies is important in multiple respects. First, MNEs shared many interests with other factions of the business community, and the extent to which being an MNE is crucial in explaining their political activities requires historical contextualization. External threats in specific historical contexts were often crucial in incentivizing the executives of MNEs to organize politically and to acknowledge that their companies had something in common to defend, despite sectoral specificities or different corporate nationalities.

Second, thanks to case studies of companies and business associations, the business history literature has opened the black box of "business interests." While, overall, most MNEs were among the main promoters of what historian Quinn Slobodian has termed a "globalist" agenda, supporting free trade and unrestricted investments flows, nondiscrimination rules, the avoidance of double taxation, and the protection of private property,[5] some corporations and sections of the business community opposed "globalist" views because they sought national protection from international competition, or because they expected to gain from imperial structures. Multinational enterprises, depending on their nationality and competitive (dis)advantages, did not support trade and investment freedom in all circumstances. Consequently, the perspective of business history reveals that there was nothing inevitable about the imposition of a "globalist" world order since it was repeatedly challenged by labor unions, nongovernmental organizations (NGOs), nationalistic political figures, and members of the business community.

This chapter investigates how MNEs organized politically in various associations, and traces the impact that these strategies had on societies from the nineteenth to the twenty-first centuries. Section 5.2 discusses MNEs' collective political activism from the apex of the first globalization wave to the Great Depression and World War II. Section 5.3 focuses on the rebuilding of globalization in the decades after 1945 in the context of European integration, the Cold War, and decolonization. Section 5.4 examines MNEs' renewed political activism in the face of the challenges of the 1970s, and how the "globalist" agenda appeared to be hegemonic in the 1990s. Finally, the chapter assesses the significance of these past trends in the context of the resurgence of economic nationalism from the 2000s.

5.2 Navigating Deglobalization Waves: From the Apex of the First Global Economy to World War II

Foreign direct investment (FDI) grew rapidly during the first global economy. The creation of chambers of commerce abroad, aimed at providing information and contacts for business leaders, paralleled the resulting economic integration. The British Chamber of Commerce and the American Chamber of Commerce, both in Paris, were created respectively in 1873 and 1894.[6] In the late nineteenth century, even local chambers of commerce, whose focus had previously been primarily on local infrastructures and lobbying, began to develop activities aimed at facilitating international commerce. Regular congresses of chambers of commerce of the British Empire were organized from 1886, and, starting in 1905, the International Congress of Chambers of Commerce and Commercial and Industrial Associations held large conferences every other year.[7]

International bankers, merchants, and shipping companies, among other early MNEs, took advantage of these meetings to promote the development of transport infrastructures, unification of calendars, and the standardization of business documents and practices, and to advocate for the nondiscrimination of foreign businesses.[8] Other cosmopolitan elite networks, consulates, colonial administrations, and the like facilitated the establishment of subsidiaries in Latin America, Asia, and Africa. While the services chambers of commerce provided were often limited to rich merchants, bankers, and business owners, their discriminatory nature was exacerbated in colonial contexts, excluding members based on their race or origin.[9]

When it came to gaining market share, developing critical infrastructure such as railroads, or securing concessions to exploit natural resources in the Global South, foreign investors often perceived their peers as competitors rather than political partners. Companies did not hesitate to develop their own lobbying channels or to seek the targeted help of their home government to secure contracts or concessions. Moreover, the arrival of foreign capital was often met with some degree of resistance, since FDI was perceived as a form of economic domination by foreign powers. Local businesses, as was the case in Japan, organized to restrict Western investments.[10] In 1877, Indian nationalist elites established the Bengal National Chamber of Commerce to challenge the status of the Bengal Chamber of Commerce created by British merchants forty-four years earlier. This episode was an early example of nationalist business countermovements.[11]

In the context of increased geopolitical rivalries between European nations at the turn of the twentieth century, some groups of foreign investors even capitalized on local nationalist sentiments against imperial powers to gain market shares over their competitors. This was, for instance, the case of German businesses producing consumer goods in India who exploited anti-British sentiments to appeal to Indian customers.[12]

Within the context of the economic recession between 1873 and 1896 that impacted Europe and the United States, as well as rising tariffs, Western MNEs both participated in various business associations and monitored the economic policies of their home states.[13] Once companies in the same industrial sector started acting collectively to promote higher or lower tariffs, other industries had no other choice but to organize themselves.[14] Moreover, industrial associations regrouped into centralized national business associations. The National Association of Manufacturers (NAM) in the United States was created in 1895 to reconcile diverging interests between free-traders and protectionists, promote probusiness policies, and lobby the US government to establish a department of commerce.[15] The US Chamber of Commerce was established in 1912 in coordination with the US government to foster cooperation regarding regulation and antitrust policy enforcement.[16] In Germany, the free-trade Bund der Industriellen was set up in 1895 in order to counter the protectionist positions of the Centralverband Deutscher Industrieller, created in 1876.

Since membership fees were often set according to the revenues of the companies, MNEs played a leading role in these national associations. Moreover, large MNEs could second staff to the various committees established by business associations much more easily than small and medium enterprises. It was nevertheless more their sectoral characteristics, their technological advances in comparison to those of foreign competitors, and the size of their internal market rather than a clearly identifiable "globalist" agenda that ultimately determined their political stance.

In addition to the need to coordinate various interests and guide national economic policy, strikes and the rising power of the labor movement certainly prompted business leaders to increasingly cooperate and triggered the creation of specialized antilabor organizations (i.e. employer's associations).[17] Multinational enterprises in the cotton and shipping industries pioneered the creation of international business associations to regulate market share and face international labor activism.[18]

World War I proved transformative in making business executives operating in belligerent countries aware of the specific "multinational" dimension of their companies since they had to face blockades and the confiscation of enemy-based properties. The US declaration of war on Germany in 1917 had significant consequences, as the country had been the most important host economy for German FDI. The US government introduced the Trading with the Enemy Act to restrict trade and sequestered investments made by German companies and other enemy countries. The war economy and the grip that the involved national governments had on economic life strongly incentivized MNEs to participate actively in national and imperial business associations.[19]

Key aspects of economic diplomacy became increasingly coproduced by governments and private actors with some executives of MNEs acting as diplomats with semiofficial mandates.[20]

The creation of the League of Nations in 1920 opened a new front for MNEs' political activism. The League modeled its economic interventions on the inter-Allied economic cooperation seen in World War I. It organized economic conferences and technical commissions in a great variety of domains ranging from transportation to statistics and taxation, all of which were of significant interest to MNEs.[21] At the center of MNEs' reactions to these new challenges was the creation of the International Chamber of Commerce (ICC). While the ICC was organized like a federation of national business associations and aspired to be the "international parliament of business," its leadership was in fact dominated by the executives of large Western MNEs.[22] In particular, the ICC's US Committee was very influential and dominated by MNEs including General Electric and the Radio Corporation of America. The association provided US MNEs with a back door through which to influence the economic initiatives of the League of Nations, which the United States never joined. Similarly, the creation of the International Labour Organization (ILO) in 1919, whose first convention limited daily labor to eight hours, triggered the creation of the International Organization of Industrial Employers (IOIE).

While the IOIE's focus was limited to labor issues, MNEs largely benefited from the ICC's activities in the domains of standardization and transportation, as well as in combatting the discrimination against foreign companies and double taxation. The ICC also developed specific services for MNEs such as the International Court of Arbitration, created in 1923, and the publication of standardized business terms in the "Incoterms" in 1936.[23]

The ICC was, therefore, simultaneously a lobby association, a service provider, and an international arena in which businesses engaged in private diplomacy for their own benefits. European industrial interests that felt underrepresented by the ICC created their own international business association in 1927 called the Council of Directors of European Industrial Federations.[24] Japanese MNEs had been active in the ICC since 1923, under the leadership of companies like the Mitsui group, hoping it would help the country's "development on the stage of the world economy."²⁵ Under the chairmanship of Alberto Pirelli, the heir to the Italian tire company of the same name, the ICC launched a diplomatic offensive in China in 1929 to cultivate this market, and a national Chinese committee of the ICC was created in 1931, just four years after an Indian National Committee joined the organization.²⁶

The ambition of the League of Nations to restore global free trade proved short-lived with the onset of the Great Depression in 1929, as well as the burgeoning of fascism in Europe and aggressive militarism in Japan. Rising tariffs and decreasing international trade were just the most obvious economic manifestations of the "anti-globalism" momentum that impacted MNEs in the 1930s. Tight controls on capital flows were progressively introduced, while imports and exports became increasingly submitted to clearing agreements. Alliances were shifting depending on economic and political evolutions and foreign investors were not immune to geopolitical rivalries. In Argentina, when US companies started in the 1920s to take over formerly British-owned infrastructure investments such as water networks and railroads, the British Chamber of Commerce in Buenos Aires took advantage of the fear against the "Colossus of the North" to lobby for British companies. Within the British Chamber of Commerce itself, interests were far from homogeneous. British MNEs that had invested in manufacturing in Argentina were favorable to tariffs, opposing the views of British trading companies that imported goods to the Argentinian market.²⁷

Navigating nationalism became a central preoccupation, and MNEs were at the forefront of designing strategies to secure their international businesses. Some of the strategies to deal with political risks were carried out individually, such as hiding the nationality of the company using front shareholders or duplicating their headquarters to secure their international business in case of a war.²⁸ Joining forces in international cartels was also a way to secure trade while mitigating the problems of overproduction and price drops and providing an alternative private solution to state planning and protectionism.²⁹

When facing fascism and Nazism, individual CEO attitudes ranged from assertive support to resistance and boycott in a few cases, but adaptation was probably the most widespread strategy. In 1937, the ICC organized its congress in Berlin. The incoming president of the ICC, IBM's leader T. J. Watson, spoke of promoting "World Peace through

World Trade." The German market was significant for IBM, which had invested heavily in the country.[30] Watson used this trip to Europe to nurture political contacts and open new IBM branches. He acknowledged later that the ICC had been useful for the global development of his firm by enabling him "to make acquaintances and friendships."[31]

World War II created specific operational challenges and a moral dilemma for companies. The US and British governments expropriated German and Japanese assets. Headquarters under regimes of strict capital control experienced tremendous difficulties in repatriating their profits. Consequently, many MNEs chose to reinvest in Germany, thus sustaining the Nazi regime. Moreover, as discussed in Chapter 7, when money transfers were authorized, the profits were often taxed twice – in both the host and home countries – resulting in what MNEs' executives denounced as "double taxation." As a result, foreign investors established dedicated business interest associations. The Swiss Industrie-Holding reported that it had been "born out of necessity" during World War II, when President Franklin D. Roosevelt promulgated an executive order to freeze targeted enemy assets in the United States, including those of Swiss MNEs suspected of being a cover for German capital.[32] In a similar vein, the Committee of British Industrial Interests in Germany was established with the objective of regaining full control of German subsidiaries after the war and its membership was limited to British companies.[33]

Organizing on a national basis remained important even for MNEs, as their executives needed their home governments' diplomatic assistance to negotiate profit repatriation and possible compensation in cases of nationalization. As emphasized in Chapter 13, the nationality of MNE managers and shareholders therefore once again became an important issue and many associations established adhesion criteria related to the company's nationality, while some MNEs limited access to those shares with voting rights to national citizens.

5.3 Getting Globalization Back on Track after 1945: Europeanization, Decolonization, and the Cold War

After 1945, as national governments were the main source of regulation, and the reestablishment of a free trade and capital flows could be attained only through bilateral or multilateral international conventions, MNEs had every interest in cultivating their national influence. Consequently, they actively participated in national business associations, which had played a crucial role in coordinating the war economy and benefited from official consultation rights with governments. The US Chamber of Commerce helped implement the Marshall Plan aid package that contributed to European reconstruction,[34] while many US MNEs increased their FDI in European countries.[35] As analyzed in Chapter 8, MNEs and national business associations also closely monitored the process of market integration in Europe launched in 1957 with the Treaty of Rome as well as the international negotiations within the General Agreement on Tariffs and Trade framework aimed at putting globalization back on track.

The postwar years also saw the apex of a broad consensus in Western Europe on the need for embedding market forces, be it by the coordination of private interests and self-discipline, or through regulation and economic planning as determined by the state in question and its institutional specificities. By coalescing with larger portions of the business community, MNEs' executives could present their interests as democratic and aligned with national interests which, in turn, justified business significant influence on national politics. The importance of speaking with one voice in such circumstances also explains why, in the case of apparently divergent interests with other portions of the business community, MNEs' representatives were often willing to negotiate pragmatic compromises, sometimes including selective protectionism and subsidies for smaller companies working for the internal market or the agricultural sector.[36]

In the United States, executives from large companies such as IBM, Standard Oil, DuPont, General Electric, and General Motors were influential on the NAM's board of directors and various committees, and from 1961 onwards, all its presidents were from a large US MNE, even though around 80 percent of the NAM's members were small and medium enterprises (SMEs) with fewer than five hundred employees.[37] Many MNEs' executives also participated in the so-called New Deal coalition that tolerated cooperation with labor and the US government.[38]

The division of labor that was established progressively with the waves of creation of business associations from the nineteenth century was further strengthened and institutionalized during the postwar years. Peak-level trade associations became central actors in the formulation of economic policies and foreign economic relations. Employers' associations focused on negotiating with national labor unions in the context of full employment and oversaw issues related to social policies, while sectoral trade associations targeted the regulations that would specifically impact the industries that they were representing. In the context of this division of labor, the associations that exclusively represented MNEs focused after World War II on facilitating foreign investments through the spread of investment protection treaties and the creation of investment risk guarantees, as well as the implementation of agreements banning double taxation.

Political risks had far from disappeared. The Egyptian nationalization of the Suez Canal in 1956 was a good reminder that the governments of decolonized countries might threaten the operations of MNEs in the future. In the absence of international conventions protecting foreign properties, MNEs once again needed the protection of their home states. Overall, Western governments widely supported their large companies in perpetuating colonial privilege or conquering foreign markets when the Cold War and decolonization reshuffled the decks of established trade and business relations. Such support ranged from military and covert interventions to facilitating the establishment of contracts through diplomatic assistance and the provision of export and investments guarantees.[39] The symbiosis between the political and economic spheres was reinforced structurally by the existence of strong national elite networks, with the same people involved in politics, business associations, and on the boards of several national companies.[40] However, governmental support did not prevent Western MNEs from experiencing nationalizations or restrictions, as especially from the 1960s many former European colonies regained the property of their natural resources, while governments in Latin America and Asia introduced restrictions over FDI flows.

When official relations were tense politically, businesses sometimes established their own networks of private bilateral diplomacy. For example, German companies with economic interests in communist

Eastern European countries set up the Ost-Ausschuss der Deutschen Wirtschaft in 1952.[41] In the late 1940s, the ICC renewed its effort to clear the way for FDI and promoted the idea of an "International Code to Protect Foreign Investments."[42] Some of its sections, in particular the United States Council of the ICC, were active promoters of freedom for trade and investments flows.[43] In the 1960s, the ICC created a joint commission with chambers of commerce of communist countries that sustained East–West contacts throughout the Cold War.[44]

Multinational enterprises created additional international business associations with more specific aims. An example was the International Association for the Promotion and Protection of Private Foreign Investments (APPI), established in 1958, in which the lawyers of US and European companies and large banks drafted laws to set up a benchmark for bilateral and multilateral treaties for investment protection.[45] During the 1950s and 1960s, private advocacy forums were also established. The most famous was Bilderberg, an annual high-profile secretive conference established in 1952 to allow business and political elites from the United States and Europe to exchange views on the evolution of the global economy as well as to monitor the influence of communism in the context of the Cold War. These private advocacy forums mostly contributed to strengthen cohesion amongst US and European elites and facilitated the exchange of information.[46]

Overall, the proliferation of business associations as well as the varieties of political issues prompted MNEs to engage in multilevel lobbying. Since it was difficult for single companies to dictate policies, even powerful MNEs such as IBM and Nestlé were ubiquitous in national and international business associations alike, in addition to being able to lobby governments in their own names. Acting collectively often proved more efficient, as emphasized in 1948 by a US lawyer working at the ICC, arguing that Standard Oil and other large investors could in fact use ICC's legitimacy to "cloak" their particular interests.[47] As business historian Geoffrey Jones has highlighted, Unilever was active in a whole range of national and international business associations to engage with European policymakers.[48] Unilever also contributed to the establishment of the Committee of British Industrial Interests in Germany and the Dutch Industrial Interests in Germany in 1947, and the firm's overseas taxation managers were key experts on the ICC's fiscal committee for many decades. Family dynasties also stand out with involvement in associations. The Watson family provided two presidents of the ICC: T. J. in the 1930s and his son Arthur K. in the 1960s, and no fewer than four generations of Sweden's Wallenberg family were active in the ICC with three being elected president.[49]

During the 1950s and 1960s, although MNEs certainly enjoyed significant power, the "globalist" agenda was far from fully realized. While the economic impact of FDI in the Global South varied, the promotion of investment treaties and bilateral taxation agreements by MNEs contributed to empower foreign investors at the expense of host governments through legal instruments and to drain wealth back to their headquarters based in the West. For these reasons, many countries, especially in Latin America, refused to sign such treaties during the postwar period, while the governments that were pursuing import substitution policies to foster endogenous growth increased their control of inward FDI, as discussed in Chapter 14.

Moreover, while MNEs were willing to secure their access to foreign markets, they were not always willing to grant reciprocity in their home countries. Keidanren, the association representing Japanese big business, opposed inward FDI to Japan in the 1950s and 1960s.[50] Such protectionist attitudes did not prevent Japanese business associations, which had been expelled from the ICC during World War II, to reintegrate the ICC in the late 1940s and to host the ICC's congress in 1955, welcoming about one thousand business leaders from all over the world to Tokyo.[51]

The impact of FDI on home economies also started to be questioned in the United States and Britain by the mid 1960s, as these countries were by far the main capital exporters at the time, and they experienced increasing balance-of-payments deficits. In the views of US and British policymakers, FDI had a substitution effect, which meant fewer exports from MNEs' home economies and justified some degree of capital controls, which were introduced or strengthened during the second half of the 1960s. Such policies were at odds with British and US MNEs' interests, which vehemently protested them.[52] These controls ultimately remained modest, especially when it came to large MNEs that could finance their investments by borrowing in the host countries.

This was nevertheless a first sign that the interests of domestic MNEs and their home states might sometimes be perceived as antagonist, a trend that would strengthen in the following decade.

5.4 From Global Challenges in the 1970s to the Short-Lived "Globalist" Hegemony

By the turn of the 1970s, MNEs had become the subject of public debate. In academia, the field of international business emerged in the 1960s to analyze MNEs' international operations. The ICC made "the multinational company" the theme of its congress in Istanbul in 1969. The specific terminology – MNE or the transnational company – used to characterize companies that had established subsidiaries abroad soon spread beyond specialized circles and became employed by a variety of often politically hostile groups. Moreover, when the economic crisis following the oil price rises of the 1970s hit Western economies, labor representatives accused MNEs of destroying jobs through restructurings and relocations and requested better information on their international operations and plants' profitability, as well as the right to negotiate with the headquarters.

Multinational enterprises were also criticized by governments in the Global South regarding their role in perpetuating unfair economic relations. Their leaders argued for the New International Economic Order (NIEO) at the United Nations (UN) assembly and for better control of their own resources, and, when appropriate, at the expense of foreign investors.[53] Criticism of MNEs was also widespread within religious circles, with liberation theology taking hold in Latin America and several European religiously inspired NGOs denouncing the negative impact of MNEs on development. Some scandals, such as the role of the US-based telecommunication MNE ITT in the overthrow of the democratically elected Allende government in Chile, also fueled their condemnation. In response, several international organizations started preparatory work to introduce international corporate guidelines in the early 1970s. The UN Centre on Transnational Corporations was created in 1975 and emerged as an additional sign of the regulatory risks that MNEs faced at the time.

This context prompted a massive counteroffensive on the part of MNEs' executives and many business associations sponsored task forces to follow all discussions targeting this specific type of company and to establish ties to civil servants in charge of the negotiations.[54] In the late 1960s, US and European pharmaceutical MNEs created new associations to safeguard their industry interests, particularly in response to challenges from developing countries regarding drug pricing.[55] Multinational enterprises also coalesced within existing international associations that benefited from official consultation rights with the international organizations in charge of drafting the codes, such as the ICC and the Business and Industry Advisory Committee, created in 1962 to influence the Organisation for Economic Co-operation and Development (OECD).

In the 1970s, the ICC welcomed business leaders from newly independent countries in Africa and Asia as members. The first non-Western businessman (from India) was elected as the ICC's president in 1969. The presence of Global South elites helped the ICC neutralize potential conflicts within the business community and contributed to create a united front to oppose the NIEO. To further emphasize the global unity of business the ICC wanted to embody, Mexico City was chosen to host the congress of the ICC in 1963, followed by New Delhi in 1965, Istanbul in 1969, and Rio de Janeiro in 1973, in spite of the brutal dictatorship that ruled Brazil at the time. Beyond symbols, however, it was doubtful that businesses from the Global South enjoyed the same political weight in international business associations. Latin American companies, for example, were organized in hemispherical business associations such as the Inter-American Council for Trade and Production, created in 1941, and remained relatively marginal in the ICC. Since 1963, US-based MNEs active in Latin America had been organized separately under the chairmanship of David Rockefeller in the Business Group for Latin America, and MNEs were active in various business associations across the continent.[56] Here again, unity was built pragmatically against an external threat – that is, international organizations and various governments' attempts to increase control on private enterprise and FDI. Concurrently, outdated forms of international business gatherings like the British Congress of Chambers of

Commerce of the Empire, which had been created during the heydays of colonialism in the nineteenth century, were disbanded in the 1970s.[57]

The 1970s context of widespread criticism against MNEs also reinvigorated the interest of business executives in financing and participating in think tanks to defend the preservation of free enterprise against state intervention and to promote the enforcement of global trade and investment rules. Some directors of MNEs had much earlier contributed to the financing of neoliberal think tanks, such as the Mont-Pèlerin Society, and participated in keeping the conservative spirit alive.[58] In the 1970s, though, larger portions of the business community embraced a forthrightly neoliberal agenda and networks espousing such an ideology soon developed worldwide.[59]

Simultaneously, the economic crisis exacerbated tensions between various business sectors in the United States and Western Europe. Such issues undermined the efficiency of national business associations in the 1970s, with the interests of SMEs as well as economic sectors working exclusively for the internal market being at odds with the perpetuation of MNEs' "globalist" agenda. Divergent national interests plagued the Union of Industrial and Employers' Confederations of Europe (UNICE), created in 1952 to represent Business in the context of European economic integration. In response, the permanent secretaries of business associations from Austria, Denmark, Germany, the Netherlands and Switzerland, which defended the interests of MNEs and export industries, joined forces and met secretly on a yearly basis in order to fight nationalist and protectionist policies at the European level, both within the UNICE and through the influence of their national diplomats in international arenas.[60] Overall, the commitment of US and European MNEs to free trade was pragmatic and could shift depending on the circumstances. For instance, when it came to facing Japanese competition in the automobile market, European MNEs did not hesitate to organize and lobby for protectionism.[61]

The disagreements within business circles and the organizational limitations of large business associations prompted the increased empowerment of CEOs as political figures. Such a trend was first visible in the United States, where the Business Roundtable, a group comprised of the chief executives of America's largest corporations, was established in 1972 to encourage business leaders to take a more active role in politics.⁶² Actually, for each new issue that arose, organizing in small groups of chief executives appeared to be an appropriate solution to bypass the difficulty of finding consensus within widely encompassing business associations as well as fostering direct cooperation with high-ranking civil servants and politicians at home and abroad. By this logic, new private advocacy forums were created. At the initiative of US business leader David Rockefeller, the Trilateral Commission, composed of American, European, and Japanese delegates, was set up "to foster closer cooperation among these core industrialized areas of the world with shared leadership responsibilities in the wider international system."⁶³

Once the governments of the seven main capitalist economic powers of the world started the so-called G7 in 1975, meeting on a regular basis in response to the economic crises that followed the surge of oil prices in 1973, private summitry of business paralleled the takeoff of this new form of public summitry that allowed for relaxed exchanges, reintroducing political agency and supranational cooperation in economic matters. In 1973, following the iconic visit of President Richard Nixon to China in the previous year, the US Department of Commerce initiated the creation of the United States–China Business Council. It gathered representatives of American MNEs and aimed at promoting and facilitating trade between the United States and China. The International Vienna Council, established in 1978, pursued similar goals by gathering businesspeople from Western capitalist countries and political elites in charge of economic planning from the Eastern Europe socialist bloc.⁶⁴ Despite increased contacts, the collaboration between executives of Western MNEs and political elites from the Middle East, China, and the Soviet Union remained relatively limited, not the least because they experienced very different types of business–government relations. As a matter of fact, most chief executive clubs gathered MNEs from the United States and Europe.

From the 1980s, traditional business associations such as the ICC also lost some of their relevance to the advantage of private advocacy forums dominated by individual chief executives. This process was epitomized in the establishment of the European Roundtable of Industrialists in 1983, which aimed at supporting the European Commission into enforcing a single European market that would advantage large MNEs. This initiative helped circumvent the roadblocks at the governmental level, providing chief executives with renewed goodwill and making them the new problem solvers, including when it came to political issues.[65] The former 1971 European Management Symposium was rebranded as the World Economic Forum in 1987, highlighting once more that CEOs alongside political leaders ambitioned to make a difference on the world stage.

Multinational enterprises achieved significant success in preserving their economic leeway, avoiding meaningful international regulation. The 1976 OECD guidelines for MNEs and the 1977 ILO Tripartite Declaration of Principles concerning Multinational Enterprises and Social Policy only provided nonbinding recommendations, while the idea of a UN code of conduct targeting MNEs was abandoned in the early 1990s after years of obstruction from Western MNEs and their government officials. The dissolution of the UN Centre on Transnational Corporations in 1992 can be seen as a further symbol of the MNEs' power in those years.[66] By that time, the wide network of groups of chief executives and think tanks that had successfully defended MNEs against international regulation in the 1970s had gone on the offensive to promote the interests of foreign investors. By the same token, they also promoted radical views regarding free enterprise and market reforms, and against social and environmental regulations.

The accession to power of Margaret Thatcher in Britain and Ronald Reagan in the United States, respectively in 1979 and 1981, contributed to put deregulation rather than regulation on the political agenda. Moreover, the increased need of many countries in the Global South to secure loans from the International Monetary Fund and the World Bank incentivized their governments to provide guarantees to foreign investors and to liberalize their economies – a set of policies often described as the "Washington Consensus" as they were promoted by international institutions based in Washington, DC. In the 1980s and 1990s, the Keidanren increasingly supported the opening of the Japanese domestic market to FDI. This policy shift was initiated by large MNEs in the electronics and automobile industries, which wanted to avoid protectionism abroad for their FDI and anticipated possible competitive gains at home.[67]

Investment treaties proliferated during the 1990s as did the use of investor–state dispute settlements. Such treaties were increasingly used by MNEs in the 2000s to contest state decisions in the domains of sustainability, public health, and the provision of public services.[68] For instance, the tobacco MNE Philip Morris sued the state of Uruguay for mandating that the company adopt health warnings that covered 80 percent of the packaging, while French conglomerate Vivendi sued Argentina for modifying water concession contracts and regulating the price for consumers. Both Philip Morris and Vivendi lost their cases, but such lawsuits put governments under considerable pressure. The fall of the Berlin Wall in 1989 ultimately seemed to confirm the uncontested hegemony of Western global capitalism, sealed by the creation of the World Trade Organization (WTO) in 1995. In the 1990s and 2000s, numerous political scientists identified a crisis in traditional national business associations, which seemed to be abandoned by MNEs, which were portrayed as the almighty winners during the heyday of late twentieth-century globalization.[69]

That hegemony of the "globalist" agenda was short-lived, however. Some discontent was already palpable at the end of the 1990s, as seen in the large gatherings of citizens who started to denounce the perceived lack of democratic legitimacy of the WTO and of international summits like the G7. Moreover, small and medium-sized companies, the agricultural sector, and industries failing to benefit from globalization increasingly called for a return to protectionism. The disputed legitimacy of US-style globalization and the rise of China's economic and political importance resulted in inaction at the WTO, which proved unable to overcome conflicts between the main trading blocs.[70] Tensions spiked again after the global financial crisis in 2008, which triggered a new cycle of public outrage against large banks. The political appeal of anti-globalization stances contributed to major political events such as the 2016 Brexit vote, which led Britain to leave the European Union, and the election of Donald Trump, who capitalized on anti-immigrant sentiments and protectionist rhetoric during his campaign in the United States in the same year.

These recent trends have demonstrated that the so-called globalist agenda had been mostly promoted by large European and US MNEs and was very much connected to the hegemony of the United States.

Once the hegemony of the United States was called into question, "globalist" principles were scrambled as well. For reasons of national security and trade rivalry, the US government since the first Trump administration has increasingly monitored and limited the activities of foreign MNEs. While Trump was primarily concerned with Chinese MNEs, the subsequent Biden administration blocked a major acquisition by a Japanese MNE, despite Japan being a political ally of the United States. The Covid-19 pandemic of 2020 and the full-scale Russian invasion of Ukraine in 2022 further contributed to challenging the viability of global value chains. In 2022, the United States banned the imports of communication equipment from Huawei and four other Chinese companies, and the takeover of US Steel by Nippon Steel was temporarily halted in 2024. In response to increased restrictions, Chinese MNEs have developed their own lobbying channels toward EU institutions and the US Congress.[71]

Paradoxically, the obstruction capabilities of MNEs remained evident when it came to the regulatory power of European states and Western-created international organizations, as the watering down of the 2021 OECD minimum tax on MNEs and of the 2024 European Directive on the Duty of Vigilance illustrated. The rule of law that favored the protection of MNEs' investments still impacted the ability of national governments to provide public goods and pursue the greening of their economies. Regarding investment protection treaties, some Western governments indeed discovered that the legal tools promoted by their predecessors and the MNEs' headquartered in their countries could be used against them. For instance, in 2021, the Germany-based energy company RWE used the legal protection provided by the Energy Charter Treaty to sue the Dutch government, which had to pay 1.4 billion euros for the phasing out of coal power plants. Moreover, the voice of individual business leaders, such as Tesla, Space X, and X chief executive Elon Musk, mattered more than ever in politics, not least due to their grip on strategic industries and media. Billionaires such as cofounder of Microsoft Bill Gates developed ambitions to offer private solutions to solve humanitarian and health issues in the Global South.

It therefore appears that we are witnessing competing forms of globalization, with major economies like China and the United States that have escaped the rules of global economic governance developing alternative trade and investment relations. China, in particular, has been able to control inward and outward FDI and to align the activities of MNEs with its developmental goals, as detailed in Chapter 3. Consequently, in a multipolar world characterized by the rise of Chinese and Indian MNEs, *multilatinas*, and others, as well as extreme wealth concentration in the hands of a few CEOs, the international business associations of the twentieth century are less relevant to understand global politics. As network analyses have shown, elite clubs such as the World Economic Forum have tended to remain largely US- and Europe-centered, with only a slight increase of corporate elites from the Global South.[72] Moreover, it might be speculated that big-tech companies, predominantly headquartered in the United States and China, and whose production is highly internationalized, are likely to pursue agendas that differ substantially from those of MNEs of earlier generations. The immense financial resources and monopolistic power these companies command may enable them to operate independently from business associations, and to develop direct and privileged relationships with governments.

5.5 Conclusion

This chapter has shown how MNEs have been active politically to defend their ability to conduct business around the world. Their business leaders have often defended their interests in a collective fashion, constantly readapting their collective organizations to the changing political circumstances from the time of empires to the collapse of the first globalization, postwar reconstruction and decolonization, the phase of a second globalization, and, ultimately, to the return to economic nationalism since the 2010s. Political hardships, such as wars and attempts to regulate them in the 1970s, were important drivers of their political activism.

Depending on economic and geopolitical circumstance, MNEs pragmatically adapted their strategies to sustain their global operations, ranging from the establishment of international cartels to the promotion of free trade and international competition. Key impacts on societies were the diffusion of standards on a global scale since the nineteenth century, the generalization of national and international regulations that facilitated and protected international investments after 1945, as well as a general lowering of taxation on MNE profits with the elimination of double taxation.

The forms of MNE collective actions paralleled the organization of world politics, so that they could engage with nation-states, international organizations, and political summits. Multinational enterprises often pragmatically stressed their nationality and coordinated with larger portions of the national business community when they needed the goodwill of national governments. From the 1970s onwards and the start of the second wave of globalization, US and European MNEs increasingly coalesced internationally within elitist forums and promoted a "globalist" agenda without much compromise. The power of individual chief executives has raised questions in terms of political accountability and democracy, as well as about the willingness of MNEs to share political influence with other companies. Some legacies of this period are still visible today, with the perpetuation of obstructionist policies when it comes to social and environmental regulation and the concentration of power and influence in the hands of a few extremely wealthy billionaires. Moreover, the legal devices that have favored the protection of MNE investments continue to impact the sovereignty of certain states while incentivizing others to stop complying with international rules of law.

It must also be emphasized that the "globalist" agenda was very much related to the hegemony of the United States and Western Europe. Over time, and especially in the 1970s and the years since 2010, the political power of MNEs and the legitimacy of their political agenda have been disputed by various groups and individuals such as labor unions, NGOs, government officials, or SMEs. Moreover, while US and European MNEs and their business associations have depicted free trade, the protection of foreign property, and agreements preventing double taxation as universal rules connected to freedom, they have not hesitated on multiple occasions to seek protection from their home states when facing new competition. Multinational enterprises from other countries, such as Japan, only embraced the globalist credo once they prioritized access to foreign markets and global value chains over the protection of their home markets.

These obvious double standards, and the rise of MNEs from the Global South, as well as the growth of China as an economic, political, and military force, contributed to make Western-led business associations and elite clubs less relevant in the twenty-first century. The resurgence of nationalist policy agendas in the United States and several European countries has, in part, been facilitated by a small number of media and technology MNE executives acting independently and cultivating privileged relationships with increasingly authoritarian political leaders. Meanwhile the overwhelming majority of the previously "pro-globalist" chief executives of MNEs have assumed a more muted public posture, frequently exhibiting alignment with these evolving political orientations and publicly reversing earlier commitments to sustainability, diversity, and free trade. International trade and FDI remain heavily influenced by geopolitical trends, and that is a reality MNEs will have to face in the future, as they did in the past.

Notes

1. Lefebvre, P. "Penser l'entreprise comme acteur politique," *Entreprises et histoire*, 104, 3 (2021), 5–18.
2. Rollings, N. "'The Vast and Unsolved Enigma of Power,' Business History and Business Power," *Enterprise & Society*, 22, 4 (2021), 893–920.
3. Culpepper, P. D. *Quiet Politics and Business Power: Corporate Control in Europe and Japan*, Cambridge, MA, Cambridge University Press, 2011.
4. Rollings, N. "Government and Regulators," in da Silva Lopes, T., Lubinski, C., and Tworek, H. (eds.) *The Routledge Companion to the Makers of Global Business*, New York, Routledge, 2020.
5. Slobodian, Q. *Globalists: The End of Empire and the Birth of Neoliberalism*, Cambridge, MA, Harvard University Press, 2018.
6. Green, N. L. *The Other Americans in Paris: Businessmen, Countesses, Wayward Youth 1880–1941*, Chicago, IL, University of Chicago Press, 2014.
7. Dilley, A. "The Politics of Imperial Commerce: The Congress of Chambers of Commerce of the Empire, 1886–1914," *Sage Open*, 3, 4 (2013). https://doi.org/10.1177/2158244013510304.
8. Ridgeway, G. L. *Merchants of Peace: The History of the International Chamber of Commerce*, Boston, MA, Little, Brown and Company, 1959, 21–25.
9. Thompson, A. "The Power and Privileges of Association: Co-ethnic Networks and the Economic Life of the British Imperial World," *South African Historical Journal*, 56, 1 (2006), 43–59.

10. Mason, M. *American Multinationals and Japan: The Political Economy of Japanese Capital Controls, 1899–1980*, Cambridge, MA, Harvard University Press, 1992, 3.
11. Maru, A. H. "The Development of Employers' Organisations in India," *International Labour Review*, 27, 2 (1933), 220–236, 224.
12. Lubinski, C. *Navigating Nationalism in Global Enterprise: A Century of Indo-German Business Relations*, Cambridge, Cambridge University Press, 2022.
13. Winkler, H. (ed.), *Organisierter Kapitalismus: Voraussetzungen und Anfänge*, Gottingen, Vandenhoeck and Ruprecht, 1974.
14. Galambos, L. *Competition & Cooperation: The Emergence of a National Trade Association*, Baltimore, MD, Johns Hopkins University Press, 1966.
15. Delton, J. A. *The Industrialists: How the National Association of Manufacturers Shaped American Capitalism*, Princeton, NJ, Princeton University Press, 2020.
16. Phillips Sawyer, L. "Trade Associations, State Building, and the Sherman Act: The US Chamber of Commerce, 1912–25," in John, R. R. and Phillips-Fein, K. (eds.) *Capital Gains: Business and Politics in Twentieth-Century America*, Philadelphia, University of Pennsylvania Press, 2016, 181–196.
17. Eichenberger, P. "Employers of the World, Unite! The Transnational Mobilization of Industrialists around World War One," in Milan, M. and Saluppo, A. (eds.) *The Dark Side of the Belle Epoque: Political Violence and Armed Associations in Europe before the First World War*, London, Routledge, 2021, 97–114.
18. Robins, J. E. "A Common Brotherhood for Their Mutual Benefit: Sir Charles Macara and Internationalism in the Cotton Industry, 1904–1914," *Enterprise & Society*, 16, 4 (2015), 847–888.
19. Olukoju, A. "An Imperial Clearing House for Commercial Information and Suggestions: The British Imperial Council of Commerce, 1911–1925," *Itinerario*, 47, 2 (2023), 240–256.
20. Hogan, M. J. "Corporatism," in Hogan, M. J. and Paterson, T. G. (eds.) *Explaining the History of American Foreign Relations*, Cambridge, Cambridge University Press, 2004, 137–148.
21. Lynch Dungy, M. *Order and Rivalry: Rewriting the Rules of International Trade after the First World War*, Cambridge, Cambridge University Press, 2023.
22. David, T. and Eichenberger, P. "A World Parliament of Business? The International Chamber of Commerce and Its Presidents in the Twentieth Century," *Business History*, 65, 2 (2023), 260–283.
23. Bertilorenzi, M. "The International Chamber of Commerce: The Organisation of Free-Trade and Market Regulations from the Interwar Period to the 1960s," in Coppolaro, L. and Mechi, L. (eds.) *Free Trade and Social Welfare in Europe Explorations in the Long 20th Century*, London, Routledge, 2020, 90–108.

24. Rollings, N. and Kipping, M. "Private Transnational Governance in the Heyday of the Nation-State: The Council of European Industrial Federations (CEIF)," *Economic History Review*, 61, 2, (2008), 409–431.
25. Fletcher, W. M. *The Japanese Business Community and National Trade Policy, 1920–1942*, Chapel Hill, University of North Carolina Press, 1989, 28.
26. Yi-Tang, L., David, T., and Eichenberger, P. "'In the Interest of Your Bank and Our Country': Two Encounters between China and the International Chamber of Commerce," *Modern Asian Studies*, 57, 4, (2023), 1387–1414.
27. Goodwin, P. B., Jr. "Anglo-Argentine Commercial Relations: A Private Sector View, 1922–43," *Hispanic American Historical Review*, 61, 1 (1981), 29–51.
28. Forbes, N., Kurosawa, T., and Wubs, B. *Multinational Enterprise, Political Risk and Organisational Change: From Total War to Cold War*, London, Routledge, 2019.
29. Bertilorenzi, M. "Legitimising Cartels: The Joint Roles of the League of Nations and of the International Chamber of Commerce," in Fellman, S. and Shanahan, M. (eds.) *Regulating Competition: Cartel Registers in the Twentieth-Century World*, New York, Routledge, 2016, 30–47.
30. Jones, G., Ballor, G., and Brown, A. "Thomas J. Watson, IBM and Nazi Germany," *Harvard Business School*, Case 807-133, revised September 30, 2021.
31. Belden, T. G. and Belden, M. R. *The Lengthening Shadow (The Life of Thomas J. Watson)*, Boston, MA, Little, Brown and Company, 1962, 197.
32. Pitteloud, S. "Industrie-Holding: Creating a Community of Interest among Swiss 'Multinationals,'" *Revue suisse d'histoire*, 69, 3 (2019), 400–417.
33. Wubs, B. "A Dutch Multinational's Miracle in Post-war Germany," *Jahrbuch für Wirtschaftsgeschichte / Economic History Yearbook*, 53, 1 (2012), 15–41.
34. Schaufelbuehl, J. M. "Becoming the Advocate for US-Based Multinationals: The United States Council of the International Chamber of Commerce, 1945-1974," *Business History* 65, 2 (2023), 284–301, at 286.
35. Wilkins, M. *The Maturing of Multinational Enterprise: American Business Abroad from 1914 to 1970*, Cambridge, MA, Harvard University Press, 1974.
36. Pitteloud, S. *Les multinationales suisses dans l'arène politique (1942–1993)*, Geneva, Droz, 2022.
37. Delton, *The Industrialists*, 7–10.
38. Schaufelbuehl, "Becoming the Advocate," 286–287.
39. Badel, L. *Diplomatie et grands contrats: L'Etat français et les marchés extérieurs au XXe siècle*, Paris, Publications de la Sorbonne, 2010.
40. David, T. and Westerhuis, G. *The Power of Corporate Networks: A Comparative and Historical Perspective*, New York, Routledge, 2015.

41. Jüngerkes, S. *Diplomaten der Wirtschaft: Die Geschichte des Ost-Ausschusses der Deutschen Wirtschaft*, Osnabruck, Fibre, 2012.
42. Slobodian, *Globalists*, 136–142.
43. Schaufelbuehl, "Becoming the Advocate for US-Based Multinationals."
44. David, T., Eichenberger, P., and Kott, S. "The International Chamber of Commerce and the Creation of a Pan-European Economic Space during the Cold War," *Contemporary European History*, First View (2025), 1–17. DOI: https://doi.org/10.1017/S0960777325101112.
45. Batselé, F. "Foreign Investors of the World, Unite! The International Association for the Promotion and Protection of Private Foreign Investments (APPI) 1958–1968," *European Journal of International Law*, 34, 2 (2023), 415–447.
46. Carroll, W. K. and Sapinski, J. P. "The Global Corporate Elite and the Transnational Policy-Planning Network, 1996–2006: A Structural Analysis," *International Sociology* 25, 4 (2010), 501–538.
47. Ross, G. T. May 1948, Harvard Business School Manuscript Collection, Baker Library, Winthrop W. Aldrich Papers, 1918–1973, Box 43, folder "Chamber of Commerce, International, 1948." Memorandum on the International Chamber of Commerce, 4–5.
48. Jones, G. *Renewing Unilever: Transformation and Tradition*, Oxford, Oxford University Press, 2005, 332–339.
49. David and Eichenberger, "A World Parliament of Business?" 267.
50. Mason, *American Multinationals and Japan*, 153.
51. Kimura, M. "The Return of Japanese Business to the World Community: The International Chamber of Commerce after the Second World War," *Journal of Shibusawa Studies*, 14, (2001), 17–40.
52. Rollings, N. "Multinational Enterprise and Government Controls on Outward Foreign Direct Investment in the US and UK in the 1960s," *Enterprise & Society*, 12, 2 (2011), 398–434.
53. Ogle, V. "State Rights against Private Capital: The 'New International Economic Order' and the Struggle over Aid, Trade, and Foreign Investment, 1962–1981," *Humanity: An International Journal of Human Rights, Humanitarianism, and Development*, 5, 2 (2014), 211–234.
54. Pitteloud, S. "Unwanted Attention: Swiss Multinationals and the Creation of International Corporate Guidelines in the 1970s," *Business and Politics*, 22, 4 (2020), 587–611.
55. Turberg, P. "Le patronat ouest-européen et américain et la structuration internationale de l'industrie pharmaceutique, 1963–1971," *Relations Internationales*, 180, 4 (2020), 75–90.
56. Scheider, B. R. *Business Politics and the State in Twentieth-Century Latin America*, Cambridge, Cambridge University Press, 2004, 46–49.
57. Dilley, "The Politics of Imperial Commerce," 2.
58. Phillips-Fein, K. *Invisible Hands: The Making of the Conservative Movement from the New Deal to Reagan*, New York, Norton, 2009.

59. Salles-Djelic, M.-L. "Marketization: From Intellectual Agenda to Global Policy Making," in Salles-Djelic, M.-L and Sahlin-Andersson, K. (eds.) *Transnational Governance*, Cambridge, Cambridge University Press, 2006, 53–73.
60. Iberg, L. "Fighting for a Neoliberal Europe: Swiss Business Associations and the UNICE, 1970–1978," *Business History*, 65, 2 (2023), 366–381.
61. Ballor, G. "Liberalisation or Protectionism for the Single Market? European Automakers and Japanese Competition, 1985–1999," *Business History* 65, 2 (2023), 302–328.
62. Waterhouse, B. C. *Lobbying America: The Politics of Business from Nixon to NAFTA. Politics and Society in Twentieth-Century America*, Princeton, NJ, Princeton University Press, 2014, 76–105.
63. Luna, M. and Velasco, J. L. "Power without Representation: The Coherence and Closeness of the Trilateral Commission," in Salas-Porras, A. and Murray, G. (eds.) *Think Tanks and Global Politics: Key Spaces in the Structure of Power*, New York, Palgrave Macmillan, 81–106, 83.
64. Morival, Y. "Forger une élite économique transrideau de fer. Le Club de Vienne et la promotion de la coopération économique pendant la guerre froide," *20 & 21 Revue d'histoire*, 153, 1 (2022), 91–104.
65. Cowles, M. G. "Setting the Agenda for a New Europe: The ERT and EC 1992," *JCMS: Journal of Common Market Studies*, 33, 4 (1995), 501–526.
66. Müller, M. "Beaucoup de bruit pour rien? L'organisation des Nations Unies et la régulation des multinationales 1974–1992," *Revue d'histoire diplomatique*, 137, 1 (2023), 27–48.
67. Yoshimatsu, H. *Internationalization, Corporate Preferences and Commercial Policy in Japan*, Basingstoke, Palgrave Macmillan, 2000, 161–165.
68. Perrone, N. M. *Investment Treaties and the Legal Imagination: How Foreign Investors Play by Their Own Rules*, Oxford, Oxford University Press, 2021.
69. Streeck, W., Grote, J. R., Schneider, V., and Visser, J. (eds.) *Governing Interests: Business Associations Facing Internationalization*, London, Routledge, 2006.
70. Orford A. "How to Think about the Battle for the State at the WTO," *German Law Journal*, 24, 1 (2023), 45–71.
71. Oprysko, C. "Companies in Crosshair over China Ties Boost Lobbying," Politico.com, retrieved October 16, 2024. www.politico.com/newsletters/politico-influence/2024/07/26/companies-in-crosshairs-over-china-ties-boost-lobbying-00171460.
72. Carroll and Sapinski, "The Global Corporate Elite."

Further Reading

David, T. and Eichenberger, P. "'A World Parliament of Business'? The International Chamber of Commerce and Its Presidents in the Twentieth Century," *Business History*, 65, 2 (2023), 260–283.

Perrone, N. M. *Investment Treaties and the Legal Imagination: How Foreign Investors Play by Their Own Rules*, Oxford, Oxford University Press, 2021.

Pitteloud, S. "Unwanted Attention: Swiss Multinationals and the Creation of International Corporate Guidelines in the 1970s," *Business and Politics*, 22, 4 (2020), 587–611.

Schaufelbuehl, J. M. *Crusading for Globalization: US Multinationals and Their Opponents since 1945*, Philadelphia, University of Pennsylvania Press, 2025.

Slobodian, Q. *Globalists: The End of Empire and the Birth of Neoliberalism*, Cambridge, MA, Harvard University Press, 2018.

6

Multinationals and Dictatorship

6.1 Introduction

The unprecedented integration of global markets between the 1860s and 1929 known as the first globalization took place at a time of important changes in the global political arena.[1] The first one is the consolidation of the nation-state as the dominant political unit. After centuries of dominance of pluri-cultural empires without clear territorial borders or stable capital cities, by the second half of the nineteenth century most societies accepted a division of the world into sovereign countries with well-defined borders, currencies, and basic cultures. The second one is the consolidation of the political systems that dominated the twentieth century. Absolute monarchies, tribal systems, or theocratic regimes were gradually (and often violently) replaced by liberal democracies or dictatorial regimes.

Countries classified as "democracies" after the 1860s were far from being perfect ones. Important segments of the population were legally disenfranchised based on gender, wealth, or ethnic origin. Having made this caveat clear, countries considered as "democracies" are those in which the executive (president or prime minister) and the legislative powers (parliament or congress) filled their positions after contested elections, in which voters were not coerced to vote for any candidate, and in which those competing for political power had freedom to campaign. In such a system, the executive rules under laws discussed and approved by the legislative power and an independent judicial power (the courts) makes sure the laws approved by the legislative power are consistent with the constitution. In contrast, in a dictatorship, the ruler comes to power through noncontested elections or simply no elections, has power over the legislative and judicial branches of the government, and the opposition has no way to contest the power of the executive.² Despite these generalities, it is worth emphasizing that during the long period between the 1870s and early 2000s, there was a variety of both democratic and dictatorial regimes representing a wide range of ideologies. In this environment, multinational enterprises (MNEs) expanding their operations across borders inevitably dealt with democratic or dictatorial regimes.

This chapter explores how MNEs originating in rich Western countries related with and strategized under dictatorial regimes. It covers the long period of time from the 1860s to the early 2020s, which is the era in which modern MNEs and the modern democracies and dictatorships dominated the world economy and polity. The chapter shows how in some circumstances the MNEs found ways to adapt their operations to the needs of the dictators, while in others the MNEs actively participated, either promoting coups that put dictators in power or legitimizing a dictatorial regime. The chapter also uncovers how MNEs often sympathized with dictatorial policies when they entailed repressing labor unionism or bringing order into a previously chaotic society. Dictators eager to promote foreign direct investment (FDI) were usually more efficient at establishing an MNE-friendly environment than a democratic regime. An alliance with a dictatorship, however, was also determined by the relations between the MNEs' home countries and the host country's dictator. As the chapter shows, geopolitical considerations overruled economic ones.

The chapter is organized covering an era divided into the following subperiods: the first global economy (1860s–1930s), World War II, the Cold War (1948–1989), and the post–Cold War authoritarianism (1989–2010s). Covering such long period of time implies some generalizations and simplifications, but the chapter offers telling examples that illustrate important trends.

6.2 Dictatorships and Foreign Capital in the First Global Economy (1860s–1930s)

The first global economy in which the world economy integrated itself like never before thanks to a combination of technological advances and pro-globalization policies adopted around the globe coincided with an era of deep political transformations. This period partially overlaps what political scientist Samuel Huntington called the First Democratization Wave (1828–1926), a period during which the world witnessed unprecedented expansion in suffrage and the creation of twenty-eight new democracies.[3] Imperfect as they were, the new democratic regimes did not rule over the majority of the world's population and the violent revolutions or civil wars taking place in many countries that had previously increased suffrage shows enormous discontent among important segments of the population.

During the first global economy, several dictators ruling relatively newly created countries saw in globalization an opportunity for economic growth and consolidation of their nation-states. This was particularly true for the case of countries rich in natural resources in high global demand. Impatient to enjoy the benefits of globalization, a breed of nineteenth-century dictators promoted policies favoring foreign direct FDI in the natural resources export sector and related infrastructure. Some of these rulers believed that development could not wait and that ruling with an iron fist was a necessary means to eliminate obstacles to foreign investment and make the most out of the export of the richness nature had blessed their countries with. Some of the best examples of this type of pro-globalization dictatorial regimes in this period can be found in Latin America. After their wars of independence from Spain (1808–1833), most Latin American countries fell into civil wars between those defending the mercantilist, pro-clerical system inherited from Spain (mainly the so-called conservatives) and those who looked at Britain or the United States as a source of inspiration and advocated for an export-led growth economic model that ditched Spain's heritage, including the role of the Catholic Church (mainly the so-called liberals). This process had its own national particularities, but after these civil wars most Latin American countries were ruled by liberal-minded elites, mainly represented by an authoritarian figure, that adopted a pro-foreign market economic regime in which MNEs were going to play an important role.

The quintessential example of a pro-globalization dictatorial regime in the first global economy is that of Mexico's Porfirio Díaz (1876–1910). Díaz took power after decades of economic and political instability that destroyed, impoverished, and fragmented Mexico. For Díaz, recovery and national unity were possible only through a strong government and a prosperous economy. The strong government required not only a capable, disciplined, loyal, and well-armed military force, but also infrastructure (mainly communications and transportation) that allowed the government to repress insurrections. Díaz also understood that in order to have a strong and loyal political coalition he needed to reward his members with rents, something he believed could be achieved only by a prosperous economy pushed by foreign investment.[4] Following this political logic, Díaz adopted an open-door policy to foreign investors that translated into a wave of investments in infrastructure (mainly roads, telecommunications, water, sewage, and railways), agriculture, mining, and oil.[5] Foreign investment "bought" the loyalty of regional leaders who supported Díaz's agenda. For this to work, in return for the MNEs' investments, Díaz offered a friendly and safe environment in which threats from labor organizations was violently neutralized and the property rights of private firms respected.

Díaz's strategy worked. By the turn of the century, Mexico was the darling of MNEs and had become one of the world's largest recipients of FDI. The economy grew handsomely with a couple of years reaching levels of 8 percent. In return, some MNEs went as far as appointing Díaz to their corporate boards, as was the case of US-based insurance company Equitable or by appointing his son as a director, as happened with British engineering contractor MNE Pearson & Son. In fact, Weetman Pearson, the head of Pearson & Son, developed a personal relationship with Díaz and his firm was in charge of crucial infrastructure and oil projects.[6] In the long term, however, some US MNEs and members of the Mexican elite resented what they perceived was a favorable policy by Díaz toward British investors and a small internal circle. This discontent eventually led some of the Mexican elites who felt excluded to rebel against Díaz and overthrow him in 1910, starting a civil war known as the Mexican Revolution.

Similar patterns can be found with other Latin American authoritarian rulers eager to modernize their countries through export promotion, as in the cases of Peru's Augusto Leguía (1919–1930), Chile's Carlos Ibáñez (1927–1931), and Argentina's Domingo Sarmiento (1868–1874), just to name a few important representatives.[7] An illustrative case of a dictator going to an extreme to favor foreign MNEs is Venezuela's Juan Vicente Gómez (1908–1935). In 1918, shortly after the discovery of important oil reserves, the Venezuelan minister of development proposed a change in the legislation that would increase the until then low taxes on crude production. The MNEs immediately protested, and Gómez responded by firing the minister and asking the MNEs to write the oil legislation themselves.[8] It has been said that Gómez told the MNEs, "You know about oil. You write the legislation. We're amateurs in this area."[9] The MNEs' written legislation ruled the Venezuelan oil sector between 1922 and 1944, a period during which that country became a major global player in the oil industry.

Foreign MNEs were often open about their preference for dictatorial regimes over democratically elected ones. A very telling example comes from the representatives of Pearson & Son when negotiating an oil concession with the Colombian government. These negotiators had already worked with Mexico's Díaz and were frustrated by the fact that in order to gain a concession in Colombia they had to navigate the complicated maze of competitive politics. When reporting back to London, one of the negotiators openly stated, "I have no doubt that you realize that the sort of concession that we are trying to get does not appeal to any government, and that it is very difficult to obtain it in a country enjoying a real parliamentary system; it is in my mind only easy in countries of a one man government like Mexico under Díaz, Venezuela under Gómez, or Colombia under [the previous authoritarian government of] Reyes."[10]

An extreme case of affinity between a foreign MNE, its home government, and dictators ruling the host country during this period is that of the US MNE United Fruit Company, which produced and marketed bananas in Central America. Boston-based United Fruit was the product of a merger of several banana-producing and banana-marketing firms operating in Central America and the Caribbean. Between the late nineteenth and early twentieth centuries most of the countries in this region were ruled by dictators who were also interested in promoting exports through FDI (except for Costa Rica). The economies of most of these countries was highly dependent on the export of one or two products (mainly bananas, coffee, and sugar) exported mostly to the United States. United Fruit created a vertically integrated structure that included a steamship fleet, ports, railways, telegraph lines, roads, and company towns (including basic services such as hospitals, schools, and security). The firm built its so-called Banana Empire in times of unchallenged US power in the Caribbean Basin. Washington did not hesitate to send the marines whenever US interests were at risk or to support a friendly government. Before 1945, the United States had already invaded Honduras (1903, 1907, 1912, 1919, 1924), the Dominican Republic (1903, 1914, 1916), Haiti (1914, 1915), Guatemala (1920), and El Salvador (1932). In this environment, the Central American dictators were eager to be on Washington's side and United Fruit took advantage of the corrupt nature of those rulers to earn concessions through bribery or by promoting coups (like in Honduras in 1906) and even an international war (e.g., Honduras and Guatemala in 1917). Before and during World War II, both the Central American dictators and United Fruit played a role in keeping the region surrounding the strategically important Panama Canal stable, something that certainly benefited the geopolitical interests of the United States. The alliance between the Central American right-wing dictators and the United States continued smoothly until the 1970s.[11]

Latin American dictators' favorable policies toward MNEs created a backlash by those who considered those regimes as "sellouts" to foreign interests. During the 1920s, nationalist political movements emerged all over the continent led by charismatic leaders who created coalitions composed of labor unions, urban middle classes, and intellectuals. The Great Depression caused by the 1929 crash exacerbated the process, leading to many populist movements to take power and reverse the until then dominant pro-foreign investment policies. New policies in the 1930s and 1940s included the expropriation of foreign property in the natural resources and utilities sectors and the development of a new import substitution industrialization model. Some dramatic cases radically reversed the environment for MNEs, such as the Mexican oil sector. In 1917, the Mexican revolutionary government changed the constitution and declared the subsoil the property of the nation. Using this constitutional right, in 1938 left-leaning Mexican president Lázaro Cárdenas sided with striking oil workers by decreeing the expropriation of all foreign properties in the oil industry, with which he created Petróleos Mexicanos (PEMEX), a new state-owned company. The MNEs strongly protested this action and requested help from the US and British governments, which responded through economic sanctions and demands for compensation. After lengthy negotiations, the foreign oil MNEs were compensated, but the state-owned monopoly remained, controlling the Mexican oil industry.

During the 1920s and 1930s, Europe also experienced a backlash against globalization. The first big event was the establishment of the Soviet Union in 1922 after a revolution and civil war that started in 1917 that put an end to the monarchy and established a communist regime. This new country had a revolutionary universalist anti-capitalist agenda that inspired many countries around the world and also created panic among many others. On the other side of the political spectrum there were also new anti-globalization movements. In 1922 Italy's Benito Mussolini started a fascist dictatorship, and later in 1933 National Socialist leader Adolf Hitler did the same in Germany. These leaders came to power with an isolationist nationalist agenda that distrusted traditional big business and was skeptical of the benefits of globalization. For many on the European right, the fascists' and Nazis' anticommunist credentials compensated for their anti-globalization and economic interventionist agenda. Foreign MNEs did not play a significant role in the rise to power of the fascists and Nazis, but they had an increasingly favorable image of those leaders due to their repression of left-wing unionism and the economic growth generated by their policies. For instance, James Mooney, president of US-based automobile manufacturer MNE General Motors Overseas Operations, showed open sympathy toward Hitler, was Hitler's guest on several occasions, and received in 1938 the Grand Cross of the German Eagle Order for his service to the Third Reich. This was the highest recognition a foreigner could receive in Nazi Germany, and Mooney was the second recipient after Mussolini. Other US business leaders receiving the same recognition later included International Business Machines' (IBM) chief executive Thomas Watson and industrialist and openly antisemitic Henry Ford. General Motors became an important provider of vehicles and warplane components to the German armed forces manufactured by its subsidiary Opel using forced labor. Ford Motor Company's plants even used prisoners from Nazi concentration camps.[12]

Despite their ideological affinities with some elements of the Nazi agenda, foreign MNEs operating in Germany soon realized that the Nazis' nationalist policies also brought obstacles for their operations. By the mid 1930s, the German government imposed increasingly complex regulations on repatriation of profits and restrictions on access to foreign exchange. Additionally, members of the Nazi Party increasingly became an annoyance for foreign managers because they constantly sought to intervene in the MNEs' operations to align them with the Nazis' long-term policy goals. Frustrated by this situation, US oil MNE Sinclair Oil sold all its European operations, but others complied by reinvesting their profits within Germany, as in the cases of Standard Oil of New Jersey (SONJ), which invested in shipbuilding, or IBM in real estate, while Ford complied with a 1933 "all German" regulation that demanded all components of the automobile industry be manufactured in Germany. Some foreign investors even declared that they preferred the straightforward Nazi interventionism to the not-so-clear uncertain New Deal interventionism of the United States.[13]

6.3 MNEs and Dictators during World War II

Germany's invasion of Poland in 1939 started one of the most major disruptions of international trade and foreign investment in history. Between 1939 and 1941, American MNEs continued operating in the Axis countries (Germany, Italy, and Japan), but faced increasing demands by the host governments to cooperate with the war effort. Given that Britain declared war against Germany after the invasion of Poland, British MNEs faced challenges from the start. One example is Anglo-Dutch consumer goods MNE Unilever, which responded to the war by completely separating its British and Dutch sides. After Germany invaded the Netherlands in 1940, communications between both parts of the company faced violating the British Trading with the Enemy Act, while at the same time the Nazi authorities did their best to "Germanize" Unilever's Dutch branch, where they applied Aryanization policies by which Jewish staff had to be replaced by "Aryan" personnel.[14]

Japan's attack on Pearl Harbor in 1941 that led the United States to join the Allied Powers against the Axis Powers changed the environment for American MNEs operating in the Axis countries. Expressions of sympathy toward Hitler from American corporate leaders stopped and turned hostile. Thomas Watson of IBM even returned his medal to Hitler.[15] Soon in 1942, a congressional committee was formed to investigate the deals several of them had made with German corporations to prevent access to crucial technology to other firms. The prewar deals with German corporations were problematic in two ways. First, they would have allowed American firms to join German cartels (permitted in Germany, but not in the United States). And second, they would have permitted Germany to access goods and technology crucial for the war effort. Although leaders from several firms like General Electric, DuPont, and Alcoa & Dow were called to testify, SONJ received the most media attention and had its reputation more tainted than the rest. Since 1927, SONJ had increased its investments in research and development through acquisitions of smaller firms or partnerships.[16] One of the world's most innovative corporations in the petrochemical industry was Germany's IG Farben, with which SONJ signed some patent agreements, some of them through a third company. The leadership of SONJ was aware of potential problems once the war broke out with Germany's invasion of Poland, but the situation inevitably worsened once the United States joined the war. The Truman Committee (in charge of the investigation) accused SONJ of making a deal with IG Farben that both helped the Germans and hurt the United States in the conflict. The SONJ leadership agreed to release all its patents and share knowledge with the US government, but the reputational damage was done.[17]

Multinational enterprises that had their homes in dictatorial regimes were also affected by World War II. For instance, German pharmaceutical and skin care products manufacturer MNE Beiersdorf responded to the Nazi anti-Jewish Aryanization policies by transferring its Jewish staff members to neighboring Holland, while simultaneously reorganizing its ownership structure by turning its Swiss affiliates into more central units than the German ones. The company conducted these strategies in great secrecy, allowing it to continue operations in Germany despite anti-Jewish policies and abroad despite anti-Nazi feelings.[18] Other German MNEs also used this strategy of hiding or cloaking their real nationality through complex ownership structures when operating abroad.[19]

6.4 MNEs and Dictators during the Cold War (1948–1989)

The end of World War II brought changes that strongly affected the relationship between MNEs and dictatorial regimes. First, the start of the Cold War between the United States and the Soviet Union influenced Western countries' policies toward their MNEs. Second, the decolonization of former European empires led to the creation of new nations often ruled by leaders who blamed the West for their poverty and held grievances against the existing economic system and its main actors, including multilateral institutions, the financial sector, and Western MNEs. Third, a new wave of revolutionary movements (sympathetic to the communist bloc) emerged around the world and aimed to change the status quo through a combination of strategies that included guerrilla warfare and participation in electoral politics. The perceived menace from these political movements (legal or illegal) created a sense of threat in the Western powers that led them to support sympathetic dictatorial regimes over those that had been elected but were less strongly allied to the West. In this environment, nationalist governments that wanted to develop an economic policy that included higher demands to foreign MNEs or their expropriation were considered by Washington as actors whose policies were favorable to the Soviet Union and therefore needed to be stopped. This led to an alliance between Western powers, Western MNEs, and right-wing segments of the host countries against governments developing a nationalist agenda, whether they were allied to the Soviet Union or not. The examples that follow illustrate these dynamics.

In 1951, Iran's monarch Mohammed Reza Pahlavi confirmed the election of Mohammed Mossadegh as Iran's prime minister. Mossadegh had had a long political career in which his popularity rested on his nationalist opposition to what he considered extremely generous concessions awarded decades before to British oil MNE Anglo-Iranian Oil Company (AIOC) to exploit Iranian crude oil.[20] Mossadegh came to power after creating a coalition of parties (the National Front) around ideas of liberalism, nationalism, and secularism, bringing together the urban educated middle class, university students, and the bazaar (small businesspeople).[21] Soon after taking power, Mossadegh decreed the nationalization of Iranian oil, which naturally faced immediate opposition from the AIOC and the British government. The British soon approached the United States, whose government disliked Mossadegh's actions and shared the concern with the British that Iranian success would encourage other governments to follow through. Additionally, they feared Mossadegh would push Iran into the Soviet sphere. After lengthy negotiations, in 1953, the British and US governments (through the International Bank of Reconstruction and Development) made Mossadegh an offer by which they would accept the nationalization of the Iranian oil industry in exchange for keeping a high degree of control in the hands of the AIOC. Mossadegh refused the offer, an action that British and US officials portrayed as proof of his intransigence. Both US and British MNEs encouraged their governments to act against Mossadegh and abandon any further negotiation.[22] In 1953, the British Secret Service, the US Central Intelligence Agency (CIA), and segments of the Iranian elite aligned with Reza Pahlavi to oust Mossadegh and replaced him with the young shah, who ruled Iran as a dictator until 1979.

A second covert action involving the CIA when the properties of US MNEs were in danger took place in Guatemala in 1954. After decades of being ruled by a dictator who strongly supported the activities of United Fruit Company in 1951, Guatemala elected Jacobo Arbenz as president. This election was remarkable in several aspects. First, it was the first time in Guatemalan history in which an elected president gave power to another elected president after finishing his term. Second, Arbenz was not a member of Guatemala's traditional upper landowning class but belonged to the country's small middle class. After coming to power, Arbenz envisioned a program of modernization of the economy that included agrarian reform by which he would distribute large landholdings to small peasants. This project clashed with the interests of Guatemala's landowning class and United Fruit Company. United

Fruit had been present in Guatemala since the early twentieth century and had been awarded land concessions by previous dictators ruling the country.[23]

United Fruit had enormous economic power in Guatemala. Around half of the country's exports were bananas, with around 80 percent of them controlled by United Fruit. The firm operated in Central America and the Caribbean and had built a vertically integrated structure that included company towns, plantations, railways, telegraph networks, and a steamship fleet. The firm achieved this through direct investments, mergers and acquisitions, and concessions awarded by dictators. Guatemala was no exception and before Arbenz came to power, the firm had very friendly relations with the dictators that preceded him.[24]

In 1952, the Guatemalan Congress approved the Agrarian Reform Law, which allowed the government to confiscate uncultivated parts of large plantations for redistribution. Arbenz maintained that his program followed the American-led agrarian reform in post–World War II Japan, but to his retractors he was just a communist. United Fruit actively promoted this image, particularly after the first expropriations of the MNE's unused lands in March 1953. For these expropriations, the government offered a compensation of US $1,185,000, an amount United Fruit protested was too low, claiming that the lands were worth US $19,335,000. The government countered that the amount had been calculated based on the company's tax documents, so either the amount was fair, or the company had cheated on its tax forms. Unsatisfied with this argument, United Fruit took the case to the Guatemalan Supreme Court, but also requested help from Washington.[25]

To convince American legislators that tiny Guatemala was a threat to the United States, United Fruit used public relations firm Bernays (owned by publicist Edward Bernays, considered a genius in marketing) and developed a strategy that included free tours for journalists and White House staff to Guatemala, the production of the documentary film *Why the Kremlin Hates Bananas* screened to the media and legislators, and the publication of a book titled *Report on Guatemala* distributed to all members of the US Congress.[26] In the end, United Fruit's strategy of creating fear around Arbenz was a success. President Dwight Eisenhower of the United States approved a destabilization plan by which the CIA assisted a rebel army to overthrow Arbenz. Unprepared and with limited resources, Arbenz was overthrown in 1954, and the new dictatorship reversed his reforms.[27]

A similar case took place in Chile, where the MNEs allied themselves with those promoting a coup against a democratically elected president to install a dictatorship. In 1970, Salvador Allende was elected Chile's president with an agenda of income redistribution and economic nationalism. Allende was also the world's first Marxist elected in democratic elections in history, but made clear that he would respect the constitution and would be subject to the legislative and judicial powers. In the Cold War environment, this did not convince many in Washington, particularly US Secretary of State Henry Kissinger, who approved plans to prevent Allende from taking oath or overthrowing him if unsuccessful in the first effort. The plan included channeling CIA funds to the opposition newspaper *El Mercurio*, providing intelligence and resources to members of the armed forces and paramilitary groups to create chaos and eliminate so-called constitutionalists among the military, and organizing economic warfare in the form of blocking foreign loans to Chile and Chilean exports in addition to creating a scarcity of consumer goods.[28] The foreign MNEs actively participated in the economic sabotage with the US-based copper MNEs Anaconda and Kennecott (which controlled 80 percent of an industry that represented 60 percent of Chilean exports) were instructed to be intransigent toward labor unions and spread false rumors about the government's policy.[29] The US-based telecommunications International Telegraph and Telephone Company (ITT) even offered money to the CIA (which the latter rejected), but the two collaborated closely to sabotage the Allende government. In 1972, after a series of documents showing the collusion between the CIA and ITT was leaked by the *Washington Post*, Allende expropriated ITT.[30] This, however, did not prevent the military coup of September 11, 1973, in which Allende died, which started the seventeen-year dictatorship of Augusto Pinochet, who brutally repressed the political movement that surrounded Allende. After ousting Allende, Pinochet imposed an economic model friendly toward foreign MNEs and returned the expropriated properties of domestic and foreign investors, except for the highly lucrative copper industry, which remained in government hands.[31]

The CIA also helped overthrow the nationalist Sukarno regime (1945–1967) in Indonesia, partially to protect American MNEs in that country. Although Sukarno was democratically elected in 1956, he led some constitutional reforms that turned his regime into a semi-dictatorial one. In 1963, he called for renegotiations on taxes and royalties paid by foreign oil MNEs, generating the first signals of opposition from Washington. Even though an agreement was reached in 1964, Sukarno went on a spree of expropriating foreign firms. Washington threatened to cut aid, but initially did not do it, fearing this would lead Sukarno toward the Soviet bloc. Pressured by some legislators, in August 1965, President Lyndon B. Johnson cut US aid to Indonesia, after which Sukarno approached the Indonesian Communist Party followed by a Soviet promise to deliver fighter jets. This led the United States to engage in covert actions against Sukarno and overthrow him in 1965. Evidence of MNEs' participation in this coup is not as clear as in the cases of Iran, Guatemala, or Chile. However, after Sukarno's fall, the new leader, Suharto, opened the door to foreign investment, starting a thirty-year-regime infamous for its high levels of corruption.[32]

Western MNEs found ways to support the Western-backed right-wing dictatorial regimes that overthrew governments that clashed with the Western powers' interests once these dictators were in power. For instance, one of the dictatorial regimes most notoriously known for its human rights abuses was the Argentine military dictatorship that ruled that country between 1976 and 1982. This regime came to power after overthrowing a populist president (Isabel Martínez de Perón) who had the support of strongly belligerent labor unions. The dictatorship practiced rampant torture and the "disappearance" of members of the opposition. It has been calculated that between nine thousand and thirty thousand people "disappeared" during the regime and more than a hundred thousand went into exile.[33] During this terrorist regime, the Argentine government kept the German MNEs Siemens (technology and infrastructure), and Mercedes Benz (automobile manufacturing) constantly informed about secret anti-subversive operations and the same firms provided the government with detailed lists of their workers, including their political affiliations. The Argentine security forces also gave Mercedes information they could only have obtained through interrogation or torture of detained workers as well as information about when some of the detainees would be freed. In addition, Mercedes employed as part of its staff an individual who had worked at a clandestine detention center, who was later accused of kidnappings and torture.[34] The German automobile manufacturer MNE Volkswagen did the same with the Brazilian authorities after the 1964 coup that started a right-wing dictatorship, in addition to collaborating with government kidnapping actions through the firm's private security apparatus.[35] In the case of Ford in Argentina, the MNE went beyond sharing information with the government and allowed tortures to be conducted on the firm's premises.[36]

The alignment of agendas between the MNEs, their home governments, and the Latin American 1970s dictatorships was clear from the start of those regimes. Just two days after the 1976 coup, the United States recognized the Argentinean new military government and permitted the approval of a US $127 million payment from the International Monetary Fund. This was followed by other rescue packages in the following years, which the Argentine government needed as a result of economic mismanagement.[37] Something similar happened with the Pinochet regime, which increased its foreign debt from US $2,862 million in 1975 to US $3,597 million in 1979. While Chile's debt with private banks in 1974 represented 19 percent of the total, by 1983 it was 83 percent, showing the favorable view the private international financial sector had of Pinochet's regime.[38]

Ford Argentina experienced good times during the dictatorship, despite the deindustrialization process that country went through during that regime.[39] This MNE went from being Argentina's tenth company in terms of sales in 1976 to the second one in 1980. These were years of harsh repression against labor unionism, something the firm's leadership openly justified as necessary. In 1976, the Ford subsidiary's president in Argentina expressed to the media that "the terrorists are not only the guerrilla members in the mountains or the streets. They are also at the assembly line, threatening workers and telling them how to produce every day. [Productivity has increased thanks to] the success of the current efforts by the armed forces." A few months later, in a speech at the inauguration of a new plant, the same president said that "Ford Motor Argentina believed in the *Proceso de Reorganización Nacional* [the name the military regime gave to its policies] because it saw in it a vehicle for the country to find its true path. [We have] faith in this country because we saw it shaking, and then we saw it recovering from chaos towards a new way of life."[40] German MNE Siemens also showed its support for the Argentine dictatorship by having its CEO meet with members of the German Federal Ministry of Economic Affairs to argue that thanks to the new Argentine regime, Siemens's productivity in Argentina had increased 100 percent. He added that the dictatorship was providing much-needed stability to the country. On other occasions, Siemens and Daimler Benz went as far as to argue that actions against the Argentine dictatorship that would affect their operations would eventually generate unemployment in Germany.[41] Playing an even more direct role, German petrochemical MNE BASF made efforts to "clean" the image of the Brazilian dictatorship in Germany by providing German journalists with lavish trips to Brazil in order to convince them to change the narrative of the Brazilian government as a "genocidal" one.[42]

It is worth highlighting that the alliance between the MNEs, their home governments, and the repressive right-wing regimes was not set in stone but depended on whether this alliance made sense for the political and corporate calculations of each of the three actors. For instance, the seemingly solid alliance between the Central American dictators, United Fruit, and Washington faced challenges during the 1970s oil crisis. As net oil-importing poor countries, these small republics were strongly affected by the 1974 Arab oil embargo. The inflation created by the sudden oil scarcity led labor unions to go on strike and demand higher wages and better working conditions. Some of those strikers worked for the banana industry dominated by US MNEs United Brands Company (the conglomerate that purchased United Fruit in 1970) and Standard Fruit Company (United Fruit's traditional competitor). Risking an economic crisis turning into a political one, the Central American governments requested the foreign MNEs to comply with the workers' demands in addition to a renegotiation of the existing contracts to favor domestic producers.

In 1974, following the example of the Organization of the Petroleum Exporting Countries (OPEC) and pressured by the economic crisis, the Central American republics plus Panama and Colombia created the new Banana Export Countries Union (UPEB in its Spanish acronym). Through UPEB, the banana-producing countries sought to collectively negotiate higher taxes, something the MNEs immediately opposed followed by protests in Washington and a threat of an export strike. Geopolitics at that point, however, were different from previous decades. The US government did not want to alienate right-wing allies in Central America, bananas were not a strategic good, and the banana companies' interests paled in comparison to those of the major US corporations facing inflation and oil scarcity. A new type of alliance emerged in which the US government requested the MNEs simply comply with the new demands of right-wing governments that temporarily allied themselves with labor unions.[43]

6.5 Post–Cold War Authoritarianism and Multinational Enterprises

With the collapse of the Soviet Union and the communist bloc (1989–1992) and the adoption of market reforms in China after 1977, the world went through a transition that affected the political environment for MNEs. A democratization wave ended the Latin American dictatorships and in the communist bloc replaced the previous communist regimes with pro-market elected ones (with some of them eventually morphing into kleptocratic oligarchic dictatorial ones). Without the Soviet threat, several long-allied dictators were suddenly abandoned by the Western powers, as in the cases of Philippines' Ferdinand Marcos and Chile's Pinochet. In other countries in which repressive regimes enjoyed favorable Western policies, the new era delegitimized such support. This was the case of South Africa, a country that in 1948 created a globally condemned racist regime (apartheid) that favored the white minority while discriminating against the black majority. The latter was even disenfranchised from participating in the electoral process, so despite the existence of a parliament and elections, the apartheid regime cannot be classified as a democracy.

The repulsive nature of the apartheid regime made it a target of boycotts in Western countries by different NGOs despite the South African's regime staunch anticommunist nature. Such boycotts succeeded at making some MNEs leave the country. Between 1984 and

1990, 212 US MNEs left South Africa, including major ones such as General Motors and Eastman Kodak. Others like IBM left but continued distributing their services through domestic firms. Others remained, as in the cases of Royal Dutch Shell (Shell), Unilever, and Johnson & Johnson.[44] The case of Shell is illustrative of how an MNE navigated calls for boycott and its own corporate interests. The firm openly showed its opposition to apartheid but portrayed boycott initiatives as harmful to the black population (some of them owners of independent gas stations). It also emphasized internal policies of promotion of black employees and pointed out that its operations were not directly aiding repressive policies. In this way, it showed itself as looking for (nonviolent) ways to achieve the end of apartheid. Whenever it had the opportunity, Shell highlighted violent antiapartheid manifestations around the world and classified some as "terrorism."[45]

The new global economy created after the 1980s also led to a new type of Western tolerance toward dictatorships. The clearest example is the People's Republic of China, which despite its economic openness remained solidly controlled by the Chinese Communist Party. China's enormous importance as the new "workshop of the world" and the place to be for many Western MNEs explains why the West shrugged off the repression against prodemocracy demonstrators in Beijing's Tiananmen Square in 1989. China was too big and powerful to be affected by boycotts by NGOs or to be reprimanded by Western countries increasingly dependent on China's manufacturing production and insatiable consumption. The Tiananmen Square massacre did not deter MNEs from investing in China in the following years and the Chinese government justified the repression as a necessary measure to keep the political stability required for economic growth.[46]

The rise of China and other emerging economies in the early twenty-first century came together with the arrival of new MNEs located in those countries. For the first time in history, major MNEs such as Sinopec, CCNP, or Gazprom did not originate in the traditional capital-exporting countries of Western Europe, the United States, Canada, or Japan, but included countries like China or Russia ruled by authoritarian governments. The close relationship between some of these MNEs with their governments led to increasing distrust on their operations, which was exacerbated with the trade war between the United States and China that started in the late 2010s. This was the case of Chinese telecommunications MNE Huawei, which in 2017 was barred from providing services to the United States Department of Defense. The US government gradually eliminated Huawei from operating in other areas, and in 2021 Huawei was no longer allowed to receive new equipment licenses in the United States. In the 2010s the US government showed a renewed interest in human rights violation in China that contrasted with the silence of the times of the Tiananmen Square massacre. By the late 2010s the United States imposed sanctions on Chinese firms or individuals who benefited from exploiting the forced labor of the Muslim Uyghur minority in China.[47]

Political tensions between the West and Russia in the early 2020s also changed the environment for MNEs operating in that country. Since the fall of the Soviet Union, Russia had opened its doors to foreign investors in a period in which the country also gradually became increasingly authoritarian. Former KGB agent Vladimir Putin took power in 2000 and has followed a strategy of amassing political power since then. The tensions with the West reached a critical point in 2022 with Russia's full-scale invasion of Ukraine, which was a continuation of a conflict that had started in 2014. The Western powers responded swiftly with economic sanctions and a mass divestiture process of Western MNEs, with more than one thousand companies reducing their investments in Russia in the following two years.[48] The China and Russia examples show how once political tensions emerge between world powers, competition for global supremacy can go on the way of the potential economic benefits for the MNEs operating in those countries. While the MNEs and Western powers were willing to tolerate Chinese authoritarianism in the 1980s and 1990s, the consolidation of China as a competitor to Western supremacy changed the equation. Although with a much smaller economy, Russia's global ambitions and its interference in Western domestic politics also made of this country unwelcome territory for Western MNEs. Similarly, the much-celebrated MNEs in emerging markets in the 1990s and early 2000s became potential threats in the West when originating in these new world powers.

6.6 Conclusion

Between the late nineteenth and early twenty-first centuries, MNEs have operated in countries with dictatorial regimes and negotiated with them. Western MNEs showed a degree of sympathy toward dictatorial regimes because of their repressive policies against labor unionism and the order they imposed in the society. However, this relationship soured when due to geopolitical calculations or international conflicts the MNEs' home countries were at odds with the dictatorial regimes. An alignment of agendas between the MNEs, their home countries, and the dictators was necessary for the MNEs to benefit from dictatorships. When the agenda of one of the three actors did not align with those of the other two, a dictatorship could become a threat for the MNEs. The rise of MNEs originating in dictatorial regimes in the early twenty-first century added a level of complexity because of the close relationship of those firms with their home governments. By the early 2020s, the world seemed to be sliding toward increasingly repressive regimes, which makes an analysis of how MNEs have historically responded to them more relevant.

Notes

1. Jones, G. *Multinationals and Global Capitalism: From the Nineteenth to the Twenty First Century*, Oxford, Oxford University Press, 2005.
2. Cheibub, J. A. Gandhi, J., and Vreeland, J. R. "Democracy and Dictatorship Revisited," *Public Choice*, 143 (2010), 67–101.
3. Huntington, S. *The Third Wave: Democratization in the Late Twentieth Century*, Norman, University of Oklahoma Press, 1991.
4. Haber, S., Maurer, N., and Razo, A. *The Politics of Property Rights: Political Instability, Credible Commitments, and Economic Growth in Mexico, 1876–1929*, Cambridge, Cambridge University Press, 2003, 357.
5. Gómez-Galvarriato, A. and Recio Cavazos, G. "A Business History of Mexico: Continuities and Changes," in Lluch, A., Monsalve Zanatti, M., and Bucheli, M. (eds.) *A Business History of Latin America*, New York, Routledge, 2025, 119–121.
6. Garner, P. *British Lions and Mexican Eagles: Business, Politics, and Empire in the Career of Weetman Pearson in Mexico, 1899–1919*, Stanford, CA, Stanford University Press, 2011.
7. Bucheli, M. "Multinational Companies in Latin American History," in Lluch, A., Monsalve Zanatti, M., and Bucheli, M. (eds.) *A Business History of Latin America*, New York, Routledge, 2025, 233–250.

8. McBeth, B. *Juan Vicente Gómez and the Oil Companies in Venezuela, 1908–1935*, Cambridge, Cambridge University Press, 1983.
9. Betancourt, R. *Venezuela: Oil and Politics*, Boston, MA, Houghton Mifflin, 1978, 27.
10. Bucheli, M. "Negotiating under the Monroe Doctrine: Weetman Pearson and the Origins of US Control of Colombian Oil," *Business History Review*, 82, 3, (2008), 529–553, 542.
11. Bucheli, M. "Multinational Corporations, Totalitarian Regimes and Economic Nationalism: United Fruit Company in Central America, 1899–1975," *Business History*, 50, 4 (2008), 433–454.
12. Basualdo, V., Berghoff, H., and Bucheli, M. "Crime and (No) Punishment: Business Corporations and Dictatorships," in Basualdo, V., Berghoff, H., and Bucheli, M. (eds.) *Big Business and Dictatorships in Latin America: A Transnational History of Profits and Repression*, New York, Palgrave, 2021, 1–34.
13. Wilkins, M. "Multinationals and Dictatorship: Europe in the 1930s and Early 1940s," in Kobrak, C. and Hansen, P. (eds.) *European Business, Dictatorship, and Political Risk, 1920–1945*, New York, Berghahn, 2004, 22–38.
14. Wubs, B. *International Business and National War Interests: Unilever between Reich and Empire, 1939–45*, New York, Routledge, 2008, 59–132.
15. Wilkins, "Multinationals," 36–37.
16. Larson, H. "Contours of Change: Standard Oil Company (New Jersey), 1882–1950," *Nebraska Journal of Economics and Business*, 8, 3 (1969), 3–19.
17. Larson, H., Knowlton, E., and Popple, C. *New Horizons: History of Standard Oil Company (New Jersey) 1927–1950*, New York, Harper and Row, 1971, 405–408.
18. Jones, G. and Lubinski, C. "Managing Political Risk in Global Business: Beiersdorf, 1914–1990," *Enterprise & Society*, 13, 1, (2012), 85–119.
19. Wilkins, "Multinationals," 26–27.
20. Bamberg, J. *British Petroleum and Global Oil 1950–1975: The Challenge of Nationalism*, Cambridge, Cambridge University Press, 2000.
21. Axworthy, M. *Revolutionary Iran: A History of the Islamic Republic*, New York, Penguin, 2019, 47–49.
22. Abrahamian, E. *Oil Crisis in Iran: From Nationalism to Coup d'Etat*, Cambridge, Cambridge University Press, 2021.
23. Bucheli, M. and Jones, G. The Octopus and the Generals: The United Fruit Company in Guatemala, *Harvard Business School Case* No.805-146, revised October 11, 2022.
24. Bucheli, M. *Bananas and Business: The United Fruit Company in Colombia, 1899–2000*, New York, New York University Press, 2005.
25. Schlesinger, S. and Kinzer, S. *Bitter Fruit: The Story of the American Coup in Guatemala*, Cambridge, MA, Harvard University Press, 1999.

26. "Why the Kremlin Hates Bananas," Sponsored by United Fruit Company, produced and directed by John Suderland, narrated by Edward Tomlinson, 1953. www.youtube.com/watch?v=SZtAKHnqkf4, accessed June 5, 2024.
27. McCann, T. *An American Company: The Tragedy of United Fruit*, New York, Crown, 1976.
28. Hitchens, C. *The Trial of Henry Kissinger*, New York, Verso, 2002, 56.
29. Kornbluh, P. *The Pinochet File: A Declassified Dossier on Atrocity and Accountability*, New York, New Press, 2013.
30. United States Senate, Select Committee to Study Governmental Operations with Respect to Intelligence Activities, *Covert Action in Chile*, Washington, DC: US Government Printing Office, 1975.
31. Llorca-Jaña, M. and Miller, R. "Business History in Chile in the Nineteenth and Twentieth Centuries," in Lluch, A., Monsalve Zanatti, M., and Bucheli, M. (eds.) *A Business History of Latin America*, New York, Routledge, 2025, 71–91, at 82–84.
32. Kim, J. "US Covert Action in Indonesia in the 1960s: Assessing the Motives and Consequences," *Journal of International and Area Studies*, 9, 2 (2002), 63–85.
33. Crenzel, E. "Dictadura y desapariciones en Argentina: memoria, conocimiento y reconocimiento del crímen," *Intersticios*, 1, 2 (2007), 159–178.
34. Stephan, M. "A Typology of the Collaboration between Multinational Corporations, Home Governments, and Authoritarian Regimes: Evidence from German Investors in Argentina," in Basualdo, V., Berghoff, H., and Bucheli, M. (eds.) *Big Business and Dictatorships in Latin America: A Transnational History of Profits and Repression*, New York, Palgrave, 2021, 237–261, at 254–257.
35. Kopper, C. "Business as Usual under a Military Regime? Volkswagen do Brasil and the Military Dictatorship in Brazil (1964–1980)," in Basualdo, V., Berghoff, H., and Bucheli, M. (eds.) *Big Business and Dictatorships in Latin America: A Transnational History of Profits and Repression*, New York, Palgrave, 2021, 319–344.
36. Basualdo, E. and Basualdo, V. "Confronting Labor Power: Ford Motor Argentina and the Dictatorship (1976–1983)," in Basualdo, V., Berghoff, H., and Bucheli, M. (eds.) *Big Business and Dictatorships in Latin America: A Transnational History of Profits and Repression*, New York, Palgrave, 2021, 215–236.
37. Basualdo, V. "Business and the Military in the Argentine Dictatorship (1976–1983): Institutional, Economic, and Repressive Relations," in Basualdo, V., Berghoff, H., and Bucheli, M. (eds.) *Big Business and Dictatorships in Latin America: A Transnational History of Profits and Repression*, New York, Palgrave, 2021, 35–62, at 39.
38. Bohoslavsky, J. P. "Banking Southern Cone Dictatorships," in Basualdo, V., Berghoff, H., and Bucheli, M. (eds.) *Big Business and Dictatorships in Latin*

America: *A Transnational History of Profits and Repression*, New York, Palgrave, 2021, 185–214, at 200.
39. Lanciotti, N. "A Business History of Argentina: Family Firms, Business Groups, and Foreign Multinationals, 1875–2010," in Lluch, A., Monsalve Zanatti, M., and Bucheli, M. (eds.) *A Business History of Latin America*, New York, Routledge, 2025, 35–52, at 45–46.
40. Basualdo, "Business and the Military," 227–228.
41. Stephan, "A Typology," 250–254.
42. Gray, W. "Stabilizing the Global South: West Germany, Human Rights, and Brazil, 1960–1980," *German Yearbook of Contemporary History*, 2 (2017), 119–135.
43. Bucheli, "Multinational Corporations," 446–450.
44. Jones, G. and Reavis, C. *Multinational Corporations in Apartheid-Era South Africa: The Issue of Reparations*. Harvard Business School Case No. 804-027, revised January 10, 2013.
45. Minefee, I. and Bucheli, M. "MNC Responses to International NGO Activist Campaigns: Evidence from Royal Dutch/Shell in Apartheid South Africa," *Journal of International Business Studies*, 52 (2021), 971–998.
46. Yee, L. C. Chinese Defense Minister Says Tiananmen Crackdown Was Justified, Reuters. www.reuters.com/article/world/chinese-defense-minister-says-tiananmen-crackdown-was-justified-idUSKCN1T3034, accessed September 4, 2024.
47. Uyghur Human Rights Project. US Sanctions Tracker. https://uhrp.org/sanctions-tracker, accessed August 13, 2025.
48. Yale School of Management, Chief Executive Leadership Institute, "Over 1,000 Companies Have Curtailed Operations in Russia: But Some Remain. https://som.yale.edu/story/2022/over-1000-companies-have-curtailed-operations-russia-some-remain, accessed August 13, 2025.

Further Reading

Billstein, R., Fings, K., Kugler, A., and Levis, N. *Working for the Enemy: Ford, General Motors, and Forced Labor in Germany during the Second World War*, New York, Berghahn, 2000.

Dosal, P. *Doing Business with the Dictators: A Political History of United Fruit in Guatemala, 1899–1944*, Lanham, MD, Scholarly Resources, 1993.

Kinzer, S. *All the Shah's Men: The American Coup and the Roots of Middle East Terror*, Hoboken, NJ, John Wiley, 2003.

Kobrak, C. and Hansen, P. (eds.) *European Business, Dictatorship, and Political Risk, 1920–1945*, New York, Berghahn, 2004.

Turner, H. A. *General Motors and the Nazis: The Struggle for Control of Opel, Europe's Biggest Carmaker*, New Haven, CT, Yale University Press, 2005.

BORIS GEHLEN AND
CHRISTIAN MARX

7

Multinationals and Taxation

7.1 Introduction

In the wake of the global financial crisis of 2007–2008, it was reported in 2010 that multinational enterprises (MNEs) like the tech companies Google, Amazon, Facebook, Apple, and Microsoft, as well as the coffee-house chain Starbucks had avoided paying taxes on a large scale by exploiting tax loopholes. Coming during one of the most serious crises in global capitalism, this revelation provided evidence for criticism of globalization and inequality. Public outrage was fueled in particular by the "immoral" behavior of MNEs.[1]

Nowadays, MNEs have a range of instruments to reduce their tax burden. The logic behind complex techniques such as transfer pricing, profit shifting, and thin capitalization is ultimately always the same: MNEs offset profits, patents, or turnover internally among business units in different countries so that a small share of their revenues is reported in locations where taxes are relatively high, while a larger share is recorded where tax rates are particularly low.[2] In one case, Apple had an Irish subsidiary collect income from global activities, which Apple then – due to loopholes and lax enforcement of tax laws – was able to transfer to another subsidiary in Bermuda, where the revenues were taxed at extremely low rates. Although the formal tax rate in Ireland was 12.5 percent, Apple's effective tax rate was only 0.005 percent, according to European Union (EU) calculations. It was not until September 2024 that the European Court of Justice ruled that Ireland had to recover up to 13 billion euros (US $14.4 billion) in back taxes from Apple. However, it was not Apple's tax avoidance practice as such, but rather the tax advantages granted by the Irish state that were deemed to be unlawful state aid and a violation of competition law.[3]

This example presents elements that typically arise in discussions on MNEs and taxation. Differences in tax levels, tax principles, and tax collection processes among tax jurisdictions – nation-states, their constituent states, and even municipalities – provide the basis for tax planning by MNEs. In legal terms, tax planning is regarded as a lawful and legitimate way for companies to minimize their tax burden. In contrast, tax evasion refers to illegal practices that are prosecuted by the state under criminal law; tax avoidance denotes a legal but not quite legitimate practice.[4]

This chapter analyses the tensions that arise when the economic rationale of MNEs, together with taxation regimes and law, comes into conflict with the public perception of fairness. Multinational enterprises, like all companies, regard taxes as costs, and cost reduction is their guiding principle. Business historians have thus always dealt with tax issues when they write individual company histories. More recently, they – as well as social scientists – have systematically analyzed tax planning and tax evasion and contributed to broader discussions about the emergence of tax havens, the shifting agendas of political institutions and the effects of these developments on state capacity as well as on income and wealth inequality.[5] This body of research has documented how MNEs have used their market power in conflicts with nation-states, influenced legislation and international standardization, and developed international strategies to avoid taxes.

For nation-states, taxes are revenues. Multinational enterprises depend in their home and host countries on public goods (infrastructure, legal certainty, education, and research) and can benefit from state support in times of crisis. Consequently, MNEs are expected to exhibit a minimum level of tax compliance. But not every nation seeks to tax companies heavily. Governments may favor lower tax rates in order to keep companies in the country to secure jobs, promote growth, or attract capital. Historically, such rationales have led to tax competition between states, especially in the twentieth century. Tax competition in turn has increased the opportunities for

MNEs to engage in tax arbitrage. In order to reduce this tax arbitrage, nation-states have strived for international coordination and harmonization on a bilateral level and within global organizations – like the League of Nations or the Organisation for Economic Co-operation and Development (OECD) – with varying degrees of intensity since the interwar period. In general, however, states have mainly pursued their own national interests and have sought to preserve the competitiveness of their domestic MNEs. Thus, national and subnational tax authorities have always been both opponents and partners of MNEs.

Since the modern tax state predates the rise of modern MNEs, tax planning by MNEs and state tax practices have been shaped by significant path dependencies – meaning that groundbreaking decisions from the past continue to influence the present. It has proven to be difficult to substantially change established principles of taxation, especially when it comes to international harmonization. Overall, mainly incremental changes have been implemented, except in cases of violent regime change, as Chapter 6 in this book and other studies have shown.[6] Back in the nineteenth century, tax authorities established tax systems that were tailored to the financial needs of their jurisdictions, and did not take into account the yet-unknown characteristics of MNEs. Moreover, tax authorities took different approaches to enforcement, with regard to the determination of both tax rates and tax bases. The latter may be determined either according to the residence principle (the location of the registered office) or the source principle (the location where profits are generated). Moreover, the unit subject to taxation may be the entire entity (e.g. group or holding), or an individual firm. Taxes can be levied on profits, turnover, and/or the use of a location. Owners or shareholders are subject to income tax on dividends or profit distributions. Taxation principles that have been established since the nineteenth century have played a significant role in the construction of the global tax architecture. The complex amalgamation of different taxation systems has provided MNEs with numerous opportunities to reduce or avoid taxes.

The spread of tax havens and the resulting reduction of the MNE's tax burden has benefited them and their shareholders, as these trends have increased investment opportunities, profits, and market power.

The further liberalization of international capital movements since the 1970s has helped place pressure on conventional economic and tax policy standards, stimulated tax competition between locations, and resulted in a race to the bottom entailing deregulation, tax cuts, and, ultimately, the reduction of state revenue and room for maneuver. The proliferation of tax havens and their use by wealthy individuals, MNEs, and political elites has helped shape a global capitalism order marked by various detrimental effects: increasing wealth and income inequality between and within national economies, the relative weakening of labor income in favor of capital income, and the reduction of state social benefits and state capacity in general.[7]

7.2 National Corporate Taxation until World War I

Tax planning and taxes in general were not a central issue for nineteenth-century MNEs, but they were the focus of attention of nation-states and tax authorities at the subnational level. The question of whether and how companies should be taxed became particularly relevant for the major capital exporters, such as Britain, Germany, France, and the United States, whose standard-setting taxation principles had lasting implications for MNEs. In all these countries, companies were taxed at relatively low rates before 1914.[8]

In Britain, companies were taxed like any other "person" subject to a general income tax – no matter whether income was generated at home or abroad. In this respect, the case of free-standing companies (FSCs) – which were a specific type of MNEs with small headquarters in their home countries (such as Britain) and operations abroad – is relevant. Most FSCs generated their profits abroad but were taxed in Britain. This included FSCs operating in British colonies. Although the colonies were given increasing fiscal autonomy, British tax policy allowed them no access to the FSCs' profits. In sum, this taxation system implied a financial transfer from the colonies and other territories to Britain.[9] The justification was somewhat contrived; in British tax practice not only the domicile of the FSCs mattered, but also the fact that relevant decisions were made in London. This notion of control, however, was not clearly defined in British tax law, but rather employed as a matter of tax practice.[10]

Furthermore, many of the tax havens that still exist today arose from the British common law tradition and the world of the empire with its legal inequalities. The coexistence of centralized nation-states, multiethnic contiguous empires, and overseas empires with their colonies, protectorates, settlements, and dominions fostered a legal pluralism. The local administrations in overseas territories had considerable leeway in drafting commercial and tax laws. The British Empire provided a convenient umbrella of political stability for investors. Multinational enterprises with their headquarters, subsidiaries, and production sites in different parts of the empire took advantage of the legal inequalities, which enabled tax avoidance on a global scale.[11]

While tax policy in the British Empire helped increase the colonial power's revenues and the British government granted limited autonomy to its colonies, France wanted at first to keep the financial burden on French taxpayers as low as possible and to limit the transfer of funds from France to its colonies. The French government therefore prevented companies from setting up sham headquarters in the colonies and thereby avoiding taxes.[12] In the French tax system, the source of income was regarded as more relevant than the headquarters location, or residence. Similar models were adopted in Belgium and many other countries in Eastern and Southern Europe, and in Latin America. However, because tax authorities at that time had little power to gather information on MNEs' income abroad or in the colonies, MNEs from countries such as France or Belgium were able to employ tax planning early on.[13]

In the United States, taxation of both individuals and corporations was based on citizenship. All businesses incorporated under US laws were taxed in the United States, no matter whether profits were earned at home or abroad. United States activities of companies incorporated in other jurisdictions were also taxed in the United States. Domestic companies were subject to the residence principle, while foreign companies were subject to the source principle. Consequently, subsidiaries of US MNEs were taxed in the United States if they were incorporated in the United States but were taxed in their host countries if they were established there under local law. The German subsidiaries of IBM, Ford, and General Motors were founded or acquired under German law in the 1920s; obviously US home-based taxation was an incentive for this strategy.

In Germany, income from foreign subsidiaries that were effectively managed by German companies was taxable in the German Reich, which increased tax revenue at the expense of host countries. However, as in the British case, vague formal criteria left room for interpretation and gave German-based MNEs – in coordination with the tax authorities – a certain leeway for tax planning. By and large, these examples show that many tax states, albeit in different ways, at first turned to domestic MNEs to increase their own tax revenues.

In federal states such as Canada, Switzerland, and the United States, there was not just one authority that taxed companies, but rather several.[14] This resulted in tax competition even among local authorities, as seen in Switzerland, where each canton pursued its own tax policy. Since the late nineteenth century, Swiss bankers and lawyers have specialized in wealth management. Together with managers in the tourism industry, they sought to transform Switzerland into a resort destination for international high society, and they entered into a lively competition with Belgian bankers in order to attract financial wealth, especially from France and Germany. When the French state attempted to hinder this activity in 1907 by asking the Swiss and Belgian governments to implement an automatic exchange of tax information, the two countries' authorities refused, invoking banking secrecy. International tax competition was thus at first a phenomenon generated by states whose governments used taxation policy as an instrument to attract money from abroad. Soon enough MNEs benefited from the structures established based on this rationale.[15] Early tax havens attracted financial holdings such as the Company for the Construction of Railways in Turkey, which was effectively controlled by Deutsche Bank and facilitated the international financing of the Baghdad Railway.[16]

The US state of Delaware provides an illustration of a subnational tax strategy. To attract new businesses, it adopted the General Corporation Law in 1899 – a liberal regime for establishing corporate structures. Even in the 2020s a disproportionately large number of US companies and their subsidiaries are registered there. Delaware offers a streamlined incorporation process, and its corporate court system is seen as business friendly. In addition, intangible assets held by companies registered in Delaware are exempt from taxation there, while royalty payments to companies in Delaware are tax-deductible in other states.[17] This mixture of attractive institutions and tax advantages has secured Delaware's position as an internal US tax haven.

7.3 Deglobalization? Double Taxation and the Increase in Tax Havens during the Interwar Period

On a global scale, the scope of tax arbitrage was still negligible until World War I. In December 1917, the British- and Dutch-owned Shell tried to preempt a Dutch tax law by changing the distribution of profits between the British and Dutch portions of the company. The company wanted to report only 5 percent of the revenue generated in Britain to Dutch tax authorities, rather than 60 percent. In this way, Shell aimed to avoid taxes in the Netherlands on income that had already been taxed in Britain; the sole purpose of this proposal was to avoid taxes. Although this tax strategy was vehemently criticized by the public and ultimately overturned by the courts, in the political arena, the central problem related to the taxation of MNEs after World War I had emerged: double taxation.[18]

World War I fundamentally changed the taxation of MNEs. States financed the war and other expenditures by imposing higher taxes in general. Corporate tax rates skyrocketed in many countries immediately after the war and remained high throughout the 1920s. From 1913 to 1918, they rose from 5.8 to 30 percent in Britain, and from 1 to 12 percent in the United States.[19] Not least due to double taxation, MNEs suffered under unprecedented tax burdens. They had to contend with different jurisdictions, new types of taxation, variations in tax principles, and more assertive and efficient tax authorities. In contrast to the prewar period, there was no longer a level playing field regarding tax costs.

The aforementioned case of Shell exemplifies these trends. After the company's internal efforts to reduce taxes had failed, it advocated for a tax reduction in the Netherlands and became a vociferous supporter of international tax treaties designed to prevent double taxation. In the interwar period, tax planning was no longer an internal matter for individual companies, but rather it became the subject of negotiations involving politicians, tax authorities, and lawyers. Tax authorities and governments generally could not stay abreast of the MNE tax-planning strategies, and they often had to rely on the expertise of the companies' tax advisors. Meanwhile, tax bureaucracies were progressively expanded and professionalized during the interwar period. Taxation became a locational factor and a matter of competitiveness for both nation-states and MNEs.

Many governments also introduced progressive taxation, which meant that taxpayers with higher incomes – including corporations – were subject to higher tax rates than those with lower incomes. Multinational enterprises therefore looked for loopholes in national tax laws.[20] French and British MNEs reacted immediately to the additional tax burden. When tax rates increased in France after World War I, a number of colonial businesses relocated their tax domicile from France to the colonies.[21] Some British FSCs – for example, Bombay Electric Supply, Adelaide Electric, and Lonely Reef Gold Mining Company of Rhodesia – relocated their tax domiciles from Britain to the former host countries as well. Joseph Nathan and Company, a producer of powdered milk, converted a former branch office in New Zealand into the independent Glaxo Manufacturing Company Limited in order to avoid double taxation. Likewise for tax reasons, the Anglo-Continental Supply Company Limited moved its registered office to France.[22]

Some British MNEs incorporated holding companies or set up subsidiaries as independent companies to save on taxes. Others – including Olympic Portland Cement and the binational Shell – changed their profit distribution, and some even decided to sell some of their investments for tax reasons. The Imperial Continental Gas Association (ICGA), a European gas supply company headquartered in London, was particularly inventive. Its executives founded the Utility Loan Company in Britain, which granted loans to the Belgian divisions of ICGA. The ICGA's Belgian units paid interest (taxed at a low rate) to the British parent company, but they paid no dividends (taxed at a higher rate), which reduced revenues for the Belgian tax authorities. Moreover, no income tax was due in Britain if foreign subsidiaries retained their profits. Thus, in 1930, ICGA converted its Belgian branches into subsidiaries that could build up reserves by retaining profits. The company justified its strategy in 1931, describing itself as "one of the most unfortunate victims of double taxation," since both Belgian and British tax authorities had taxed its income.[23]

During the 1920s and 1930s, the establishment of holdings in tax havens grew in importance. In Switzerland, for example, the number of offshore holding companies and trusts increased enormously after 1920.[24] One reason was the Swiss banking secrecy law, which was tightened in the 1930s in response to pressure from the French government and Swiss social democrats – and still provided sufficient protection from unwanted disclosures, thanks to the political connections of Swiss banks and industries.[25] Even though not many tax havens emerged in this period, some countries attracted significant flows of foreign capital. For example, capital amounting to 5 to 10 percent of French GDP was placed in Swiss tax havens during the interwar period.[26] Belgium reinforced its position as a hub for global electrification: Electrical holding companies based there, like Sofina and the Empain Group, increased their global investments, due in part via the business-friendly Belgian taxation system.[27] The Netherlands also attracted many international holding companies.[28]

Those small open economies acting as tax havens presented MNEs with further advantages; for instance, German companies were able to transfer assets to neutral states in the 1920s. Germany's largest chemical company, IG Farbenindustrie, founded the financial holding company IG Chemie in Basel in 1928 to facilitate access to capital and to secure its international property rights. Its managers welcomed the lower tax burden as a side benefit. The ability to cloak business activity afforded German MNEs greater investment freedom during both the interwar era and the war period.[29] Meanwhile, with the sole purpose of tax savings, the American Silica Gel Corporation and the British-based Rio Tinto founded a joint holding company in Switzerland in 1929, which managed the property of their European subsidiaries in Britain, Germany, and France, while management decisions were still made by the company's London Overseas Organisation Central Office.[30] Taken together, the increased tax burdens of the interwar period and the incentives presented by the tax havens drove further internationalization.

Tax havens and double taxation exacerbated international tax inequality. On the initiative of the British, French, and Dutch governments, the League of Nations addressed the problem of double taxation in the 1920s. However, the League's ambitions to decrease tax competition and tax avoidance were soon abandoned, due to obstruction by the states that benefited from fiscal evasion.[31] Economists and lawyers, some of them MNE advisors, analyzed the problems systematically and concluded that the best way to build an international tax architecture was via bilateral agreements between nation-states. However, by 1939, there were only twenty double taxation agreements, mostly between friendly neighboring states, or between colonial states and their colonies or former colonies.[32]

In the 1920s and 1930s, tax havens developed not only in geographical and cultural proximity to the main capital exporters (as in the cases of Liechtenstein, Luxembourg, and the Channel Islands), but also in more distant countries, including Bermuda and the Bahamas. It was in this period, especially within the British Empire, that offshore financial centers and foreign trade zones were implemented as free-market experiments.[33] In contrast, as described previously, France did not provide for tax havens.[34] The creation of tax havens outside of Western countries was therefore linked to the policies colonial powers pursued to maintain their empires after World War I.

In general, during the interwar period, economic-nationalist or imperial motives often played a decisive role in international tax policy. For example, Britain found itself on the defensive in the discussions at the League of Nations because it insisted on the residence principle as other principles would have reduced its tax revenues.[35] Meanwhile, the Dutch government had no particular interest in a double taxation agreement with the German Reich that would include greater transparency, due to the large sums of assets that German companies managed in the Netherlands.[36] Although German tax officials suspected that German companies were using their Dutch subsidiaries to avoid paying taxes in the Reich, they lacked information from the Netherlands with which to investigate the companies. The German-Dutch clothing company C&A, for instance, took advantage of this situation.[37]

7.4 Reconstruction, Decolonization, and the Expansion of the Offshore Economy (1945–1970s)

Global power relations were destabilized as a result of World War II, not least due to its triggering of decolonization movements. However, governments still set the rules for taxing MNEs – again, according to their understanding of national interests. Britain responded to the persistent problem of double taxation in 1957 with the Overseas Trade Corporation. This new tax status reduced the tax burden of MNEs such as Shell, British Petroleum, and Dunlop, in some cases considerably, but it was abolished again in 1965 for fiscal reasons. Ultimately, it gave many British MNEs space to adapt organizationally to the postcolonial world. Operational business units in the colonies and former colonies were now replaced by subsidiaries that were incorporated in the host countries.[38]

The Japanese government implemented – at the insistence of the US occupying power – a capital gains tax with the tax reform of 1949 but abolished it by 1953. In Japan, as in Germany, the primary objective of tax policy was to enable companies to accumulate capital.[39] Thus, German MNEs were able to quickly rebuild their foreign investments, and Japan was able to increase outward foreign direct investment (FDI) – albeit on a rather small scale. National tax authorities took different paths, but the regimes they established were tailored to the needs of their domestic MNEs.

Overall, corporate taxation was not a major public concern in the traditional home countries of MNEs. In view of the enormous postwar growth rates of GDP in most countries of the Global North, which both reduced domestic social inequality and increased state capacity, fierce battles over the distribution of wealth were almost nonexistent in these societies. Most of them became high-tax welfare states.[40] As the aforementioned British case indicates, decolonization was a major challenge that changed the international tax system. With the liberalization of foreign trade and exchange controls, FDI increased worldwide (with US MNEs in the lead until the 1970s), along with opportunities to shift investments in order to take advantage of tax benefits.

The period from 1945 to 1975 saw significant growth in offshore tax havens and offshore financial centers, due in particular to decolonization and the desire of former colonies to attract investment. A group of lawyers, accountants, and former politicians and diplomats succeeded in persuading governments to establish the legal framework for a wide array of avoidance and offshore practices. As a result, "offshoring" became a multinational business in itself, often described as the "avoidance industry," even if the original business model of this sector had focused on consulting in general, not tax avoidance in particular.[41]

Since geographical and/or cultural factors play an important role in MNE investment decisions, it is no coincidence that the earliest tax havens emerged in Europe, in the territories of the British Empire, and in jurisdictions close to the United States. Accordingly, tax havens in Asia and the Middle East (for example, Hong Kong, Singapore, the United Arab Emirates) have become more important since the rise of the "tiger economies" in the late 1970s, and later, of China and India.[42] United States MNEs were already using new tax havens in the Western Hemisphere by the 1950s. For example, an unspecified pharmaceutical MNE, most likely Pfizer, set up a sales organization for foreign markets in Panama in 1955, thereby shifting profits within the company from the United States to a location with a more favorable tax environment.[43]

Meanwhile, the traditional tax havens, above all Switzerland, were keen to expand their locational advantages as capital hubs and attract as many European headquarters of US MNEs as possible.[44] The City of London also envisioned the development of offshore finance as a way to halt a decline triggered by the weakening British economy, a weak currency, and decolonization. When in September 1957, the Bank of England accepted the proposition that transactions undertaken by British banks on behalf of a lender and borrower from abroad were not to be officially viewed as having taken place in Britain, it sanctioned a new type of credit and capital market. British banks, especially Midland Bank, had been engaged in the Eurodollar business – that is, using US dollar deposits placed in London to grant loans in sterling or another currency instead of transferring the dollars to the US Federal Reserve System – since 1955. The decision of the Bank of England legalized this practice. Since Eurodollar transactions took place in London, the emerging Eurodollar market was not subject to regulation by authorities in any other countries, and it became an effectively unregulated or "offshore" credit and capital market.[45]

The end of European colonial rule presented further opportunities. Many former colonies were willing to offer favorable investment options, such as low taxes, to attract capital.[46] French colonial and postcolonial jurisdictions remained an exception, after attempts to establish special tax regulations for the colonies in the 1920s and after

1945 failed due to the steadfast resistance of the Ministry of Finance.[47] But the United States, the Netherlands, and Britain promoted the development of tax havens in their spheres of influence through active nonintervention. Decolonization, the dismantling of capital movement restrictions, and international tax arbitrage went hand in hand.[48]

Curaçao in the Netherlands Antilles provides a well-documented example.[49] Like other tax havens, it attracted capital via business-friendly legislation, political stability, and fiscal autonomy. The Dutch-American tax treaty was extended to the Netherlands Antilles in 1955 and exempted payments of dividends, interest, and royalties from the United States to the Antilles from the US withholding tax. As a result, more than two hundred US corporations founded "paper corporations" in the capital city of Willemstad in the 1960s and 1970s, through which they borrowed money from foreign investors and lent it to US corporations. European MNEs, including Royal Dutch Shell (Shell), Rio Tinto-Zinc, ITE-Imperial Corporation, BASF, Bayer, Hoechst, Siemens, and Sperry Rand, took advantage of this tax loophole as well – primarily to carry out low-tax investments in the United States.[50] Curaçao and other tax havens essentially functioned as capital hubs. In contrast, holding companies in Switzerland and other established tax havens tended to act as tax-privileged headquarters for the European operations of US MNEs in particular. From the mid 1950s to the mid 1970s, the number of holding companies registered in Switzerland rose eightfold, from around two thousand to sixteen thousand.[51]

Postwar attempts to reach an agreement on combating international tax arbitrage began in the 1950s and built on discussions from the 1920s. The principles outlined by the League of Nations in 1923 were incorporated into OECD drafts of models for tax conventions in the 1960s and 1970s. In response to the OECD initiatives, between 1969 and 1980 a working group of experts within the UN prepared several reports on tax treaties between developed and developing countries, culminating in the first UN Model Double Tax Convention in 1980. Although the core components addressed in the OECD and UN model agreements were similar, there were some fundamental differences, as the OECD is an international organization of primarily capital-exporting countries, while the UN agreement was designed for developing countries that are primarily capital importers.[52] In addition, informal coalitions of tax authorities – like the "Group of Four" set up by France, Germany, Britain, and the United States in 1969 – tackled the issue of tax treaties, but they did not make much progress, because the views of the MNEs and their nation-states of origin were usually aligned. For example, genuinely Dutch MNEs (Philips) and MNEs with strong ties to the Netherlands (Unilever and Shell) always had relatively close relationships with the Dutch negotiators. The same organic ties existed between players in the Swiss "avoidance industry" and Swiss diplomats. In contrast, US and Swiss diplomats disagreed with regard to greater tax transparency, as in the US view, Swiss law was responsible for the loss of tax revenues in the United States. Although the United States has repeatedly sought to address tax avoidance in the OECD since the 1960s and has targeted Switzerland in particular, it was to take half a century and the consequences of the financial crisis of 2007–2008 for effective changes to be made – not least because MNEs, tax havens, and many of the experts and politicians involved benefited materially from the existing constellation.[53]

7.5 Decreasing Tax Rates, Increasing Tax Avoidance: Ambivalences of the Second Globalization Wave

During the 1980s, as governments deregulated and liberalized their economies, there was a shift to tax-cutting with the hope of promoting economic growth by attracting foreign capital – a policy generally supported by MNEs. Simultaneously, public debt tended to increase, as MNEs fought politically against tax increases and relocated their tax base, or at least threatened to do so. Tax competitiveness became a relevant locational factor in a globalized world. Due to these trends, statutory tax rates fell from 49 percent (1985) to 24 percent (2018) on average globally, as did the effective tax rates on capital and corporate profits. Meanwhile, the effective tax rates on labor income rose throughout the world. The share of MNE profits that was shifted to tax havens increased, while ever more tax havens emerged worldwide. Tax shelters – like Luxembourg and Ireland – were even promoted within the framework of the EU. Offshore centers including the British Virgin Islands, Bermuda, the Cayman Islands, the Channel Islands, Hong Kong, Singapore, and Luxembourg were not only tax paradises for wealthy individuals; they became hubs for FDI.[54] In 2018, ten of the twenty-two most important countries of origin for FDI were tax havens. The British Virgin Islands invested about as much as France; Luxembourg and Hong Kong each invested more than Germany, Bermuda more than Canada, and the Cayman Islands more than China.[55] These numbers and estimates strikingly illustrate the growth of tax avoidance on a global scale.[56]

The "avoidance industry" continued to professionalize, but the boundaries between MNEs, tax lawyers, auditing firms, banks, financial policy, and financial diplomacy were fluid and characterized not least by the revolving door. For example, renowned Swiss tax lawyers Raoul Lenz and Willy Staehelin were on the boards of various Swiss subsidiaries of US MNEs. Jacob Kraayenhof's career can be seen as paradigmatic. He was head of the Dutch accountancy firm Klynveld, Kraayenhof & Company from 1939 onwards and he served as a tax advisor to MNEs such as Shell, Philips, and the Thyssen-Bornemisza Group, and to the Dutch government as well. He was part of an international network of accountants that eventually merged in 1986, after his death, to form Klynveld Peat Marwick Goerdeler (KPMG) – one of the Big Four of the "avoidance industry."[57] Multinational enterprises sent their experts to support think tanks as consultants, and dispatched them to advocate for MNE interests as expert advisors during legislative processes.

Within MNEs, financial techniques were refined, and the organizational structures of tax-avoiding MNEs became more and more complex.[58] In particular, companies with high expenditures on research and development and a large number of valuable patents, brands, or franchise licenses optimized their tax burden through internal offsetting mechanisms. Already by the early 1970s, the Swiss pharmaceutical MNE Hoffmann-La Roche was criticized by the Group of Four and by Britain's Monopolies and Mergers Commission because its foreign subsidiaries paid excessive prices to the parent company for the use of the brand and patents. Moreover, Roche charged its British subsidiary around forty times the market price for the main ingredients of specific pharmaceuticals, although according to the OECD, the market price should have been the benchmark for internal allocations. Both strategies reduced the income of subsidiaries and increased taxable income in low-tax Switzerland. However, it was very difficult and expensive to prove such price manipulations. Multinational enterprises knew that and even used their tax avoidance techniques to negotiate favorable conditions at individual locations: The alleged losses were used to threaten governments with the possible relocation of subsidiaries.[59]

As a rule, such techniques worked very well in a world of bilateral tax treaties. For example, an US MNE could avoid Italian taxation by using a Swiss holding company as an intermediary for cash flows. It thus benefited from a low level of taxation because this was provided for in the bilateral double taxation agreement between Switzerland and the United States. With such "treaty shopping," MNEs were able to secure the tax constellation most favorable to them.[60]

The use of financial operations to reduce corporate taxes increased continuously – not least due to the adaptation of Western models by Asian MNEs, which were rapidly growing and spreading. Unlike FDI from Japan or South Korea, this new Asian FDI usually passed through tax havens.[61] In 2016, the most important destination countries of Chinese FDI were – in that order – Hong Kong, the United States, the Cayman Islands, and the British Virgin Islands – that is, three tax havens, and the United States as the only "real" investment destination.[62] Within China, state-owned companies became involved in tax avoidance, even though they were supposed to have a high level of tax compliance.[63] Indian MNEs, to a large extent, used tax havens to circumvent taxation and the rather inefficient economic institutions – including relatively high bureaucracy costs – in India and to benefit from the political and economic stability of offshore centers.[64] They invested mostly via Mauritius, Cyprus, the Cayman Islands, the British Virgin Islands, and the United Arab Emirates. In Central and Eastern Europe, competition for international investors intensified at the turn of the millennium, as more and more countries attracted MNEs with favorable flat tax regulations – and they in turn reduced state social benefits.[65]

It can, from a neoliberal perspective, be argued that MNEs that avoid taxes have low costs, and that their savings flow back into society in the form of investments or low prices.[66] For example, before a tax reform in 2008, China successfully offered tax incentives to promote the establishment of foreign companies. Of course, tax incentives were not the only decisive factor for MNEs to become involved in a large and fast-growing market, but China's tax policy on this issue can be interpreted as a growth-promoting factor.[67] It is possible for tax avoidance to foster increased capital productivity and the creation of jobs, but since the 1970s, tax savings seem to have primarily been used to maximize profits distributed to shareholders in the form of higher dividends – thus increasing inequality.

Wealthy individuals and global financial investors, such as Kohlberg Kravis Roberts & Company (KKR), Morgan Stanley, and the Blackstone Group, increasingly operated via tax havens; KKR alone had 217 subsidiaries registered in the Cayman Islands in 2015.[68] With the increasing mobility of capital, the number of potential tax avoiders continued to expand. What began in the nineteenth century with tax concessions for a very few privileged and wealthy people proved to be financially advantageous for MNEs after World War I and became a mass phenomenon for affluent individuals by the 1990s at the latest. For example, the notorious Panamanian consulting firm Mossack Fonseca, whose papers were leaked in 2016, specialized in anonymously managing the assets of individuals in tax havens. To this end, it cooperated with global banks such as Barclays, Deutsche Bank, and Hongkong & Shanghai Banking Corporation. Its clients were predominantly super-rich individuals from a wide range of backgrounds: influential business families, politicians, Russian oligarchs with close ties to the Kremlin, sheikhs and oil billionaires from the Middle East, famous athletes, big names from show business, and many more. In addition, arms and drug dealers, terrorists, Mafiosi, and other criminals used the clandestine structures to launder money.[69] The associated social problems – from growing wealth inequality to organized crime – were not directly attributable to the business models of MNEs, but rather to the tax avoidance structures promoted and created by both tax authorities and MNEs.

The globalization of asset management was perhaps the greatest driver of social inequality to which MNEs significantly contributed and continue to contribute. Economist Gabriel Zucman estimated that in the mid 1980s, US companies booked around 20 percent of their profits in Singapore, the Caribbean, the Netherlands, Luxembourg, Switzerland, and Ireland; for 2012, his estimate rose to more than 50 percent.[70]

According to further estimates, around 36 percent of the profits of all MNEs worldwide were booked in tax havens in 2015.[71]

This has restricted the scope of action for emerging economies. Less developed economies are more affected by MNE tax avoidance than more developed ones – not least due to the lack of legal instruments to combat tax avoidance. At the same time, as Chapter 11 in this book explores, these states have been susceptible to corruptive MNE practices. Many of them have chosen to enforce relatively low corporate taxes and covered the increasing financial requirements of public budgets with other types of taxes. As a result, inequality between the Global South and the Global North has increased.[72]

In a world with nearly free movement of capital, MNEs hold great power in both their home and host countries. The detrimental effects for states and societies were occasionally discussed before the 2007–2008 global financial crisis but were for a long time accepted as a characteristic of hyperglobalization. The revelations in the cases of the Offshore Leaks, LuxLeaks, SwissLeaks, Panama Papers, and Paradise Papers, along with the aforementioned debate on Google, Apple, and others, have increased political pressure to take action to curb the offshore economy.

One outcome was the OECD's Base Erosion and Profit Shifting initiative, along with its Country by Country Reporting initiatives, all of which aim to increase transparency for tax authorities and prevent tax avoidance by MNEs. Finally, in July 2021, the G20 finance ministers decided that large global corporations should make a fair contribution to financing society: They should pay a global effective tax rate of at least 15 percent on their profits. Initial analyses indicated that this global minimum tax (GMT) could reduce tax avoidance and that, in particular, assets in "investment hubs" would be taxed much more effectively than before.[73] However, the agreement has also been criticized because the minimum tax rate is lower than the average tax rates paid by individual US taxpayers, for example, not least due to the successful lobbying of the international "avoidance industry" and the long-lasting resistance of nation-states benefiting from tax avoidance – among others, Ireland.[74] With regard to increasing global geopolitical and economic tensions in the 2020s, it seems uncertain whether GMT will be fully implemented at all.[75]

7.6 Conclusion

Business historians have examined the relationship between tax jurisdictions and MNEs from different perspectives. For a long time, tax planning was not an intentional strategy, but a reactive one that aimed to adapt corporate strategy to the limitations and incentives of tax jurisdictions and preserve competitiveness. However, historians have highlighted the ability of MNEs to react to changing tax conditions, to develop instruments for tax arbitrage, and to influence national and international tax policy debates in their favor. In this respect, the history of MNEs and taxation from the nineteenth century to the present is a history of permanent, tense, and multilayered negotiation – with socially detrimental effects.

During World War I, increasing government spending caused tax rates to rise worldwide and led to double taxation. Since then, corporate taxation has developed into a tension-filled arena characterized by interactions between state actors, MNEs, international regulatory bodies, and not least a tax-avoidance service sector featuring tax lawyers, accounting firms, and financial diplomats. At the same time, diplomats and negotiators have advocated for international regulation, but national governments have tended to defend their domestic MNEs or their own low-tax strategy to safeguard jobs or promote growth. While in the interwar period it was mainly smaller European states that became tax havens, many former colonies joined the offshore economy after 1945. The interests of investment capital and MNEs engaged in tax planning meshed with the economic policy of the decolonized countries to create an environment in which tax havens could flourish.

In view of the massive expansion of MNEs since the 1970s, as part of the globalization and the liberalization of capital markets, many countries have lowered their tax rates to increase their economic attractiveness. However, many tax havens have continued to improve the conditions they offer to companies, and tax competition has increased. As a result, statutory tax rates have fallen throughout this period. Tax revenues from corporate income have remained broadly stable as a proportion of GDP since 1965, but as a share of total tax revenue, they have fallen continuously. Due to these developments, MNEs are being increasingly criticized for paying low taxes or none at all, and thus not contributing their fair share to societies. Even though the GMT of 2021 is supposed to be a milestone, many states have hesitated to implement its rules, and activist groups and academics have criticized the low GMT tax rate. Consequently, tax arbitrage and debates about corporate tax justice are likely to continue.

Notes

1. Jones, C., Temouri, Y., and Cobham, A. "Tax Haven Networks and the Role of the Big 4 Accountancy Firms," *Journal of World Business*, 53, 2 (2018), 177–193.
2. Beer, S., Mooij, R., and Liu, L. "International Corporate Tax Avoidance: A Review of the Channels, Magnitudes, and Blind Spots," *Journal of Economic Surveys*, 34, 3 (2020), 660–688.
3. "Apple Loses EU Court Battle over €13bn Tax Bill in Ireland," *The Guardian*, September 10, 2024. www.theguardian.com/technology/article/2024/sep/10/apple-loses-eu-court-battle-tax-bill-ireland [01.12.2024].
4. Alldridge, P. "Avoidance and Evasion," in Alldridge, P. (ed.) *Criminal Justice and Taxation*, Oxford, Oxford University Press, 2017, 25–40.
5. Ylönen, M. and Christensen, R. C. "Rediscovering the Multinational Enterprise: The Rise and Fall of 'Corporate Escape' Studies," *Review of International Political Economy*, 32, 2 (2025), 455–484.
6. Buggeln, M., Daunton, M., and Nützenadel, A. (eds.) *The Political Economy of Public Finance: Taxation, State Spending and Debt since the 1970s*, Cambridge, Cambridge University Press, 2017.
7. Slobodian, Q. *Crack-Up Capitalism: Market Radicals and the Dream of a World without Democracy*, New York, Henry Holt & Company, 2023.
8. Bank, S. A. *From Sword to Shield: The Transformation of the Corporate Income Tax, 1861 to Present*, Oxford, Oxford University Press, 2010.
9. Wilkins, M. "The Free Standing Company 1870–1914: An Important Type of British Foreign Direct Investment," *Economic History Review*, 41, 2 (1988), 259–282.
10. Picciotto, S. *International Business Taxation: A Study in the Internationalization of Business Regulation*, London, Weidenfeld & Nicolson, 1992, 5–9.
11. Ogle, V. "Archipelago Capitalism: Tax Havens, Offshore Money, and the State, 1950s-1970s," *American Historical Review*, 122, 5, (2017), 1431–1458.
12. Woker, M. "French Imperial Statecraft, Capital, Corporate Taxation, and the Tax Haven That Wasn't, 1920s–1950s," *Past and Present*, 266, 1 (2025), 188–223.
13. See Picciotto, *Taxation*, 4–13, 175.

14. Foss, N. J., Mudambi, R., and Murtinu, S. "Taxing the Multinational Enterprise: On the Forced Redesign of Global Value Chains and Other Inefficiencies," *Journal of International Business Studies*, 50, 9 (2019), 1644–1655, at 1650.
15. Watteyne, S. "The Emergence of and Threats to the Belgian Tax Haven during La Belle Époque (1890–1914)," in Guex, S. and Buclin, H. (eds.) *Tax Evasion and Tax Havens since the Nineteenth Century*, Cham, Palgrave Macmillan, 2023, 73–92.
16. Guex, S. "The Emergence of the Swiss Tax Haven, 1816–1914," *Business History Review*, 96, 2 (2022), 353–372.
17. Dyreng, S. D., Lindsey, B. P., and Thornock, J. R. "Exploring the Role Delaware Plays as a Domestic Tax Haven," *Journal of Financial Economics*, 108, 3 (2013), 751–772.
18. Beurden, T. v. "The Oil Multinational Shell's History of Using Tax Evasion Methods, Including Tax Havens and Political Pressure, 1914–1974," in Guex, S. and Buclin, H. (eds.) *Tax Evasion and Tax Havens since the Nineteenth Century*, Cham, Palgrave Macmillan, 2023, 93–109.
19. Taylor, J. "Corporation Income Tax Brackets and Rates, 1909–2002," *IRS Statistics of Income Bulletin* (2013), 284–290.
20. Guex, S. "Introduction. 'Low-Tax Predators' Rather Than 'Tax Havens': New Perspectives on the History of the International Tax Evasion and Avoidance Market," in Guex, S. and Buclin, H. (eds.) *Tax Evasion and Tax Havens since the Nineteenth Century*, Cham, Palgrave Macmillan, 2023, 11–13.
21. Woker, "French Imperial Statecraft," 20–22.
22. Mollan, S. and Tennent, K. D. "International Taxation and Corporate Strategy: Evidence from British Overseas Business, circa 1900–1965," *Business History*, 57, 7 (2015), 1061–1062.
23. Izawa, R. "Corporate Structural Change for Tax Avoidance: British Multinational Enterprises and International Double Taxation between the First and Second World Wars," *Business History*, 64, 4 (2022), 710–715.
24. Leimgruber, M. "Kansas City on Lake Geneva: Business Hubs, Tax Evasion, and International Connections around 1960," *Zeitschrift für Unternehmensgeschichte*, 60, 2 (2015), 123–140, at 128.
25. Farquet, C. "Tax Avoidance, Collective Resistance, and International Negotiations: Foreign Tax Refusal by Swiss Banks and Industries between the Two World Wars," *Journal of Policy History*, 25, 3 (2013), 334–353.
26. Delalande, N. *Les batailles de l'impôt: Consentement et résistances de 1789 à nos jours*, Paris, Seuil, 2014, 337–339.
27. Hausman, W. J., Hertner, P., and Wilkins, M. *Global Electrification: Multinational Enterprise and International Finance in the History of Light and Power, 1878–2007*, Cambridge, Cambridge University Press, 2008, 152–155.

28. Euwe, J. "Financing Germany: Amsterdam's Role as an International Financial Centre, 1914–31," in Baubeau, P. and Ogren, A. (eds.) *Convergence and Divergence of National Financial Systems: Evidence from the Gold Standards, 1871–1971*, London, Routledge, 2015, 219–240.
29. Kobrak, C. and Wüstenhagen, J. "International Investment and Nazi Politics: The Cloaking of German Assets Abroad, 1936–1945," *Business History*, 48, 3 (2006), 399–427.
30. Izawa, "Corporate Structural Change," 711–713.
31. Farquet, C. "The International Tax Evasion Market in the Interwar Period," *L'Économie Politique*, 54, 2 (2012), 95–112.
32. Mollan and Tennent, "Taxation," 1059.
33. Ogle, "Archipelago Capitalism," 1434–1437.
34. Woker, "French Imperial Statecraft."
35. Mollan and Tennent, "Taxation"; Picciotto, *Taxation*.
36. Essers, P. "The Radical Changes Made to Dutch Tax Regulations during the Second World War," in Jochum, H., Essers, P., and Englisch, J. (eds.) *Taxing German–Dutch Cross-Border Business Activities: A Legal Comparison with Particular Focus on the New Bilateral Tax Treaty*, Osnabruck, Institut für Finanz und Steuerrecht, 2015, 1–50.
37. Spoerer, M. *C&A: A Family Business in Germany, the Netherlands and the United Kingdom 1911–1961*, Munich, Beck, 2016.
38. Mollan and Tennent, "Taxation," 1066.
39. Ishi, H. "Historical Background of the Japanese Tax System," *Hitotsubashi Journal of Economics*, 29 (1988), 11–14.
40. Hürlimann, G., Brownlee, W. E., and Ide, E. (eds.) *Worlds of Taxation: The Political Economy of Taxing, Spending, and Redistribution since 1945*, Cham, Palgrave Macmillan, 2018.
41. Ogle, "Archipelago Capitalism," 1436.
42. Hines, J. R. J. "Treasure Islands," *Journal of Economic Perspectives* 24, 4 (2010), 103–125.
43. Ogle, V. "Governing Global Tax Dodgers: The 'Group of Four' and the Taxation of Multinational Corporations, 1970s–1980s," *Business History Review*, 97, 3 (2023), 547–574, at 561.
44. Leimgruber, "Kansas City."
45. Schenk, C. R. "The Origins of the Eurodollar Market in London. 1955–1963," *Explorations in Economic History*, 35, 2 (1998), 221–238.
46. Ogle, V. "'Funk Money': The End of Empires, the Expansion of Tax Havens, and Decolonization as an Economic and Financial Event," *Past and Present*, 249, 1, (2020), 213–249.
47. Woker, "French Imperial Statecraft."
48. Mollan, S. and Sævold, K. "Private Empires: The Development of Offshore Commercial and Financial Services in Tax Havens, 1955–1979," *Enterprise & Society* 26, 3 (2025), 1112–1151.

49. Beurden, T. v. and Jonker, J. "A Perfect Symbiosis: Curacao, the Netherlands and Financial Offshore Services, 1951–2013," *Financial History Review*, 28, 1 (2021), 67–95.
50. Gehlen, B. and Marx, C. "'I Am a Professional Tax Evader': Multinationals, Business Groups, and Tax Havens, 1950s to 1980s," in Schönhärl, K., Hürlimann, G., and Rohde, D. (eds.) *Histories of Tax Evasion, Avoidance and Resistance*, London, Routledge, 2022, 221–239.
51. Leimgruber, "Kansas City," 128.
52. Eden, L. "Taxing Multinationals: Three Lenses on International Tax Cooperation" (Comments on UN Resolution 77/244, Promotion of Inclusive and Effective International Tax Governance at the United Nations) (March 16, 2023). http://dx.doi.org/10.2139/ssrn.4394624.
53. Leimgruber, "Kansas City."
54. Bullough, O. *Butler to the World*, New York, St. Martin's Press, 2022.
55. Lejour, A. "The Rise of Tax Havens and Conduit Countries from the Early 2000s," in Guex, S. and Buclin, H. (eds.) *Tax Evasion and Tax Havens since the Nineteenth Century*, Cham, Palgrave Macmillan, 2023, 149.
56. Zucman, G. *The Hidden Wealth of Nations: The Scourge of Tax Havens*, Chicago, IL, University of Chicago Press, 2015.
57. Gehlen, B. *Die Thyssen-Bornemisza-Gruppe: Eine transnationale business group in Zeiten des Wirtschaftsnationalismus (1932–1955)*, Paderborn, Schöningh, 2021, 179.
58. Eden, L. "Taxes, Transfer Pricing, and the Multinational Enterprise," in Rugman, A. M. and Brewer, T. L. (eds.) *The Oxford Handbook of International Business*, 2nd edition, Oxford, Oxford University Press, 2009, 591–620.
59. Pitteloud, S. and Donzé, P.-Y. "Swiss Multinationals versus the French Welfare State? The Social Security Deficit, European Integration, and the Battle for 'Fair' Drug Prices (1970–1990)," *Contemporary European History*, 34, 1 (2025), 1–20.
60. Ogle, "Governing Global Tax Dodgers," 563.
61. Contractor, F. J. "Tax Avoidance by Multinational Companies: Methods, Policies, and Ethics," *Rutgers Business Review*, 1,1, (2016), 34–36.
62. Pereira, V., Temouri, Y., Jones, C., and Malik, A. "Identity of Asian Multinational Corporations: Influence of Tax Havens," *Asian Business & Management*, 18 (2019), 325–336.
63. Tang, T. Y. H. "A Review of Tax Avoidance in China," *China Journal of Accounting Research*, 13, 4 (2020), 327–338.
64. Mukundhan, K. V., Sahasranamam, S., and Cordeiro, J. J. "Corporate Investments in Tax Havens: Evidence from India," *Asian Business & Management*, 18, 5, (2019), 360–388.
65. Ther, P. *Die neue Ordnung auf dem alten Kontinent: Eine Geschichte des neoliberalen Europa*, Berlin, Suhrkamp, 2014, 114–116, 124–128.

66. Hines, "Treasure Islands."
67. Lu, B. and Wang, Y. "Multinationals' Profits in China: Impact of Tax Avoidance," *Journal of International Money and Finance*, 140 (2024), 102990.
68. Kutera, M. "The Role of Tax Havens in Tax Avoidance by Multinationals," in Choudhry, T. and Mizerka, J. (eds.) *Contemporary Trends in Accounting, Finance and Financial Institutions*, Cham, Springer, 2018, 111–121.
69. "Mossack Fonseca: Inside the Firm That Helps the Super-Rich Hide Their Money," *The Guardian*, April 8, 2016.
70. Zucman, G. "Taxing across Borders: Tracking Personal Wealth and Corporate Profits," *Journal of Economic Perspectives*, 28, 4 (2014), 121–148.
71. Tørsløv, T. R., Wier, L. S., and Zucman, G. "The Missing Profits of Nations," *Review of Economic Studies*, 90, 3, (2023), 1499–1534.
72. Johannesen, N., Tørsløv, T. R. and Wier, L. S. "Are Less Developed Countries More Exposed to Multinational Tax Avoidance? Method and Evidence from Micro-Data," *World Bank Economic Review*, 34, 3 (2020), 790–809.
73. Hugger, F., González Cabral, A. C., Bucci, M. B., Gesualdo, M., and O'Reilly, P. *The Global Minimum Tax and the Taxation of MNE Profit (OECD Taxation Working Papers 68)*, Paris, Organisation for Economic Co-operation and Development, 2024.
74. "Ireland Ends 12.5% Tax Rate in OECD Global Pact," *The Guardian*, October 7, 2021. www.theguardian.com/world/2021/oct/07/ireland-poised-to-drop-125-tax-rate-in-oecd-global-pact accessed January 12, 2024.
75. "Trump Win Puts Global Corporate Tax Deal 'in Peril,'" *Financial Review*, November 11, 2024. www.afr.com/world/north-america/trump-win-puts-global-corporate-tax-deal-in-peril-20241111-p5kpi4, accessed January 12, 2024.

Further Reading

Guex, S. and Buclin, H. (eds.) *Tax Evasion and Tax Havens since the Nineteenth Century*, Cham, Palgrave Macmillan, 2023.

Izawa, R. "Corporate Structural Change for Tax Avoidance: British Multinational Enterprises and International Double Taxation between the First and Second World Wars," *Business History*, 64, 4, (2022), 704–726.

Mollan, S. and Tennent, K. D. "International Taxation and Corporate Strategy: Evidence from British Overseas Business, circa 1900–1965," *Business History*, 57, 7 (2015), 1054–1081.

Ogle, V. "Governing Global Tax Dodgers: The 'Group of Four' and the Taxation of Multinational Corporations, 1970s–1980s," *Business History Review*, 97, 3 (2023), 547–574.

Picciotto, S. *International Business Taxation: A Study in the Internationalization of Business Regulation*, London, Weidenfeld & Nicolson, 1992.

8

Multinationals and Market Integration

8.1 Introduction

For economic thinkers on both the political left and right, market integration – like free trade – has long promised economic growth, peace and stability, business opportunities, and increased living standards.[1] Multinational enterprises (MNEs), companies operating across national borders through structures of parents and subsidiaries, have been especially attracted to the possibility of lower costs for doing business, improved efficiency, larger consumer markets, and more economies of scale afforded by market integration. By operating across national borders from the nineteenth to twenty-first centuries, MNEs have been drivers of standardization in practice and trade liberalization in politics in some cases, resulting in price convergences of products and the integration of markets, even across international borders. In other cases, they have motivated protectionism and the implementation of tariff and nontariff barriers to shield domestic industry from international competition and investment. Consequently, MNEs have shaped both the economic and political dimensions of market integration on global and especially regional scales.

While regional market integration simultaneously challenges globalization and facilitates it, the markets shaped by MNEs have tended to favor certain actors, like big business and MNEs themselves, over others, often inciting backlash by the "losers" as in the widespread public protests on the streets of Seattle against the World Trade

Organization (WTO) in 1999 and the British referendum on membership in the European Union (EU) (Brexit) in 2016 against what Euroskeptic Britons perceived to be threatened national democratic sovereignty, job losses, increased immigration, and competition with other EU member states over regional resources. Such events keep MNEs squarely at the center of debates about globalization and its social consequences.

Many economists and political scientists have theorized the agreements and policies that have created free trade areas and customs unions, but the approaches of business history make possible a deeper and richer granular analysis of market integration. Firm-level analysis unveils the complex behavior of the primary agents of market integration and the trade-offs and uncertainties MNEs must navigate. For instance, it was not always clear whether regional integration should be interpreted as protectionist or as a springboard for globalization. Business history scholarship demonstrates that MNEs will do always adopt a generic rational economic behavior. On the contrary, it illustrates the wide variety of responses to market integration, depending for instance on MNEs' competitive (dis)advantages, their nationality, and their organizational adaptability. Ultimately, the way MNEs respond to this process in terms of business strategies and political involvement resulted in different impacts for various communities and stakeholders, beyond aggregate cost-benefit analysis. Moreover, deep engagement with the history of individual firms reveals the trade-offs and tensions between economic gains for MNEs as a whole entity in contrast to consequences for specific subsidiaries. The business historical approach taken by this chapter illuminates not only the economic dimensions of market integration but its social, political, and cultural dimensions as well, thus also revealing some origins of discontent.

This chapter builds on work by scholars like political scientist Joseph Nye, who has examined the role of MNEs in global political integration.[2] It also draws on the rich scholarship of business historian Geoffrey Jones, who has historicized the ways MNEs have facilitated both economic and political integration, to show how MNEs have played a key role in integrating markets, and that market integration has produced a range of social consequences.[3] Section 8.2 discusses the roots of market integration in the nineteenth century and MNEs' crucial role, for instance through the establishment of transatlantic communication networks or international cartels. Section 8.3 focuses on European integration and its various phases since 1945 and analyses the role of MNEs as both rule takers and rule makers. Section 8.4 considers the multiplication of trade zones around the world and discusses MNEs' strategies in their regional business environments. Section 8.5 focuses on societal impacts. Section 8.6 concludes.

8.2 Multifaceted Market Integration since the Nineteenth Century

Beginning with what Geoffrey Jones has termed "proto-multinationals" in the early "age of empire," MNEs and their predecessors have operated as forces for market integration since the seventeenth century, connecting imperial centers like Britain and the Netherlands to their overseas colonies in South and Southeast Asia, initially through the British and Dutch East India Companies. Elsewhere in the seventeenth century, the Hudson's Bay Company exchanged European trade goods like tobacco shipped from Brazil to Lisbon for beaver pelts from indigenous North Americans, thereby shaping indigenous Americans into consumers and integrating an emerging international market with imperial Europe and its colonial economies.[4]

By the nineteenth century, MNEs helped integrate the markets of nascent nation states and federations, like Germany and the United States. While contemporary thinkers like German political theorist Friedrich List extolled the advantages of trade treaties for economic development, Geoffrey Jones uncovered the forced market integration of India, China, and Japan with imperial Britain and the West including an emergent and aspirational United States with early interests in the Pacific.[5] Subsequently, in the late nineteenth century, the railroad and telegraph industries were dominated by a small group of MNEs, like the German telecommunications multinational Siemens, positioned to capitalize on the new technologies and business opportunities of the Second Industrial Revolution, giving rise – together with trade agreements like the Franco-British Cobden Chevalier Treaty of 1860 and the international gold standard – to the first global economy. Multinational enterprises trading in commodities dominated industries like oil and mining, and "managing agencies" or "free-standing companies" in commodities like rubber further consolidated international markets across vast geographies throughout the nineteenth and twentieth centuries. Nineteenth-century standardization and developments like the creation of the global General Postal Union in 1874 further supported multinational business.

After World War I, international cartels consolidated markets.[6] The war also motivated the creation of early international organizations like the League of Nations, which delegated trade policy and arbitration to MNEs.[7] Cartels operating across borders, like the International Copper Cartel and the Spanish-based General Association of Sugar Manufacturers, functioned as private forms of market integration, which set standards for products and production and harmonized prices across their activity.[8] In fact, cartels like the International Aluminum Cartel functioned as an alternative form of integration.[9] As a result, some national and regional policymakers even supported cartels over competition in the early twentieth century because they believed cartels expedited market integration and its attendant social benefits.[10]

After World War II, efforts to integrate regional markets intensified, even as international organizations worked to develop a global economy. The following pages discuss MNEs and market integration in four major regions of the globe, social outcomes, and the relationship between regional market integration and globalization.

8.3 European Integration and the Economic and Political Strategies of MNEs

By the twentieth century, the business and economic project of market integration became a (geo)political one, creating new business environments for MNEs as well as new opportunities for international policy influence. In the wake of World War II's decimation of the European continent, economic, social, and political reconstruction was shaped by the United States in Western Europe and by the Soviet Union in Eastern Europe. By extending Marshall Aid funds to Western European countries in 1948, the United States drove economic integration through its Organization for European Economic Cooperation (later renamed the

Organisation for Economic Co-operation and Development [OECD]), after which six Western European countries formed the European Coal and Steel Community in 1951 and the European Economic Community (EEC) in 1957, which aimed to achieve collective peace and prosperity through "ever closer union" by creating a common market.

Many MNEs from the United States took advantage of market integration in Western Europe by establishing subsidiaries that could operate across the EEC's customs union.[11] United States MNEs nevertheless primarily organized their operations regarding countries' locational advantages, for instance by establishing their European headquarters and R&D facilities in countries with sufficient skilled labor and low taxation rates, including those outside the EEC, such as Switzerland, which has not joined the EEC, or Britain, which joined the EEC only in 1973.[12] They saw European integration as a process in the making, and often, optimistically, anticipated its geographical extension. British MNEs also increasingly invested in the six member countries of the EEC, while the Commonwealth countries' relative importance decreased by the 1960s.[13]

In direct response to Marshall Aid from the United States, the Soviet Union created the Council for Mutual Economic Assistance in 1949 to offer support for reconstruction and created a Soviet trade bloc in Eastern Europe. While state-owned enterprises functioned as MNEs across the Soviet bloc, private Western MNEs like Fiat invested in socialist economies from the 1960s.[14] In 1960, non-EEC member states in Western Europe formed the rival European Free Trade Association (EFTA) to offer an alternative to the EEC's supranationally governed customs union and to foster trade both between EFTA countries and with their global partners, respectively.

Path dependency mattered in explaining MNEs' ability to take advantage of market integration. United States MNEs in the pharmaceutical sector, such as Dow, Monsanto, and DuPont, which had few investments in Europe before 1939, adopted a coherent Europewide organization when entering the European market after 1945, while automobile manufacturers such as General Motors and Ford had to deal with their existing numerous and independent national subsidiaries. Only in 1967 did Ford develop a coherent strategy to organize its European operations.[15] European MNEs experienced similar challenges. Unilever, headquartered in both Britain and the Netherlands, and one of the largest and most internationalized MNEs, employed about two hundred thousand people in Europe and should have theoretically been ideally positioned to take advantage of European integration. Nevertheless, Unilever struggled over three decades to turn a nationally based soap and detergents business into a regionally based one, although this product was easily standardized, contrary to food products, for which different national consumption patterns were more pervasive.[16] The persistence of nontariff barriers despite the establishment of a customs union was an important factor to explain such inertia, as well as organizational rigidities related to managerial concerns to preserve local autonomy and avoid social unrest that plant closures would have triggered. Ultimately, US-based companies took advantage of the opportunity of the regional integrated market. This "American challenge" was sometimes perceived as a threat to European economies and societies, especially in France,[17] even if foreign direct investment (FDI) was allowed to continue to flow from the United States into the region.[18]

Business leaders did not passively witness the political discussions and negotiations regarding market integration in Western Europe. Some of them, such as Unilever, were Euro-enthusiasts from the start[19] and established clubs such as the European League for Economic Cooperation with the aim of promoting integration.[20] Businesses and their national associations coalesced to mirror the European integration process. The Union of Industrial and Employers' Confederations of Europe (UNICE, now Business Europe) benefited from formal consultation rights in EEC institutions, so this association was of great interest for European MNEs, despite the difficulty to find consensus beyond national lines.[21] United States MNEs also increasingly engaged with European institutions by establishing contacts in Brussels.[22]

European MNEs, while sometimes raising concerns over US competition, advocated for a liberalization of trade and financial flows.[23] The process of European integration within the European Steel and Coal Community and, later on, the EEC, was nevertheless from the very start divisive within the business community, including its most internationalized segments, for several reasons. First, the meaning of European integration was far from unequivocal, and its future developments were rather unpredictable, particularly regarding the degree of political integration with possible fiscal and social harmonization. Second, even from an economic perspective, regional integration was assessed very differently, with some companies considering that integration within the EEC was a welcome first step in the direction of more trade and economies of scale and advantages to withstand US competition. Other portions of the business community preferred a free-trade zone over a customs union that would establish a common tariff toward third-member countries and favored broader trade and financial integration within more universal institutions, such as the OECD or the General Agreement on Tariffs and Trade.

In Western Europe, the EEC completed its customs union in 1968, two years earlier than originally promised in the founding Treaty of Rome in 1957, and it continued the requisite legislative harmonization to maintain its common market into the 1970s. The economic downturn and the inflation that plagued European economies, as well as increasing global competition, further incentivized MNEs to rationalize and reorganize their production, both regionally and internationally. Plant closures by MNEs put European labor unions on the defensive, as, for instance, in the case of Opel, which led German labor unions to advocate for employment protection.[24] In the face of labor concerns regarding restructurings by MNEs, the EEC commission put the Vredeling Directive (named after EEC commissioner Henk Vredeling) on the agenda, which aimed at achieving industrial democracy by protecting and providing information to the employees of multinational subsidiaries. Individual MNEs as well as the UNICE successfully advocated against it.[25] Multinational enterprises were usually rather critical of social supranational regulations.

By the 1980s, the EEC's Executive Commission argued the economic and social crises of that decade demanded deeper integration to deliver on the EEC's promises of ensuring the peace and prosperity of its member states and their citizens, especially in contrast to the socialist, especially Soviet, world. Consequently, with influence from business associations like the Confederation for British Industry, the Commission developed a plan to complete a single internal market across the EEC, which would ensure the free movement of goods, services, capital, and labor across member states and could undergird an eventual currency union.[26]

Participation by MNEs was essential to the Commission's plan, which explains its solicitation of business input by gathering the leaders of companies together into sectoral and transnational forums. These included the European Roundtable of Industrialists, established in 1983 by seventeen chief executives of European MNEs. Commission vice president Etienne Davignon created several business forums in the late 1970s and early 1980s for executives from carmakers, retailers, technology producers, and industrialists to serve as EEC "policy consultants," where they advocated for regional market integration.[27] Many European MNEs also adapted their business strategies to the internal market for better and worse. Automobile manufacturer MNEs like Volkswagen and BMW were early supporters of the single market, although commercial banks like Paribas seemed ambivalent.[28] Through their regional business strategies, by doing business across member state borders, making acquisitions, and building supply chains, European MNEs facilitated regional market integration, especially by setting de facto standards and influencing legislative norms as well. Many also formed sectoral clubs with partner and rival firms – as automakers did by creating the Committee of Common Market Automobile Constructors (CCMC), which simultaneously advocated for internal liberalization and protections against rival Japanese carmakers, and banks did in forming the Associated Banks of Europe Corporation – for the purpose of sharing information and ultimately lobbying EEC and later EU policymakers.[29] Disagreements within these business interest associations confirms MNEs are not monolithic groups and do not experience policies and business environments in the same ways. The CCMC ultimately dissolved due to the French PSA Group's rejection of the trade liberalization supported by other members and its insistence instead on protections against foreign competitors.[30]

European MNEs also advocated for collective research and development initiatives and investment in regional infrastructure like transcontinental rail networks to enable the so-called four freedoms: the free movement of goods, services, capital, and labor. But not all European companies benefited from regional market integration. Geoffrey Jones and Peter Miskell uncovered how the British–Dutch firm Unilever had to restructure its business to face the European market and its many challenges, including divergent demand and political obstacles to rationalization.[31] Through this business historical case, Jones and Miskell underscore the importance of studying regional market integration through a firm-level analysis, which illuminates the different ways how companies experienced market integration.

The European single market was declared complete in 1992 after an intensive program of market integration to remove all nontariff barriers between member states, to which some EFTA member states eventually joined with the creation of the European Economic Area and on the foundation of which the EEC launched plans for Economic and Monetary Union and established the EU. While early attempts to regulate MNEs in the EEC had not been adopted in the proposed Vredeling Directive of 1983 to achieve industrial democracy by protecting and providing information to the employees of multinational subsidiaries, the commission did pair the single market with a social charter in 1989 to ensure labor, consumer, and environmental protections.[32] That pharmaceutical MNEs worked to influence the EEC/EU and its member states in setting drug prices reveals how MNEs often embraced a "pick and choose" strategy regarding market integration and its supranational rules. Pharmaceutical MNEs fiercely advocated against a centralized EU database on drug prices that would have allowed tax authorities to document MNE use of transfer prices. They were nevertheless not opposed to a deepening of European integration in other domains and actively promoted mutual recognition regarding the commercialization authorizations of new drugs and a general extension of patent protection.[33]

8.4 Trade Zones around the Globe

By the early 1990s, the European single market seemed to have delivered on its promise of mitigating the stagflation and high unemployment of the 1970s. But the EEC/EU had not been as committed to the principle of liberalization in its external relations as it had been within its internal market: competitors and foreign investors alike decried protectionism that smacked of a discriminatory and protectionist "Fortress Europe" with high external tariff "walls" around an internally liberalized market.

Argentina and Brazil resolved to build on the market-oriented structures of the Latin American Free Trade Association (LAFTA), created in 1960 to foster trade within the region, and the Latin American Integration Association to form a closer economic bloc of their own, in the process of which they debated whether the EEC was a model or a rival.[34] The global liberalization of capital and commodity markets incentivized further defensive regionalization. In 1991, Argentina, Brazil, Paraguay, and Uruguay agreed to go deeper than LAFTA had gone and agreed to the Treaty of Asunción to create what was known as Mercado Común del Sur in Spanish or Mercado Comum do Sul in Portuguese (MERCOSUR/L) to eliminate internal tariff barriers and create a free trade zone by 1994, with pressure from business lobbying.[35] While the bloc added full and associated members during the 1990s and 2000s, it did not deepen its economic integration beyond a common market. In 2004, in opposition to the neoliberal free trade-ism of MERCOSUR/L and the proposal to create the even larger Free Trade Area of the Americas, Venezuelan president Hugo Chávez spearheaded the creation of an alternative bloc with Fidel Castro in Cuba based on the socialist logic of cooperative – rather than comparative – advantage, called the Bolivarian Alliance for the Peoples of Our America (ALBA), which Bolivia, Nicaragua, and several Caribbean countries also joined.[36] Many ALBA members, like Bolivia, became associated states of MERCOSUR/L in the 2010s and even applied for membership in the "Southern Common Market."

Some international business scholars have described Latin America as the ideal natural experiment to study MNEs and markets since the bloc's liberalization, privatization, and focus on trade and attracting foreign investment were designed to incentivize MNE activity. Not only did Latin American countries drop the average tariff in the region from 51.8 percent in the 1980s to 13.2 percent by the early 1990s, and reject state interventionism, but MERCOSUR/L further facilitated economies of scale.[37] Many Latin American state-owned companies were privatized in this period, and MNEs – carmakers in particular – responded quickly to expand their business in the region, resulting in a fivefold increase in intraregional trade in the 1990s and a tenfold increase during its first decade.[38] Retail MNEs from Europe and the United States, including Ahold, Carrefour, and Walmart, seized on consumer demand and ease of distribution in MERCOSUR/L and expanded so aggressively into Latin America that they dominated food retail in some countries by the early 2000s, expanding consumer choice at the expense of forcing some local firms out of business. However, some local competitors such as Chile-based Cencosud remained powerful and indeed became MNEs themselves with an extensive business across the region.

Overall, however, the efficiency gains, knowledge transfers, and modernization promised by the regional bloc did not materialize. Instead, push and pull forces created "regional automotive spaces" in Latin America, as in Europe and Asia.[39] In Brazil, as in China, a large market combined with industrial policies that blocked exports "pulled" automaker MNEs toward developing economies with high inhabitant to vehicle ratios, where automobile manufacturers could benefit from both robust labor markets and burgeoning consumer markets.

Turning to North America, in 1988, the United States and Canada formed a trade agreement called the Canada–United States Trade Agreement. Within a few years, these northern partners recognized the opportunity of a proximate cheap labor market and included Mexico in the new North American Free Trade Agreement (NAFTA) signed in 1994, which promised to progressively eliminate barriers to trade and investment to enable the free movement of goods and services across the three signatories. Even in an era of peak neoliberalism, ratifying NAFTA in the United States and Canada required the addition of two adjoining agreements on labor and environmental protection. Business historian Benjamin Waterhouse has shown the lobbying and political pressure MNEs applied on policymakers in the United States in favor of NAFTA.[40] Others have shown that Mexican peak business associations played a key role in the NAFTA negotiations and even served as links between United States MNEs and Mexican firms.[41]

The North American Free Trade Agreement accelerated a process already underway in the region – a geographic division of labor – in a way that critics argued maximized the interests of MNEs.[42] Moreover, unlike MERCOSUR/L's common market, which had a common external tariff, NAFTA's free trade bloc "facilitated, reinforced, and culminated a process of structural transformation" with more intensive market integration thanks to more MNE activity across borders.[43] While United States carmakers like Ford had established production in Mexico earlier in the twentieth century, many more were motivated anew by NAFTA to make greenfield investments to move manufacturing into Mexico to benefit from the lack of tariffs.[44] Foreign direct investment into Mexico increased sixfold after 1994.[45] Between 1990 and 2000, auto imports coming from Mexico increased from 5 to 13.5 percent. Largely because of this shift in the North American auto industry, by the 2000s, the United States ran a significant trade deficit with Mexico. Beyond cars, Mexico also became a destination for Asian electronics producers, which accessed the large consumer markets of North America by producing in Mexico so they could meet the minimum requirements of regional production to fall under the preferential trade agreement.[46] Manufacturing by US and Canadian MNEs in Mexico created jobs in the country; these jobs were not high paying, but they did boost employment rates and contribute to the local economy.[47] Multinational enterprises that invested in Mexico for its consumer markets sometimes caused significant societal damage, however, as Nestlé did when resisting food labeling for consumer health and safety amid Mexicans' struggle with obesity.[48]

In Southeast Asia, the Association of Southeastern Asian Nations (ASEAN) was established in the wake of decolonization by Indonesia, Malaysia, the Philippines, and Singapore, as well as by Thailand. With the founding Bangkok Declaration in 1967, these countries pledged to cooperate in economic, social, cultural, technical, and educational matters and to jointly pursue peace, freedom, and prosperity by upholding the rule of law and abiding by the United Nations Charter. As was the case with early European international organizations like the European Coal and Steel Community and the EEC, the creation of ASEAN was also initially motivated by the perceived threat of communism during the early years of the Cold War. As a result, the Southeast Asian bloc worked to align itself closely with market-oriented allies and international organizations and to promote cross-border business activity.

Not until the mid 1970s did ASEAN's economic ministers meet to outline the contours of their economic cooperation. The resulting Bali Concord I of 1976 established a trade framework between the bloc's members, as well as cooperation on basic commodities, large-scale industrial development, and the pursuit of new joint export products to "eliminate poverty, hunger, disease, and illiteracy ... and improve the living standards of their peoples" and "contribute to the establishment of a New International Economic Order."[49] Subsequent Bali Concords increased the number of ASEAN's members and deepened the commitments between them to create a customs union and – with the addition of free movement of capital and labor – a common market. In their approach to market integration, ASEAN's economic ministers demonstrated their desire for neither a mere free trade agreement nor an EU-style supranationally governed single market.[50]

Some "local" Southeast Asian MNEs, like Thailand-based Siam Cement Group, capitalized on the advantages afforded them by the regional trading bloc.[51] Japanese MNEs led the way, however, for investment in production in the relatively cheap ASEAN labor market.[52] Japanese manufacturing MNEs, including Mitsubishi, Toyota, and Nissan, built production plants in the Philippines, Thailand, and Malaysia. Mitsubishi proposed the implementation of "Brand to Brand Complementation" in 1988, which allowed Japanese carmakers to increase parts production in the region and establish a pan-ASEAN production chain, with common standards throughout: Toyota produced diesel engines and body panels in Thailand, steering and radiators in Malaysia, transmissions and meters in the Philippines, and gasoline engines and clutches in Indonesia. In this way, Japanese MNEs like Mitsubishi and Toyota "were promoters and users of ASEAN economic integration," by building value chains and facilitating standardization across the region as noted in Chapter 4. European-based retail MNEs like Belgium-based Delhaize (now Netherlands-based Ahold Delhaize) and Britain-based Tesco also saw ASEAN as a growth opportunity, although they had to divest in the early 2020s after years of unprofitable business.

Despite criticism that ASEAN designed its economic framework to benefit foreign rather than local firms, the bloc further deregulated its markets in the 1990s to attract more FDI and launched the ASEAN Industrial Cooperation scheme, which required 30 percent local equity but enabled production optimization.[53] Such policy innovations and the elimination of tariffs between ASEAN member states also contributed to a broader shift from import substitution to export substitution, in which industrialization was accelerated by subordinating domestic production of necessary goods in favor of producing nontraditional primary and manufactured products to boost export-led growth.[54] But increasing volumes of trade across the bloc was relatively slow: ASEAN agreements covered only 1 percent of intra-ASEAN trade by 1990. This was largely the result of stark differences between member state economies, weak infrastructure investment, and few indigenous MNEs.[55] The bloc was strengthened with the accession of Vietnam, Laos, Myanmar, and Cambodia in the 1990s. And by the 2020s, ASEAN's economic strength and geographic location positioned it to benefit from the "derisking" and "friendshoring" initiatives undertaken during heightened geopolitical tensions and trade wars between the West and China by joining global supply chains.[56] Meanwhile China emerged as ASEAN's largest trading partner, with Chinese MNEs such as BYD, Geely, Tencent, Alibaba, and Huawei driving the region's economic integration and digital transformation.

These regionally constructed cases of market integration in Southeast Asia, Latin and North America, and Europe span the spectrum of market integration, with NAFTA and now the United States–Mexico–Canada Agreement (USMCA) (which replaced NAFTA in 2020) reflecting free trade, and the European single market representing the deepest form of market integration. While each of these regional blocs formed around trade agreements, they diverged in their economic systems (socialism vs. capitalism) and degrees of integration, just as the firms operating within and across them differed in their strategies.

By the 2000s, although there was much talk of "the global," in reality more than half of the global economy (by output) had been broken up into regional blocs, characterized as much by external competition as internal liberalization.[57] As Chapter 1 explains, deglobalization, which gained momentum in the wake of the global financial crisis in 2008 and has continued through the economic, political, security, and pandemic crises of the 2010s and 2020s, appears to some to be a return to regionalization.[58] The twenty-first-century creations of the African Continental Free Trade Area and the Regional and Comprehensive Economic Partnership only increased the number of preferential trade agreements with which the WTO has to contend or accommodate, such that by 2021, every WTO member was also party to at least one regional trade agreement, resulting in twenty-eight separate preferential trade blocs of proximate and/or contiguous countries, all of which threaten the homogeneity of the global economy.[59] In this way, regional trading blocs present a challenge to globalization while simultaneously offering a stepping stone to it.[60] Business historians have shown how MNEs expanded beyond their home countries' borders long before regional economic frameworks were in place, but they have also shown how MNEs played key roles in shaping regional economic integration and even the contours of bloc agreements.

8.5 Market Integration and Society

The four regional cases of market integration discussed in the previous section highlight the ways MNEs have contributed to, benefited from, and even struggled against regional market integration, from the free trade area of NAFTA, to the common markets of ASEAN and MERCOSUR/L, to the full economic and monetary union of the EU. A comparison of the social consequences of these cases further illuminates the ways MNEs have contributed to and benefited from market integration and its social consequences.

While classical economic theory would expect the 84 percent increase in trade made possible by NAFTA and the related boost in productivity and specialization from the 1990s to the 2020s to be beneficial for everyone, the distribution of the costs and benefits of economic integration has largely been uneven.[61] And while the United States, Canada, and Mexico had very different economies, they came to share similar social problems in the 1990s and 2000s, namely rising income inequality, slow growth, and, paradoxically in the case of the United States, rising productivity paired with falling real wages.[62] According to some observers, NAFTA opened the floodgates of FDI outflows from the United States and Canada to Mexico, and with that FDI went jobs, reflecting the differences in factor mobility. General Motors, for example, closed plants in both the United States and Canada and transferred significant manufacturing to Mexico to take advantage of cheaper labor. Ford also closed some plants in the United States, but while this was partly explained by shifting production to Mexico, other factors including declining demand for certain models and increased automation, also played a role.[63] The fact that China joined the WTO in 2001 and that the twenty-first century has been characterized by increasing automation better explains the frustration of US workers whose jobs were offshored to China and automated rather than relocated to Mexico within NAFTA.

In the United States in the 1990s and early 2000s, there was significant public backlash against NAFTA for having created a generation of disaffected workers until their self-styled champion Donald Trump renegotiated a very similar deal with the USMCA in 2020, albeit this time with a few more labor protections. In the 1990s, NAFTA skeptics predicted that "economic dislocation" in the Mexican agricultural sector would also give rise to migration to the United States, which has since become a core element of US political debates about immigration.[64] After NAFTA was signed in 1994, Mexico experienced a major exchange rate crisis that damaged its economy and society. In sum, NAFTA's free trade framework accelerated trends already underway in MNEs, exacerbated the social problems of rising inequality and falling wages, and did not substantively increase Mexico's GDP, despite it being the recipient of most inward FDI and achieving a trade surplus with the US.[65] There were both winners and losers of market integration in North America.

Although the Southern Common Market represents integration deeper than a mere free trade area, MERCOSUR/L has been described as a "failure of Latin American neoliberalism" for contributing to the development crises of the 2000s, exacerbating wealth inequality, and precipitating political instability in the region. Many citizens of Latin American countries viewed MERCOSUR/L as having been created by and for economic elites, including MNEs, at the expense of everyone else, especially in member states in which foreign investors controlled key economic sectors with seeming impunity. Proponents of the bloc argued its creation reflected the democratic will of Latin Americans, but scholars have since shown its early formation was driven by economic and political elites like conservative Mexican president Felipe Calderón.[66] While economists have documented increasing wealth inequality across the region since the bloc's formation, others have demonstrated convergences in GDP and productivity between MERCOSUR/L member states.[67]

International Monetary Fund reports in the 1990s optimistically predicted that ASEAN was set to provide a "giant leap forward" to the economies of Southeast Asia.[68] In practice, the 1997 Asian financial crisis devastated the region. The bloc's industrial powerhouse, Thailand, stagnated as it experienced multiple political crises and emerged as a classic example of the "middle income trap." Under its repressive communist government, Vietnam, however, flourished, benefiting from the strategies of US MNEs to diversify their business beyond China. Furthermore, as with all trade liberalization, there have been winners and losers, down to the firm level.

Most economically integrated of the four regions covered in this chapter is the EU, with its single market and Economic and Monetary Union. Even accounting for the Great Recession, Brexit, and Covid-19 crises, EEC/EU GDP grew by almost three times from 1990 to the present, thanks in large part to growing its membership from six founding countries in 1957 to twenty-eight member states in 2013, before contracting to twenty-seven members in 2020 with the departure of Britain, a move that has taken a greater toll on the British economy than that of the EU. While EU cohesion and regional development policies ameliorated some of the starkest structural differences between European economies, and reduced inequality between member states, total productivity declined in many EEC and EU member states during the period of regional market integration. Meanwhile the shock therapy imposed on former Soviet states in the 1990s caused significant economic dislocation. The capacity for supranational governance set the EU and its single market apart from other regional blocs, and could have, in principle, been directed at mitigating the possible social consequences of trade liberalization. However, in both Western and Eastern Europe resentment fueled the growth of populist, right-wing political parties.[69]

8.6 Conclusion

This chapter has used historical evidence to illuminate the ways MNEs have in some cases supported and contributed to, in other cases opposed, and in many – although not all – cases benefited from market integration since the nineteenth century. It has also historicized the democratic debates, geopolitical tensions – from armed conflict in Europe to trans-Pacific trade and chip wars – and social problems of inequality and stagnation that emerged from this history. Multinational enterprises have long been drivers of international economic integration: While they used the opportunities of empire to globalize in the nineteenth and early twentieth centuries, many regionalized their business in the later twentieth century.

As business history demonstrates, MNEs have contributed to regional market integration and the formation of regional economic blocs, which have paradoxically partitioned the global economy into smaller units and undermined the liberal international order. But they have also maintained global value chains during periods of deglobalization and global economic fragmentation, thereby contributing to globalization. Especially across the four global regions discussed here, MNEs have facilitated market integration with varying social consequences: In the case of free trade areas like NAFTA, market integration had the potential both to create jobs and exacerbate inequality. The common markets of MERCOSUR/L and ASEAN allowed endogenous flows of goods, services, capital, and labor while retaining the ability to control the external boundaries of the market. The EU's capacity for supranational governance through intergovernmental decision-making made possible some collective regulation of capitalism, even to the point of economic protectionism.

In each of these contexts, MNEs cultivated privileged access to policymakers to advocate against fiscal and social harmonization. This significantly undermined trust not only in MNEs but also in national and transnational governance. In addition to their contributions to standardization through their operations and trade liberalization through political activities like lobbying, MNEs have simultaneously contributed to interconnectivity and helped insulate economies from both nation-state and intergovernmental regulation.

Notes

1. Palen, M-W. *Pax Economica: Left Wing Visions of a Free Trade World*, Princeton, NJ, Princeton University Press, 2024.
2. Nye, J. S. "Multinational Enterprises and Prospects for Regional and Global Political Integration," *The Annals of the American Academy of Political and Social Science*, 403, 1 (1972), 116–126.
3. Jones, G. *Multinationals and Global Capitalism from the Nineteenth to the Twenty-First Century*, Oxford, Oxford University Press, 2005.

4. Carlos, A. M. and Lewis, F. D. "Marketing in the Land of Hudson Bay: Indian Consumers and the Hudson's Bay Company, 1670–1720," *Enterprise & Society*, 3, 2 (2002), 285–317.
5. Jones, *Multinationals*, chapters 2 and 6.
6. Hewitt, L. "'Monopoly Menace': The Rise and Fall of Cartel Capitalism in Western Europe, 1918–1957," unpublished PhD dissertation. Princeton University, 2023.
7. Clavin, P. and Dungy, M. "Trade, Law, and the Global Order of 1919," *Diplomatic History*, 44, 4, (2020), 554–579.
8. Fellman, S. and Shanahan, M. "Beyond the Market: Broader Perspectives in Cartel Research," *Scandinavian Economic History Review*, 68, 3, (2020), 195–203.
9. Bertilorenzi, M. *The International Aluminium Cartel: The Business and Politics of a Cooperative Industrial Institution (1886–1978)*, London, Routledge, 2016.
10. Hewitt, "Monopoly Menace."
11. Wilkins, M. "American Business in Europe," in Bonin, H. and de Goey, F., (eds.) *American Firms in Europe: Strategy, Identity, Perception, Performance 1880–1980*, Geneva, Librairie Droz, 2009.
12. Leimgruber, M. "'Kansas City on Lake Geneva': Business Hubs, Tax Evasion, and International Connections around 1960," *Zeitschrift Für Unternehmensgeschichte*, 60, 2 (2015), 123–140.
13. Rollings, N. *British Business in the Formative Years of European Integration, 1945–1973*, Cambridge, Cambridge University Press, 2008.
14. Komornicka, A. *Poland and European East–West Cooperation in the 1970s: The Opening Up*, London, Routledge, 2023.
15. Tolliday, S. "American Multinationals and the Impact of the Common Market: Cars and Integrated Markets, 1954–67," in Amatori, F., Colli, A., and Crepas, N. (eds.) *Industrialization and Reindustrialization in XXth Century Europe*, Milan, Franco Angeli, 1999, 383–393.
16. Jones, G. and Miskell, P. "European Integration and Corporate Restructuring: The Strategy of Unilever, c.1957–c.1991," *Economic History Review*, 58, 1 (2005), 113–139.
17. Servan-Schreiber, J.-J. *Le Défi Américain*, Paris, Denöel, 1967.
18. Schaufelbuehl, J. M. *Crusading for Globalization: US Multinationals and Their Opponents since 1945*, Philadelphia, University of Pennsylvania Press, 2025.
19. Jones, G. *Renewing Unilever: Transformation and Tradition*, Oxford, Oxford University Press, 2005, 334–336.
20. Ramírez Pérez, S. M. "Crises and Transformations of European Integration: European Business Circles during the Long 1970s," *European Review of History*, 26, 4 (2019), 618–635.

21. Morival, Y. "Reassessing the Historical Dynamics of European Business Associations: The Genesis of UNICE, Late 1940s to 1970s," *Business History*, 66, 6 (2024), 1394–1411.
22. Cowles, M. G. "The EU Committee of AmCham: The Powerful Voice of American Firms in Brussels," *Journal of European Public Policy*, 3, 3 (1996), 339–358.
23. Schaufelbuehl, J. M. "The Transatlantic Business Community Faced with US Direct Investment in Western Europe, 1958–1968," *Business History*, 58, 6 (2016), 880–902.
24. Fetzer, T. "Reversing Gear: Trade Union Responses to Economic Crises at Opel (1974–1985)," *Business History*, 59, 1 (2017), 141–157.
25. Petrini, F. "Demanding Democracy in the Workplace: The European Trade Union Confederation and the Struggle to Regulate Multinationals," in Kaiser, W. and Meyer, J.-H. (eds.) *Societal Actors in European Integration: Polity-Building and Policy-Making 1958–1992*, London, Palgrave Macmillan, 2013, 151–172.
26. Rollings, *British Business*.
27. Ballor, G. and Salén, R. "In Search of Unicorns: Lessons from Past European Industrial Policy and Business Forums in High Tech," *Council for European Studies Conference Paper* 2024.
28. Ballor and Salén, "In Search of Unicorns."
29. Drach, A. "An Early Form of European Champions? Banking Clubs between European Integration and Global Banking (1960s–1990s)," *Business History*, 66, 1 (2024), 287–310.
30. Ballor, G. "Liberalisation or Protectionism for the Single Market? European Automakers and Japanese Competition, 1985–1999," *Business History*, 65, 2 (2023), 302–328.
31. Jones, and Miskell, "European Integration."
32. Warlouzet, L. *Governing Europe in a Globalizing World: Neoliberalism and Its Alternatives after 1973*, London, Routledge, 2018, chapter 3.
33. Pitteloud, S. and Donzé, P. "Swiss Multinationals versus the French Welfare State? The Social Security Deficit, European Integration, and the Battle for 'Fair' Drug Prices (1970–1990)," *Contemporary European History*, 34, 1 (2025), 1–20.
34. Kellogg, P. "Regional Integration in Latin America: Dawn of an Alternative to Neoliberalism?," *New Political Science*, 29, 2 (2007), 194–195.
35. Benítez, G. J. "Business Lobbying: Mapping Policy Networks in Brazil in Mercosur," *Social Sciences*, 7, 10, (2018), 198.
36. Christensen, S. F. "The Influence of Nationalism in Mercosur and in South America: Can the Regional Integration Project Survive?" *Revista Brasileira de Política Internacional*, 50, 1, (2007), 139–158, at 142.

37. De La Torre, J. R, Esperança, J. P., and Martínez, J. I. "Organizational Responses to Regional Integration among MNEs in Latin America," *Management International Review*, 51, 2 (2011), 244.
38. US Council on Foreign Relations, "Mercosur: South America's Fractious Trade Bloc," December 18, 2023.
39. Obaya, M. "Multinational Companies in MERCOSUR: Building up a Peripheral and Hierarchical Regional Automotive Space," in Sebesta, L. and Doyle, N. (eds.) *Regional Integration and Modernity: Cross-Atlantic Perspectives*, Lanham, MD, Lexington, 2014, chapter 9.
40. Waterhouse, B. C. *Lobbying America: The Politics of Business from Nixon to NAFTA*, Princeton, NJ, Princeton University Press, 2013.
41. Schneider, B. R. "Why Is Mexican Business so Organized?" *Latin American Research Review*, 37, 1 (2002), 77–118.
42. Blecker, R. A. "The North American Economies after NAFTA: A Critical Appraisal," *International Journal of Political Economy*, 33, 3 (2003), 5–27.
43. Frischtak, C. "Multinational Firms' Responses to Integration of Latin American Markets," *Business and Politics*, 6, 1 (2004), 9.
44. Wilkins, M. and Hill, F. E. *American Business Abroad: Ford on Six Continents*, Detroit, MI, Wayne State University Press, 1964.
45. De La Torre, Esperança, and Martínez, "Organizational Responses to Regional Integration among MNEs in Latin America," 245.
46. Frischtak, "Multinational Firms' Responses to Integration of Latin American Markets."
47. Trachtenberg, D. "Local Labor-Market Effects of NAFTA in Mexico: Evidence from Mexican Commuting Zones," *IDB Publications*, November 20, 2019.
48. Saliba, F. "How Nestlé Tried to Undermine Mexico's Anti-obesity Policy," *Le Monde*, July 3, 2022.
49. ASEAN, Bali Concord I, 1976.
50. Pelkmans, J. "ASEAN's Economic Integration Model: A Conceptual Approach," Centre for International Law Executive Summary, December 2014.
51. Pananond, P. "The Making of Thai Multinationals: A Comparative Study of the Growth and Internationalization Process of Thailand's Charoen Pokphand and Siam Cement Groups," *Journal of Asian Business*, 17, 3 (2001), 41–70.
52. Ambashi, M. "ASEAN as an FDI Attractor: How Do Multinationals Look at ASEAN?" Economic Research Institute for ASEAN and East Asia working paper no. 2016-04 (2017).
53. Cox, R. "Explaining Business Support for Regional Trade Agreements," in Cox, R. (ed.) *Business and the State in International Relations*, Boulder, CO, Westview Press, 1996.

54. Meier, G. M. "Export Substitution and Multinational Enterprises," in Cairncross, A. and Puri, M. (eds.) *Employment, Income Distribution and Development Strategy: Problems of the Developing Countries: Essays in Honour of H. W. Singer*, London, Palgrave Macmillan, 1976, 140–153.
55. Cockerham, G. B. "Regional Integration in ASEAN: Institutional Design and the ASEAN Way," *East Asia*, 27, 2 (2010), 165–185.
56. Cerdeiro, D. A., Kamali, P., Kothari, S., and Muir, D. V. "The Price of De-risking Reshoring, Friend-Shoring, and Quality Downgrading." IMF Working Papers 2024, 122 (2024).
57. Slobodian, Q. *Globalists: The End of Empire and the Birth of Neoliberalism*, Cambridge, Mass, Harvard University Press, 2018.
58. O'Neil, S. K. *The Globalization Myth: Why Regions Matter*, New Haven, CT, Yale University Press, 2023.
59. WTO Committee on Regional Trade Agreements. www.wto.org/english/tratop_e/region_e/timeline_100th_e.pdf.
60. Sideri, S. "Globalisation and Regional Integration," *European Journal of Development Research*, 9, 1 (1997), 38–82.
61. Ciuriak, D. "Winners and Losers in International Economic Integration: The Distributional Effects of NAFTA," in *ASEAN-Canada Forum 2008*, ISEAS, 2010, 158–194, at 159. http://dx.doi.org/10.2139/ssrn.1532881.
62. Blecker, "The North American Economies after NAFTA."
63. Hakobyan, S. and McLaren, J. "Looking for Local Labor Market Effects of NAFTA," *Review of Economics and Statistics*, 98, 4 (2016), 728–741.
64. Durán, C. R. "NAFTA: Lessons from an Uneven Integration," *International Journal of Political Economy*, 33, 3 (2003), 50–71.
65. Gálvez, A. *Eating NAFTA: Trade, Food Policies, and the Destruction of Mexico*, 1st edition, Oakland, University of California Press, 2018.
66. Heine, J. "Regional Integration and Political Cooperation in Latin America," *Latin American Research Review*, 47, 3 (2012), 209–217.
67. Bulmer-Thomas, V., Coatsworth, J. H., and Conde, R. C. (eds.) *The Cambridge Economic History of Latin America*, Cambridge, Cambridge University Press, 2006.
68. Larsen, F. "ASEAN in the World Economy," in Hicklin, J., Robinson, D., and Singh, A. (eds.) *Macroeconomic Issues Facing ASEAN Countries*, Washington, DC, International Monetary Fund, 1997.
69. Berend, I. *Economic History of a Divided Europe: Four Diverse Regions in an Integrating Continent*, London, Routledge, 2020.

Further Reading

Ballor, G. *Enterprise and Integration: Big Business and the Making of the Single European Market in the 1980s–1990s*, Cambridge, Cambridge University Press, 2026.

Chase, K. A. *Trading Blocs: States, Firms, and Regions in the World Economy*, Ann Arbor, University of Michigan Press, 2005.

Narula, R. "Multinational Firms, Regional Integration and Globalising Markets: Implications for Developing Countries," MERIT-Infonomics Research Memorandum Series 2001-036.

Rugman, A. "Globalization, Regional Multinationals and Asian Economic Development," *Asian Business and Management*, 9 (2010), 299–317.

de la Torre, J., Esperança, J. P., and Martinez, J. "Organizational Responses to Regional Integration among MNEs in Latin America," *Management International Review* 51 (2011), 241–267.

Part III

Stakeholders

THOMAS FETZER

9

Multinationals and Labor

9.1 Introduction

In the debate on the impact of multinational enterprises (MNEs) on society, the labor question, embedded in the wider controversy about the implications of economic globalization for inequality and social justice, has occupied a prominent role. Today, in the academic as well as in the public policy realms, this debate is dominated by social scientists and business analysts focusing on the contemporary period, and it is characterized by a range of heated controversies: Are MNEs, as far as labor is concerned, a source of progressive development, or rather a generator of a race to the bottom? Can corporate social responsibility help improve employment conditions, or is it a merely a whitewashing PR exercise? Do footloose MNEs undermine national labor regulation and trade union strength, or can they be reined in by new forms of countermovements? While addressing crucial questions, these controversies frequently appear based on rather sterile dichotomies that lack nuance and a sense of contextual complexity. At the same time, the preponderant emphasis is on the post-1990 period, while little interest is shown in historical insights and perspectives.

This chapter engages with these debates by placing them in a longer-term historical framework, highlighting the crucial contributions of the work of historians and historically minded social scientists for our understanding of the relationship between MNEs and labor. It will be demonstrated that many contemporary dynamics can be better understood if they are traced back further in time, not only because this allows giving contemporary analyses greater contextual nuance and temporal depth, but also because a historical perspective can help us identify periods of contingency in which specific actors, under specific contextual conditions, played a crucial role in shaping subsequent developments while foreclosing alternative paths.

The chapter proceeds in two steps. First, it reviews scholarship concerned with the impact of MNEs on employment and labor conditions, distinguishing between developing and developed countries (Sections 9.2 and 9.3), while a separate section (Section 9.4) will address the question of corporate social responsibility. In Sections 9.5 and 9.6, the chapter then surveys work addressing the challenges posed by MNEs for organized labor, as well as the responses to these challenges by trade unions and other bodies of worker interest representation at both the national and transnational levels. The conclusion will tease out implications of the chapter for the broader debate on the relationship between MNEs and societies.

9.2 The Labor Impact of MNEs in Developing Economies

While MNEs today employ millions of workers around the world, their relative significance as employers in developing countries was perhaps never as great as during the first global economy in the late nineteenth and early twentieth centuries when a small number of giant firms gained often monopolistic control over huge labor-intensive plantations and mines across countries of the Global South. And, as this occurred embedded in a wider colonial or quasi-colonial political and economic context, this is also the period that gave rise to different notions associating MNEs with labor exploitation.

At one level, exploitation referred in a straightforward way to a host of abusive practices, ranging from forced labor recruitment and brutal, hazardous working conditions to structural racial discrimination vis-à-vis Indigenous workers. In a formal colonial context, the case of the Belgian Congo was particularly notorious. The horrors of Anglo-Belgian India Rubber Company's "red rubber" system of imposing extraction quotas on villages, backed up by a system of armed guards and prison camps punishing noncompliance, have been well documented, while

Lever Brothers' palm groves exploited cheap and often forced African labor in direct contradiction to its own corporate self-image of socially responsible capitalism.[1]

Although taking place in formally independent territories, labor abuse was equally widespread in Central and South American countries. United Fruit became the paradigmatic case not only of state capture by MNEs, but also of exploitative labor relations characterized by hazardous working conditions and systematic racial segregation resembling Jim Crow practices in the United States South.[2] Disregard for worker safety, racial discrimination, and the conscious use of ethnic division to play off different groups of workers, including migrants, against each other, were also common in the large oil and mining MNEs, as well as in the livestock and transport industries. Protests against such exploitative practices were at the origin of a string of large-scale strikes between 1900 and 1930 in Mexico, Chile, Colombia, and elsewhere, and collusion by MNEs in the violent repression of these strikes helped spur the creation of independent trade unions in these countries, as discussed in Chapter 14.

At a second level, arguments regarding exploitation also became part of debates about the wider developmental impact of MNEs in host societies in the Global South. While MNEs often paid higher wages than could be earned in domestic agriculture, the enclave character of the large mines and plantations, and their strong focus on exports without follow-up product processing, entailed new spatial inequalities while developmental benefits remained limited. Inside the firms themselves, there were few efforts toward the skill development of local workers, as Western expatriates – with greatly superior pay and racially segregated housing – were brought in to handle the newest technology and occupy senior managerial positions. These dynamics have been documented for colonial and noncolonial settings alike, from the French-controlled Suez company in Egypt and Dutch MNEs in Indonesia to the large mineral extraction companies in Latin America, although there were also differences in degree between different industries.[3] In India, these problems were exacerbated by the employment displacement effects of imperial trade and investment integration, in particular in the textile sector, soon giving rise to debates about colonial economic drain and the Swadeshi boycott campaigns, as shown in Chapter 12. Elsewhere too, next to broader debates about tax concessions and government–MNE collusion, the "labor enclave" argument fed emerging agendas of economic nationalism.

With the onset of deglobalization from the 1930s and the subsequent decolonization processes of the 1950s and 1960s, the labor impact of MNEs in developing countries radically changed. Employment levels plummeted, as many MNEs in the primary sector were nationalized or put under different types of government control if they did not divest on their own; the resistance of a few large US firms like ITT and United Fruit, colluding in CIA-orchestrated coups in Guatemala, Iran, or Chile, did not fundamentally alter this dynamic. Indeed, MNEs came at times to be targeted in major strikes that focused on broad political issues rather than workplace conflicts – for example, in postindependence Ghana and Nigeria.[4] This trend further accelerated with the spread of dependency theory and economic nationalism across the Global South during the 1960s and 1970s, as Marxist interpretations gained traction that considered MNEs as micro-scale mirror images of global core–periphery patterns cementing uneven development.[5]

Under these new conditions, labor relations in MNEs came to focus on the challenges to align corporate objectives with broader state-mandated development agendas. For firms in manufacturing, opportunities arising from import-substitution policies required investment in workforce skill development, as well as building up networks of local clients and suppliers against the backdrop of government requirements to create spillover effects of MNE investment for local economies, including in terms of employment creation. The key challenge was to move toward the indigenization of staff at the expense of Western expatriates, in particular with regard to high-level managerial and technical positions. Depending on country, industry, and company contexts, this was sometimes a success, as subsidiary management became decentralized and the employment of expatriate staff was significantly reduced without major disruptions to corporate operations. In other cases, indigenization was approached as a form of window dressing, while yet other firms made significant efforts to provide in-company training and educational facilities and were still experiencing major difficulties. The contrasting fate of the two Unilever subsidiaries in India and Indonesia illustrates this diversity – while the Indian affiliate had become one of India's biggest firms and had almost ceased the use of expatriate managers by the mid 1960s, the Indonesian subsidiary first substituted Dutch for British expatriates, then fully reversed this before ending up under government supervision with a near-complete loss of its sales.[6]

The onset of the second global economy from the 1980s again brought fundamental transformations. The liberalization of global trade and investment regulation entailed renewed massive growth of investment and employment by MNEs in developing countries, including in new geographical areas (most notably China), while rekindling concerns about exploitation and the labor–development nexus. However, these debates were different from the first global economy in that, as far as Western MNEs were concerned, most activity was now concentrated in manufacturing, rather than in natural resources. Accordingly, exploitation charges against MNEs now frequently relied on juxtapositions of labor compensation in production locations and global retail prices for branded goods (most frequently information technology products), although such notions were difficult to translate into benchmarks to define exploitation.

The International Labour Organization's (ILO) core international labor standards, enshrined in conventions on the prohibition of forced and child labor and the right to association and collective bargaining, as well as the prohibition of gender and race discrimination in employment and pay, became a more straightforward measure of exploitation. Since the 1980s, there have been multiple instances of violations of these standards by MNEs, including forced overtime, child labor, hazardous working conditions, and refusal of the right to join labor unions. Workplace discrimination has also been a recurring issue, not least in relation to the treatment of migrant workers. Multinational enterprises' involvement in racial discrimination practices has been well documented in a number of countries, most extensively in the case of South Africa.[7] Health and safety problems have been particularly acute in labor-intensive sectors; some of the most egregious cases of violations occurred in the apparel industry – for example, the Rana Plaza collapse of a garment factory in Bangladesh in 2013 that killed more than one thousand people and caused massive public backlash.

While these abuses attracted justified outrage, it would be misleading to suggest that they were a unique feature of MNE operations, as the overwhelming majority of cases of ILO convention violations occurred in local situations rather than involving MNEs. Indeed, the most systematic and longitudinal research for the second global economy demonstrates that, on balance, MNE presence was associated with stronger rather than weaker protection of labor rights in developing countries. There was also a great deal of variation across countries and sectors, as labor rights protection strongly depends on domestic legal and political contexts.[8]

The debate on the broader labor–development nexus also shifted in significant ways. Expatriate staffing, for many decades one of the key contentious issues, lost much significance in relation to operations of Western MNEs, while it was now inherited by Japanese and, later, Chinese MNEs. In recent years, a great deal of tension on this question has been reported specifically with regard to the operations of Chinese MNEs in Africa, as discussed in Chapter 3.

With the overall shift from resource extraction to manufacturing, the main debate on the labor–development nexus in the second global economy has focused on whether integration into MNEs and global production networks allows countries to climb up the value-added ladder, including with regard to pay, labor conditions, and employee skill development. On the aggregate level, the evidence is overall positive, as per capita income growth has been particularly marked in countries with extensive integration into global production networks; stronger MNE presence in developing countries has thus, on average, been a significant factor in global poverty reduction and reduced between-country income inequality.[9] However, the picture is uneven. While some countries' reliance on an MNE-driven development path has been a success story, other countries have been trapped in low-value-added segments of global production networks, which, while allowing for basic improvements, pose limitations in terms of potential for further upgrading of wage and skill levels. Most studies conclude that much depends on the interaction between MNE strategies and host country development policies, as shown in Chapter 4.[10]

9.3 The Labor Impact of MNEs in Developed Economies

Compared to developing countries, the labor impact of MNEs in developed economies remained limited until after the post-1945 period when manufacturing replaced natural resources as the dominant domain of MNE investment. In Britain, for example, employment in affiliates of US manufacturing MNEs increased sevenfold between the early 1930s and the early 1960s, to constitute about 5 percent of the country's overall manufacturing workforce. Subsequent decades then witnessed further growth.[11] Key concerns in relation to MNE impact were also quite different from developing countries, as MNEs were often concentrated in technologically advanced industries; typically, public anxiety about the rising presence of US MNEs in Western Europe in the 1960s focused on perceived dangers of technological dependence rather than on the violation of basic labor standards.

In developed economies, the oldest labor–MNE debate was related to arguments that MNEs imported alien labor practices clashing with host country traditions; this argument targeted specific practices derived from MNE home country patterns, and it can be found in misgivings over US-owned firms' import of Fordist production methods in the early post-1945 period, as much as in later debates about Japanese "just-in time" manufacturing approaches of the 1980s, or in contemporary concerns over labor practices of state-owned Chinese MNEs.

From the 1970s, however, as many developed economies acquired significant levels of inward and outward foreign direct investment (FDI), the salience of alien labor practice arguments became supplanted by concerns over production geography of MNEs and their ability to shift assets across borders. Major debates unfolded about whether MNEs were exporting jobs, and whether, bargaining "in the shadow of exit," they played off workers and countries against each other, seeking lower labor costs and light regulation. These concerns emerged somewhat earlier in the United States, where controversies about "capital flight" of US-owned firms had already reached a first culmination point in the late 1960s and early 1970s.[12] In Western Europe, these debates took off with the completion of the European Union's (EU) single market in the mid 1980s and accelerated in the wake of the integration of the former Council for Mutual Economic Assistance countries during the 1990s.

In the United States, the debate on job exporting and MNE-induced downward pressure on wages was particularly vivid, feeding into wider academic and public controversies about the labor-related impact of the expansion of global economic integration; the title of one influential analysis – "Are your wages now set in Beijing?" – captured the essence of decades of debate.[13] By the 2020s, key findings appeared rather clear – first, the overall labor share of national income in developed economies had fallen since the 1990s; second, among wage earners, job losses and income drops predominantly hit less educated workers and those performing routine tasks; third, next to technological advancement, globalization was a key driver behind these changes, as anticipated in adaptations of the mainstream Stolper–Samuelson theorem related to the distributional domestic effects of market liberalization policies.[14]

Within this debate, the specific role of MNEs evidently focused on offshoring. Macro surveys were at pains to emphasize that offshoring could not be equated with a run to low-wage economies, as employment at US MNE affiliates remained concentrated either in other high-income countries or, with growing incidence, in emerging middle-income countries. Neither did it imply that MNEs deserted the United States – while foreign employment shares of US-based MNEs grew significantly, the overall share of MNEs among private-sector employers in the United States remained rather stable from the 1980s, and the share of affiliates of foreign-owned MNEs modestly increased. Indeed, in many instances, offshoring dynamics went hand in hand with some employment growth in domestic locations, while the wage premium paid by US MNEs, compared to the US private-sector average, appears to have further increased since the 2000s.[15]

However, more fine-grained analyses of offshoring related to specific skill and occupational groups in the context of the wider US labor market did confirm significant distributional effects. Offshoring may not negatively affect aggregate employment and pay in US MNEs themselves, but going beyond the confines of the firm demonstrates that it does frequently crowd out jobs in other domestic firms in the same industry or region. Moreover, occupational and industry studies also highlighted that MNE offshoring is associated with the depression of wages for workers performing routine tasks in the US labor market, particularly those in the lower-middle bracket of income distribution, thus contributing to the polarization trend in the US labor market over the past decades.[16] Apart from the wider social and political implications of such polarization, even the more measurable economic costs – for example, externalized costs for employee training and skill development – have raised important questions about how MNEs can be made accountable, not least with regard to the taxation of their revenues as analyzed in Chapter 7.

Overall, both historical work and social science work demonstrate that the labor impact of MNEs in developed economies has unfolded through two countervailing dynamics since World War II. On the one hand, with important differences across sectors and corporate countries of origin, MNEs have sought to take advantage of cross-country labor cost and regulatory differentials. This has not only consistently been highlighted in surveys of investment allocation decision-making, but also through case study research. For example, RCA's corporate production relocation strategy has been characterized as the "seventy-year quest for cheap labor," while research on McDonald's European affiliates has documented systematic practices of curtailing collective labor rights.[17] Case study research on the European automobile industry in the 1980s and 1990s has highlighted how MNEs, in particular United States–owned firms Ford and General Motors (GM), have systematically used locational competition for investment to apply pressure on established labor conditions.[18]

On the other hand, and particularly so in high-tech sectors, such dynamics have remained tempered by the need to retain skilled and motivated workforces – this, taken together with larger average firm size, has ensured that most MNEs have continuously paid a wage premium compared to domestic employers in developed economies. Indeed, corporate models built on paradigms such as diversified quality production could turn labor into a competitive asset, rather than a cost, to ensure customer loyalty in higher-value-added market segments not primarily driven by price competition.[19]

Importantly, the study of the labor impact of MNEs needs to be connected to wider considerations of the changing social and political contexts – the public and policy focus on control of MNEs in the 1970s created very different conditions compared to the post-1990 neoliberal paradigm of competition states seeking to attract mobile capital.[20] Moreover, research on the labor impact of MNEs in developed economies points to the need for analytical emphasis on social and political contestation – from the local workplace to transnational networks. In the following, these themes are explored in more detail in relation to corporate social responsibility and the role of labor unions.

9.4 MNEs and Corporate Social Responsibility

Corporate social responsibility (CSR), the idea that the societal function of business firms ought not to be confined to profit maximization, but ought to include wider stakeholder (e.g. employees, suppliers, local communities) interests, is a much-hyped concept today. Yet, as the work of business historians has highlighted, its origins go back to the nineteenth century when firms like Cadbury, Bosch, and Tata instituted comprehensive employee welfare programs and sought to contribute to wider social progress through a range of philanthropic initiatives.[21] Importantly, however, these early forms of CSR had an overwhelmingly local focus and rarely addressed labor issues from an international perspective. Indeed, in sectors such as food processing, there were at times glaring contradictions between home-country CSR models and the appalling treatment of labor in colonial locations providing raw materials, such as in the case of Lever Brothers' palm fruit plantations in Congo. Cadbury too became embroiled in a public scandal over the use of forced laborers in the West African island plantations of Sao Tomé and Principe, which provided a large part of the company's cocoa beans, although Cadbury subsequently did take active steps to shift to alternative supplier locations.[22]

Emphasis on the international labor dimension of CSR became more pronounced in the post-1945 period, against the backdrop of growing consumer affluence in North America and Western Europe, as well as the emergence of new social and political movements associated with the New Left, which created a significant market potential for business models focused on notions of ethical consumption. In many cases, such as Whole Foods or The Body Shop, concern for the poor in the developing world was part of a wider ethical package that also included health- and environment-related goals.[23] Alternatively, labor conditions in the Global South could also become the central focus of ethics-driven business models; this was most clearly articulated by firms associated with the fair trade movement that offered long-term supplier contracts with guaranteed minimum prices and a community premium to farmers in developing countries.

Many of these firms started out as niche market businesses but over time often experienced significant growth – fair trade brands, for example, had achieved significant market shares of coffee and chocolate sales in North America and Western Europe by the early 2000s, as they drew on independent product certification and labeling to enter mainstream retailing. In the process, major controversies ensued over whether this represented a dilution of purpose – while firms were now able to enhance the appeal of ethical consumption beyond earlier niches, this also came with glaring examples of "image laundering" – firms faced the dilemma of either remaining "pure" but probably marginal, or aligning and compromising with the mainstream.[24]

By the 1990s, ethical consumption and CSR models also became connected to wider political debates about the transnational regulation of MNEs. These debates had earlier resulted in a range of generic codes of conduct for MNEs in the framework of the ILO and the Organisation for Economic Co-operation and Development, but were now redirected toward the level of individual firms, most notably through the United Nations Global Compact launched in 2000. By the 2010s, thousands of MNEs had followed the trend, adopting CSR codes for their global value chains and monitoring compliance through internal audits or multi-stakeholder initiatives involving nongovernmental organizations (NGOs) and consumer groups; a separate professional reporting industry (e.g. the Global Reporting Initiative) emerged to cater to the new CSR performance market.[25]

The academic and public debates about these forms of transnational private governance of MNE production chains have been highly controversial. Some observers highlighted the potential of such governance models to improve labor rights and conditions particularly in developing countries, as MNEs could set in motion a trading-up dynamic of labor-related capacity building or even step in where host countries were unwilling or unable to protect employee rights. On the other hand, critics likened transnational CSR codes of MNEs to a whitewashing public relations exercise, which, moreover, undermined state regulatory capacities and detracted attention from the nefarious role organized business played in its inhibition of regulation mandated by international organizations.[26]

Empirical research on contemporary CSR practices in MNEs points to a very heterogeneous picture – best-practice examples of firms turning CSR into a competitive asset coexist with bad-practice CSR characterized by low-quality audits and poor monitoring of supplier chains. Moreover, impact varies across sectors, countries, and CSR types. For example, CSR programs designed by corporations themselves frequently focus on the monitoring of minimal labor standards while falling short in relation to the right to freedom of association (collective bargaining, right to strike, etc.); the latter area is better addressed in cases where CSR initiatives are codesigned by external stakeholders.[27] Differences in product market destinations also matter – the growing significance of South–South value chains, for example, diminishes the external pressure potential of NGOs and consumer groups predominantly located in Western countries. Studies of horticultural South–South value chains, for example, point not only to opportunities for trading diversification, but also to dangers of economic and social downgrading for producers and workers in developing countries, especially in Africa.[28]

Beyond highlighting the diversity of CSR practices, empirical research also points to the need for a nuanced understanding of the relationship between CSR and state regulation. On the one hand, much evidence was found to indicate that CSR practices in MNEs function best if they are supported by strong regulatory capacities in host states. On the other hand, the very nature of CSR as microlevel governance inevitably leaves regulatory gaps that can be filled only through statutory means; this is particularly relevant in cases of MNEs operating in sectors with limited exposure to public and consumer scrutiny.[29]

9.5 MNEs and Organized Labor at the Domestic Level: Reshaping Interest Representation Strategies?

Public debates about the labor impact of MNEs have always also been debates about how to tame the new global leviathans, and labor unions have played a key role in these debates. The core question has been whether the emergence and growth of MNEs has entailed a weakening of trade unions and other bodies of employee interest representation, and, at the same time, how the new MNE challenge has reshaped the strategies of organized labor.

Much contemporary writing on the alleged need to confront MNEs through radical new forms of labor internationalism notwithstanding, the predominant focus of organized labor strategies toward MNEs has been on the domestic level. This is little surprising in the case of MNEs in the resource extraction and service industries, which are tied to specific locations and markets. But even in manufacturing where cross-border relocation and offshoring have been common, organized labor has frequently been able to build up strength to deal with MNEs domestically – as even the most footloose companies, such as the US electronics MNE RCA, have experienced over decades of corporate relocation exercises.[30]

In historical perspective, indeed, while MNEs did frequently cause setbacks and defeats for organized labor, their domestic engagement often also served as a catalyst for mobilization. This complex dynamic can already be observed for the first global economy, particularly in Latin America, where major strikes in United States–owned mining MNEs paved the way, with much suffering, toward the creation of independent trade unions in Chile, Mexico, and elsewhere (see also Chapter 14 in this volume). In the United States, United Autoworkers strikes at GM, Chrysler, and Ford brought a significant breakthrough toward industrial unionism during the 1930s.[31] In 1970s Spain, labor relations in MNE subsidiaries were an important battleground for the emergence of independent trade unions in the transition from autocratic dictatorship to liberal democracy, and similar dynamics have been observed for a range of other countries in the 1980s, from Brazil and South Korea to South Africa.[32] Of course, beyond these high-profile cases, battles for trade union recognition and collective bargaining have been a day-to-day occurrence for worker representatives in many MNEs – while the notorious anti-union stance of United States–owned manufacturing MNEs in Western Europe and Japan had been blunted by the 1960s and 1970s, a subsequently emerging new crop of union-hostile MNEs, from McDonald's to Starbucks and Amazon, has been a continuous challenge for organized labor to this day.[33] Recently, collective labor rights have also emerged as a concern in relation to Chinese-owned MNEs, mostly with regard to subsidiaries in developing countries.[34]

Beyond these fundamental issues of independence and recognition, organized labor also faced continuous challenges arising from the import of labor relations practices from MNEs' home countries. In Western Europe, for example, "Americanization" was much debated already in the 1950s and 1960s, and this was superseded by widespread concerns about "Japanization" in the 1980s and 1990s.[35] Such imports could indeed pose severe problems and constraints for trade unions, most importantly the danger that collective interest representation capacities were undermined through practices targeting individual workers or small employee groups – from performance-related pay, employee share programs, and workforce attitude surveys pioneered by US MNEs, to Japanese team work and quality circles. Still more problematic were systematic attempts to ignore or circumvent legally mandated practices of worker representation, most notoriously exemplified by many US MNEs' resistance against statutory codetermination, in particular with regard to union representation in company boards.[36]

However, organized labor also frequently succeeded in domesticating labor relations imports; in Scotland, for example, trade unions were faced with a clear strategy of marginalizing shop-floor unionism in the 1950s and 1960s in many US MNEs, but were able to "blunt the edge of aggressive American management techniques."[37] Moreover, the home–host country dichotomy was not always so clear – decentralized plant bargaining in German subsidiaries of US MNEs, for example, was frequently welcomed by local labor representatives, but was resisted by national union bureaucracies fearful of deleterious effects for overall union structures and strategies.[38] Much also depended on the broader historical context; in Europe, again, the apogee of trade union power during the 1960s and 1970s created more favorable conditions to reign in MNEs than later decades when many unions, albeit with significant cross-country differences, experienced membership losses and a decline in workplace strength and political influence.[39]

It is also noteworthy, as explored in Chapter 13, that "foreignness" of MNE practices could at times be turned into an asset, enabling labor representatives to frame concerns in the language of nationality.

Charges of Yankee imperialism against US MNEs became staples of labor rhetoric around the world from the first major strikes against United States–owned mining and plantation firms in Latin America in the early twentieth century, while juxtaposing references to allegedly peculiar national heritage – from "British craftsmanship" to "German quality work" and "Swiss labor peace" were also frequently deployed. While this was not always successful in achieving short-term aims such as preventing plant closures or lay-offs, it underpinned longer-term strategies to legitimize trade union objectives in the eyes of workforces, as well as external stakeholders, from consumers and local governments to wider public opinion.[40] In some corporate contexts like at Ford and GM Europe, labor representatives recurrently deployed narratives of national identity, autonomy, and solidarity in campaigns to defend production and employment levels, as well as country-specific trade union rights and practices.[41]

Nationality at times also mattered in a wider political economy sense. Labor union campaigns could become associated with the nationalization of MNEs, such as in the Mexican oil industry in the 1930s, or with Renault and British Leyland in Europe's post-1945 automobile industry. In different contexts, organized labor also engaged in campaigns for capital controls and import restrictions to reign in MNE offshoring, most notably in the United States (in the late 1960s and early 1970s) and Britain (from the mid 1970s to the mid 1980s), although none of these campaigns achieved meaningful success.[42]

From the 1960s, especially in manufacturing MNEs, organized labor was confronted with the new challenges of geocentric restructuring and creating integrated corporate networks, along with the cross-border standardization of products, either regionally, or, from the 1990s, sometimes also on a global scale. This meant that collective bargaining and union actions in different subsidiaries of the same firm became much more interdependent – in an ambiguous way. On the one hand, strikes in any given location, especially if targeting a strategic part of the MNE production network, could have massive repercussions across borders and thus enhance the short-term power of organized labor. On the other hand, the greater capacity of geocentric MNEs to switch investments and production across locations meant that, in the longer term, recurrent "labor trouble" in a specific location could induce firms to reduce operations and/or to deploy such exit threats in collective bargaining processes. The relevance of this ambiguity for trade union militancy is borne out by strike patterns in the global automobile industry since the 1930s, which demonstrate, important cross-country differences notwithstanding, that organized labor exploited corporate network vulnerabilities particularly during times of production and employment expansion, while militancy declined when operations in particular countries/regions stagnated or shrank.[43]

Beyond the question of militancy, the new geocentric corporate networks also posed a range of other challenges, not least because of the growing opaqueness of headquarter–subsidiary decision-making processes, which often diluted organized labor's domestic influence capacities. Trade union responses to this were shaped by country-specific contexts. In Britain, for example, United States–owned MNEs' transition to European production networks from the 1970s first transformed union strategies from exclusive emphasis on strikes toward broader public and political pressure, while later, in the context of the wider political onslaught on union power in the 1980s and 1990s, MNE-based union representatives were in the forefront of debates to endorse law-backed instruments of interest representation. In Germany, on the other hand, the preempting of codetermination rights through European management coordination was instrumental in shifting union and works council strategies toward "shadow" management through which labor representatives could actively challenge corporate product and investment decision, as well as toward new legal strategies to secure production and employment in German locations. For example, at several points during the 1990s, Ford and Opel work councils, going beyond the purview of their regular statutory rights, concluded legally binding agreements with subsidiary management that listed specific earmarked future investments and production allocations for German plants.[44]

9.6 MNEs and Organized Labor: Toward New Forms of Cross-Border Collective Action?

Ever since the 1848 Communist Manifesto, labor internationalism has inspired academic and public debate, and the question of the emergence of a new form of such internationalism in MNEs has added a significant layer to this debate. Today, many business and industrial relations scholars consider this question as pertaining exclusively to the period of the second global economy since the 1990s. Many observers point to historically unprecedented global production chains to argue for the necessity of enhanced cross-border labor cooperation in MNEs, while skeptics highlight obstacles to such a scenario, from management resistance and a lacking legal framework for transnational collective bargaining, to the embeddedness of trade unions in distinct national labor relations systems.[45] Both sides barely pay any attention to pre-1990s developments.

By contrast, historical scholarship has demonstrated that attempts at cross-border trade union coordination in MNEs can be traced back to the early post-1945 period when first transatlantic networks occurred that focused as much on geopolitical as on economic aspects – US unions used MNE networks as one route in their multipronged strategy to contain the communist influence on the Western European left.[46] By the 1960s, however, this dynamic was supplanted by efforts at a wider transnational coordination of union strategies to address the MNE challenge.

Historical work has addressed two different dimensions of this dynamic. One strand of scholarship has focused on the role of trade unions in the context of attempts to establish a transnational regulatory framework for MNEs, which occurred in a variety of international organizations, from the OECD and the ILO to the United Nations. On the regional level, particular attention has been paid to debates about MNE regulation in the European Community (later the EU) in the wider framework of the development of a European social and employment policy. There is general agreement that trade unions were the main actor pushing these efforts, although the ambitiousness of union agendas remains somewhat clouded. However, strong resistance by employer associations, driven not least by direct MNE lobbying, either diluted the regulatory scope and teeth of adopted codes (the OECD and the ILO) or obstructed regulatory processes altogether, as in the case of a planned European Community scheme for transnational worker consultation.[47]

The other strand of literature has directly focused on the company level. Case studies of the automobile (Ford and GM) and chemical industries (Saint-Gobain) have reconstructed ambitious agendas for the cross-border coordination of collective bargaining and mutual strike support, which, while predominantly driven by US unions, also enlisted widespread support from among local labor representatives in Western Europe. However, they encountered the staunch resistance of national union leaderships – at Ford and GM, for example, German and British union leaders were fearful of the formation of breakaway car industry unions along the model of the US United Auto Workers union; this resistance, alongside opposition from Ford and GM management, effectively buried company-level coordination agendas by the mid 1970s.[48]

Regardless of these different emphases, historical work thus highlights that trade union efforts to address the MNE challenge at the transnational level emerged long before the onset of the second global economy, and that the 1960s and 1970s can perhaps even be considered as a crucial period of missed opportunities in this regard. More importantly still, such a historical perspective also helps us better understand the subsequent developments of the 1990s and 2000s and, in general terms, the conditions under which post–World War II cross-border trade union cooperation initiatives in MNEs were more or less likely to succeed.

Again, company case studies of Ford and GM in Europe provide excellent material to explicate these trends, as the late 1990s and early 2000s witnessed a series of successful cross-border union cooperation efforts in both firms through newly created European works councils, which, while only having a legal mandate for worker consultation, turned into agents of transnational bargaining with Ford and GM management.[49] Compared to the 1960s and 1970s, however, the agenda of cross-border cooperation was not anymore focused on broad ambitions for collective bargaining coordination, but much more narrowly, and defensively, on how to share production cutbacks and limit union concessions in corporate restructuring exercises. In other words, the success of cross-border union cooperation was predicated on economic self-interest to limit investment and job losses – a pattern that had been absent in the growth context of the period before the mid 1970s. Crucially, moreover, investment and job competition affected local labor representatives evenly and left them without alternative domestic influence channels, translating into a shared sense of a "risk community."[50] These were conditions not frequently found in this combination, and Ford and GM were accordingly often singled out as best-practice cases in the scholarship on European works councils; however, it should be added that transnational agreements with headquarters management – even if less ambitious and elaborate – were also concluded in a range of other MNEs.[51]

By the early twenty-first century, moreover, in line with the growing significance of manufacturing MNEs in developing countries during the second global economy, transnational agreements of a very different kind also came to be concluded by global trade union organizations in different industries. Compared to the European pattern, these agreements focused much less on the cross-border coordination of corporate restructuring, but predominantly on the protection and promotion of minimum ILO labor standards in MNE affiliates in developing countries; while these agreements added an important new layer of transnational trade union cooperation in MNEs, they frequently resembled corporate social responsibility codes more than the outcomes of classic union–management bargaining.[52]

9.7 Conclusion

Ever since the first global economy of the late nineteenth century, MNEs have been influential in shaping labor conditions and practices not only within their own corporate boundaries, but also through their supply chains and their wider impact in home and host locations alike. However, as this chapter highlights, the analysis of this impact needs to place MNEs into a wider stakeholder context, including governments, international organizations, and, notably, labor unions.

This chapter has made the case for a historically informed analysis of the MNE–labor nexus, highlighting the extreme diversity of MNE business and labor models, and questioning frequently held assumptions in contemporary debates about the allegedly unprecedented nature of challenges posed by MNEs today. Patterns of labor exploitation and abuse in MNE supply chains can be traced back to the first global economy, while concepts of MNEs providing blueprints for upward harmonization in labor standards have originated long before the race-to-the-top hype of the 1990s.

Moreover, such a historical perspective can shed new light on contemporary dynamics themselves, as indicated by the evolution of transnational regulation and transnational trade union cooperation. The reconstruction of failed past attempts in this regard points to missed historical alternatives, especially during the 1970s, while also illuminating the changing contextual conditions under which more contemporary labor union initiatives have been more or less likely to succeed.

The historical analysis of the MNE–labor nexus thus defies easy conclusions – labor challenges of MNE business activity have been very different in developing and developed economies, as well as across different industries, while broader MNE home and host country contexts have greatly mattered too. Multinational enterprises have been at the source of progressive as well as exploitative labor practices. As far as the relationship between MNEs and organized labor is concerned, it clearly appears that many MNEs have sought to exploit spatial mobility patterns to exercise pressure on local workers and trade unions whenever possible. However, while this has entailed fundamental new challenges, organized labor has sought to rein in negative impacts, both in developing and in developed countries. Future researchers are called upon to explore this diversity in more depth and detail especially where there are gaps in available scholarship, from the exploration of labor relations in subsidiaries of MNE in developed economies during the first global economy, to the analysis of alternative and fair trade business models since the 1960s.

Notes

1. Harms, R. "The End of Red Rubber: A Reassessment," *Journal of African History*, 16, 1 (1975), 73–88.
2. Colby, J. "Banana Growing and Negro Management: Race, Labour and Jim Crow Colonialism in Guatemala, 1884–1930," *Diplomatic History*, 30, 4 (2006), 595–621.
3. Piquet, C. "The Suez Company's Concession in Egypt, 1854–1956: Modern Infrastructure and Local Economic Development," *Enterprise & Society*, 5, 1 (2004), 107–127.
4. Decker, S. "Africanization in British Multinationals in Ghana and Nigeria, 1945–1970," *Business History*, 92, 4 (2018), 691–718.
5. Hymer, S. "The Multinational Corporation and the Law of Uneven Development," in Bhagwati, J. N. (ed.) *Economics and World Order*, London, Macmillan, 1972.
6. Jones, G. "Multinational Strategies and Developing Countries in Historical Perspective," *Harvard Business School Working Paper*, 10–076, 2010.

7. Decker, S. "Postcolonial Transitions in Africa: Decolonization in West Africa and Present Day South Africa," *Journal of Management Studies*, 47, 5 (2010), 791–813.
8. Mosley, L. *Labor and the Global Political Economy*, Oxford, Oxford Research Encyclopedia of Politics, 2017.
9. Dollar, D. and Kraay, A. "Spreading the Wealth," *Foreign Affairs*, 81 (2002), 120–133.
10. Narula, J. and Dunning, J. H. "Multinational Enterprises, Development and Globalization: Some Clarifications and a Research Agenda," *Oxford Development Studies*, 38, 3 (2010), 263–287.
11. Jones, G. *Multinationals and Global Capitalism: From the Nineteenth to the Twenty First Century*, Oxford, Oxford University Press, 247–248.
12. Sheehan, M. "The AFL-CIO, the US Balance of Payments, and the End of the Post–World War II Liberal Order, 1965–1973," *Enterprise & Society*, 25, 4 (2024), 1190–1213.
13. Freeman, R. B. "Are Your Wages Set in Beijing?" *Journal of Economic Perspectives*, 9, 3 (1995), 15–32.
14. Bivens, J. "Globalization, American Wages and Inequality," *EPI Working Paper* 279, 2007.
15. Hines, J., Foley, F., Malatoni, R., and Wessel, D. "Multinational Activity in the Modern World," in Foley, F., Hines, J., and Wessel, D. (eds.) *Global Goliaths: Multinational Corporations in the 21st Century Economy*, Washington, DC, Brookings Institution Press, 2021.
16. Oldenski, L. "Offshoring and the Polarization of the US Labour Market," *ILR Review*, 67, 3 (2014), 734–761.
17. Cowey, J. *Capital Moves: RCA's Seventy-Year Quest for Cheap Labor*, New York, New Press, 2001.
18. Fetzer, T. *Paradoxes of Internationalization: British and German Trade Unions at Ford and General Motors 1967–2000*, Manchester, Manchester University Press, 2012, 37–48.
19. Sorge, A. and Streeck, W. *Diversified Quality Production Revisited: The Transformation of Production Systems and Regulatory Regimes in Germany*, MPIfG Discussion Paper 16/13, 2016.
20. Sauvant, K. P. "The Negotiations of the United Nations Code of Conduct on Transnational Corporations," *Journal of World Investment and Trade*, 16, 1 (2015), 11–87.
21. Jones, G. *Deeply Responsible Business: A Global History of Value-Driven Leadership*, Cambridge, MA, Harvard University Press, 2023, chapters 1–4.
22. Jones, *Deeply Responsible Business*, 33–36.
23. Jones, *Deeply Responsible Business*, chapter 8.
24. Moore, G. "The Fair Trade Movement: Parameters, Issues and Future Research," *Journal of Business Ethics*, 53, 1/2 (2004), 73–86.

25. Bartley, T. "Transnational Corporations and Global Governance," *Annual Review of Sociology*, 44 (2018), 145–165.
26. Bartley, "Transnational Corporations and Global Governance."
27. Anner, M. "Corporate Social Responsibility and Freedom of Association Rights: The Precarious Quest for Legitimacy and Control in Global Supply Chains," *Politics & Society* 40 (2012), 609–644.
28. Barrientos, S. "Shifting Regional Dynamics of Global Value Chains: Implications for Economic and Social Upgrading in African Horticulture," *Environment and Planning*, 48, 7 (2016), 1266–1283.
29. Anner, "Corporate Social Responsibility."
30. Cowey, *Capital Moves*.
31. Lichtenstein, N. *Walter Reuther: The Most Dangerous Man in Detroit*, Urbana: University of Illinois Press, 1995.
32. Silver, B. *Forces of Labor: Workers' Movements and Globalization since 1870*, Cambridge, Cambridge University Press, 2003, 54–64.
33. Royle, T. *Working for McDonalds in Europe: The Unequal Struggle?* London, Routledge, 2000.
34. Yang, Y. "Racing to the Bottom? Chinese Foreign Direct Investment and Collective Labor Rights," *International Interactions*, 49, 6 (2023), 962–988.
35. Zeitlin, J. *Americanization and Its Limits: Reworking US Technology and Management in Postwar Europe and Japan*, European University Institute, Working Paper RSC No. 99/33, 1999.
36. DeVos, T. *US Multinationals and Worker Participation in Management*, London, Aldwych Press, 1981.
37. Knox, B. and McKinlay, A. "Working for the Yankee Dollar: American Inward Investment and Scottish Labour, 1945–1970," *Historical Studies in Industrial Relations*, 7 (1999), 25.
38. Fetzer, T. "Exporting the American Model? Transatlantic Entanglements of Industrial Relations at Opel and Ford Germany (1948–1965)," *Labor History*, 51, 2 (2010), 173–191.
39. Hyman, R. *Understanding European Trade Unionism*, London, Sage, 2001.
40. Pitteloud, S. "'American Management' vs. 'Swiss Labour Peace': The Closure of the Swiss Firestone Factory in 1978," *Business History*, 64, 9 (2022), 1648–1665.
41. Fetzer, *Paradoxes of Internationalization*, chapter 3.
42. Fetzer, *Paradoxes of Internationalization*, 122–125.
43. Silver, *Forces of Labor*, 43–47.
44. Fetzer, *Paradoxes of Internationalization*, chapter 4.
45. Streeck, W. "The Internationalization of Industrial Relations in Europe: Prospects and Problems," *Politics & Society*, 26, 4 (1998), 429–459.
46. Fetzer, "Exporting the American Model?"
47. Warlouzet, L. *Governing Europe in a Globalizing World: Neoliberalism and Its Alternatives Following the 1973 Oil Crisis*, London: Routledge, 2018.

48. Fetzer, *Paradoxes of Internationalization*, chapter 5.
49. Fetzer, *Paradoxes of Internationalization*, chapter 5.
50. Fetzer, *Paradoxes of Internationalization*, chapter 5.
51. Telljohann, V., Costa, I. D., Müller, T., Rehfeldt, U., and Zimmer, R. "European and International Framework Agreements: New Tools of Transnational Industrial Relations," *Transfer*, 15 (2009), 505–525.
52. Telljohann et al. "European and International Framework Agreements."

Further Reading

Fetzer, T. *Paradoxes of Internationalization: British and German Trade Unions at Ford and General Motors 1967-2000*, Manchester, Manchester University Press, 2012.

Jones, G. *Deeply Responsible Business: A Global History of Value-Driven Leadership*, Cambridge, MA, Harvard University Press, 2023.

Oldenski, L. "Offshoring and the Polarization of the US Labour Market," *ILR Review*, 67, 3 (2014), 734–761.

Royle, T. *Working for McDonalds in Europe: The Unequal Struggle?* London, Routledge, 2000.

Silver, B. *Forces of Labor: Workers' Movements and Globalization since 1870*, Cambridge, Cambridge University Press, 2003.

PAULA DE LA CRUZ-FERNÁNDEZ

10

Multinationals and Gender

10.1 Introduction

The history of multinational enterprises (MNEs) has largely been written without a focus on gender. However, MNEs are not neutral spaces – managerial strategies, corporate structures, consumer markets, and the goods that circulate within them are embedded in evolving cultural norms and societal values. The ways of understanding the difference between men and women's roles in society inform and codify ideas about femininity and masculinity and shape expectations for all business and economic actors. Given their global reach, MNEs have been subject to both various cultural contexts and a powerful vector of norms transmission. This chapter shows how gender roles and value systems have been negotiated within the transnational spaces that MNEs have generated from 1850s through the opening decades of the twenty-first century.

The thematic approach of this chapter emphasizes how gender is deeply embedded across various industries – and not only those associated with femininity – and time. Section 10.2 examines how ideologies of domesticity and other gender-informed value systems have been foundational to the markets of MNEs. Consumer goods and technologies such as sewing machines, food storage products, and other household appliances became symbols of gendered labor and spaces, and were perceived as more significant for women than men (and vice versa) in economic, social, and cultural life. Section 10.3 is focused on gendered economies and considers the operations of large

MNEs that played a significant role in shaping agricultural economies in Latin America and contributed to the industrial transformation in the region. These companies not only transformed economic structures, but also gendered everyday life. Section 10.4 further discusses gender representation in management and leadership within MNEs that have traditionally been seen as more feminine spaces, and male-dominated sectors such as banking and computing. It provides insights into the policies of selected MNEs on gender equality and female representation in executive and board-level roles since the 1990s.

10.2 The Gendered Technologies of MNEs from the 1850s

Technological advancements have long mirrored and reinforced societal gender norms. As historian Ruth Oldenziel stressed, technologies reflect norms and roles expected of men and women in society. In different time periods, sewing machines were seen as key household and domestic technologies, plastic storage containers (commonly referred to as Tupperware) became a feminine symbol, and computers were masculinized. These technologies carried distinct gendered connotations, traits that were also widely disseminated across global markets and commonly reinforced by the distribution and selling strategies of MNEs. Furthermore, the impact of MNEs on reinforcing gender identification was combined with other systems of ordering – and othering – such as tiering notions of Western progress and industrial prowess that ended up framing these technologies as superior and reinforcing cultural hierarchies globally. As local economies engaged with global economic relations, cultural interactions began incorporating local nuances into the gendering of technologies.[1]

The case of the sewing machine and the history of the Singer Sewing Machine Company provides one of the earliest examples of such global gendering of technology. Incorporated in 1863, Singer quickly established itself as a global leader in the sewing machine industry. While other companies were also exporting sewing machines, Singer had established manufacturing plants in Europe including Russia, and developed a distribution network capable of reaching every corner of the globe by the 1910s.[2] Singer's marketing and distribution system internationally developed according to the industry's primary market, domestic sewing.[3]

Women were pivotal in shaping the company's corporate structure from manufacturing to distribution and marketing strategies. Ongoing ideals about domesticity and household management, rooted in Victorian ornamentalism, industrial modernity, and middle-class consumerism, associated sewing with a feminine sphere. Singer magnified and perpetuated these domesticity ideals through its design, manufacturing, marketing, and sales processes, embedding gendered expectations into the very fabric of the industry's global operations. The family-sized machine became one of the most important products in Singer's lineup in the United States and abroad. Singer included women in the production process of sewing machines, particularly in sampling machines and by decorating and creating furniture around the technology to seamlessly into households.

Perhaps the most visible part of Singer's role in disseminating ideas on femininity – such as nurturing, family traditions, ornamenting, and domestic expertise – had to be found in its marketing and sales strategies. One of the company's earlier strategies involved showcasing its machines at international and regional industrial exhibitions. At these events, as well as in the hundreds of stores worldwide, embroidery and sewing demonstrations were often conducted by women – either employees or family members – who were knowledgeable about home sewing, dressmaking, household linens, and embroidery decorations among other practices included in the domesticity canon. Many of these women were not officially recorded as employees, which is another indication of the blurred line between the domestic and the economic spheres. These demonstrations allowed potential clients to see firsthand the types of products they could create with a Singer machine, and women contributed to effectively adapt the product to domestic markets and strengthen the brand's appeal.[4]

However, Singer's expansion was not without challenges. In some regions, such as India, domestic sewing was neither traditionally a women's trade nor inherently tied to the household. In Japan, the sewing machine initially faced resistance because it was not well suited for making kimonos, a highly skilled trade that did not easily adapt to this technology. Despite these challenges, the global spread of Western fashion and the idealization of domesticity as a feminine pursuit eventually took hold, even in countries like India and Japan, by the 1920s.[5]

Within the period of the Great Reversal and beginning of the second global economy, Tupperware, headquartered in Orlando, Florida, and others in the food industry and kitchenware were among those that sought to understand the market deeply to drive their business strategies. Tupperware took advantage of white middle-class domesticity ideals that were prevalent in the mid twentieth century in the West as the company sought to target housewives in the US and abroad.[6] Although the concept of domesticity had evolved since the late nineteenth century, it continued to position women as the primary managers of the home. Within this framework, food storage was seen as a woman's duty and an extension of her role in nurturing and sustaining the family. Tupperware capitalized on this by offering women a product that not only promised to make this responsibility easier and more efficient but also symbolized modernity through the use of plastic goods, reflecting sophistication and progress.

Tupperware's global manufacturing expansion began with its first facility in Massachusetts in the 1940s and soon extended internationally with plants in Britain, Belgium, Australia, Canada, France, Japan, Mexico, Brazil, and India. Though women were part of the production process, especially in the testing and processing orders stages, their role was noteworthy in the marketing domain. In particular, Brownie Wise developed the concept of Tupperware parties, a direct selling model akin to the US cosmetics giant Avon's sales strategy. In recognition of her achievements, Wise was the first woman to appear on the cover of the US magazine *BusinessWeek* in 1954. Wise and Tupperware's sales force of women transformed the company into a household name and achieved record-breaking sales.

Tupperware's headquarters dedicated a building to managing and planning these parties, which became central to the company's operations. For decades, women made up the majority of Tupperware's sales force and allowed the company to enter more than twenty countries by the 1960s. The strategy of using parties to socialize and demonstrate the usefulness of plastic food containers to housewives was employed globally. The company's marketing strategies did more than sell a product; they spread the idea that effective food storage was an essential part of a woman's domestic role.[7] Tupperware parties thus became social gatherings that celebrated domesticity and subtly reinforced traditional gender roles.

Such marketing efforts built sales up and solidified brand recognition worldwide. The history of Tupperware in Indonesia only two decades after it started distribution in the mid 1990s shows the brand's global reach and adaptability. By 2015, Indonesia had emerged as the largest market for Tupperware at a moment when Tupperware started losing traction in Western markets – though this trend has continued, leading to the company's bankruptcy in 2024. The expansion into Indonesia's households and food practices may be attributed to Tupperware's effective engagement with housewives, who not only became key consumers but also pivotal salespeople, with more than two hundred and fifty thousand women involved in direct selling by that time.[8] Tupperware parties in Indonesia mirrored those in other countries, serving as social gatherings where women could connect, share product knowledge, and contribute financially to their households.

Building a female sales force worked for Tupperware worldwide regardless of women's position in local contexts. In India, where Tupperware entered kitchens in 1996, the company's sales force soon became 100 percent female. At first, the company faced significant challenges, such as assuming women would work outside the home to sell their kitchenware, which led to limited success in rural areas especially. To overcome these challenges, Tupperware formed alliances with other MNEs, such as Procter & Gamble, and adapted its strategy from the 2000s onward. Tupperware began creating products specifically designed for the Indian market, such as spice containers and multi-cookers and, thanks to its female sales force model, highlighted its positive impact on the empowerment and status of women as business owners. This strategy leveraged the traditional roles of women in household management and childcare, reframing these responsibilities as opportunities for entrepreneurial growth and social mobility. Tupperware successfully expanded to fifty-nine cities across twenty-two states by the 2010s.[9]

Still, there is a deeply problematic side to how international business embeds goods and practices in a discourse of empowerment. While household technologies were marketed as labor-saving starting in the nineteenth century, they often led to women being encouraged to take on even more domestic work and the labor itself remained unpaid and undervalued. Multinational enterprises like Singer or Tupperware, or Electrolux (headquartered in Sweden and owner of brands and companies like the US Kelvinator since 1968), and Hoover (headquartered in the US with a factory in Britain since the early twentieth century and with subsidiaries in Latin America, Africa, and elsewhere in Europe by the 1960s) were not just selling appliances – they were promoting a vision of modernity that reinforced the perception that certain skills and economic roles were inherently feminine.[10] As a result, this limits the recognition of women's broader economic contributions and their standing in the global workforce and management ranks.

The global production and marketing of other products like hygiene goods have been and continue to be predominantly managed by men, yet remained rooted in narratives of femininity and the control of women's bodies. Tampax, founded in 1936, and Unilever, which became significantly involved in the development of feminine products in the 1970s, are examples. Although the invention and patenting of tampons are credited to Dr. Earle Haas, it was Tampax's female founder, Gertrude Tendrich, who played a pivotal role in introducing the first tampons to the public. By emphasizing the freedom and comfort of using sanitary protection, Tendrich transformed what had previously been a taboo topic into a conversation about women's health. During the 1940s, as World War II pushed more women into the workforce, the need for reliable menstrual protection grew. Similar to the marketing of sewing machines and plastic containers, Tampax leveraged its global organizational skills and resources to create an educational program and thus to reach women in multiple countries. Tampax sent women employees to colleges, schools, and trade shows to teach women about tampons and their use. The necessity to involve women to establish the social acceptance of tampons became clear as other MNEs, such as Unilever, entered the market.[11]

In the 1970s, Unilever developed Lyogel, a "superabsorbent" and odor-reducing material to go in tampons. To do so, the global company gathered crucial insights from women about their menstrual experiences, preferences, and attitudes to ensure that its product met practical and cultural needs. The business involvement in this process addressed practical management and production concerns but also reshaped cultural narratives around menstruation, emphasizing comfort and convenience while also stigmatizing periods and turning natural biological processes into something seen as shameful or dirty.[12]

Menstrual product development over time and their global dissemination underscores these companies' significant role in creating feminine versus masculine worlds. The marketing of condoms under the Durex brand by the London Rubber Company is deeply intertwined with male-centered discourses of sexuality, disease prevention, and sexual freedom. Founded in the 1920s, Durex became a global leader in condom production by the 1970s, with marketing strategies that often played on masculine ideals of control and responsibility while also linking the brand to public health narratives, particularly during the HIV/AIDS crisis in the 1980s. Interestingly, in the early 1960s, the London Rubber Company employed public relations techniques to undermine confidence in the oral contraceptive pill, positioning condoms as a safer, more reliable option for birth control.[13] In 2020 the cleaning and household products industry player and owner of brands such as Lysol and Finish, Reckitt Benckiser, acquired Durex. Their condoms are sold in more than 140 countries. Contemporary discourse around the brand is more inclusive and addresses mutual sexual pleasure and shared responsibility in sexual health. However, not until the 1980s did companies like the Female Health Company, now part of Veru Healthcare, address gender equality in more meaningful ways by designing products specifically with the female body in mind.[14] Still, female condoms remain more expensive, harder to find, less widely used, and less prominently advertised.[15]

Many other consumer goods reflected how MNEs navigated and exploited gender norms within global consumer cultures. Some even shaped consumers' perceptions from a very young age. Consider the example of Mattel, founded in 1945 in the United States, which rapidly grew to become a global leader in the toy industry. Mattel established manufacturing plants and affiliates in numerous countries during the 1980s, including South Korea, Japan, the Philippines, Thailand, and several European and Latin American nations.[16] Mattel's strategy was to adapt the ways Barbie dolls dressed and looked to local cultures. An example was the introduction of Barbie dressed in a sari for the Indian market. Mattel opened its first office in the country, in Mumbai, in 1988, ahead of this nation's economic liberalization that began in 1991. Nevertheless, adaptation was limited to clothing and skin color while Mattel kept promoting strongly stereotyped body ideals. Barbies were skinny, tall, and had large breasts and slim waists.[17] Moreover, Barbie's impact on little girls' representations regarding women empowerment has been ambiguous. The doll indeed simultaneously represents evolving ideals of independence, career aspirations, and contemporary womanhood while also embodying the traditional roles, particularly when portrayed as a housewife or in a dependent relationship with her boyfriend, Ken.

Another domain in which MNEs shaped the global consumer culture was the movie industry, which after being led by European studios became dominated by Hollywood from the 1920s. The "big five" so-called majors – Paramount, Warner Bros., RKO, 20th Century Fox, and Metro-Goldwyn-Mayer – flourished in the 1930s. Feminized labor was essential for this industry, women often occupying low-paid positions such as secretaries, seamstresses, milliners, embroiderers, maids, and telephone operators.[18] During the interwar years, actors and actresses' autonomy was restricted as they were usually contractually bound to act exclusively for a specific studio. While women occasionally occupied prominent positions such as movie director – Dorothy Arzner was the single female director in Hollywood in the 1930s – the movie industry remained male-dominated up to the twenty-first century, as the burst of the "me-too" movement in the years 2020s to denounce structural sexist violence indicated.

Already in the first half of the twentieth century, Hollywood movies were distributed far beyond the United States. While Hollywood recruited "exotic" actors and actresses to make their films appealing for international markets, diversity had strict limits, with African-Americans and Asians being kept off-screen.[19] Moviemakers also paid attention to what was socially and politically accepted in foreign markets and adapted the content of their films accordingly. Between 1930 and 1969, the Motion Picture Production Code, established by the industry association, prohibited scenes considered immoral, such as scenes featuring nudity and sex between people of different ethnicities or in gay relationships, and discouraged showing unmarried couples in bed or the voicing of criticism of the institution of marriage. So-called independent movies, made by producers beyond the Hollywood cluster, sometimes sharply challenged mainstream societal norms, but they remained at the margins of global marketing and movie distribution. In India, an alternative global movie industry was established in the late 1940s, and Bollywood movies soon became distributed internationally, especially in communist and nonaligned countries, but they were highly gendered and sexist in their portrayal of women stereotypes and frequently featured physical violence against women contributing to spread gendered romantic ideals just like their Western counterparts.[20]

Feminist film critics of the 1970s denounced the "male gaze" dominating the global movie industry. Some major film producers, including Walt Disney, whose films had become icons of childhood, became criticized for spreading heteronormative stereotypes and ideas such as "what is beautiful is good," picturing wicked witches or stepmothers as ugly.[21] In response, Disney belatedly started to develop movies in which women were more diverse and had more agency such as *Mulan* in 1998 and featured its first black princess in 2009 in *The Princess and the Frog*. *Mulan* was nevertheless criticized in China for spreading Western ideals. Moreover, when Disney's CEO spoke out in 2022 to criticize a law in California aimed at preventing sexual and gender education in schools, Florida's governor, Ron DeSantis, threatened to revoke Disney's fiscal privileges in Central Florida.[22] These episodes illustrated how changing the status quo might be challenging and demonstrate the strong incentives for global film companies to conform rather than challenge established norms.

Beyond culture and products manufactured specifically for the domestic sphere, the marketing of most consumer goods was gendered. For instance, Ford – which founded in 1903 a Brazilian subsidiary and had manufacturing plants in Europe, Latin America, and Asia by the mid twentieth century – leveraged its brand to promote automobiles as symbols of progress and modernity. Ford in Brazil shows how discourses of modernity and masculinity were central to embedding the automobile into society. Addressing urban life and targeting businessmen, the automobile would be seen not just a tool of transportation but a symbol of male identity and progress.[23] In the United States, after

World War I – and even more so after World War II – the automobile progressively emerged as a symbol of independence for women, and carmakers understood they could create new models for this specific customer segment. Cars allowed women greater freedom of movement and participation in public life. Furthermore, the automobile became even more parts of women's lives as it became framed as a necessity for most domestic roles, such as shopping, childcare, and social visits.[24] This example also underscores mixed impacts in terms of gendered roles and freedom for women.

These MNEs' histories are not a straightforward narrative of cultural imperialism but rather a reflection of how local identities are reconfigured within globalizing business. Despite Barbie's Western origins, the doll's presence in India became a complex symbol that mediated between global consumer culture and local traditions. Brazil's goals to modernize and industrialize integrated well with the symbolism and meaning that Ford automobiles conveyed. Whether through adaptation, localization, or the full implementation of foreign technologies and their cultural meanings, MNEs and their managerial forces play a significant role in bringing technology and cultural values and symbols to the global marketplace.

10.3 Gendered Economies, Everyday Life, and Labor

If products and marketing can be gendered, MNEs' management of their workforce and foreign operations can be as well. This section focuses on how MNEs operating within gendered home and host economies reinforced or altered these dynamics.

Multinational enterprises, like United Fruit Company in the Caribbean and Central America, exploited labor and resources in their host economies, which in turn resulted in significant social and cultural interactions. By prioritizing gender-specific skills and managing labor according to established norms, MNEs negotiated and continue to shape labor distribution across borders, reinforcing underlying and evolving social gender roles. A similar pattern can be seen in other industries like oil extraction in Mexico, where foreign entrepreneurs and, ultimately, large MNEs such as Royal Dutch Shell (Shell) and Standard Oil dominated until the nationalization of the industry in 1938 by President Lázaro Cárdenas. From the lowest ranks to the executive, company roles were legally and culturally reserved for men.[25]

Although women were not found as workers in the railroads of United Fruit Company or in oil extraction operations in Mexico, nor were they managing oil posts, communications, or distribution branches at the turn of the twentieth century, this did not mean they were absent from oil fields. As environment and Latin America historian Myrna Santiago has explained, they were full of women. They were mothers, sisters, wives, or daughters of workers and executives. They performed all sorts of labor as well: domestic, informal-sector, entertainment, and sex work, as well as political, cultural, and ideological work. In contrast to the wives of the executives, Mexican women, particularly those from Indigenous and working-class backgrounds, often took on supplementary work, including sex work, to support their families as their husbands labored in the oil fields and faced exploitation and marginalization.[26] Their daily lives were also transformed as household management trends and practices needed to adapt to the new labor forms and consumption patterns. Similarly, the railroad industry in Mexico, which was crucial to the country's economic development and integration with the United States, brought profound and lasting changes to the local economies, restructuring labor dynamics with local women increasingly involved in paid and unpaid work supporting the rail industry and the communities around it.[27]

United Fruit Company, which dominated Central American economies from the early twentieth century and is discussed in Chapter 6, illustrates how some MNEs could exert significant economic and social influence in the region.[28] The local societies the company operated within were not merely passive recipients of this economic power. Similar to the oil fields, the company relied heavily on a diverse local workforce that incorporated gender-specific labor practices, as well as explicit policies based on class and race, as migrants from regions close to the mainland (most coming from having labored at the canal zone) and the Caribbean, with men primarily engaged in the physically demanding work of banana cultivation, while women often took on roles that supported the daily lives of these workers, including domestic labor and sex work. The company recognized the necessity of maintaining a stable workforce, which indirectly supported these gendered labor dynamics.

One of the most revealing ways to understand how MNEs interacted with local societies and to highlight the important role of locals is by examining company towns. These towns, built and managed by corporations, serve as key sites where these companies not only controlled economic activities but also shaped gender roles, family dynamics, and broader social relations within the communities. Labor historians Angela Vergara and Thomas Miller Klubock, in their studies of company towns in the nineteenth and twentieth centuries across the Americas, show how MNEs were conductors of socially imbued urban visions and cultural ideologies, typically from north to south (but also from east to west, for example, within the United States). For instance, by constructing homes for managers and workers, along with stores, schools, healthcare facilities, and spaces for socialization, these towns became environments of work and everyday life.[29]

In Chile, mining communities emerged around US copper companies in towns across the Andes. Examples of these were Chuquicamata, initially developed in 1910 by the Chile Exploration Company and later acquired by the US-based Anaconda Copper Company in 1923, and El Teniente, acquired by the US-based Braden Copper Company in 1904 and later a subsidiary of Kennecott Copper Corporation. Housing provided by these companies to recruit and maintain a stable labor force was segregated by race and class, with better accommodations reserved for American managers and their families while local workers lived in more modest quarters.[30]

In these company towns, the concept of "gender compromises," which refers to how gender roles were negotiated, is relevant to understand the interactions between MNEs and local societies.[31] By controlling the town's infrastructure, services, and social life, MNEs like Braden Copper Company and United Fruit Company fostered a form of corporate paternalism that left workers and their families dependent on the company for their livelihood and well-being. However, locals often played an active role in these processes, initiating or participating in efforts to improve living conditions and ease daily life such as the development of recreational areas or healthcare facilities, which in turn helped maintain labor stability. For instance, Braden Copper Company, in its effort to maintain a stable and disciplined workforce, funded the Escuela Vocacional in the late 1920s, a skill training facility for young women specializing in trades like sewing or cooking. The school required marriage for enrolling and for certain benefits such as using the daycare facilities dedicated to the workers' children.[32] Local women actively participated in these initiatives and even initiated some. They also developed clinics and other family focus services. These efforts not only supported and grounded their expected domestic roles in the community, but also illustrated the reinforcing dynamics between local gender norms and corporate-driven programs.

A similar dynamic was evident in Fordlândia, Ford Motor Company's ambitious but ultimately unsuccessful attempt to create an idealized American community in the Amazon. Ford's plan for Fordlândia included the promotion of traditional US family structures in the 1920s, and there were concerted efforts to "civilize" local women according to US standards of domesticity. However, the predominantly male workforce led to social issues, including conflicts over relationships with local women, illustrating the tensions that arose when foreign gender norms clashed with local realities. Fordlândia failed to be a profitable rubber production project, partly due to a lack of expertise in tropical agriculture. Pest infestations and poor yields then fueled worker discontent and increased tensions within the community.[33] Whether in the mining towns of Chile or the isolated outposts of the Amazon, MNEs' interactions with local communities through the establishment of company towns impacted how social and cultural perceptions of gender, race, and class hierarchies unfolded even after foreign companies stopped operating.

Beyond paternalist welfare programs, the organization and functioning of subsidiaries' factories often reflected or established a gendered division of labor. For example, in the Argentine meatpacking industry during the early twentieth century, the incorporation of women into the labor force reflected both traditional gender roles and new economic realities. As historian of Argentina Mirta Zaida Lobato explains in her study "Cathedrals of Corned Beef," traditional ideas about women's roles were reinforced, but in a way that fit the changing industrial landscape. By 1914, women made up 6 percent of the workforce in meatpacking plants, growing to 25 percent by 1935. They worked in lower-paid positions within the production process like conservation, packaging, and making other meat products.[34] Meatpacking is a good example as it showed that MNE subsidiaries created new opportunities for women while perpetuating and reinterpreting a division of labor that already existed in the host society. More recently, US-based MNEs operating in Mexican *maquiladoras*, as production and assembling plants of export goods in the Mexico–United States border region are commonly known, also found in Central American countries, have been criticized for exploiting local *machismo* practices, reinforcing patriarchal relations while benefiting from cheap female labor.[35]

10.4 Gendered International Management

Feminist scholars have made the case that hierarchical organizations – and MNEs in particular – are significant sites of male dominance.[36] Indeed, like products and technologies in international business, management is inherently gendered. The representation of women in high-level leadership positions has remained uneven across regions and industries, both in emerging and in developed countries. Historical data, when available, and recent data – including Morgan Stanley Capital International, the Emerging Markets, World, and All Country World Index indices – reveal that while women's presence in roles such as CEOs, board chairs, CFOs, and directors have gradually increased over time, the numbers remain far from achieving parity.[37]

Women, through marriage in particular or through their role in educating future business heirs, have been central to maintain elite networks and perpetuate family businesses. However, few businesswomen, especially at the beginning of the twentieth century, could be found in corporate networks. But progressively and especially toward the end of the twentieth century, an increased number of women made it to top executive positions in a number of countries, including Argentina, Chile, and Switzerland.[38] Being present, however, is different than being recognized as linchpins of organizations. Even with the implementation of quotas or other initiatives, when women do break into the corporate elite, they often find themselves in noncentral roles or viewed through a gendered lens, regardless of the similar steps they might take to succeed as their male counterparts. Recruitment and selection processes for board members often rely on established networks, which traditionally have been only male, thereby excluding women. The perception and biased views of women's roles as primarily family-oriented also continue to shape and define who enters executive ranks.[39]

An iconic example of a businesswoman in a company that grew internationally, Ruth Handler, the cofounder of Mattel and the creator of the iconic Barbie doll, operated in a business world where female leadership was rare and often unwelcome, particularly in the male-dominated toy industry, which often viewed women's contributions with skepticism. Business historians Valeria Giacomin and Christina Lubinski explain that Handler's innovative vision and determination allowed her to carve out a space not only for herself but also for a product that would go on to challenge gender norms on a global scale. Feminism, with its emphasis on equality, autonomy, and the dismantling of patriarchal structures, provided a framework through which Handler could assert her identity and leadership in a male-dominated industry. Her creation of Barbie – despite later controversies over the doll's body shape and other features – was also a cultural statement. Handler believed in the importance of providing young girls with a tool to imagine a more diverse and empowered future, one in which girls could envision themselves in various roles.

The case of French fashion designer and businesswoman Gabrielle "Coco" Chanel is another iconic example. Within the high couture millinery, she began designing and crafting ladies' hats and selling them in France and Spain in the early twentieth century. She operated in an industry dominated by men and frequently faced criticism and ostracism for wanting to be there. Despite these challenges, Chanel revolutionized the fashion industry with her commitment to comfortable, women-focused fashion. Chanel introduced groundbreaking innovations such as the use of jersey fabric for elegant dressing – a material previously reserved for men's undergarments – and the creation of Chanel No. 5, a fragrance developed with Ernest Beaux that was untraditional for its incorporation of synthetic substances and its focus on women. She established Parfums Chanel in partnership with the Wertheimer brothers, positioning her perfume and fashion business among the most high-profile companies in the industry.

Chanel's business venture was not immune to ethical issues, including workers' wage protests and her controversial involvement with Nazi Germany, leading to operational challenges when she was in exile before returning to France and relaunching the business in the mid 1950s.[40]

Chanel is iconic in terms of gender and management, both because she was a woman in a male-occupied business world and because the transformative impact of her creations (emphasizing practicality and independence) challenged the restrictive norms governing women's fashion. Female executive leadership within the company remained scant until the turn of the twenty-first century when Françoise Montenay was appointed CEO.[41] Since then, several key leadership roles, including CEOs and presidents, have been held by women. Notably, Virginie Viard served as the creative director from 2019 until her departure in 2024.[42]

The 1940s and 1950s were marked by a dual dynamic in which women participated in and fought for their place in business, the workplace, and politics, while simultaneously reinforcing and perpetuating gender-restrictive norms. This period laid the groundwork for the renewed growth of feminism in the 1960s (sometimes known as the Second Wave to distinguish it from nineteenth-century feminism, which focused on voting and property rights). The feminists of this era were concerned with gender equality, workplace rights, reproductive rights, and challenging traditional domestic roles at the same time the idealized image of the housewife surged.[43] The duality represented a complex panorama where MNEs could benefit from more women entering the workplace and the opening of new consumption trends and markets. Yet despite the growing gains for equality, women still faced significant challenges in attaining positions of power.

The cosmetics industry was also an unavoidable sector in which women have been particularly impactful, both in leadership and in shaping the market. As business historian Katina Manko has argued, Avon's business model provided women with an unprecedented opportunity to earn their own income at a time when economic autonomy for married women was severely restricted. Avon operated only in the United States and Canada before World War II, but after opening in the US territory of Puerto Rico in 1954, it rapidly expanded internationally. The iconic Avon Lady was more than just a sales agent; she symbolized a path to financial independence in an era when married women in many countries, such as Italy, were barred from formal employment, even with their husbands' approval, but still within the limits of restrictive domesticity.[44] Women had to navigate societal expectations that deemed it inappropriate for women to work for personal gain rather than humanitarian causes.[45]

Despite these barriers, many Avon representatives, including those from minority communities, built successful businesses in the United States and abroad. In the late 1950s, Ecuadorian and Brazilian women joined Avon's sales force in those countries, becoming part of the MNE's extensive women-led network. These women uniquely understood the aspirations and values that cosmetics could help bring to life for their female clientele.[46] Avon representatives, much like Singer saleswomen and instructors across the globe, were not only salespeople but also integral parts of the companies' structures, serving as vital links between the MNE and its consumers in remote areas. For Avon, saleswomen were responsible for collecting payments, managing credit lines, and adhering to supply schedules established by the company in the United States. Their influence extended further, shaping Avon's corporate structure by informing product development, advertising strategies, and the company's overall image.

In other regions, the entry of foreign cosmetics companies also transformed local economies and management. In China, after the opening up of the economy after 1978, MNEs played a large role in the country's burgeoning beauty industry and influencing gendered consumer culture. Companies like Japan-based Shiseido, US-based Avon and Mary Kay, and French-based L'Oréal not only introduced international products and business practices but also helped reshaped the country's standards of femininity, beauty, and sociocultural aspirations that resonated with Chinese consumers. These companies invested heavily in advertising and built sales force structures that closely mirrored those in other countries. Shiseido, the first foreign cosmetics firm to enter China in 1981, and Avon, which entered in 1990, both leveraged a network of women sales representatives and women-led and women-focused marketing campaigns that rapidly succeeded among Chinese growing consumer culture.[47] Chinese companies and female entrepreneurship rose significantly during this period. One notable example was Yue-Sai Kan, who in 1992 created the first Chinese cosmetics brand with factories in Shenzhen and Shanghai. L'Oréal acquired Yue-Sai in 2004, by which time the Chinese cosmetics industry had expanded significantly, with more than 3,500 licensed manufacturers, including 703 foreign-invested companies.[48]

Female leadership made significant strides across various industries worldwide, extending beyond traditionally feminine-associated sectors and paving a way for a greater presence and visibility in the twenty-first century. In India, a number of women have served on the board of the Coorla Spinning and Weaving Company in Mumbai since 1930. Lady Rachel Workman MacRobert, an American-born woman who married into a Scottish-Indian business family, served on the board of the British India Corporation – one of India's largest firms – in the mid twentieth century. Sumati Morarjee led Scindia Steam Navigation Company Limited, India's largest shipping company, from the 1950s to the 1980s, becoming one of the richest working women globally.[49] In Spain, several women have risen to prominent leadership positions in major companies, including Carmina Ramis of Carmina Shoemaker, a family-managed company since the 1960s; Ana Botín, CEO of the MNE Banco Santander since 2014 when her father (also president of the bank) died; and Juana Roig, since 2018 head of the e-commerce division of Spain's largest supermarket chain, Mercadona.[50]

However, despite these exceptional cases in both traditionally feminine and male-dominated sectors, the obstacles of gendered societies and economies persist, continuing to shape corporate structures and vice versa. Research on Scandinavian MNE banks, for instance, has revealed how senior managers often perpetuate hegemonic masculinity by emphasizing the supposed challenges women face when seeking an international career – such as the impact of motherhood – thereby reinforcing a gendered division in management responsibilities.[51] Another study of Norway's computer industry shows that women in the twenty-first century remain in the minority due in part to how advertising has historically portrayed women's roles in the industry. Advertisements have often reinforced traditional gender roles, depicting men as the primary users and developers of technology, while women are shown in more passive or supportive roles. Norway's educational system has supported this portrayal by steering women away from technical fields like computer science and engineering, prompting them to pursue careers traditionally seen as more appropriate for women.[52] As gender scholars have shown, computers are a highly internationalized industry, with global supply chains and MNEs playing a dominant role in shaping its workforce and marketing narratives and often replicating or deepening the gendered expectations of women's and men's social roles.[53]

From another perspective, however, MNEs were sometimes positive forces for female employment opportunities. It has been argued that foreign affiliates from countries with a more gender-equal culture tend to employ proportionally more women and appoint more female managers, and also that their example may encourage locally owned firms to follow suit.[54] In many countries and regions in which US and European MNEs have operated over recent decades, including Japan, South Korea, the Middle East, and much of Latin America and Africa, they were much more comfortable employing women in senior management positions than local firms. In Japan, large numbers of women with career aspirations chose to work for MNE affiliates rather than local firms, where career progress was and is very difficult.[55] However it is also true that the international transfer of human resource management practices, including the employment of women in senior positions, is constrained by the local social and cultural environment, as well as by law. In South Korea, where informal networks and informal institutions facilitate women's social exclusion from career progression in locally owned firms, MNE affiliates serve as role models by adopting and implementing gender equality-related policies to reduce social exclusion, but the local context still constrains the progress that could be made.[56]

By the twenty-first century, many MNEs in the United States and Europe at least recognized the importance of embedding DEI into their organizational frameworks, acknowledging the various dimensions of diversity (race, neurodiversity, gender, Indigenous identity) and the potential for MNEs to become exemplars of inclusive workplaces. European MNEs such as Diageo, Sodexo, Nestlé, and Schneider Electric have made significant progress in increasing gender diversity, with women holding substantial portions of their board and executive roles. Unilever began investigating the low percentage of women in its management in the late 1950s, although there was little progress in recruiting women to its management training programs until the 1980s, and even then retaining female talent was a major problem.[57] For example, at Unilever, women comprised 15 percent of the Unilever Leadership Executive (ULE) in 2023, with 36 percent of senior management roles being held by women. By the end of 2023, women made up 37 percent of Unilever's total workforce of 128,000. The implementation of gender quotas on corporate boards has also played a critical role in driving this change and this approach ensures that women have greater representation and influence within the highest levels of corporate governance.[58] In the United States, after Tampax was acquired by Procter & Gamble (P&G) in 1997, P&G made efforts to increase gender diversity across its organization, including within its leadership teams.[59]

However, equality policies also entailed growing political risk after the return of Donald Trump as president of the United States in 2025. As seen with quota systems, MNEs may need to align with regulations that respect diverse identities to operate. But these come under threat with authoritarian tendencies and even mandates to dismantle diversity, equity, and inclusion (DEI) initiatives and regulations. Meanwhile, women, despite DEI programs and vocal social movements, continue to raise and denounce the lack of equality within management and the bias inherent in workspaces – such as in the court case Nestlé lost against a female manager who endured years of gender bias and discriminatory practices.[60] The effectiveness of efforts addressing gender inequality depends on the company, region, and industry and scholars of international business argue it also requires moving beyond human resources and addressing deeper, holistic structural organizational changes.[61]

10.5 Conclusion

Across various global business contexts, gender has played a significant role in shaping the practices and structures of MNEs, both internally within management and externally in the market. This chapter has used historical evidence to show the need to understand gender and cultural dynamics of both the home and host economies and to analyze their interactions in the operations of MNEs. The MNE can be viewed as a "gender accomplice," not merely imposing foreign (gender) values and norms, but becoming entangled in the local context, actively shaping, sustaining, and still creating the very gender norms that define societies within different sectors, countries, and markets.

Multinational enterprises have impacted gender norms through the products they distribute and market distinctively for male and female consumers, through their gendered organization of production and company town and through their hiring practices, offering or restricting opportunities for women. The relationship between MNEs and gender norms records no single pattern – while some would challenge more restrictive gender norms, at other times, MNEs' organization may create more hybrid systems, including MNEs adaption to local contexts. Some MNEs have offered more work opportunities for women than local firms, or have challenged gender stereotypes in host economies with new products. Nevertheless, their need to comply with local law requirements and their primary goal of appealing to customers (and therefore when deemed necessary compromising with existing discriminatory norms) often limited such positive impacts. Moreover, when foreign MNEs did challenge local gender norms, it often triggered reactions against a perceived cultural imperialism. Gender is not just a by-product of MNE operations but a lens through which we can understand further the broader social and cultural transformations these companies generate.

The chapter shows how through the waves of globalization, gender-specific norms have both persisted and evolved, and remained contextual and part of the system, a factor that explains the enduring, continuous and reinvented forms of gender inequality across all business forms over time. During the first wave of globalization up to 1929, MNEs, through the establishment of global distribution and marketing of home appliances like the sewing machine or by influencing everyday life in company towns, played a crucial role spreading Western ideals of domesticity. Deglobalization from the 1930s did not halt such transfer and exchange – as MNEs pursued strategic adaptations or operating in countries undergoing social and cultural transformations, management, marketing, and labor composition evolved according to ongoing discourses, transnationally. For example, in company towns in the

Americas, from Canada to Chile, corporate-driven welfare structures in the 1930s supported gendered family roles and divisions of labor.

From the 1960s onward, the presence of women in leadership roles within corporate structures increased and gender-sensitive policies and efforts became more prevalent among MNEs, reflecting broader shifts toward gender equality. However, despite some progress, gender equity remains insufficient both regarding production and consumption. Geographically, at the local and international levels, systemic biases and deeply ingrained gender norms continue to influence workplace dynamics and corporate practices.

A key concept in discussions about MNEs and gender, from the mid nineteenth century until the twenty-first century, is domesticity, historically seen as a private and gendered sphere. Women have always been involved in business, but the association of certain skills with femininity and masculinity has often rendered their contributions invisible or scattered. Domesticity, as part of a patriarchal system, and evolving alongside global capitalism, has been a way to define masculine and feminine economic spaces and access also within the context of the MNE.

Notes

1. Domosh, M. *American Commodities in an Age of Empire*, New York, Routledge, 2006.
2. Godley, A. "Selling the Sewing Machine around the World: Singer's International Marketing Strategies, 1850–1920," *Enterprise and Society*, 7, 2 (2006), 266–314.
3. De la Cruz-Fernández, P. "Multinationals and Gender: Singer Sewing Machine and Marketing in Mexico, 1890–1930," *Business History Review*, 89, 3 (2015), 531–549.
4. De la Cruz-Fernández, P. "Manufacturing and the Importance of Global Marketing," in Da Silva Lopes, T., Lubinski, C., and Tworek, H. J. S. (eds.) *The Routledge Companion to the Makers of Global Business*, New York, Routledge, 2019, 410–423.
5. Gordon, A. *Fabricating Consumers: The Sewing Machine in Modern Japan*, Berkeley, University of California Press, 2012.
6. "The Wonderful World of Tupperware," accessed August 14, 2024. http://archive.org/details/6164WonderfulWorldOfTupperwareThe00005007.

7. Clarke, A. J. *Tupperware: The Promise of Plastic in 1950s America*, Washington, DC, Smithsonian Books, 2001.
8. Elsya, P. and Indriyani, R. "The Impact of Product Knowledge and Product Involvement to Repurchase Intention for Tupperware Products among Housewives in Surabaya, Indonesia," *SHS Web of Conferences* 76, 2020, 01037. https://doi.org/10.1051/shsconf/20207601037.
9. Singh, H. and Aggarwal, N. "Tupperware: Achieving Sustainable Development Goals through Elevating Socio-economic Status of Women in India," *International Journal of Business Performance Management*, 13, 1 (2012), 18–27.
10. D'Antonio, V. "From Tupperware to Scentsy: The Gendered Culture of Women and Direct Sales," *Sociology Compass*, 13, 5, (2019), accessed June 1, 2025. https://doi.org/10.1111/soc4.12692.
11. Røstvik, C. M. "Mother Nature as Brand Strategy: Gender and Creativity in Tampax Advertising 2007–2009," *Enterprise & Society*, 21, 2 (2020), 413–452.
12. Jones, G. *Renewing Unilever*, Oxford, Oxford University Press, 2005, 285–287.
13. Borge, J. *Protective Practices: A History of the London Rubber Company and the Condom Business*, Montreal, McGill-Queen's Press, 2020.
14. Veru Healthcare. "The Female Health Company. A Leading Men's and Women's Health and Oncology Company," accessed November 5, 2024. https://verupharma.com/wp-content/uploads/2017/01/Veru-Investor-Deck_Jan2017.pdf.
15. Terlikowski, J. and Forbes, A. ""Female" Condoms Cost Too Much: A Call for HIV Prevention Equality for Receptive Sex Partners," accessed November 5, 2024, www.thebody.com/article/female-condoms-cost-too-much-a-call-for-hiv-preven.
16. Grewal, I. "Traveling Barbie: Indian Transnationalities and the Global Consumer," in Grewal, I. (ed.) *Transnational America: Feminisms, Diasporas, Neoliberalisms*, Durham, NC, Duke University Press, 2005, 80–120.
17. Grewal, I. *Transnational America: Feminisms, Diasporas, Neoliberalisms*, Durham, NC, Duke University Press, 2005.
18. Stamp, S. "What Happened to Women in Histories of Hollywood?" *Journal of Women's History*, 33, 3 (2021), 162–172.
19. Sheth, S., Jones, G., and Spencer, M. "Emboldening and Contesting Gender and Skin Color Stereotypes in the Film Industry in India, 1947–1991," *Business History Review*, 95, 3, (2021), 496–506, 488.
20. Sheth, Jones, and Spencer, "Emboldening," 496–506.
21. Bazzini, D., Curtin, L. Joslin, S., Regan, S., and Martz, D. "Do Animated Disney Characters Portray and Promote the Beauty–Goodness Stereotype?" *Journal of Applied Social Psychology*, 40, 10 (2010), 2687–2709.

22. Reuters, *Why Is Ron DeSantis in a Feud with Disney World Florida?*, May 25, 2023, www.reuters.com/world/us/escalating-battle-between-ron-desantis-walt-disney-2023-04-26.
23. Wolfe, J. *Autos and Progress: The Brazilian Search for Modernity*, Oxford, Oxford University Press, 2010.
24. Scharff, V. *Taking the Wheel: Women and the Coming of the Motor Age*, Albuquerque, University of New Mexico Press, 1992.
25. O'Brien, T. F. *The Century of US Capitalism in Latin America*, Albuquerque, University of New Mexico Press, 1999.
26. Santiago, M. "Women of the Mexican Oil Fields: Class, Nationality, Economy, Culture, 1900–1938," *Journal of Women's History*, 21, 1 (2009), 89.
27. Francois, M. "Housekeeping, Development, and Culture in Porfirian Chihuahua and Sonora," *Mexican Studies*, 27, 2 (2011), 281–324.
28. Joseph, G. M., LeGrand, C., and Donato Salvatore, R. *Close Encounters of Empire: Writing the Cultural History of US-Latin American Relations*, Durham, NC, Duke University Press, 1998.
29. Dinius, O. J. and Vergara, Á. (eds.) *Company Towns in the Americas: Landscape, Power, and Working-Class Communities*, Athens, University of Georgia Press, 2011.
30. French, J. D. and James, D. (eds.) *The Gendered Worlds of Latin American Women Workers: From Household and Factory to the Union Hall and Ballot Box*, Durham, NC, Duke University Press, 1997.
31. Rosemblatt, K. A. *Gendered Compromises: Political Cultures & the State in Chile, 1920–1950*, Chapel Hill, University of North Carolina Press, 2000.
32. French and James, *Gendered Worlds*.
33. Grandin, G. *Fordlandia: The Rise and Fall of Henry Ford's Forgotten Jungle City*, New York, Henry Holt and Company, 2010.
34. Lobato, M. "Women Workers in the 'Cathedrals of Corned Beef': Structure and Subjectivity in the Argentine Meatpacking Industry," in French, J. and James, D. (eds.) *Gendered Worlds*, 54–71.
35. Fernandez Kelly, M. P. "Making Sense of Gender in the World Economy: Focus on Latin America," *Organization* 1, 2 (1994), 249–75.
36. Acker, J. "Hierarchies, Jobs, Bodies: A Theory of Gendered Organizations," *Gender & Society* 4, 2 (1990), 139–58.
37. "Women on Boards and Beyond: 2023," accessed September 11, 2024. www.msci.com/research-and-insights/women-on-boards-and-beyond-2023.
38. Ginalski, S., Salvaj, E., Pak, S., and Taksa, L. "Women in Corporate Networks: An Introduction," *Business History*, 66, 8 (2024), 2050–2071.
39. Wright, C. E. F. "Good Wives and Corporate Leaders: Duality in Women's Access to Australia's Top Company Boards, 1910–2018," *Business History*, 66, 8 (2024), 2072–2094.

40. Jones, G. and Grandjean, E. "Coco Chanel: From Fashion Icon to Nazi Agent," *Harvard Business School Case* No. 318–139, revised October 6, 2023.
41. Weisman, K. "A Round of Applause as Chanel Sa Confirms Montenay as New CEO: Montenay's Step Up at Chanel Sa Praised," *WWD* 173, June 27, 1997. https://login.lp.hscl.ufl.edu/login?url=https://www.proquest.com/trade-journals/round-applause-as-chanel-sa-confirms-montenay-new/docview/1445728469/se-2.
42. Fine, J. B. "Chiquet in Charge: Chanel's New President Maureen Chiquet Has a Solid Vision of Where the Company Should Go – and a Lot Riding on Her Ability to Get It There," *WWD Beautybiz*, 190 (53), September 1, 2005. https://login.lp.hscl.ufl.edu/login?url=https://www.proquest.com/trade-journals/chiquet-charge/docview/231180476/se-2.
43. Smith, B. G. and Robinson, N. (eds.) *The Routledge Global History of Feminism*, New York, Routledge, 2022.
44. Scarpellini, E. "Transnational Beauty: Avon International and the Case of Italy," *Journal of Modern Italian Studies*, 28, 1 (2023), 113–142.
45. Manko, K. *Ding Dong! Avon Calling! The Women and Men of Avon Products, Incorporated*, Oxford, Oxford University Press, 2021.
46. Moura, S. "Try It at Home: Avon and Gender in Brazil, 1958–1975," *Business History*, 57, 6 (2015), 800–821.
47. Hopkins, B. E. "Western Cosmetics in the Gendered Development of Consumer Culture in China," *Feminist Economics*, 13, 3–4 (2007), 287–306.
48. Western Cosmetics. "Yue-Sai Kan 靳羽西," n.d. Yue-Sai Kan, accessed September 2, 2024. www.yuesaikan.com.
49. Tumbe, C. "Women Directors in Corporate India, c. 1920–2019," *Business History*, 66, 8 (2024), 2133–2136.
50. "Historia de Carmina Shoemaker," accessed September 3, 2024. www.carminashoemaker.com/historia.
51. Frenkel, M. "Gendering the MNC," in Dörrenbächer, C. and Geppert, M (eds.) *Multinational Corporations and Organization Theory: Post Millennium Perspectives*, Leeds, Emerald, 2017, 357–388.
52. Halrynjo, S. and Teigen, M. "Gender Quotas for Corporate Boards: Do They Lead to More Women in Senior Executive Management?" *Gender in Management: An International Journal*, 39, 6, 2024, 761–777.
53. Misa, T. J. *Gender Codes: Why Women Are Leaving Computing*, Hoboken, NJ: John Wiley & Sons, 2011.
54. Tang, H. and Zhang, Y. "Do Multinationals Transfer Culture? Evidence on Female Employment in China," *Journal of International Economics*, 133, (2021), 103518, https://doi.org/10.1016/j.jinteco.2021.103518.
55. Pudelko, M. and Tenzer, H. "From Professional Aspirations to Identity Confirmation and Transformation: The Case of Japanese Career Women

Working for Foreign Subsidiaries in Japan," *Human Resource Management Journal*, 34, 3 (2024), 599–626.
56. Horak, S. and Suseno, Y. "Informal Networks, Informal Institutions, and Social Exclusion in the Workplace: Insights from Subsidiaries of Multinational Corporations in Korea," *Journal of Business Ethics* 186, (2023), 633–655.
57. Jones, *Renewing Unilever*, 226–227.
58. Lluch, A. and Salvaj, E. "Women May Be Climbing on Board, but Not in First Class: A Long-Term Study of the Factors Affecting Women's Board Participation in Argentina and Chile (1923–2010)," *Business History*, 66, 8, (2024), 2095–2122.
59. Røstvik, "Mother Nature as Brand Strategy."
60. "Nestle to Pay Ex Manager $2.2 Million over Bullying Case, Tages-Anzeiger Reports," February 11, 2023, accessed January 15, 2025, www.reuters.com/markets/europe/nestle-pay-ex-manager-22-mln-over-bullying-case-tages-anzeiger-2023-02-11.
61. Newburry, W., Rašković, M., Colakoglu, S. S., Gonzalez-Perez, M. A., and Minbaeva, D. "Diversity, Equity and Inclusion in International Business: Dimensions and Challenges," *AIB Insights* 22, 3 (2022), https://doi.org/10.46697/001c.36582.

Further Reading

De la Cruz-Fernández, P. *Gendered Capitalism: Sewing Machines and Multinational Business in Spain and Mexico, 1850–1940*, London, Routledge, 2021.

Dean, H., Perriton, L., Taylor, S., and Yeager, M. "Margins and Centres: Gender and Feminism in Business History," *Business History*, 6, 1, (2023), 1–13.

Hicks, M. *Programmed Inequality: How Britain Discarded Women Technologists and Lost Its Edge in Computing*, Cambridge, MA, MIT Press, 2017.

Jones, G. *Beauty Imagined: A History of the Global Beauty Industry*, Oxford, Oxford University Press, 2010.

Santiago, M. I. *The Ecology of Oil: Environment, Labor, and the Mexican Revolution, 1900–1938*, New York, Cambridge University Press, 2006.

11

Multinationals and Corruption

11.1 The Challenges of Corruption

Corruption in business has serious negative consequences for societies. It diminishes confidence and trust and so discourages investment. It promotes inefficient spending and the waste of resources. Among the most negative consequences, especially in developing countries, is poor-quality building construction. Corruption distorts economic activities by, for example, helping one sector of the business community grow at the expense of others. Socially, corruption encourages inequality as the well connected can exploit the system. It facilitates organized crime. Typically, corruption weakens rather than strengthens democracy. Yet some scholars have suggested corruption can bring positive benefits through enhancing efficiencies in complex bureaucracies and enhancing knowledge spillovers.[1] In a study of corruption and development in South Korea and the Philippines, political scientist David Kang argued that if there was a balance of power between a small set of business and government elites, as in South Korea, bribery and corruption can reduce transaction costs and so promote economic growth.[2]

Business historians have shown that the phenomenon of corruption was seen in business long before multinational enterprises (MNEs) appeared. Eighteenth-century Britain – the home of the Industrial Revolution – was full of fraudsters and financial scandals like the South Sea Bubble.[3] The officials of Britain's East India Company in India in the eighteenth and early nineteenth centuries were notoriously corrupt.[4] The constitution of the United States made bribery one of the two explicit crimes that could merit impeachment.[5] Corruption and fraud remained a prominent feature of US business even as the United States became the world's largest and richest economy.[6]

Yet it is not as straightforward as it seems to identify corruption. The nongovernmental organization (NGO) Transparency International's working definition is "the abuse of *entrusted* power for private gain," which assumes the initial presence and later erosion of social trust in entities with power.[7] A more focused definition is the widely cited conception by political scientist Susan Rose-Ackerman of corruption as "the misuse of public power for private gain."[8] However, the sharp distinction between the public and the private, which this definition assumes, does not apply to many countries in the developing world, which have been described as "patrimonial" states.[9] An alternative to focusing on power as such is the concept of "corrupt entrepreneurship," which has seen entrepreneurs both creating and exploiting institutional voids that they profit from, as well as employing cultural resources to legitimize themselves.[10]

Another complicating factor is that corruption can take many forms: Bribery, embezzlement, and nepotism are all forms of corruption. There is a particularly important distinction between "grand" corruption – which occurs at the highest levels of power – and petty corruption – which involves lower-level functionaries and is sometimes termed "facilitating" payments as it involves speeding up, simplifying, or reducing the costs of routine procedures.[11] This chapter focusses on grand corruption, primarily because there is no obvious way of establishing whether and how frequently low-level employees of MNEs engaged in petty corruption. This does not mean that petty corruption was not of major consequence for societies. As economist Antonio Argandoña argues, facilitating payments is "a cancer that has harmful consequences."[12] They especially harm small businesses, hamper economic development, and are likely to grow in scale over time.

A greater complication still is the culturally embedded nature of corruption. What is regarded as corruption in one country and time might not be regarded as corruption in another country and time. In the contemporary United States, the extensive lobbying of government by business and donations to politicians and political action committees might be regarded as forms of corruption but are never treated as such. More generally, the dividing line between a bribe and normal business expenses or appreciation gifts is not sharp.[13] It has been suggested that in Confucius-influenced cultures such as China, Japan, and South Korea there is a strong sense of hierarchy and duty. This does not mean that corruption is accepted, but "gifts" are often given to others as a demonstration of respect.[14]

This chapter proceeds in the following fashion. Section 11.2 offers a historical survey of corrupt strategies by MNEs. Section 11.3 provides a case study of MNEs and corruption in Africa. This is chosen because the egregious impact of MNEs on countries with weak governance structures is particularly apparent. Section 11.4 looks at attempts to control corruption both by the MNEs themselves and through international law and organizations. Section 11.5 concludes.

11.2 MNEs and Corruption over Time

A consistent picture of MNE engagement in corruption is (by definition) hard to ascertain. It is silent unless exposed in a legal case, by an investigative journalist, or by a business historian with access to corporate archives. An aggregate statement of how much MNEs have engaged in corruption over time is impossible, therefore. Instead, this chapter will rely heavily on studies of known cases of corporate corruption. The sample is as a result idiosyncratic in that it consists of firms whose corrupt strategies have been exposed. There is no way of knowing the cases of "successful" corrupters who have never been caught.

A working assumption is that corruption flourished especially, although certainly not entirely, in contexts where there were weak institutional environments.[15] The international business literature has debated whether MNEs are passive takers or active agents of corruption in such environments, but with most of the literature focused on how MNEs based in "clean" Western countries responded when investing in allegedly more corrupt developing markets.[16] A business history and firm-level perspective allows a clearer view of the role of MNEs as active agents.

As Chapter 1 shows, MNE investment was heavily concentrated in the nonaffluent world before World War II, and mainly engaged in commodities and related services, so it is likely that historically forms of corruption were quite widespread. The securing of concessions from autocratic and corrupt governments in the non-Western world often involved bribery before World War II. As Chapter 6 notes, the actions of US-based United Fruit Company in Central America were classic in this regard. As business historians Ishva Minefee and Marcelo Bucheli have observed, often the actions of United Fruit – and other companies such as Standard Oil of New Jersey – outside the United States were not seen in the contemporary United States as corrupt.[17] Subsequently, during the Cold War, the United States government turned a "blind eye" to companies bribing the leaders of countries identified as pro-Western, whether in Central America, Indonesia, or the Congo.[18]

A well-documented corruption scandal occurred in Meiji Japan involving the German electrical goods MNE Siemens. In 1914 a former employee of Siemens' Tokyo office was found guilty by a German court of having stolen company documents and attempted extortion. Evidence collected during the trial revealed that Siemens (as well as its British competitor Vickers) paid large bribes to high-ranking naval officers to secure orders.[19] The Japanese navy was one of the largest spending departments, so it was likely that the sums involved were substantial. The practice of naval officers accepting "commissions" dated back to at least the 1890s, and the legal system was ambiguous about their legitimacy. Although heavy sentences were passed on Mitsui employees involved in handling illicit payments, they were overturned by the appeal court.[20]

The defense industry, alongside public works and construction, saw extensive use of bribery by MNEs. This was because the industry was primarily based on large contracts signed with governments, and so bribing a key politician or bureaucrat could deliver lucrative returns. During the interwar years and subsequently Vickers and its British competitor Armstrongs (which merged in 1927) cultivated relations with domestic and international elites. The strategy of using bribes in Turkey, Venezuela, and elsewhere was sanctioned by the British government.[21]

After World War II there were more spectacular instances of corruption in the armaments industry. The US aerospace MNE Lockheed made extensive use of bribery to negotiate the sale of aircraft in Japan,

Germany, and the Netherlands between the 1950s and the 1970s. In the context of the Cold War and a booming demand for fighter jets, Lockheed invested a huge amount of money in a new jet, the F-104 or Starfighter, which was launched in 1954. The plane had major drawbacks, including that complex electronics were necessary to keep the aircraft stable, and, since pressurizing equipment was removed to save on weight, pilots had to wear uncomfortable space suits. When the US Air Force bought only a few planes, Lockheed turned to international markets, but despite some redesign the plane still had limited attractions to foreign militaries. Lockheed's executives resorted to irregular sales methods.

In countries around the world, Lockheed's strategy was to identify intermediaries with connections to the highest reaches of governments who could sway purchase decisions, for a price, and with access to a pool of funds that could not be tracked too closely. In the Netherlands, Lockheed acquired the services of Prince Bernhardt, who had married into the Dutch royal family and who accepted payments through a variety of intermediaries. In Indonesia, Lockheed made generous contributions to a "Widows and Orphans Fund" with close ties to senior figures in the Indonesian air force. In Saudi Arabia, Lockheed paid bribes to the Saudi arms dealer Adnan Khashoggi, who the company recruited when he was only twenty-six years old in 1964, before he made a fortune serving as a middleman between the Saudi royal family and Western companies.[22] In the end, Lockheed sold more than two thousand Starfighters overseas; it managed to sell fewer than three hundred to the US Air Force.[23]

In Japan, Lockheed spent US $10 million on bribes by 1976 through its Tokyo representatives and a large trading company, the Marubeni Corporation. The company worked with a secret agent named Yoshio Kodama, a hard-line ultra-right nationalist and underworld figure who had been imprisoned by the Americans for war crimes, but who emerged in the 1950s and 1960s as a close associate of several prime ministers.[24]

Although the use of bribery and corruption by MNEs in the international arms industry attracted the greatest headlines, the practice was evident in different industries. During the 1950s and 1960s, for example, the competing German sportswear firms Adidas and Puma engaged in widespread bribery aimed at getting their sports shoes on the feet of athletes. The context was the amateur rules of all the world's sports associations that prohibited direct commercial sponsorship. During the 1970s and 1980s Horst Dassler, the leading member of the Dassler family that owned Adidas, also diversified into sports sponsorship on his account, engaging in bribery and corruption to capture the leaderships of sports associations such as the Fédération Internationale de Football Association and eventually the International Olympic Committee and open them to sports sponsorship. Dassler operated the business first through a company registered in Monte Carlo, Société Monégasque de Promotion Internationale and subsequently though a joint venture called International Sport and Leisure (ISL) with Dentsu, Japan's largest advertising firm, based in Lucerne, Switzerland. Bribery was legal in Switzerland in this period. When the ISL collapsed into bankruptcy in 2001, long after Dassler's death, it was discovered that the company had paid out US $120 million in bribes to leading sports officials to secure marketing and television rights contracts.[25]

Dassler's use of Monte Carlo and Switzerland was part of a much wider trend that facilitated corporate corruption. The offshore financial centers in the Caribbean and elsewhere – such as Hong Kong, which provided the basis for the extensive "roundtripping of Chinese FDI" grew exponentially from the 1980s. They were not only tax havens, but also opaque and secretive. They provided means for MNEs to engage in corruption with no public scrutiny. This was the case of US energy trader Enron, which went bankrupt in 2011 following major accounting fraud. As several studies have shown, the corporate culture grew progressively more corrupt over the course of the 1990s.[26] Enron's fraudulent accounts were made possible by extensive use of international financial centers. The company used phony "prepay" transactions to hide US $8 billion in debt, each transaction of which was knowingly facilitated by a major financial institution. JPMorgan Chase and Citigroup were among the banks that used offshore shell companies they secretly controlled to provide billions of dollars in cash loans to Enron while allowing Enron to characterize the loans on its books as income from trading deals it had secured with those offshore entities.[27]

Many of the MNE corruption scandals in this period involved the use of offshore financial centers. In 2010, for example, Britain's BAE Systems, a defense contractor, was fined US $400 million for conspiring to defraud the United States by misrepresenting its enforcement of the Foreign Corrupt Practices Act. According to court documents, BAE made a series of substantial payments to shell companies and third-party intermediaries that were not subjected to the degree of scrutiny the company told the US government they would face. BAE admitted that it regularly retained "marketing advisors" to assist in securing sales of defense items without scrutinizing those relationships. In fact, BAE took steps to conceal its relationships with some of these advisors and its undisclosed payments to them. After 2001, BAE contracted with and paid advisors through various offshore shell companies beneficially owned by BAE. BAE also encouraged certain advisors to establish their own offshore shell companies to receive payments from BAE while disguising the origins and recipients of these payments.

In 2001 BAE established a company in the British Virgin Islands (BVI) to conceal its marketing advisor relationships, including who the advisor was and how much it was paid, and to assist advisors in avoiding tax liability for payments from BAE. It subsequently used the BVI entity to make payments totaling more than £135 million after 2001, knowing that there was a high probability that part of the payments would be used to ensure that BAE was favored in foreign government decisions regarding the purchase of defense articles. The US court also learned that BAE provided substantial bribes to an official in the Kingdom of Saudi Arabia (KSA) who could influence arms purchases. In 2001/2002, BAE transferred more than £10 million to a bank account in Switzerland controlled by an intermediary, aware that there was a high probability that the intermediary would transfer part of these payments to the same KSA official.[28]

As the BAE example demonstrates, despite the introduction of much stricter anticorruption policies within MNEs as well as the growth of international regulation over the past two decades (see Section 11.4), a striking number of examples of major corruption by leading MNEs have surfaced. Between 1998 and 2001 managers at the US and British subsidiaries of Swiss-based ABB paid bribes to officials in Nigeria, Angola, and Kazakhstan. In 2006 Statoil, a Norwegian oil and gas company, entered a consulting services contract with an offshore company based in Britain whose purpose was to channel funds to a top Iranian official in the oil and gas industry. Statoil was to pay more than

US $15 million in bribes over an eleven-year period. The arrangement helped Statoil secure several contracts in Iran.[29] In 2005 it was discovered that US retailer Walmart had spent US $24 million in bribes to facilitate the construction of Walmart stores in Mexico. In 2010 the German automobile manufacturer Daimler was fined US $185 million in criminal and civil penalties in the United States for engaging in widespread bribery in its subsidiaries. According to court documents, Daimler made hundreds of improper payments worth tens of millions of dollars to foreign officials in at least twenty-two countries – including China, Croatia, Egypt, Greece, Hungary, Indonesia, Iraq, Ivory Coast, Latvia, Nigeria, Russia, Serbia, Montenegro, Thailand, Turkey, Turkmenistan, Uzbekistan, Vietnam, and others – to assist in securing contracts with government customers for the purchase of Daimler vehicles.[30] In 2013 it was revealed that the Chinese affiliate of the British-based pharmaceutical company GlaxoSmithKline (GSK) had engaged in widespread bribery. The scandal unfolded after a clandestine sex tape of GSK's China chief executive was circulated. In 2014 GSK was fined £297million by a Chinese court for bribing officials with cash, as well as offering gifts, including prostitutes, to doctors and other officials to boost sales of its products. In 2016 the firm was also fined US $20 million by the US Securities and Exchange Commission for its bribing strategy in China.[31]

French companies were also regularly indicted for bribery and corruption. In 2010 the telecommunications company Alcatel-Lucent agreed to pay Costa Rica US $10 million in reparations for the social damage caused by its payment of US $2.5 million in bribes to provide cell phone service to the country. In 2013 French oil MNE Total agreed to pay US $398 million to settle a US criminal and civil allegation that it had paid bribes between 1995 and 2004 to win oil and gas contracts in Iran. In 2018 French engineering company Alstom was fined £6.5 million by a British court after it was established that the British affiliate bribed Lithuanian politicians and officials at a Lithuanian power plant. This came after a decade of other corruption scandals. In 2015 Alstom was sentenced to a US $772 million fine in the United States for violating the Foreign Corrupt Practices Act after investigators found it had paid at least US $75million of bribes to secure contracts worth billions of dollars. Alstom attempted to conceal the scheme by routing bribes through middlemen with code names such as "Mr. Geneva."³²

What is striking in many of these cases is that corruption was not driven by aberrant managers or ethically depraved chief executives, but was the product of system-wide features of corporate cultures. In 2008 Siemens (again) was revealed to be engaged in widespread and systematic foreign bribery in at least ten countries between 2001 and 2007. The US Securities and Exchange Commission fined the company US $1.6 billion having established that between 2001 and 2007 dubious payments had been made in 5,468 cases, including 4,283 incidents of corruption. Offenses before 2001 were not investigated. The company's entire management board was replaced.

Siemens's modus operandi was, as in many cases, to bribe through intermediaries. Bribes for two Italian officials were channeled through an intermediary based in Dubai. Intermediaries in Cyprus and Dubai were used to bribe Venezuelan officials. Officials in Israel, mainland China, and Vietnam were bribed using Hong Kong-based consultants. In contrast, in relation to a Venezuelan metro project, Siemens used a business consultant who had advised former Venezuelan presidents and so was known to be an established insider. The bribes reached intermediaries through different means. The bribes for the two Italian officials, for example, were drawn from secret funds held in Liechtenstein. Bribes for Vietnam officials were sent from the United States to a Singapore account controlled by the Hong Kong-based consultant.³³

In the case of Siemens, the company gave business historian Hartmut Berghoff access to its archives, and so a clearer picture can be seen of how corruption took hold of the company. Berghoff reveals a multilayered picture. He established that nearly three-fifths of the bribes originated with the telecommunications division of the company, which faced intense competitive pressures. The division responded by investing in several countries, especially Nigeria and Greece, whose business cultures were notoriously corrupt. However Siemens's power generation division was the second largest briber, and it became Siemens most profitable division after a boom for gas turbines took place after 1999. Siemens's order book was both full and profitable, yet the managers resumed to bribing, among others, managers of Italy's semipublic energy company ENEL and the state-owned Israeli energy company IEC.

Berghoff identifies more systematic factors. First was a shift in the geography of the firm's business. In 1980 most of Siemens's sales were in industrialized countries, but thereafter its business shifted toward countries with corruption issues. By 1997 thirty of the thirty-five most corrupt countries accounted for nearly two-fifths of total Siemens sales. Berghoff also points to the corporate culture of Siemens, which had many long-serving managers intensely loyal to each other and to the company. Many of them believed, Berghoff notes, that "facilitating bribery was in the best interest of the firm." It was assumed that competing firms paid bribes and giving up the practice would result in falling sales.[34]

There are clear parallels between the case of Siemens and the bribery scandal of the Dutch-registered aviation MNE Airbus. In 2020 Airbus agreed to pay a record US $4 billion to the governments in the United States, France, and Britain in fines to settle foreign bribery charges accrued between 2008 and 2015. The case documented the use of large bribes to win contracts in Ghana, Sri Lanka, Malaysia, Taiwan, and Indonesia. For example, Airbus offered US $16.84 million to the wife of an executive of Sri Lankan Airlines to purchase ten aircraft and to lease an additional four planes. Airbus operated though BPs or agents who provided services as intermediaries between the company and its potential buyers. Parts of the organization concerned with international sales developed their bribery strategy through appointing BPs who were close associates of Airbus customers. The intermediaries received indirect bribe payments through commissions and sometimes directly in cash. To avoid Airbus's compliance structures, the identity of some of the BPs was concealed, and documentation was created to disguise illicit payments. These practices became embedded in the corporate culture. Like Siemens, unethical behavior was rationalized and normalized within the MNE.[35]

It would be a mistake to conclude this section with the impression that MNE bribery has been confined to gold-plated Western MNEs. One of the greatest bribery scandals of the first two decades of the twenty-first century concerned Brazilian MNE construction firm Odebrecht. The firm admitted to US prosecutors that it paid US

$800 million in bribes throughout Latin America to win infrastructure contracts. The scheme led to the downfall of several presidents, including Dilma Rousseff in Brazil. In 2016 Odebrecht settled with legal authorities in the United States, Brazil, and Switzerland for US $4.5 billion.[36] As the following section will discuss further, recent decades have also seen examples of corruption in Africa and elsewhere by Chinese MNEs.

11.3 MNEs and Corruption in Africa

To pursue the question whether MNEs are passive takers or active agents of corruption, it is worthwhile to examine the corrupt practices of MNEs in Africa. Today Transparency International ranks Sub-Saharan Africa as the worst region for corruption. South Sudan, Somalia, Equatorial Guinea, and the Democratic Republic of Congo are among the most corrupt countries in the world.[37]

In the era of European colonization foreign MNEs might be seen as exploitative rather than corrupt. This is most vividly seen in Congo, under the personal rule of King Leopold II of Belgium after 1885, and a Belgian colony between 1908 and 1960. The Union Minière du Haut-Katanga, created in 1906 to exploit Congo's mineral resources, was highly exploitative, forcing up to a quarter of a million men into its service in its first thirty years. Britain's Lever Brothers secured a huge concession and created Huileries du Congo Belge, where forced laborers were whipped with twisted hippo hides and their wives and children kidnapped if they refused to work.[38] These foreign MNEs did not need to bribe and corrupt government officials because they were fully supported by colonial administrations.

This situation changed as African states became independent. Many governments were interventionist and began insisting that foreign MNEs sold some of their equity to local shareholders. Restrictions on the use of expatriates spread. Exchange controls were introduced. The response of many Western MNEs was to divest from their African subsidiaries. The companies that sought to stay began to develop strategies to manage the new situation.

This was the case of Dutch MNE Heineken. After independence, Heineken developed an accounting method for its African affiliates using an intermediary company that created two types of profit: One was officially declared to the local governments, while the largest part was hidden and transferred to an affiliate in Switzerland. Heineken persisted in Africa and sometimes had very profitable businesses, but as investigative journalist Olivier Van Breemen observes in his history of the company in Africa, "fraud and other controversial practices have played a significant role in that survival strategy." Heineken's biggest market was Nigeria, where Van Breemen found "senior managers, both Dutch and Nigerian, indulging in all kinds of controversial deals and shady business practices in order to enrich themselves." The Nigerian affiliate was described as "rotten to the core, with fraud and corruption happening at every level." Overall, this author concludes, "Heineken appears not to have adapted its business practices to the culture of fraud, corruption and self-interest – it appears to have an active hand in creating it."[39]

Various African countries also featured prominently in a corruption scandal involving British Leyland, Britain's largest motor vehicle manufacturer in the 1970s, which became partly state owned in 1975. In May 1977 the British newspaper *Daily Mail* published a story that the company was engaged in bribery in Nigeria and elsewhere to secure orders for its vehicles. A Nigerian government investigation caused anguish in the British government, which sought to suppress the story. The British high commissioner in Lagos observed "that firms competing in the Nigerian market have to follow the local rules or lose out. This is recognized throughout British business. It would be all the more damaging if we ourselves take action putting British commercial interests at risk."[40] The British foreign secretary recommended against any investigation as the situation in "area is very sensitive and the dangers of raising any further doubts or suspicions are considerable."[41]

The Nigeria story turned out to be the tip of the iceberg. The British government's complicity was disguised after it was discovered that *Daily Mail*'s story was based in part on forged letters from a former executive anxious to monetize his information. However, decades afterwards it was discovered in government archives that the British government at the highest level knew about and connived in the global use of bribery by British Leyland. At a meeting of government ministers after the *Daily Mail* story was published, the chancellor of the Exchequer noted that there "was no doubt that bribery had been going on for years on a large scale in the Middle East and Africa and that organizations responsible to government (including defense sales and nationalized industries) had been involved." Another minister informed the meeting that 10 percent of Britain's trade "probably involved some type of practices which we would normally consider improper in this country." Prime Minister James Callaghan decided to keep the information undisclosed because "given the heavy reliance of the British economy on exports, it might be more difficult for us to accept as high standards in this matter as, for instance, the Americans." Subsequently a private report produced for British government ministers revealed that British Leyland used a "slush fund," managed in Lausanne, which made payoffs around the world totaling £4.2 million a year. Most of the payments were made to sell Land Rovers and buses to governments in Iran, Iraq, and other Middle Eastern countries, and for bribery in Nigeria. The firm also sold a fleet of overpriced military Land Rovers to the national guard in Saudi Arabia for approximately £5 million, of which £700,000 was secretly passed as a 15 percent "commission" via Switzerland to an account at Chase Manhattan Bank, belonging to a Mr. N. Fustic, the brother-in-law of the commander of the national guard, Prince Abdullah bin Abdul Aziz, the future king.[42]

The use of bribery by Heineken and British Leyland paled in comparison with MNEs involved in commerce and commodities. In the late 1950s British officials had "a strong suspicion of corrupt dealings" undertaken by the large trading house A. G. Leventis, owned by Greek Cypriot brothers with head offices in Manchester and Paris, and a large business in West Africa. The firm was believed to be closely associated with prominent Nigerian politicians and political parties.[43]

A prominent example was the British trading company Lonrho, which flourished in postcolonial Africa. Although founded in 1909, until 1961 its activities were primarily concentrated in mining, ranching, and real estate in the British colony of southern Rhodesia (now Zimbabwe). Subsequently, under the colorful leadership (and part ownership) of Roland W. ("Tiny") Rowland, the company diversified across central, east, and south Africa, often acquiring existing assets. Rowland's relationships with influential African leaders were at the center of its business strategy. A British Foreign Office report in 1969 observed that the company had "employed bribery" in Malawi, Zambia, Zaire, Ghana, and Sierra Leone.[44]

One of the most well-documented cases of corruption in commodities concerned Equatorial Guinea, where significant quantities of oil were discovered in the 1990s. In 2004 the US Senate Permanent Subcommittee on Investigations released a report on corruption in the country involving the use of its oil revenues. The investigation established that Riggs Bank, a long-established US bank based in Washington, DC, helped government leaders in Equatorial Guinea siphon oil revenues to accounts set up for them in DC. Between 1995 and 2004, Riggs oversaw at least sixty accounts containing up to US $700 million. Some were government accounts, and others were private accounts of President Teodoro Obiang Nguema, other government officials, and their families. In 1999 Riggs helped the president establish Otong, SA, an offshore corporation incorporated in the Bahamas. In 2001 Riggs helped establish Awake Limited, another offshore corporation in the Bahamas owned by two of the president's sons. Riggs assisted the funneling of millions of dollars in the government accounts to such offshore tax shelters. Riggs was fined US $25 million for failing to report suspicious transactions made to the Equatorial Guinea accounts.[45]

The subcommittee's report also established that leading US oil companies such as Exxon Mobil and Amerada Hess, which had driven the county's growth to be the third largest oil producer in Africa, made payments into the personal accounts of Equatorial Guinea officials that were used for land purchases, office leases, and the education of the children of the country's leaders. The subcommittee was able to document payments of US $4 million made by oil companies to support more than one hundred Equatorial Guinea students studying internationally, most of whom were the children or relatives of powerful officials.[46]

As in the case of Heineken, Riggs and the oil MNEs encountered a well-established culture of bribery and corruption in Equatorial Guinea. The government, economy, and legal system of the country were controlled by President Nguema Mbasogo and a small number of his close associates, mostly drawn from the Esangui clan or the province of Mongomo. They had established a system to siphon off the wealth of the country. The group first used the machinery of state in the early 1980s to expropriate – without compensation – the rich agricultural farmland on Bioko Island, mostly owned by Spaniards and Portuguese, which was redistributed to the Nguema/Mongomo group. What Riggs Bank and the oil companies did in the 1990s was to facilitate rather than create the position of the corrupt elite and enable it to flourish on a large scale by providing channels for illicit payments from the oil industry to be deposited in the United States and offshore financial centers. The result was a country that by 2010 had a high per capita income and 60 percent of its population living in dire poverty and that regularly came near the top of Transparency International's ranking of corrupt countries.[47]

The MNE that especially specialized in bribery and corruption across Africa (and elsewhere) was Switzerland-based Marc Rich & Company (renamed Glencore in 1994), one of the world's largest commodity traders. Spun out of the US-based commodity trader Phillip Brothers in 1974, the company grew exponentially during the 1970s as the control of oil markets by Western oil companies was lost and replaced by spot market trading. The owners, primarily Marc Rich and Pinky Green, used their contracts in Iran to sell oil to Israel, South Africa, and other countries that faced political problems accessing oil. The company benefited from a low tax regime in Canton Zug and used its Swiss registration to deal with countries who had United Nations (UN) sanctions such as South Africa, as Switzerland was not a member of the UN until 2002. Bribery and corruption were well-documented features of its business culture.[48] "The bribes were paid," Rich told his biographer, "in order to be able to do business at the same price as other people were willing to do the business. It's not a price which is disadvantageous for the government involved in the selling or buying country."[49]

After Marc Rich left the company in 1994, Glencore continued to engage in widespread bribery, especially but not only in its oil division. In 2022 it pleaded guilty to violating the Foreign Corrupt Practices Act and agreed to pay a US $1.1 billion fine to the United States government. Glencore admitted to a decade-long scheme to make and conceal corrupt payments and bribes through intermediaries for the benefit of foreign officials in multiple countries. The principal countries concerned were Nigeria, Cameroon, Ivory Coast, Equatorial Guinea, and the Democratic Republic of Congo, as well as Brazil and Venezuela.

Glencore and its subsidiaries admitted to making approximately US $79.6 million in payments between approximately 2007 and 2018 to intermediary companies to secure improper advantages to obtain and retain business with state-owned and state-controlled entities in Nigeria, Cameroon, Ivory Coast, and Equatorial Guinea. Glencore concealed the bribe payments by entering sham consulting agreements, paying inflated invoices, and using intermediary companies to make corrupt payments to foreign officials. For example, in Nigeria, Glencore entered into multiple agreements to purchase crude oil and refined petroleum products from Nigeria's state-owned and state-controlled oil company. Glencore and its subsidiaries engaged two intermediaries to pursue business opportunities and other improper business advantages, including the award of crude oil contracts, while knowing that the intermediaries would make bribe payments to Nigerian government officials to obtain such business. In Nigeria alone, Glencore and its subsidiaries paid more than US $52 million to the intermediaries, intending that those funds be used, at least in part, to pay bribes to Nigerian officials.[50]

In 2022 Glencore pleaded guilty and was fined US $335 million by the British government for bribing government official for access to oil cargoes in Africa. Britain's Serious Fraud Office found that Glencore had paid bribes worth US $29 million to secure access to oil in Cameroon, Equatorial Guinea, Ivory Coast, Nigeria, and South Sudan. The presiding judge noted that Glencore developed a culture "in which bribery was accepted as a part of the West Africa's desk's way of doing business. The corruption is of extended duration. It was endemic amongst traders on that particular desk."[51] In 2023 nearly two hundred of the world's biggest asset managers sued Glencore in London's High Court for failing to disclose in its 2011 prospectus for its listing on the London Stock Exchange and its 2013 prospectus for its merger with Xstrata that bribery and corruption were prevalent in its subsidiaries.[52]

Glencore's business in the Democratic Republic of Congo came under special scrutiny. After 2007 it worked with Israeli entrepreneur Dan Gertler to acquire extensive mining rights. Gertler arrived in the Congo in 1997 as a rough diamond dealer and became strongly associated with President Joseph Kabila. He was cited in a 2001 UN investigation for giving the president US $20 million to buy weapons to equip his army against rebel groups in exchange for a monopoly on the country's diamonds. He subsequently became a key figure in granting mining rights in the country, A US government estimate was that the lost revenues to Congo associated with Gertler's deals from 2010 to 2012 alone were about US $1.36 billion, or approximately half the nation's entire healthcare budget during that period. The Paradise Papers, a leaked cache of documents from secretive offshore law firms, documented how Glencore became associated with Gertler. Glencore loaned Gertler US $45 million in 2009 to secure control of the Toronto-listed Katanga copper mine in the southeast of the country. Gertler, whose previous diamond monopoly in Congo was described by the UN as a "disaster" for the country, then represented Glencore as the key negotiator with Congolese authorities. The relationship ended in 2017 and in that year the US government placed Gertler on its sanctions list, accusing him of undertaking more than US $1 billion worth of corrupt mining and oil deals in the Congo, saying they undermined economic growth and the rule of law in the country.[53]

As Chapter 3 shows, the past two decades have seen fast growth of Chinese MNE activity in Africa. In 2020 alone, it is estimated that Chinese companies were responsible for 31 percent of infrastructure projects on the African continent. Although there is little solid scholarship on the strategies of these MNEs, there is anecdotal evidence that they have followed in the footsteps of their Western counterparts. According to a report by consulting firm McKinsey in 2017, 60 percent to 87 percent of Chinese firms they had sampled said they had paid a "tip" or bribe to obtain a license in connection with business transactions in Africa.[54] The use of bribery by Chinese MNEs in Africa and other regions has been well documented.[55] As latecomers to MNE activity in Africa and in other parts of the world, Chinese companies learned to emulate the tactics of their Western antecedents.

The case of Africa provides suggestive evidence concerning whether MNEs respond to corruption as the cost of doing business or exacerbate it. The evidence, which remains fragmentary and dependent on individual case studies and government inquiries about scandals, supports the later interpretation. Heineken, Riggs Bank, Exxon and Glencore are not a representative sample of the thousands of MNEs that have invested in Africa over the past century, but they were very significant business enterprises, and their engagement in and facilitation of corruption in two of Africa's most corrupt countries – the Democratic Republic of Congo and Equatorial Guinea – is worthy of note.

11.4 Contesting Corruption

Although many large MNEs have extensive company histories, few of them provide details corporate engagement in bribery and corruption, and corporate policies toward them. Geoffrey Jones's history of the consumer goods MNE Unilever does contain some information. Unilever had an extensive business spread over developing as well as rich countries. During the mid 1970s Unilever's board confirmed that it would "never criticize management for any harm which may result to the business" for not engaging in bribery and corruption of public officials. This was a long-standing policy, and the company has never appeared in a major corruption scandal. However, there was a caveat. In some countries small "facilitating" payments were made to secure things like the passage of baggage through customs. While the company banned grand corruption then, it did permit petty corruption, which it defined in 1980 as "small payments made to minor officials to procure or expedite the legitimate performance of their normal functions."[56]

In 1976 the Shell Group formulated its formal Statement of Business Principles, which also banned the taking and accepting of bribes.[57] However, anecdotal evidence suggests that Shell continued to engage in corruption in certain contexts. In 2010 Shell was fined US $30 million by US regulators for employing Panalpina, a Swiss shipping and logistics company, to pay Nigerian officials to speed drilling rigs and other equipment through customs.[58]

During the later twentieth century, and in the wake of the Foreign Corrupt Practices Act in 1976, many other MNEs introduced formal regulations and compliance procedures, but it is less clear how well rules were enforced. Berghoff's study of the Siemens scandals in the 1990s and 2000s is again informative. He writes that during the 1990s managers repeatedly had to sign declarations that they would observe the law, but they were filed away and were "sometimes the object of ridicule." It did not help that in Germany bribes to foreign officials could be deducted from taxes until 1999 and, if paid to people in business, until 2002. After foreign corruption was criminalized in Germany between 1998 and 2002, Siemens paid increased attention to the issue "but only slowly and without any real commitment on the part of senior management." Berghoff reports that an effective compliance system was introduced after the scandal broke and court cases launched in Germany and the United States against the company.[59]

Germany was far from alone in allowing bribes to be deducted from taxes, at least before the 2000s. The practice was widespread in Europe. In Switzerland the practice appears to date back to World War I, when Swiss firms selling weapons to France made the argument that they needed to pay bribes to the French army. The tax authorities allowed the deductions. The practice was confirmed in Swiss courts in the 1920s, and then reaffirmed in an official circular of the Swiss tax administration in 1946.[60]

As legal scholar M. Weisman's careful analysis has shown, the United States' Foreign Corrupt Practices Act of 1977 – the first national regulation concerning global corruption – had extremely limited impact in its first decades. The key problem is that it relied on "corporate self-policing through mandatory reporting with regulatory oversight." The Act had several limitations. The bribery that was prohibited was defined as payments to public officials to "obtain or retain business." In other words, grand corruption was prohibited but not petty corruption. The Act excluded private companies from reporting bribery and left them to self-regulate. When the US parent owned less than 50 percent of the voting power of a foreign affiliate, it was also not required to report. Enron used special purpose entities, which it nominally did not control, to transfer assets off its balance sheet to conceal its liabilities. Between 1978 and 2002 only thirteen cases were initiated under the Act, two of which were dismissed or disposed of without sanctions. In 2025 the Trump administration in the United States suspended enforcing the Foreign Corrupt

Practices Act on the grounds that it would "mean a lot more business for America."[61]

From the mid 1970s the United States sought to secure agreement on illicit payments at the UN, but this was opposed by other industrialized countries as well as developing countries. A special commission of the International Chamber of Commerce drafted a report on the issue in 1977, but without the backing of governments there was no practical outcome. Only in May 1996, at a meeting convened by the Organisation for Economic Co-operation and Development (OECD), did ministers of twenty-six industrialized countries agree to ban the tax deductibility of bribes to foreign public officials.[62] In 1999 the OECD's Anti-Bribery Convention provided that members would prohibit domestic firms from engaging in bribe payments in global markets. However, it did not prohibit political contributions or oblige companies to establish proper reporting standards. There were also UN initiatives, including the Convention Against Corruption and Principle 10 of the UN Global Compact, but compliance was voluntary and there was no global judicial body.[63]

11.5 Conclusion

This chapter has demonstrated that the use of bribery and corruption was a well-established MNE strategy over a long period. There is no means of stating firmly whether the examples of grand corruption shown here were tips of an iceberg or outlandish outliers. Most probably it was nowhere near the norm, but not rare either. After all, a British government minister estimated in 1977 that one-tenth of British foreign trade involved corrupt practices. We know little about the extent of petty corruption, but it is striking that even the ethically proper Unilever permitted it, and that the Foreign Corrupt Practices Act in the United States allowed it. Nor is it possible to say whether MNEs as a category have been more or less likely to be corrupt than purely domestic firms. However, it is noteworthy the MNEs considered here – whether Siemens, Vickers, United Fruit, ABB, Glencore, Walmart, Adidas, Daimler, British Leyland, Riggs Bank, GSK, or Airbus – were giants in their respective industries when they engaged in bribery and corruption.

The industrial distribution of MNE bribery and corruption is especially skewed toward armaments and commodities, although as the examples of Adidas, Walmart, and Heineken show, it could and did take place historically in other industries. The use of bribery and corruption appears to be particularly prevalent in Africa and condoned by the home governments of the MNEs involved. Grand corruption arose especially when business involved large contracts with governments in countries and time periods when societies manifested high levels of corruption. Bribery was fueled by the pervasiveness of corruption in the host economies in which the MNEs operated, but the MNEs were active agents in the use of bribery and facilitating corruption. Corruption was also facilitated by specific features of the international economy, and in particular opaque financial centers. Regarding the mechanics of grand corruption by MNEs, the historical evidence points to the importance of intermediaries, such as Yoshio Kadama and Lockheed and Glencore and Dan Gertler.

Strikingly, although bribery and corruption are often associated in the public mind with rogue individuals, it has historically been more often the product of miscreant corporate cultures. Whether in Siemens, Glencore, or other MNEs, a part at least of the organization systemized corruption, which enabled managers to rationalize it as a source of competitive advantage, especially in countries seen as already corrupt. The prevalence of preexisting corruption, however, was significant, creating a form of path dependence. The corruption that was extensive in Nigeria, Equatorial Guinea, and elsewhere did not originate with MNEs, but the actions of some firms confirmed rather than countered it, putting large sums of money into the system and providing means for corrupt profits to be recycled elsewhere. Bribery and corruption might have reduced transaction costs in the circumstances of South Korea, but it is hard to argue that the use of corruption by MNEs in countries with fragile institutional structures, including in Africa, was anything but unproductive.

Notes

1. Humphry, J. and Schmitz, H. "Trust and Inter-firm Relationships in Developing and Transition Economies," *Journal of Development Studies*, 34,4 (1987), 32–61.

2. Kang, D. C. *Crony Capitalism: Corruption and Development in South Korea and the Philippines*, Cambridge, Cambridge University Press, 2020.
3. Griffiths, C. C. *Prosecuting London's Fraudsters 1760–1820: Swindlers, Tricksters and the Law*, London, Bloomsbury Academic, 2024.
4. Das, S. K. *Public Office, Private Interest: Bureaucracy and Corruption in India*, Oxford, Oxford University Press, 2001.
5. Tanzi, V. "Corruption around the World: Causes, Consequences, Scope and Cures," *International Monetary Fund Working Paper*, WP/98/63 (1998).
6. Balleisen, E. J. *Fraud: An American History from Barnum to Madoff*, Princeton, NJ, Princeton University Press, 2017.
7. Transparency International. "What Is Corruption?" accessed February 27, 2025, www.transparency.org/en/what-is-corruption.
8. Rose-Ackerman, S. *Corruption and Government: Causes, Consequences, and Reform*, Cambridge, Cambridge University Press, 1999, 91.
9. Zolburg, A. R. *Creating Political Order: The Party States of West Africa*, Chicago, IL, University of Chicago Press, 1966.
10. Cavotta, V. and Phillips, N. "All That Glitters: A Call for More Research on Corrupt Entrepreneurship," *Innovation*, 24, 4 (2022), 348–370.
11. Rose-Ackerman, *Corruption and Government*.
12. Argandoña, A. "Private and Public Corruption: Facilitating Payments," in dela Rama, M. and Rowley, C. (eds.) *The Changing Face of Corruption in the Asia Pacific: Current Perspectives and Future Challenges*, Cambridge, MA, Elsevier, 2017, 71–79, at 77.
13. Cuervo-Cazurra, A. "Corruption in International Business," *Journal of World Business*, 51, 1 (2016), 35–49.
14. Johnston, M. "Japan, Korea, the Philippines, China: Four Syndromes of Corruption," *Crime, Law and Social Change*, 49 (2008), 205–223.
15. Li, S. *Bribery and Corruption in Weak Institutional Environments*, Cambridge, Cambridge University Press, 2019.
16. Cooke, F. L., Wang, J., and Wood, G., "A Vulnerable Victim or a Tacit Participant? Extending the Field of Multinationals and Corruption Research," *International Business Review*, 31, 1 (2022), 101890.
17. Minefee, I. and Bucheli, M. "Combating Corruption," in Lopes, T., Lubinski, C., and Tworek, H. J. S. (eds.) *The Routledge Companion to the Makers of Global Business*, New York, Routledge, 2020, 519.
18. Minefee and Bucheli, "Combating Corruption," 516–529, at 519–520.
19. Spear, J. *The Business of Armaments: Armstrongs, Vickers and the International Arms Trade, 1855–1955*, Cambridge, Cambridge University Press, 2023, 101, 172.
20. Hunter, J. and Jones, G. "Ethical Business, Corruption and Economic Development in Comparative Perspective," in Colpan, A. M. and Jones, G.

(eds.) *Business Ethics and Institutions: The Evolution of Turkish Capitalism in Global Perspectives*, New York, Routledge, 2020, 224–245, at 233.
21. Spear, *The Business of Armaments*, 32, 328.
22. Hartung, W. D. *Prophets of War: Lockheed Martin and the Making of the Military-Industrial Complex*, New York, Nation Books, 2011, 125–127.
23. Terris, D. *Ethics at Work: Creating Virtue at an American Corporation*, Waltham, MA, Brandeis University Press, 2005, 54–65.
24. Anon, "Lockheed Scandal: Multinational Bribery and Japan," *Japan Quarterly*, 23, 2, (1976) 109–112.
25. Jones, G., Norris, M., and Kim, S. "Horst Dassler, Adidas and the Commercialization of Sport," *Harvard Business School Case* No. 316–007, revised January 28, 2020.
26. Nix, A., Decker, S., and Wolf, C. "Enron and the California Energy Crisis: The Role of Networks in Enabling Organizational Corruption," *Business History Review*, 95, 4 (2022), 765–802, at 799.
27. Salter, M.S. *Innovation Corrupted. The Origins and Legacy of Enron's Collapse*, Cambridge, MA, Harvard University Press, 2008.
28. Office of Public Affairs, US Department of Justice, BAE Systems PLC Pleads Guilty and Ordered to Pay $400 Million Criminal Fine, March 1, 2010.
29. OECD, Working Group on Bribery in International Business Transactions, Typologies on the Role of Intermediaries in International Business Transactions. Final Report, October 9, 2009.
30. Office of Public Affairs, US Department of Justice, Daimler AG and Three Subsidiaries Resolve Foreign Corrupt Practices Act Investigation and Agree to Pay $93.6 million in Criminal Penalties, April 1, 2020.
31. Spinello, R. A. *Business Ethics: Contemporary Issues and Cases*, Los Angeles, CA, Sage, 2020, 381–388.
32. Pegg, D. "Three Alstom Executives Guilty of Conspiracy to Corrupt," *The Guardian*, December 19, 2018.
33. OECD, Working Group on Bribery in International Business Transactions, 22–23.
34. Berghoff, H. "'Organized Irresponsibility'? The Siemens Corruption Scandal of the 1990s and 2000s," *Business History*, 60, 3 (2018), 423–445.
35. Boakye, D., Shaw, D., and Sarpong, D. "'The Airbus Bribery Scandal': A Collective Myopia Perspective," *European Management Review*, 19, 4 (2022), 654–670.
36. Spinello, *Business Ethics*, 380–381.
37. Transparency International, Corruption Perceptions Index 2023.
38. Marchal, J. *Lord Leverhulme's Ghosts: Colonial Exploitation*, London: Version, 2008.
39. Breemen, O. v. *Heineken in Africa: A MNE Unleashed*, London, Hurst & Company, 2018, 39, 81.

40. Memorandum by Sir Sam Falle, Lagos High Commissioner, October 29, 1977, FO 65/1930, National Archives UK.
41. David Owen to Prime Minister, November 7, 1977, FO 65/1930, National Archives, UK.
42. Leigh, D. and Evans, R. "Newspaper Hoax Masked Labour Role in Scandal," *The Guardian*, January 24, 2006.
43. Secret Memorandum by N. D. Watson, Colonial Office, April 24, 1958, C0 554/1917, National Archives, UK.
44. Cohen, A. "Britain and the Breakdown of the Colonial Environment: The Struggle over the Tanzam Oil Pipeline in Zambia," *Business History Review*, 88, 4 (2014), 737–759.
45. United States Senate Permanent Subcommittee on Investigations, Money Laundering and Foreign Corruption: Enforcement and Effectiveness of the Patriot Act. Case Study Involving Riggs Bank, July 15, 2004.
46. Subcommittee on Investigations.
47. Open Society Justice Initiative, "Corruption and Its Consequences in Equatorial Guinea: A Briefing Paper," Updated March 2010.
48. Jones, G. and Storli, E. "Marc Rich and Global Commodity Trading," *Harvard Business School Case* No 813–020, revised December 19, 2017.
49. Ammann, D. *The King of Oil: The Secret Lives of Marc Rich*, New York, St Martin's Press, 2009, 177.
50. Office of Public Affairs, US Department of Justice. www.justice.gov/opa/pr/glencore-entered-guilty-pleas-foreign-bribery-and-market-manipulation-schemesce, "Glencore Entered Guilty Pleas to Foreign Bribery and Market Manipulation Schemes," May 24, 2022.
51. Serious Fraud Office, "Glencore to Pay £280 Million for 'Highly Corrosive' and 'Endemic' Corruption," November 3, 2022.
52. Hook, L. "Big Investors Sue Glencore over 'Untrue' Prospectuses," *Financial Times*, August 31, 2023.
53. Lipton, E. and Searcey, D. "Fight over Corruption and Congo's Mining Riches Takes a Turn in Washington," *New York Times*, April 2, 2023.
54. McKinsey, "Dance of the Lions and Dragons" (June 2017). www.mckinsey.com/~/media/mckinsey/featured%20insights/middle%20east%20and%20africa/the%20closest%20look%20yet%20at%20chinese%20economic%20engagement%20in%20africa/dance-of-the-lions-and-dragons.pdf, accessed February 2, 2025.
55. Cardenal, J. P., Pablo, J., and Araújo, H. *La silenciosa conquista china: Una investigación por 25 países para comprender cómo la potencia del siglo XXI está forjando su futura hegemonía*, Barcelona, Grupo Planeta, 2011.
56. Jones, G. *Renewing Unilever*, Oxford, Oxford University Press, 2005, 158.
57. Sluyterman, K. *Keeping Competitive in Turbulent Markets, 1973–2007*, Oxford, Oxford University Press, 2007, 308.

58. "Panalpina and Shell Close to Settling Bribery Case: Report," Reuters, October 15, 2010. www.reuters.com/article/idUSTRE69E06S, accessed February 27, 2025.
59. Berghoff, "Organized Irresponsibility?"
60. Eichenberger, P. "Swiss Capitalism, or The Significance of Small Things," *Capitalism: A Journal of History and Economics*, 3, 1 (2022), 215–252, at 230.
61. Chavez, S. and Palma, S. "Donald Trump to Halt Enforcement of Law Banning Bribery of Foreign Officials," *Financial Times*, February 11, 2025.
62. Pieth, M. "International Cooperation to Combat Corruption," in Elliot, K. A. (ed.) *Corruption and the Global Economy*, Washington, DC: Institute for International Economics, 1997, 119–123.
63. Weismann, M. F. "The Foreign Corrupt Practices Act: The Failure of the Self-Regulatory Model of Corporate Governance in the Global Business Environment," *Journal of Business Ethics*, 88 (2009), 615–661.

Further Reading

Berghoff, H. "'Organized Irresponsibility'? The Siemens Corruption Scandal of the 1990s and 2000s," *Business History*, 60, 3 (2018), 423–445.

Breemen, O. v. *Heineken in Africa: A MNE Unleashed*, London, Hurst & Company, 2018.

Cuervo-Cazurra, A. "Corruption in International Business," *Journal of World Business*, 51, 1 (2016), 35–49.

Dela Rama, M. and Rowley, C. (eds.) *The Changing Face of Corruption in the Asia Pacific: Current Perspectives and Future Challenges*, Cambridge, MA, Elsevier, 2017.

Rose-Ackerman, S. *Corruption and Government: Causes, Consequences, and Reform*, Cambridge, Cambridge University Press, 1999.

Part IV

Geopolitics

CHINMAY TUMBE

12

Multinationals and Imperialism
The Indian Trajectory

12.1 Introduction

When India gained political independence from British rule in 1947, the memory of foreign rule beginning with the entry of a multinational enterprise (MNE), the East India Company, was deeply enmeshed in the national subconscious. As part of the British Empire in the early twentieth century, India was one of the largest recipients of foreign direct investment (FDI) in the world, ranked eighth in 1914 and third in 1929 (only after Canada and the United States).[1] However, hostile policies toward MNEs post Independence kept companies away from India and even led to many MNEs exiting India. By the 1980s, India was not even ranked among the top fifty FDI host economies in the world. Subsequently, and especially with the opening up of the economy in 1991, inward FDI rose, but remained far short of what China accumulated by an order of magnitude.[2] These waves of FDI flows to India over a century broadly mirror the waves of globalization discussed in Chapter 1, and yet India's lack of appetite for FDI between 1947 and 1991 can be understood only by understanding the legacy of imperialism.

The idea that MNEs and imperialism can be intertwined has a long history that may not be so obvious for today's onlookers as the objection to MNEs has reduced across the world, even in countries like India, where the two terms were once seen as synonymous. "Imperialism" is usually considered to be a set of practices that project power over a foreign entity. Between 1870 and 1945, imperialism worked through territorial annexations and leading imperial powers included Britain, France, Portugal, Spain, the Netherlands, Germany, Belgium, Italy, Russia, Japan, and the United States. As business historian Geoffrey Jones has pointed out, "imperialism involved the forcible removal of barriers to cross-border flows of capital, trade and knowledge" and thus facilitated the spread of MNEs in this time.[3] Between 1945 and 1990, imperialism was understood by other means and the United States and the Soviet Union were the major world powers. However, private-enterprise MNEs were associated with only the United States in this pairing.

The literature on MNEs and imperialism was dominant between the1960s and 1980s as many countries in Asia and Africa were decolonized. A discourse analysis of the words "Multinational" and "Imperialism" clearly shows the rise in usage of these words from the 1960s and their decline since the 1980s, in both the Google N-Gram Viewer based on the corpus of American English books and the digital archive of the Indian daily newspaper, *The Times of India*. The thematic concern was also expressed in Africa, for instance, in a 1978 paper titled "Imperialism and Multinational Corporations: A Case Study of Nigeria," which argued that MNEs were "basic units of imperialism in its contemporary neo-colonial stage" and that the impact was mediated through "foreign investment, export–import trade, and foreign aid."[4] The ire of that paper was directed toward the three largest MNEs operating in Nigeria at that time: Unilever and its autonomous affiliate United Africa Company, and Lonrho (London and Rhodesian Mining and Land Company). A few years later, another paper broadened the scope from Nigeria to all of Africa.[5]

The common theoretical apparatus used by critics of MNEs in Africa, Latin America, and Asia at that time was essentially Marxist, blaming foreign enterprises for stimulating an extractive form of capitalist development. "Imperialism" was the title of an influential treatise by Russian Marxist Vladimir Lenin in the early twentieth century, where he argued that it was "the highest stage of capitalism."[6] An anthology of the various ways in which "imperialism" was understood and interpreted in the late twentieth century was brought out in a three-volume study in 2001 entitled *Imperialism: Critical Concepts in Historical Studies*.[7] Political scientist Richard Sklar's entry on MNEs emphasized that economic power could not be separated from political power when it came to MNEs and that the costs of extraction and exploitation far outweighed the purported gains through technology and skill transfer, employment, and generation of tax revenues in the recipient country.[8] A more recent Marxist account continues this line of critique, arguing that MNEs have broadened their ambit from their erstwhile territorial zones that reflected colonial linkages to be truly global exploiters.[9]

Other views on MNEs and imperialism have emerged from business historians and management scholars in the past two decades. These narratives have shown the limits of imperialism in many contexts and the significance of adaptation to local conditions. In an article titled "The End of Corporate Imperialism" published in 2003, management scholars pointed out that the old way of doing business in the developing world by MNEs was coming to an end.[10] If pre-1990s strategies were run with an imperial mindset of selling old products in new markets, the new business landscape demanded a complete reorientation of every aspect of traditional business models. Emerging markets were to be seen as sources of technological innovation and managerial talent for operations worldwide and not just as a destination for products that were often at the end of their life cycles.

British historian David Fieldhouse was a leading critic of Marxist theories of imperialism and argued that a cost-benefit approach was more appealing to understand MNEs and that "without looking at specific cases it is generally impossible to know whether an MNC [multinational corporation] will benefit or harm a host country."[11] While older MNEs could still be criticized for pursuing monopolistic rents, newer MNEs were seen to promote free trade and competition. Fieldhouse questioned the idea of modern MNEs being part of a new imperial system and whether power from corporate headquarters could really dictate the fortunes of the host country. In this narrative, there is also much more agency given to the host country's government whose relations with the MNEs can reduce the scope for exploitation. Governments have used a variety of policy levers to keep MNEs in check ranging from antitrust laws, employment regulations, caps on profit remittances and equity participation, quotas and price controls, and the threat of outright nationalization.

Another narrative posits the coevolution of empires and MNEs as "firms compete in the product dimension, states compete in the territorial dimension."[12] Knowledge is seen as critical for success: military knowledge for empires and product technology for MNEs. And nationalism is seen as a constraint for both the state and the MNE.

In this chapter, India is used as the principal regional case study to understand the various ways in which MNEs, and imperialism have been interpreted in connection with each other. The East India Company and its role in India's colonization and India's tryst with MNEs in the twentieth century form the two major building blocks of this chapter. This is followed by a general discussion to better understand the interconnections between multinationals and imperialism, which can be valid for other regions as well.

12.2 The East India Company (1600–1874)

In India, and perhaps much of Asia, the origin of MNEs in popular discourse and culture is inevitably tied with the East India Company. Politicians and commentators weary of MNEs and foreign investment routinely invoke the ghost of the East India Company to warn citizens of how an MNE in the past had entered India for trade and then gone on to rule them. The MNE is so much a part of Indian national consciousness that an Indian-born entrepreneur, Sanjiv Mehta, in Britain in 2005 acquired enough shares to become the sole owner of the long-dormant East India Company, only to assert historical recalibration. He proceeded to build a luxury brand business using the same historical emblem and coat of arms.[13]

To be precise, there were several East India Companies (EIC) – the English version, the Dutch version (known by its acronym VOC) with substantive operations in Indonesia, the French version, and a few others. More has been written on the English East India Company than arguably any other company in the world due to its astonishing longevity and its incredible power when it ruled parts of the Indian subcontinent for a century from 1757 to 1857.

Two relatively recent books written in contrasting styles outline the broad narratives on the English EIC. Historian William Dalrymple's *The Anarchy: The East India Company, Corporate Violence, and the*

Pillage of an Empire, as the title suggests, is a story of corporate violence and plunder.[14] Economic historian Tirthankar Roy's *East India Company: The World's Most Powerful Corporation* takes an institutional approach and asks how exactly the MNE changed the manner in which business was conducted in India.[15] These books and several others provide important glimpses into the connections between MNEs and imperialism. Significant aspects are related to the EIC's monopoly status, militias, governance, hierarchy, and collaboration with local suppliers.

Chartered companies of the seventeenth-century world such as the EIC actively sought monopolies in the markets in which they operated. The EIC charter granted by the monarchy specified monopolistic rights to trade in Asia and the EIC sought monopoly-granting treaties from local rulers. These monopoly rights were renewed in successive charters over the centuries. The EIC's monopolistic tendencies in the tea trade were thwarted by the Boston Tea Party in the lead-up to the American Revolution in the 1770s. But in the opium trade, the EIC was successful for some time in enforcing a monopoly in production in eastern India while trading with China in the late eighteenth century. These monopolistic tendencies of the EIC drew flak from contemporary free-trade enthusiasts, including Adam Smith. The EIC charter was modified to end its monopoly trading rights in India only in 1813.

One explanation for the extreme monopoly-seeking conduct of the EIC has been the structure of the market it operated in.[16] High sunk costs, such as military and fortifications, and free riders – servants and interlopers – led the EIC to seek monopsony and monopoly power in India and England respectively, precisely because competition was so fierce in both places. The EIC consistently raked up multiple debts during its long existence and thus strived to carve out monopolies for itself to ensure stable financial performance.

The transition of the EIC from a trading firm in the seventeenth century to one with a large standing army in the Indian subcontinent, at its peak comprising more than one hundred thousand soldiers, has been widely discussed in Indian historiography. Its evolution can best be seen as a series of incidents and alliances dictated principally by commercial reasons. The ban on textile imports in England to prevent dumping of Indian cottons in the early 1700s led the EIC to explore new avenues of revenue generation in the Indian subcontinent. This, coupled with the disintegration of the Mughal Empire after the death of Emperor Aurangzeb (1707) led the EIC to revenue farming and contact with local mercenaries. The Anglo-French rivalry of Europe that spilled on to overseas theatres brought the EIC more firmly into the ambit of military development by the middle of the century and ultimately more aggressive territorial conquests. Most of the army comprised Indian soldiers, who often chose the EIC as a better paymaster than the other options available to them. By then, the EIC was not just an MNE with economic power; it was also a military power. Thus the EIC thereafter defined the template of MNEs that can grow to have imperial military ambitions. In fact, only when this military rule was tested by a powerful revolt in 1857 was EIC rule finally replaced by Crown rule in the Indian subcontinent.

The EIC faced well-known principal–agent problems that have been documented in the literature on MNEs and subsidiaries. In a world with relatively primitive means of transport and communications, the EIC headquarters in London found it hard to discipline its employees and outlets in distant India. One of the reasons people joined the EIC in England to work in India despite it being a land with high mortality rates was the possibility to secure large fortunes on the side. The enormous riches earned by EIC employee Robert Clive (who spearheaded victory at the Battle of Plassey in 1757) and his contemporaries in the late eighteenth century sparked a parliamentary debate in England, impeachment proceedings, and a general perception of the moral degradation of the EIC as a corrupt company. The EIC's employees routinely conducted private trade on their own account and left service to try out other pastures once enough knowledge had been gained on the Indian subcontinent.[17] This was why the monopoly in opium production could not be effectively maintained as Indian traders and EIC employees formed partnerships to sell Malwa opium from Central India to China from the western seaboard. The idea of a corrupt MNE with limited checks and balances from the side of shareholders and the need for government intervention was thus registered emphatically by the travails of the EIC.

The EIC staff comprised mainly white English officers, and despite its existence of 274 years, the EIC rarely recruited Indians in corporate services and barred Indians from the higher echelons of management.

The racial hierarchy was maintained in the bureaucracy it invented, the Indian Civil Service, where officers had to take examinations in England for posts in India. Pleas by Indians to participate in these roles went unheard. One of the foundational critiques of EIC rule in India was that by its employment practices, it conferred an economic drain on the resources of the country.[18] Officers worked in India but retired in England, where they spent their pensions. The racial hierarchy the EIC maintained was reproduced in British trading firms and other MNEs that started operating in India in the late nineteenth century. The objective of hiring locals by MNEs was put into place strongly only after direct government intervention in India after Independence in 1947.

The EIC hired Indian soldiers for its standing army. It also collaborated with Indian merchants, traders, and bankers to secure a foothold in India. Indian capital was instrumental in securing important victories for the EIC, including the Battle of Plassey in 1757. An important aspect of the eighteenth-century world was that Indian merchants flocked from their traditional bastions such as Surat in western India and Murshidabad in eastern India to EIC outposts such as Bombay and Calcutta.[19] This occurred because many Indian merchants looked at the EIC as a better business partner with easier conflict resolution mechanisms in courts of law. Multinational enterprises often need the active support of local supplier networks to conduct their operations, and the EIC demonstrated that to ample effect in the eighteenth century.

The EIC case shows that the most iconic MNE of the pre-1850 world was associated with several aspects of imperialism. These included outright military power, a projection of racial hierarchies, and an outflow of profits back to England, often reflecting corruption more than competence.

12.3 MNEs and Imperialism in Twentieth-Century India

After the revoking of the EIC's monopoly status in 1813, British merchants and trading firms began to operate more freely in the Indian subcontinent.[20] These were small family-based firms and not the MNE its and subsidiaries form of business. That began to change with the Second Industrial Revolution in the late nineteenth century, setting the stage for MNEs from several countries to operate in India during the early twentieth century.[21]

The word "Imperial" or "Empire" itself was a part of the name of some of these MNEs, such as Imperial Tobacco Company, Imperial Chemical Industries, Imperial Tea, Empire of India Assurance, Empire Jute Company, and Empire Tea. The Imperial Bank of India was formed as an amalgamation of three local banks serving the Bengal, Bombay, and Madras Presidencies respectively.[22] Indian firms also used "Empress" in the names of many of their ventures, after Queen Victoria was designated the Empress of India in 1876. The iconic Indian business house Tata's, for instance, named its cotton mill enterprise in Nagpur in Central India Empress Mills.

But the memory of the EIC was still alive, and as Indian nationalism grew, foreign enterprise was subjected to scrutiny with the word "drain" popularized in the public discourse. One way to counter "drain" was by promoting Indian-made goods and boycotting foreign-made goods. The word "swadeshi," meaning "one's own country," was marketed by the Indian freedom movement, especially after the return of Mohandas Gandhi from South Africa to India in 1915. Indian firms, until then, largely aloof from the freedom movement, began to participate in this project of economic nationalism in greater earnest.[23] The Tata group had named a mill it had purchased in Bombay Swadeshi Mills in the late nineteenth century, but by the 1930s, it was marketing some goods as "Pure Swadeshi" in order to convince its customer base that its goods were different from those of MNEs, which generally produced abroad and sold in India.

The interwar period thus gave rise to what has been called "Swadeshi capitalism," a rallying cry to counter MNEs through boycotts and promotion of locally made products.[24] Recent research has shown creative ways in which MNEs, especially non-British ones, countered this growing sentiment of economic nationalism in India.

One MNE that did extraordinarily well during the interwar period was Bata, a footwear company founded in 1894 by Tomas Bata in Zlin in what is now called the Czech Republic.[25] Bata's industrial-scale shoe production expanded in the 1920s, and Tomas Bata was popularly known as the Ford of Czechoslovakia or even as the Ford of Europe. Then, in the 1930s, during the Great Depression and amid deglobalization pressures and rising economic nationalism around the world, Bata expanded its operations to dozens of countries, including India. Partly the expansion was justified as a way to jump high tariff walls, but it was also fueled by an aspiration to provide shoes to everyone in the world.

Bata's international expansion was also aided by the important geopolitical consideration that it did not belong to a colonizing country and was hence not resented by economic nationalists. Further, to gain acceptance and legitimacy in the host country, Bata not only opened factories and stores that employed locals but also developed model townships that provided housing and public welfare services. In India, it developed its base south of Calcutta in Batanagar (Bata Town) just as Tata's had earlier built a model township in Jamshedpur (also referred to as Tatanagar).

Bata's shoe production in India began to steadily rise during the 1930s and 1940s and its township was a site of visit for local politicians as a model industrial township. It also sent Indian workers to Zlin for training and learning best practices in the field. It had consciously moved from production to "economic and social integration" with India.[26] Jawaharlal Nehru, who would later become India's first prime minister, also visited Bata's factory in Zlin to get a better understanding of its operations.

Business historian Christina Lubinski's research on German MNEs in colonial India shows the various ways in which firms such as Siemens, Krupp, and Bayer/IG Farben navigated economic nationalism in the early twentieth century.[27] Often, German MNEs aligned with the nationalistic Indians' aspirations against British imperialism and dominance. Unlike Bata, these firms belonged to a country that had its own imperial ambitions in the interwar period, and yet they were able to align with the Indian economic nationalists as Britain was perceived as the greater enemy. In strategic terms, this has been called "geopolitical jockeying."

Multinational enterprises were freely allowed to operate in India until the country got independence from British rule in 1947. Then came the restrictions, at first slowly, and they gathered steam in the 1970s, followed by a sea change in policy in the 1980s and substantial liberalization in the 1990s. The first restrictions in the 1950s and 1960s came in the form of forcing MNEs to employ more locals and to look and feel more Indian. Several MNEs even changed their names with "India" or "Hindustan" being a common adoption. Thus Imperial Tobacco Company changed its name to India Tobacco Company in 1970 and to ITC in 1974. Anglo-Dutch Lever Brothers/Unilever became Hindustan Lever, and US advertising MNE J Walter Thompson became Hindustan Thompson Associates. Hindustan Lever also appointed an Indian manager, Prakash Tandon, as its first Indian head of operations in India, which was a big deal in top management recruitment even in the 1960s. The existing racial hierarchy of MNEs often employed Europeans and Americans in top management, Anglo-Indians in middle management, and Indians lower down the order.[28] Government intervention forced several MNEs to abandon such hierarchies.

India nationalized only a few sectors, but the threat of nationalization itself was an important factor in driving many MNEs away. The Imperial Bank of India was nationalized in 1955, creating the State Bank of India, and several more were nationalized by the Indira Gandhi government in 1969. The clamor against big business, both domestic and foreign, rose in India in the 1960s with a series of reports suggesting a high concentration of corporate capital in a few hands. Foreign aid, largely from the United States, was viewed suspiciously as a prop to facilitate the entry of products of MNEs. Postwar multilateral institutions such as the World Bank and the International Monetary Fund were also seen as imperial agents. Democratically elected politicians belonging to communist parties in India routinely voiced their anguish over MNEs and imperialism. While nominally nonaligned with the Cold War bloc countries, India's tilt toward the USSR was perceptible by the early 1970s.

India turned a hard left in economic policies in the 1970s, first under the Indira Gandhi government and toward the end of the decade under Prime Minister Morarji Desai, driving several MNEs to exit the country, including US-based IBM and Coca-Cola. This was done through stringent caps on foreign equity participation to under 50 percent and restrictive rules laid out by the Foreign Exchange Regulation Act (FERA) of 1973 aimed at Indianizing corporate ownership and socializing economic policies. IBM's exit had the unintended consequence of launching several Indian firms in the computer hardware space, which then moved on to providing information and technology (IT) services.

India's IT sector flourished over the next four decades due to the entrepreneurial energy of software engineers and active government policy.

The Indian government also took the bold decision of ending product patents by the Patents Act of 1970, much to the disbelief of MNEs, especially in the pharmaceutical sector. Pharmaceutical MNEs like Pfizer and Roche spent a lot of money on research and development and expected to recover their costs by monopolizing their discoveries for a few years in the marketplace via patents. Ending product patents led to a few pharmaceutical MNEs leaving India and many others staying but not selling their patented medicines in India. Since process patents were still in place, Indian firms mastered the art of reverse engineering medicines developed in Western Europe and the United States using different processes and selling medicines at affordable rates in India and from the 1990s, even in leading export markets. The stellar rise of India's pharmaceutical sector was not dampened when the product patents regime returned in 2005 as part of World Trade Organization obligations as firms had developed critical manufacturing capabilities by then. Indian pharmaceutical firms such as Cipla were highly sought after in Africa, since their medicines used to battle vital diseases like HIV-AIDS were far cheaper than those developed in the United States and Western Europe. The emphasis on self-sufficiency in medicines by the Indian government in the 1970s and the hostile attitude toward MNEs via patent policies eventually created a vibrant Indian pharmaceutical sector that benefited not only India but also many other countries of the world by widening access to affordable medicines.

British-owned MNEs, which had been in India for a long time, navigated this storm against MNEs in India successfully using different strategies, drawing from their networks and knowledge about India.[29] The India Pakistan Burma Association, formed in 1942 and amalgamated in 1971 into the Confederation of British Industry, was an important source of market information for British firms and business interests in India. Through bulletins, it analyzed the risk perception of outsiders in the Indian business landscape against the backdrop of economic nationalism. Thus the new economic policies against MNEs in the 1970s did not surprise major British firms such as Hindustan

Lever, Godfrey Philips, Cadbury, Metal Box, and others. Some divested their shareholdings and expanded their overall share issuance for further investment while some like Hindustan Lever steadfastly maintained 51 percent foreign ownership by citing escape clauses. Hindustan Lever negotiated with the Indian government that 10 percent of its production volume would be exported (thus earning valuable foreign exchange) and that it would move to higher-technology fields (which were part of the exceptions to the rules framed under the FERA). Imperial Chemical Industries also got away with similar flexibility. In some cases, however, as with Metal Box and the metallurgy MNE Guest Keen Nettlefolds, the firms were crippled by the FERA and eventually wound up or exited India.

A study on British and US MNEs in India in the twentieth century using a "dynamic trajectories" framework shows how varied MNE strategies were in dealing with the same policy shocks against MNEs in India.[30] Some firms exited, while some successfully adapted through local responsiveness on the input side and a few others exited and reentered after liberalization in 1991.

Another study points out that foreign enterprise was not necessarily viewed suspiciously before 1991 if it belonged to Indians outside India.[31] In the 1980s, Swraj Paul, a London-based Indian-origin businessman and corporate raider, had his eye on a hostile takeover of two large Indian industrial firms – Escorts Limited and Delhi Cloth Mills. Surprisingly, the Indian government led by the Congress sided with this foreign capitalist endeavor even though it went against the interests of Indian business houses. Opposition, however, did come from communist politicians in India.

The idea of equating MNEs with imperialism took an environmental turn with the tragic Bhopal Gas tragedy in 1984 linked with Union Carbide. While the US MNE got away with compensation that was seen as meager, the lack of accountability in the whole saga soured the minds of many who were slowly warming up to the idea of actively inviting MNEs to India in the 1980s, as China had already opened its economy in 1978. Ultimately, it was a balance of payments crisis in India that led to a decisive pivot toward liberalization and globalization in 1991. This opened the floodgates to let in MNEs and with that came a new counter-allegation, that of cultural imperialism. One study on advertisements by

MNEs and Indian-owned businesses in the 1990s found limited applicability of the idea of cultural imperialism in the Indian context, but the concept has wide traction around the world, often posited as a clash of values between tradition and modernity.[32]

Overall, even as recently as in 2000, one of the most globally diversified MNEs, Nestlé, considered India to be among its toughest markets. It had stepped up its foray in India in the 1950s only after successfully using Indo-Swiss government channels.[33] Its top management saw the problem to be mainly political, as observed in this quote in a managerial memoir: "Indians have an ambivalent attitude towards foreign investors. Somewhere deep in the nation's subconscious there still linger strong reservations, which do not permit India to stand whole-heartedly behind companies like Nestlé."[34] This was contrasted with China, which backed Nestlé and consistently removed obstacles in its path. Thus the legacy of imperialism still weighed on India's political economy and attitude toward MNEs, which began to soften only post 2000.

12.4 Indian MNEs and Imperialism

While Indians often viewed MNEs suspiciously in the twentieth century, several Indian firms ventured abroad and faced a similar backlash as experienced by MNEs operating in India. In the early twentieth century, Indian businesses flourished in Southeast Asia via the South Indian Chettiar business community and in East Africa via the West Indian Gujarati business community.[35] Both these operations received major shocks in the twentieth century that forced them to relocate. Indian capitalists were seen as exploitative and extractive in many parts of the world just as the Indian economic nationalists were rallying against British enterprises. In Burma, in the 1930s, the Chettiars were leading bankers, and when the Great Depression crashed its rice economy, they came to own nearly a fifth of the gross cropped area as farmers defaulted on their loans and submitted their land as their collateral. This led to massive resentment in Burma against the Indians and eventually their ouster. Indian businesses lost millions in their exodus and the later nationalizations. The Chettiar business community received such a large shock that members of the community began to look at avenues outside business for security. Some firms still petition the government in Myanmar even today for compensation.

Decolonization in East Africa led to a change of power from British to Indigenous rule. The new ruling dispensations did not take kindly to Indian businesses, seen as foreign capitalists. In Uganda, Idi Amin ordered Indians to leave the country in the 1970s, when he came to power, and many relocated to Britain, the United States, and Canada. In other countries too the hostile climate led to emigration. Only two decades later were Indian capitalists wooed back to East Africa. The experience of Indian firms in these cases shows that Indian businesses were also at the receiving end in the narrative against foreign capitalists under the rubric of imperialism in the twentieth century.

Finally, as Indian MNEs began to march around the world post 1991, some of the investment decisions were guided more by the history of imperialism than profitability considerations per se. The case of Sanjiv Mehta buying the rights to use the EIC emblem was mentioned before. More symbolically, Tata, the largest Indian business group for a century, paid US $12 billion in 2007 to take over the British–Dutch firm Corus Steel, once mocked by British imperialists for its capability in making quality steel in the early twentieth century.[36] Tata and Indian media hailed the takeover as the case of an MNE correcting the sins of past imperialism. Unfortunately for Tata, the acquisition would prove to be a serious drain on its resources over the next decade. Its other big acquisitions in Britain, Jaguar and Tetley Tea, did better.[37]

More recently, the meteoric rise of infrastructure firm Adani in India's business landscape has led to a fallout in many countries where the Indian MNE has expansion plans. In Australia in particular, there has been tremendous backlash against a proposed large coal mining project led by Adani. The "Stop Adani" grassroots movement by environmental activists in Australia is similar to what many MNEs from Western Europe and the United States have faced in India over the decades.[38]

12.5 A Framework to Understand MNEs and Imperialism

Building on the earlier discussion of India's long tryst with MNEs, it is possible to provide a broad framework to understand the connections between MNEs and imperialism. The most basic categorization of MNEs in history is whether they had militias. Today's MNEs may not have standing armies like the EIC of the past, but many have security teams in place that may resemble local militias, especially in the mining and energy sectors. A direct or indirect projection of military power is a fundamental way in which MNEs are embroiled with imperialism.

If MNEs do not have militias, host governments and societies can still raise allegations of imperialism against them on four dimensions. First, imperialism through political interference by the MNEs has been observed in a variety of contexts: from forcing regime changes to supporting dictatorships and outright corruption retarding political development (see Chapters 6 and 11 in this volume). Second, the economic imperialism of MNEs is said to work via the profit remittances out of the country and has been the subject of major critiques around the world as a drain on the host country.

Even with no political interference or limited profit remittances, MNEs can be accused of cultural imperialism by changing the attitudes and belief systems of the Indigenous people through powerful advertising and propaganda. Nestlé's advocating for baby food products replacing breastfeeding received a massive pushback in many countries on this account. Many US MNEs are criticized for imposing Western ideals and customs, and the current popularity of K-pop and K-drama may also be seen as Korean cultural imperialism in some Asian countries. Finally, MNEs are increasingly under the scanner for their actions on the environment in host countries, especially if they are relocating "bad" practices away from the richer countries to the poorer countries to escape stringent environmental regulations.

These allegations of imperialism can lead to concrete actions by governments and civil society in host countries against MNEs. Decolonization and nationalization were popular in the middle of the twentieth century, boycotting was popular in early twentieth century India, regulations on profit remittances and equity participation are in place in virtually every country and social movements, and lawsuits (national and international) have taken place and will continue to take place on many issues, especially related to environmental change.

In response to these actions, researchers have shown a wide number of responses of MNEs against "political risk"[39] and other threats to their operations.[40] Multinational enterprises have exited markets (such as IBM and Coca-Cola from India) or chosen to stay and adapt in creative ways, as documented earlier in the case of India. To cite one example outside India, in Chile, two oil MNEs were forced by the government to join a local firm to form a three-member cartel that proved to be beneficial for the MNEs in the long run.[41] Adaptive responses have also translated into two novel MNE strategies documented by business historians: "cloaking" and "geopolitical jockeying." Cloaking strategies are used when the MNE wants to hide its true ownership identity from authorities, either at home or abroad. Cloaking was common for German firms operating abroad during the Nazi era in the interwar period.[42] And MNEs can also strategically side with economic nationalists in host countries if they are not seen as imperialists or do what is called "geopolitical jockeying."[43]

12.6 Conclusion

For a few decades after 1945, as new nations emerged through decolonization, the language of MNEs and imperialism was commonplace in discussions on international business. As the Cold War entailed one power – the USSR – that did not project MNEs onto other countries in the form of private enterprise and one power – the USA – that did, it was the United States that became the principal target in discourses on MNEs and imperialism.

If this discourse has reduced or changed substantially since the 1980s, it is partly because the old axis of MNEs mostly belonging to the United States and Western Europe has given way to a new geoeconomic world order where large MNEs exist in all continents and all major countries, including some of the poorest ones in the world. The rise of MNEs based in South Korea and China in East Asia or in India in South Asia has upended binaries of MNEs belonging only to the traditional imperial power elite that ruled much of the world between 1800 and 1945.

This change in discourse has also shifted the gaze from the two traditional dimensions of imperialism – political interference and economic drain – to cultural imperialism and environmental change. This shift also slowly moves the focus of MNEs origins away from the United

States and Western Europe toward Asia and other parts of the world. Standard Oil and United Fruit Company are giving way to Korean, Chinese, and Indian MNEs as examples of exploitative MNEs in the contemporary world. United States and European imperialism is slowly giving way to charges of Chinese neo-imperialism in Africa, as discussed in Chapter 3 of this volume.

The case of India, studied extensively in this chapter, shows how the national subconscious enmeshed with EIC-led colonization garnered a bitter reaction against MNEs for a few decades after 1947. This anti-imperialist attitude had some positive outcomes (even if not always intended as part of the policies) in nurturing domestic business sectors such as IT and pharmaceuticals and the ending of racial hierarchies in management. It also had negative outcomes as FDI can shore up growth prospects, and China's lead over India in attracting FDI certainly led to its quicker pace of economic development since the 1980s.

India finally opened up to foreign MNEs and projected its own MNEs after 1991. While country origins may change, the concept of imperialism attached to MNEs will continue to attract academic and popular attention in the twenty-first century.

Notes

1. Wilkins, M. "Comparative Hosts," *Business History*, 36, 1(1994), 18–50.
2. Tumbe, C. "Globalization, Cities and Firms in Twentieth-Century India," *Business History Review*, 96, 2 (2022), 399–423.
3. Jones, G. *Multinationals and Global Capitalism: From the Nineteenth to the Twenty-First Century*, Oxford, Oxford University Press, 2005, 19.
4. Onimode, B. "Imperialism and Multinational Corporations: A Case Study of Nigeria," *Journal of Black Studies*, 9, 2 (1978), 207–232.
5. Udofia, O. E. "Imperialism in Africa: A Case of Multinational Corporations," *Journal of Black Studies*, 14, 3 (1984), 353–368.
6. Lenin, V. *Imperialism: The Highest Stage of Capitalism*, London, Penguin Classics, 2010.
7. Cain, P. and Harrison, M. (eds.) *Imperialism: Critical Concepts in Historical Studies*, Volumes I, II, and III, London, Routledge, 2001.
8. Sklar, R. "Postimperialism: A Class Analysis of Multinational Corporate Expansion," in Cain, P. and Harrison, M. (eds.) *Imperialism: Critical Concepts in Historical Studies*, London, Routledge, 2001, 170–188.

9. Screpanti, E. *Global Imperialism and the Great Crisis: The Uncertain Future of Capitalism*, New York, Monthly Review Press, 2014.
10. Prahalad, C. K. and Lieberthal, K. "The End of Corporate Imperialism," *Harvard Business Review*, 81, 8 (2003), 69–79.
11. Fieldhouse, D. "A New Imperial System? The Role of the Multinational Corporations Reconsidered," in Frieden J. A. and Lake D. (eds.) *International Political Economy: Perspectives on Global Power and Wealth*, London, Routledge, 2000, 167.
12. Casson, M., Dark, K., and Gulamhussen, M. A. "Multinational Enterprise, Imperialism, and the Knowledge-Driven State," in Dunning, J. H. and Gugler, P. (eds.) *Foreign Direct Investment, Location and Competitiveness*, Oxford, JAI Press, 2008, 23.
13. "The Whimsical Tale of Sanjiv Mehta," *The Financial Express*, July 21, 2023.
14. Dalrymple, W. *The Anarchy: The East India Company, Corporate Violence, and the Pillage of an Empire*, London, Bloomsbury, 2019.
15. Roy, T. *The East India Company*, New Delhi, Penguin, 2012.
16. Sivramkrishna, S. "From Merchant to Merchant-Ruler: A Structure–Conduct–Performance Perspective of the East India Company's History, 1600–1765," *Business History*, 56, 5 (2014), 789–815.
17. Roy, *The East India Company*.
18. Naoroji, D. *Poverty and Un-British Rule in India*, London, Swan Sonnenschein & Company, 1901.
19. Tumbe, C. *India Moving: A History of Migration*, Gurugram, Penguin India, 2018.
20. Jones, G. *Merchants to Multinationals: British Trading Companies in the Nineteenth and Twentieth Centuries*, Oxford, Oxford University Press, 2000.
21. Wilkins, M. *The Maturing of Multinational Enterprise*, Cambridge, MA, Harvard University Press, 1974.
22. Tripathi, D. *The Oxford History of Indian Business*, New Delhi, Oxford University Press, 2004.
23. Roy, T. *A Business History of India: Enterprise and the Emergence of Capitalism from 1700*, New Delhi, Cambridge University Press, 2018.
24. Velkar, A. "Swadeshi Capitalism in Colonial Bombay," *The Historical Journal*, 64, 4 (2021), 1009–1034.
25. Pokluda, Z., Herman, J., and Balaban, M. *Bata: Across Continents*, Zlin, Thomas Bata University Press, 2022.
26. Balaban, M., Herman, J., and Savić, D. "The Early Decades of the Bata Shoe Company in India: From Establishment to Economic and Social Integration," *Indian Economic and Social History Review*, 58, 3 (2021), 297–332.
27. Lubinski, C. *Navigating Nationalism in Global Enterprise: A Century of Indo-German Business Relations*, Cambridge, Cambridge University Press, 2022.

28. Jones, G. *Renewing Unilever: Transformation and Tradition*, Oxford, Oxford University Press, 2005.
29. Aldous, M. and Roy, T. "Reassessing FERA: Examining British Firms' Strategic Responses to 'Indianisation,'" *Business History*, 63, 1, (2021), 18–37.
30. Choudhury, P. and Khanna, T. "Charting Dynamic Trajectories: Multinational Enterprises in India," *Business History Review*, 88, 1 (2014), 133–169.
31. Varadarajan, L. *The Domestic Abroad: Diasporas in International Relations*, New Delhi, Oxford University Press, 2010.
32. Sengupta, S. and Frith, K. T. "Multinational Corporation Advertising and Cultural Imperialism: A Content Analysis of Indian Television Commercials," *Asian Journal of Communication*, 7, 1, (1997), 1–18.
33. Donzé P-Y. "The Advantage of Being Swiss: Nestlé and Political Risk in Asia during the Early Cold War, 1945–1970," *Business History Review*, 94, 2 (2020), 373–397.
34. Schwarz, F. *Nestlé: The Secrets of Food, Trust and Globalization*, Toronto, Key Porter Books, 2002, 38.
35. Tumbe, C. "Transnational Indian Business in the Twentieth Century," *Business History Review*, 91, 4 (2017), 651–679.
36. Raianu, M. *Tata: The Global Corporation That Built Indian Capitalism*, Cambridge, MA, Harvard University Press, 2021.
37. Economic Times Online, "Successful or Not, Here's How Every Deal Tata Pulled Off Played a Role in Taking India Global." October 10, 2024. Accessed on January 10, 2025. https://economictimes.indiatimes.com/news/company/corporate-trends/successful-or-not-heres-how-every-deal-tata-pulled-off-played-a-role-in-taking-india-global/articleshow/114110571.cms?from=mdr.
38. www.stopadani.com. Accessed on January 10, 2025.
39. Casson, M. and da Silva Lopes, T. "Foreign Direct Investment in High-Risk Environments: An Historical Perspective," *Business History*, 55, 3 (2013), 375–404.
40. Cuervo-Cazurra, A., Duran, P., Arregle, J. L., and Essen, M. "Host Country Politics and Internationalization: A Meta-Analytic Review," *Journal of Management Studies*, 60, 1 (2023), 204–241.
41. Bucheli, M. "Multinational Corporations, Business Groups, and Economic Nationalism: Standard Oil (New Jersey), Royal Dutch-Shell, and Energy Politics in Chile, 1913–2005," *Enterprise & Society*, 11, 2 (2010), 350–399.
42. Jones, G. *Entrepreneurship and Multinationals: Global Business and the Making of the Modern World*, Cheltenham, Edward Elgar, 2013.
43. Lubinski and Wadhwani, "Geopolitical Jockeying."

Further Reading

Fieldhouse, D. "A New Imperial System? The Role of the Multinational Corporations Reconsidered," in Frieden, J. A. and Lake, D. (eds.) *International Political Economy: Perspectives on Global Power and Wealth*, London, Routledge, 2000, 167–179.

Jones, G. *Multinationals and Global Capitalism: From the Nineteenth to the Twenty-First Century*, Oxford, Oxford University Press, 2005.

Lubinski, C. *Navigating Nationalism in Global Enterprise: A Century of Indo-German Business Relations*, Cambridge, Cambridge University Press, 2022.

Prahalad, C. K. and Lieberthal, K. "The End of Corporate Imperialism," *Harvard Business Review*, 81, 8 (2003), 69–79.

Roy, T. *The East India Company*, New Delhi, Penguin, 2012.

ALFRED RECKENDREES

13

Multinationals and Nationality

13.1 Introduction

This chapter examines how multinational enterprises (MNEs) have strategized and navigated nationality related issues historically. Multinational enterprises comprise different nationalities as they are based on operations and investments in foreign countries typically with subsidiaries registered abroad. But nationality is not just defined by the place of incorporation or the nationality of owners. Nationality encompasses citizenship, culture, history, perceptions, and legal dimensions, and the meaning and relevance of nationality change with the political context. The rich field of business history helps explain how, dependent on these contexts, nationality matters for MNEs and how MNEs strategize with and manage nationality.

In the first wave of globalization in the late nineteenth and early twentieth centuries, when MNEs emerged as significant economic actors, sometimes occupying a prominent role in political affairs, the owner's nationality, the place of incorporation, and the location of headquarters were of minimal consequence. There were few restrictions on foreign direct investment (FDI), and citizenship was pragmatically and readily changed until World War I heralded the end of what has been termed "cosmopolitan capitalism." Subsequently, states around the world embraced economic nationalism and imposed restrictions on FDI. Multinational enterprises adapted to these changes in various ways, including by disguising nationality.

In the aftermath of World War II, restrictions on FDI and protective tariffs were only gradually eased. Newly independent postcolonial states typically adopted development strategies inimical to MNEs with colonial ties. Not until the mid 1970s did an emerging trend toward FDI liberalization and new technology give rise to a second wave of globalization, which the collapse of the Soviet Union in 1991 only accelerated. Many observers then considered nationality to be an anachronistic factor in the context of MNEs. They foresaw the advent of a "borderless world" inhabited by stateless global corporations. However, in the aftermath of the global financial crisis of 2007/2008 export mercantilism and protective tariffs returned to the political toolbox, and anti-globalization policy platforms gained prominence. Concerns about national security hampered technology transfer and inward FDI. Geopolitical conflicts and the Russian war on Ukraine restricted cross-border trade, affecting global value chains and the location of MNE operations. The question of how to manage nationality became once again a focal point for MNEs.

For any MNE, nationality may manifest in various ways. Strategy scholars Yip, Johansson, and Roos suggest it "is a multidimensional phenomenon (including citizenship, history, culture, and experience) and can apply to different aspects of an [MNE] (including the past and current location of corporate headquarters, the nationality of managers, and the national location of units and subsidiaries)."[1] What might appear to be a simple definition is in fact quite complex. Nationality is often ambiguous. The nationality of the company may differ from that of the owners, or the place of registration may not coincide with the place of production. The Hong Kong and Shanghai Banking Corporation registered in Hong Kong, for example, was founded by British, US, German, and Indian shareholders; the activities of the Siemens family in Russia involved operations and decision-making without control from Germany; and the Swedish Nobel family operations modernizing the Russian oil industry had their headquarters in Russia, shareholders across Europe, and no parent or holding company in Sweden. Business historian Geoffrey Jones has provided numerous historical examples of such ambiguities, many of which still exist today.[2]

This chapter focuses on five dimensions of nationality that are relevant to MNEs; while they cannot always be clearly distinguished in practice, they serve as analytical tools. The first dimension is *corporate nationality* – typically defined by the place of incorporation (Anglo-Saxon legal tradition) or the site of headquarters (French/German legal tradition) – which determines the jurisdictions and laws to which the parent MNE and its foreign affiliates are subject, potentially affording them access to diplomatic protection. Foreign subsidiaries would possess a passport that differs from that of the parent MNE.[3] However, corporate nationality is not a fixed attribute. In response to changing conditions, firms may choose to "migrate" and incorporate in another state or relocate their headquarters. Today, an MNE among the top one hundred has, on average, "more than 500 affiliates, across more than 50 countries"; its ownership structure involves several hierarchical levels, different holding companies with subsidiaries across multiple jurisdictions, having multiple "passports."[4] As noted in Chapter 7 of this volume, this issue has globally attracted the attention of tax authorities, as tax evasion and tax planning, in addition to the intricate process of attributing profits to the place of incorporation, the seat, or the country where a product or service is sold, represent significant factors influencing tax earnings.

The second dimension is *owner nationality*, referring to the nationality of the shareholders ultimately in control. This played a crucial role in the British and US Trading with the Enemy Acts (1914, 1917) and since then in case of war between states. During decolonization and national independence after World War II, many countries in Africa and Asia imposed, for example, restrictions on the proportion of shares that foreign entities could own. These measures were implemented to foster national industries independent of foreign investors and for populist reasons.[5] Other countries have adopted approaches akin to that of the United States, where the Committee on Foreign Investment has investigated sensitive takeovers since 1975. Today, most Organisation for Economic Co-operation and Development (OECD) countries impose restrictions on FDI in sectors deemed of national security interest.[6] National security has historically been and continues to be an area where owner nationality matters, despite the difficulty of establishing the nationality of corporations with substantial foreign ownership, particularly from institutional investors.

The third dimension is the nationality constructed and perceived in accordance with the cultural values, norms, and practices espoused by its managers, or *national management styles*. Until the twenty-first century, MNEs were often dominated by directors of one nationality, demonstrating clearly who was in control.[7] However, this varied significantly in subsidiaries located in different parts of the world, reflecting different cultures and managerial approaches. The internal effects included, for example, persistent cultural and nationality tensions or even conflicts among owners or managers, in the case of cross-border joint ventures, or mergers and acquisitions.[8]

The fourth dimension is *nationality as assigned to companies* because of their products and the location of production. Foreign takeovers of iconic brands frequently attract media scrutiny, spark debates, and even elicit opposition due to the nationality of a foreign investor. The acquisitions of "British" icons Jaguar and Land Rover by India-based MNE Tata in 2008 or "German" industrial robot producer Kuka in 2016 by the China-based Midea Group prompted significant debates related to nationality. The question of what constitutes the "nationality" of a car or a robot is not semantic. It changes with the context, whether the owner, the subsidiary's place of incorporation, the location of production, or the product's history determines nationality in the public discourse. Multinational enterprises' leaders reflect on such factors and construct brand images based on associations with "national flags," such as French perfume and Italian pasta.[9] The portfolios of MNEs in household and consumer goods like Unilever, Procter & Gamble, Johnson & Johnson, and many others exemplify instances where the perceived nationality of the product does not coincide with corporate nationality, owner nationality, or location of production.

Fifth, the *relations between the home and host countries*, which evolve over time, add a further layer of complexity, and the presence of actors from third countries may influence the significance attributed to the MNEs' nationality. Business historian Christina Lubinski shows that robust opposition from the Indish national movement against the British Empire and the MNEs they perceived as representing it created opportunities for MNEs originating from Germany to strategize via employing their "Germanness."[10] Business history is particularly relevant in this context, as the attributions ascribed to a nationality are often related to friendly or hostile past relationships between nations.

Which of these dimensions might become relevant for an MNE or its subsidiaries, and how they can manage nationality, is contingent on the political background and the specific context related meaning of nationality. However, it is possible to identify turning points in history and periods in which different nationality related issues gained weight for MNEs. Section 13.2 examines the period of "Cosmopolitan Capitalism" when nationality concerns were limited. Section 13.3 surveys the decades after World War I, which were shaped by economic nationalism. Section 13.4 examines the re-internationalization after World War II until the 1970s. Section 13.5 addresses the second wave of globalization witnessing new MNEs from emerging economies and the return of economic nationalism after the financial crisis of 2007/2008.

13.2 Cosmopolitan Capitalism: Mid Nineteenth Century until World War I

In the nineteenth and early twentieth centuries, the nationality of the owner and corporate nationality were of little consequence for companies investing abroad. Many MNEs emerged from merchant activities or were established by migrants who had moved from Europe to Asia, the United States, and South America, while entrepreneurs from China and India settled elsewhere in Asia, the United States, or Britain. As Geoffrey Jones wrote, "People moved across borders as well as capital."[11] In the 1830s, investors from Belgium and France created companies with their legal seats, headquarters, and plants in different states without encountering substantial difficulties. For example, in 1837, Belgian and French shareholders established the Vieille Montagne, a zinc-melting and rolling-mill firm in Moresnet, a small neutral zone on the Prussian–Belgian border. Its legal seat was in Liège, its administration was in Paris, and its first plants were in various German states and in France.[12]

Registering a firm abroad typically involved minimal requirements. Those who registered a company were required to be residents, often lawyers or business partners, who would sell their shares to the foreign investor after registration.[13] Occasionally, directors were required to reside in the host country. In rare instances where the law mandated that directors be citizens – for example, in the US banking industry – foreign owners had to hire directors with the necessary citizenship. However, due to liberal immigration laws, changing a director's citizenship was a common practice by the end of the century. It was widely accepted and did not raise substantial concerns that the nationalities of the ultimate owners and the foreign subsidiary were not aligned. Political risk was assumed to be low. Foreign ownership had been protected through an internationally shared understanding among states since the Treaties of Westphalia (1648) and Paris (1763), which guaranteed the security of property in foreign countries during peacetime. If substantial economic interests were threatened, "gunboat diplomacy" helped protect these interests as, for example, in the British Chinese Opium Wars from 1839–1842 and 1856–1860.

Still, foreign companies investing in mining, plantations, railways, and manufacturing, as well as merchant houses and trading banks facilitating international exchange, were usually welcomed in host countries. These MNEs often originated from states with competitive advantages over the host economies. A significant investment vehicle was the free-standing company (FSC). Free-standing companies, typically registered in London by groups of investors, including non-British investors, sought to utilize the London Stock Exchange to finance their ventures in third countries.[14] The investors frequently comprised groups of large firms. The renowned Rio Tinto Company, which began with portfolio investments in South America and evolved into a significant mining MNE, was established in 1873 by a consortium led by the British merchant house Matheson & Company, the German Deutsche Nationalbank, and the British engineering firm Clark, Punchard & Company.[15] Free-standing companies typically engaged in mineral extraction and agricultural commodities in South America and colonies in Africa and Southeast Asia. Robert Fitzgerald – connecting the growth of MNEs to formal and informal imperialism and extraction of resources – estimates that "natural resources may have accounted for half of all foreign direct investment from Britain and the United States by 1914."[16] Some FSCs also invested in US industries, with significant investments made in the brewing sector.[17]

Nationality provided privileged access to resources within a colonial empire and in the hinterland of hegemonic regional powers, such as the

United States in Central and South America; Japan exclusively permitted Japanese MNEs to operate in Korea or Taiwan.[18] As colonial powers protected their zones of interest, outsiders had only limited access, particularly to mineral resources. To exploit the advantages offered by the colonial empires to companies from their own domain, Royal Dutch Shell (Shell), established in 1907, deliberately chose a dual Dutch–British nationality over merging into a Dutch company. Operating solely under the Dutch flag appeared impossible to the Royal Dutch president Henri Deterding, who noted, "We are in our business far too dependent on the British government because we have to sell a large part of our products to English colonies."[19] While dual nationality created new opportunities and helped the group become the global leader in oil, it also led to repeated power struggles between the British and Dutch directors within certain parts of the organization. Trying to counteract these tendencies, Shell aimed at involving representatives from both nationalities in most operations.

Manufacturing MNEs operated differently from resource-seeking MNEs; they did not require political negotiations over concessions and typically brought goods to host countries' markets that domestic firms could not provide. Initially, these MNEs predominantly originated from Continental Europe, and some British and US manufacturers, like the British spinning company J. P. Coats and the US sewing machine producer Singer. The relatively small size of home markets, tariff protection in the United States and Europe from the 1880s, and transportation costs collectively indicated the benefits of establishing production abroad. The rapid expansion of the French chemicals producer Solvay illustrates this dynamic.[20] The chosen organizational structures were often complex. For example, for political and for tax reasons the Germany-based Siemens and AEG used Swiss financial holding companies with investors from several European states to control their operations in South America and Southern Europe.[21] Employing nationality strategically helped reduce potential conflict.

United States-based manufacturers such as Ford, General Electric (GE), International Harvester, and Westinghouse entered Europe at the end of the nineteenth century. America-based MNEs often partnered with local firms to improve their competitive position. General Electric, for instance, cofounded the Compagnie française pour l'exploitation des procédés

Thomson-Houston (1893) with French partners to serve the French market, French colonies, and Southern Europe. Although the French company was initiated by Americans and technologically reliant on GE patents, most directors were French, and the majority of shares was owned by French. General Electric did not have formal control; it only exercised technological influence. This arrangement effectively acted as a barrier to German competitors entering the market. According to French business historian Hubert Bonin, cloaking of American roots "explains the success of the Thomson-Huston techniques all-over the French industry."[22]

There were exceptions to the generally low relevance of nationality before World War I. Situations where nationality became significant typically involved competitive pressure and strong anti-foreign sentiments. For instance, competition in domestic markets and "Buy British" initiatives led the British Parliament to introduce the British Merchandise Marks Act in 1887, attributing nationality to products labeled as "made in Germany" if they were sold in the British Empire. While this aimed to limit imports from Germany, German MNEs in India used this attribution of nationality strategically, seizing the opportunity to leverage their "Germanness" to differentiate themselves from the colonial power and gain a competitive edge over competitors from Britain.[23]

Related to nationality, there were undoubtedly home country advantages, such as the size and competitiveness of the home market, the educational system, and specific technological knowledge, which helps explain, for example, the American dominance in automobiles or the German dominance in the chemical industry.[24] Home country characteristics and advantages or disadvantages should, however, be distinguished from nationality: Countries might share certain characteristics but would still not have the same nationality. It was during the Great War that nationality began to matter seriously to MNEs.

13.3 Economic Nationalism: From World War I to World War II

World War I fundamentally changed the landscape for international business. Across Europe, the plants of foreign MNEs were ordered to produce and were often requisitioned for military needs. Belligerent states investigated the ultimate ownership of companies, and the enactment of Trading with the Enemy Acts in Britain and the United States along with similar regulations in Germany allowed the seizure of property from enemy state citizens. While German confiscations were reversed after the German defeat, Germany-based MNEs lost a significant portion of their global business, including patents and trademarks, which were subsequently absorbed by US and British firms.[25]

The era of global openness had ended. Many states adopted protectionist policies and economic nationalism to address the war's aftermath. The Versailles peace agreements and the dissolution of the Russian and Austrian-Hungarian Empires created new states and new borders and changed perceptions of nationality. European states imposed high import tariffs on semifinished products and nationalist discourse included hostility to companies originating from previously belligerent states. Legislators worldwide tightened incorporation rules. In addition to residence requirements for those who registered a new firm, many states demanded domicile and sometimes citizenship of company directors. In some cases, limits were established on the percentage of shares that foreigners could own in a company. As also immigration laws were tightened worldwide, the establishment of a company abroad became a more arduous process. Consequently, MNEs began to manage more proactively nationality-related issues, particularly corporate nationality (including the passports of the subsidiaries), the nationality of owners and managers (particularly the board of directors), and the branding of their products.

Outside of Europe, nationalists and independence movements articulated anti-imperial sentiments, focusing particularly on the British colonial state.[26] But anti-foreign sentiments and effectively anti-British policies also surged in the United States, although the implemented measures covered legally all foreign investors. Aiming at national control over the telegraph industry, the US Navy purchased control stations and vessels from the British Marconi Company and helped transfer their radio stations to the Radio Corporation of America, which permitted only a minority stake for foreign investors. The prohibition in the United States effectively resulted in the elimination of British assets in the US brewing industry. Other measures implemented in the 1930s aimed at favoring US over foreign companies – for example, by providing privileged tax rates (banking), requiring a majority ownership by US citizens (75 percent for domestic airlines), or excluding foreigners from operations (radio broadcasting).[27]

In the 1930s, MNEs from Japan, typically trading and shipping companies exporting, for example, steel scrap and raw cotton from the United States to Japan and finished cotton goods from Japan to the United States, suffered severely from anti-Japanese hostility. The US government conducted hearings, and it was heatedly debated whether Americans were "being put out of work because of Japanese textile imports, goods made with 'coolie wages'?"[28] And even more, low-priced goods from Japan were expected to outcompete US exports to third countries, resulting in manufacturing jobs lost in the United States.

Nationalist sentiments were even more prevalent in Europe, where the fear of "Americanization" was a common feature in public discourse in many countries in the 1920s, particularly in France and Germany. To support domestic industry, the French government required the detailed declaration of the origin of all imported items to be processed in France. For final products to qualify for exemption from import tariffs, they must be recognized as "domestic," meaning that at least 50 percent of all components must have been produced in France. Many MNEs therefore sought to present their subsidiaries in the host countries as domestic firms. In response to nationalist discourse (and taxation), the car manufacturer Ford adopted a multi-domestic approach. This entailed, in addition to being registered in France and Germany, the sale of 40 percent of the two subsidiaries' shares to domestic shareholders, producing as many of the components as possible at their local factories, sourcing from domestic suppliers, and offering specific models for the German and French markets. The Ford subsidiary in Britain, 40 percent of whose shares had been sold to British investors, served as the holding company for the altogether nine European Ford firms. By transforming the Ford into a "British," "German," or "French" car, they aimed at embedding themselves deeply in the host economy.[29] While embedding in the respective business community and national culture helped expand the European activities of MNEs, their approach was very different outside of Europe.[30] Here, expatriates from the MNEs' home countries typically served as directors and managers of foreign subsidiaries as in the case of the Dutch-based Heineken or Unilever in Indonesia.[31]

Other MNEs operating in Europe also used multi-domestic approaches. Oil companies typically worked with nationals as executives as their business involved close government relations. Unilever ran its European business with executives from the host country, and when General Motors assumed ownership of the British car manufacturer Vauxhall in 1925 and the large German car manufacturer Opel in 1929, the respective national management did not change substantially. The car producers continued to appear British or German to their customers despite foreign ownership. And despite being controlled by Americans, they became closely aligned with the Nazi regime after 1933.[32]

Multinational enterprises from Germany that experienced confiscation during World War I were particularly cautious; their internationalization strategies often involved cloaking their nationality. They typically contracted local solicitors and trustees to register foreign subsidiaries, serve on the board of directors, and "own" the shares. The ultimate owners and the management of these German MNEs hoped that having host country citizens as board members and trustees would provide protection in the event of another war and trustee agreements would ensure that the ultimate ownership of foreign property remained unknown to authorities and the public. A second strategic aim of cloaking was legitimizing the business in the host country.

The international activities of Beiersdorf, a producer of skin care products headquartered in Hamburg, exemplify the first strategy of cloaking nationality. From 1919 to 1934, Beiersdorf established all foreign subsidiaries with the assistance of trustees, who were citizens of the respective state and responsible for managing the subsidiaries. The US subsidiary (established in 1920) and, since 1938, a holding company in Switzerland, exercised ownership control over other foreign subsidiaries. Similarly, the Germany-based IG Farben chemical company financed and managed its foreign investments from the late 1920s via a holding company in Switzerland.[33] The trustee agreements were intended to safeguard foreign assets in an international conflict. In Beiersdorf's case, the trustees were the formal owners of the shares; the foreign subsidiaries provided internal credits to each other and shares as collateral for international loans, following the terms of the trustee agreements. The German trademarks, supply, and the licensing contracts that originated financial returns to the German headquarters were transparent. After World War II, when Beiersdorf's firms and trademarks registered abroad were seized as they had been during World War I, the board in Germany argued that the sequestered activities in the Allied- and German-occupied countries had not been owned by Germans and were, therefore, seized unlawfully. But the trustee approach ultimately did not withstand scrutiny.[34]

The activities of the German steel magnate Friedrich Flick in Polish Upper Silesia exemplify cloaking as a means to overcome liabilities resulting from the MNEs' home countries. Flick controlled several steel companies in Upper Silesia, which became part of the newly established Polish state in 1920. To disguise German ownership, he transferred the Polish shares from his holding company in Germany to trading and holding companies in the Netherlands and Switzerland belonging to his group. When the Polish government in 1926 demanded "Polonization," requiring a majority of Polish citizens on executive boards, Flick sought to protect his investments by transferring these Polish assets into a US holding company in which he appeared as a minority partner of the US company W. H. Harriman, which already had interests in Silesia and held favorable relations with the Polish government. Flick's arrangement under a US facade involved trustee letters between dozens of firms guaranteeing the minority partner ultimate ownership and full managerial control through multiple voting rights. A few years later, Flick leveraged this organizational scheme to extort financial help from the German government by threatening to disclose the German presence in Polish Upper Silesia unless he received support. He correctly calculated that the German government, fearing retaliation and pressure on the German minority in Poland to leave the country, would not risk such exposure.[35] Flick strategically utilized nationality in multiple ways to achieve his aims.

Outside of Europe, MNEs employed corporate nationality strategically for investments in colonial empires and zones of political interest (hinterland). They could choose the subsidiary through which they would make the investment; for example, the British company Lever entered Congo via a subsidiary in Belgium and the American Standard

Oil entered Bahrain via a subsidiary in London.[36] Other MNEs set up specific units in neutral Switzerland for countries in which it was politically complicated to invest. Unilever, founded in 1929 with dual Dutch–British nationality like Shell, actively used its dual nationality to accommodate the political context in the host country by choosing which of the two headquarters would control the foreign subsidiary. Sometimes it was preferable to stay within the empire; sometimes the political relations between the host country and Britain or the Netherlands favored another headquarters.[37]

On the other hand, MNEs were also able to benefit from not being connected to a colonial empire. Multinational enterprises from Germany operating in India in the 1930s created new narratives of a shared Indo-German history and the "community of Aryans" and engaged in the "Indianization" of their business in India by employing more highly qualified Indian employees. Siemens and IG Farben explored in much detail in which region they could benefit most from raising anti-British sentiments and Indian nationalism, and Krupp and Siemens developed close relationships with Tata's steel company. Considering the anticolonial interests of Indian nationalists, constructing narratives of a shared Indo-German history, and emphasizing the German origin of the Indian subsidiaries, they turned nationality into a strategic advantage from which they benefited until World War II began.[38]

13.4 From Exclusion to Integration: The Evolving Role of MNEs after World War II

After World War II, MNEs encountered even greater restrictions than after the Great War, as they lost access to many countries. The Cold War led to the formation of an isolated economic bloc, Comecon, controlled by the Soviet Union, and MNEs lost substantial assets in Eastern Europe. Reentry was largely impossible until 1990. Also China expelled foreign MNEs from its territory from 1949 to the 1980s. The opportunities for FDI in Europe further shrank because of the nationalization of significant industries in Britain, France, and Italy in the 1950s. Germany transferred energy and utilities to public ownership. And decolonization fundamentally changed the role of MNEs in large parts of Africa and Asia.

In the process of decolonization, many new states nationalized MNE affiliates in natural resources, infrastructure, and industrial sectors. Some previously British colonies such as Tanzania explicitly expropriated British owners.[39] In their pursuit of economic independence many new states launched indigenization programs and demanded MNE subsidiaries hire nationals as directors and managers and sell a part of their shares to domestic shareholders.[40] As MNEs relied on leniency by governments and political elites, their subsidiaries typically became more "national" and increasingly engaged in local management education.[41] Occasionally MNEs preferred shifting nationality. In the former Dutch colony of Indonesia, the shares of Heineken's Indonesian brewery were handed over to subsidiaries in Belgium and Luxemburg, while Unilever transferred its assets from its Dutch to its British headquarters and Shell moved its shares to an affiliate in Canada so as to distance itself to the extent possible from colonial legacy.[42] However, new opportunities could emerge from decolonization: If states adopted policies particularly unfavorable to MNEs from the colonial power, MNEs from third countries could gain advantages. For example, India's licensing system, restricting access to a limited number of companies in each industry, enabled Germany-based MNEs already present in India to diversify into different industries and prevent entry of competitors.[43]

European domestic business was protected through import tariffs and capital import controls, and states safeguarded their currencies with capital export controls. Due to massive war destructions, MNEs from Western Europe typically prioritized resources to develop the domestic business. Expanding internationally followed. Furthermore, the experience of war and the German occupation of Europe had shifted perceptions of nationality. In the first postwar decades, particularly when domestic firms or competitors from third countries offered alternatives, customers typically preferred to not buy German. Lack of competition from Europe-based MNEs and the perception of "good" and "bad" foreign investments offered space for US-based MNEs, which were in general also technologically advanced. But some European governments, like that of France in the 1960s, battled "Americanization" by bans on foreign takeovers to protect their domestic companies and for populist reasons. The role of the United States as the sole hegemon in global politics, coupled with its involvement in the Vietnam War, had fueled anti-US sentiments worldwide. Also close ties with dictatorships in Central and South America supported the view that US MNEs were representatives of "US imperialism." In Chile in 1972, the collaboration between the Central Intelligence Agency and ITT legitimized the expropriation of the latter.[44] All these developments required new approaches of how to manage nationality.

In Western Europe, Germany-based MNEs experienced nationality as a historic burden. Due to the German occupation, reestablishing business in Western Europe was challenging, if the MNE did not offer products that were very scarce or new to the respective markets. The case of skin care and adhesives producer Beiersdorf, during World War I expropriated in the United States and the British Empire and again expropriated of most international companies and trademarks after World War II, allows us to present both scenarios.[45]

In skin care, Beiersdorf aimed at cooperating with the respective firms that had taken over trademarks and production as to keep the door open for future negotiations about retaining the properties. Particularly NIVEA appeared to most consumers, due to the prewar organization of foreign subsidiaries, as a domestic brand. To protect the brand and its reputation, Beiersdorf engaged in international joint ventures and shared product knowledge with the new owners so as to avoid brand damages. Over time, they amicably took over their partners and bought back the iconic NIVEA trademark. This process was concluded by the late 1990s. Despite Beiersdorf being incorporated in Germany and owned by German shareholders, the NIVEA brand still had many nationalities. In the adhesives segment, where the company predominantly faced competition from the US 3M company, which was not yet present everywhere in Europe, Beiersdorf used foreign subsidiaries. There were two reasons for producing in the host country: import taxes and the need of direct access to the domestic business communities. The fact that the main customers were industrial companies and not end consumers reduced the relevance of nationality issues.

In general, nationality became significant to MNEs due to institutions and markets. Multinational enterprises in household and consumer goods such as Colgate-Palmolive, Nestlé, Johnson & Johnson, Procter & Gamble, and Unilever had typically grown through brand acquisitions, which was less expensive than bringing new products to competitive markets. They had to be aware of national habits and consumer tastes and thus placed their brands within the respective cultural context, using numerous distinct brand names as these names carried various associations across different languages. Unilever, by the end of the 1960s, had thousands of brands and product lines with "strong national identities built up over the years," that defined their positions in national markets.[46] The resulting national differences were reinforced by national regulations ranging from packaging to advertising.

In response to national and institutional embeddedness, US-based MNEs typically followed the multi-domestic approach that Ford, GM, and others had developed in the 1920s. When Gillette acquired Germany-based MNE Braun, known for its phonographic and kitchen appliances, shavers, and iconic design, in a friendly takeover in 1967, the *Frankfurter Allgemeine Zeitung* lamented a "national sell-out" and sighed, "Now Braun, too." But the new US owner retained the organizational structure, kept the board of directors in place, and supported employee identification with the German subsidiary. Consumers forgot quickly about the US takeover.[47] Also IBM's European strategy was based on national management, but for different reasons. IBM wanted to stay close to the respective business community to which it leased its computers and services and sought to appear as a partner struggling with similar challenges. For this reason, the subsidiaries of IBM engaged to an unusual extent in national business associations and fully accepted the systems of industrial relations in European host countries. Similarly, Unilever's leaders viewed industrial relations as the responsibility of individual operating companies and national managements. They opposed wage comparisons between countries and international union negotiations, as trade unions should not bypass national managements. This approach reinforced the perceived nationality of the company among their employees.[48]

Procter & Gamble usually operated with US expatriate managers, presenting to customers and partners the image of US energy and modernity. But in some countries, for example in Japan, this did not work. In the 1970s, P&G finally decided to change its organizational setup and employ Japanese directors and managers on all levels converting toward an organizational identity as Japanese.[49] Ford Europe, on the other hand, was challenged by rising labor and energy costs and increasing competition from within the European Common Market and Japanese car producers. It moved toward an integrated transnational corporation. Assuming consumer tastes varied only slightly between countries, it aimed at exploiting economies of scale on a global level with global products. However, Ford Europe was ahead of the times. In the context of the 1970s, departing from the multi-domestic approach, which focused on national markets, resulted in massive declines in car sales.[50]

While MNEs from Europe and North America typically aligned with national cultures in Europe and North America and did not face strong opposition, new MNEs from Asia, at first from Japan, faced skepticism and xenophobia when establishing new US and European ventures beginning in the late 1950s. Their products were often perceived as cheap and low-quality and associated with a former wartime adversary. This perception shifted dramatically in the 1970s and 1980s. "Japanese" products, particularly automobiles, consumer electronics, and photography equipment, gained a reputation for cutting-edge technology and reliability. As they gained market share, however, particularly in automotives and electronics, tensions rose in the United States. Multinational enterprises from Japan were increasingly viewed as a threat by government agencies. Advances in the semiconductor industry were even perceived as a risk to national security, while similar investments by British, French, or German-based MNEs went unchallenged. When Fujitsu attempted to acquire 80 percent of Fairchild Semiconductor from a French investor in 1986, the US commerce secretary intervened, arguing French ownership was preferable.[51]

13.5 The Second Wave of Globalization and the "Return" of Nationality after the Financial Crisis of 2007/2008

During the 1990s, the conditions for MNEs changed with the comprehensive liberalization of inward FDI in developing economies; deepening economic integration through the strengthening of various trade zones like the Association of Southeast Asian Nations, the formation of the European Union, the North American Free Trade Agreement, and others; and the General Agreement on Tariffs and Trade, as detailed in Chapter 8. Many saw the emergence of a borderless world. This was accelerated by the opening of China, the collapse of the Soviet Union in 1991, and the political transitions in Eastern Europe. New MNEs came from emerging economies like South Korea, India, Taiwan, Malaysia, South Africa, Mexico, and Brazil, as well as from China, Russia, and other countries such as the United Arab Emirates, where the MNEs were closely tied with the political elites.

Transportation and communication technology were rapidly improving, allowing for deeply integrated global supply and value chains that reduced dependency on national or regional suppliers. Competitive pressure on MNEs led to new strategies focusing on economies of scale at a global level and on developing global brands as discussed in Chapter 4. The process had started in the 1980s, in machine manufacturing, electric engineering, electronics, or automobiles, where consumer tastes between countries varied less significantly. Now it spread into multiple sectors. Cross-border mergers between MNEs, both through friendly agreement and hostile takeover, resulted in "transnational" or "global" corporations that could potentially evade the control of nation-states. But nationality remained relevant to MNEs in different domains.

As shown in Chapter 7, decisions over the location of corporate headquarters for tax reasons have a long history. Since the 1990s, tax planning has been more widely used due to tax competition between states drawing on low corporate taxes to attract FDI and the growth of tax havens. Changing corporate nationality ("migration") is a key instrument of tax planning. On the other hand, in case of foreign governments breaking contracts, or nationalization as in Venezuela in the early 2000s, MNEs used the "shield of nationality" to defend their interests by involving the governments of their home countries and by cooperating with MNEs from their home countries; collectively they could better achieve their aims.[52] Furthermore, national management styles and resulting strategic orientations impacted cross-border mergers of MNEs. For example, the failed merger of Daimler AG and Chrysler in 1998 that was finally discontinued in 2007 resulted in massive conflicts due to incompatible management styles and divergent strategic interests very much focusing on the respective national markets.

Anti-foreign sentiments continued to create barriers to entry for MNEs particularly from India and China, but also from the United

States. To protect domestic MNEs against foreign takeovers, typically the concept of "national interest" was mobilized – for example, in 2005, when US-based PepsiCo considered a takeover bid for the France-based Danone. The case sparked intense debate centered around safeguarding national interests and maintaining French economic sovereignty. The French government swiftly acted to prevent the potential takeover, considering Danone a strategic asset for France and promising to defend it against foreign acquisition. This led to a decree allowing the government to defend "strategic industries" against foreign takeovers, known as the Danone Law. The bid from the China National Offshore Oil Corporation to acquire the American oil company Unocal in 2005, and the wish of Dubai Ports World, a state-owned company, to acquire the operations of several major US ports in 2006, both faced strong political opposition in the US Congress, with concerns raised about national security and the potential loss of US control over strategic resources, leading in both cases to the MNEs eventually abandoning the acquisitions.

In 2006, while many scholars were still advocating for convergence toward "global corporations," Geoffrey Jones cautioned that the "persistent influence of nationality on international firms is one of the paradoxes of multinationals."[53] Shortly later, the responses to the global financial crisis of 2007/2008 persuaded many scholars that those who emphasized the enduring influence of nationality on MNEs might have been correct. Some MNEs survived only because of the financial security network the nation-states provided; no other institution could provide this support. Perhaps more importantly, globalization was no longer viewed as an unequivocally positive development but it was recognized that it could benefit certain industries within a country while adversely affecting others.[54]

This perspective was appropriated by anti-globalization policy platforms such as the Brexit campaign in 2016 and Donald Trump's "America First" project, which both addressed the sentiments of workers and communities afraid of losing their jobs due to global value chains and imports.[55] Nationality mattered in an unexpected way. United States subsidiaries of Japan- and Germany-based MNEs were suddenly seen as foreign companies. Accordingly, political scientist Stephen Kobrin warned in 2017 that restrictions on immigration, nationalist sentiments, raising nationalism and ethnocentrism could affect the security of global supply chains, global brand strategies, and global management.[56] Geopolitics, the Chinese threats to Taiwan, the US-Chinese trade war, and the Russian war on Ukraine only amplified these concerns.

Today, FDI is weighted more than ever against concerns over national security. The OECD states have strengthened their policies to limit foreign ownership in sectors of national security interest, including military and infrastructure, agriculture, finance, media, or natural resources. Multinational enterprises are assessed based on their home countries and ultimate ownership control. It was in reaction to a surge in takeovers by investors from China that the European Union has formulated a foreign investment screening mechanism.[57] A parallel case can be seen in China, when following the revelations by Edward Snowden, government agencies and state-owned companies were instructed to purchase locally due to the US government's use of Cisco products for espionage in China or the blocking of US-based online platforms in China.[58] National security continues to be an area in which owner nationality matters, but nationality matters in many more ways.

13.6 Conclusion

This chapter showed that nationality plays a significant role for MNEs and how they adapt their strategies and management of nationality over time. However, MNEs' nationality strategies are not merely corporate decisions; they have far-reaching societal implications. Their ability to navigate nationality and exploit legal loopholes created economic inequalities, influenced political affairs, and shaped public perceptions. The concrete societal impacts of MNEs exploiting their nationality have varied significantly across historical periods and geographical contexts. It offered opportunities for growth and expansion during periods of globalization and liberal economic policies, and it helped taking advantage of resources and labor in host countries with limited benefits for local communities. In response to decolonization after World War II, some MNEs strategically shifted their subsidiaries' nationalities to flee responsibility for colonial practices, while others capitalized on anticolonial sentiments to gain a competitive advantage.

Even today as they navigate an increasingly globalized business environment, nationality remains a crucial factor in the operations and strategies of MNEs. But MNEs are not uniformly affected by nationality issues in any given historical context. Multinational enterprises from different countries may face distinct challenges or opportunities based on factors such as political alliances, historical conflicts, or cultural perceptions. Geopolitical shifts can significantly alter the landscape and conditions for MNEs, influencing their decisions of where to incorporate, how to manage their operations, and how to present their offerings in foreign markets. Despite the increasing transnational nature of large MNEs in terms of ownership and management, and their relative independence from states, they may still rely on resources provided by their home countries during times of crisis. It can be assumed that as long as nation-states and national cultures persist, MNEs will address nationality-related issues and strategically utilize and manage nationality in various ways.

Governments face the challenge of balancing the benefits of FDI with broader societal interests. While FDI could stimulate economic growth and technological advancement, there are legitimate concerns about potential negative consequences such as loss of domestic control over strategic resources fuelling nationalist sentiments and protectionist policies. At the same time, MNEs could become instruments or pawns in geopolitical conflicts. Ambiguous nationality facilitates MNEs' ability to evade regulations and taxes by strategically locating their operations and structuring their ownership across different jurisdictions potentially depriving both home and host countries of tax revenue and undermining the effectiveness of regulatory frameworks. Strategic use of nationality with detrimental effects on the host countries' societies were made possible by the lack of global rules and norms governing MNE behavior. Effective international frameworks would, for example, limit tax competition between states and establish transparency regarding the ultimate ownership of economic resources. However, as the 2020s have progressed, the prospect of any such international collaboration has weakened rather than strengthened.

Notes

1. Yip, G. S., Johansson, J. K., and Roos, J. "Effects of Nationality on Global Strategy," *MIR: Management International Review*, 37, 4 (1997), 365–385.
2. Jones, G. "The End of Nationality? Global Firms and 'Borderless Worlds,'" *Zeitschrift für Unternehmensgeschichte*, 51, 2 (2006), 149–165.
3. Wellhausen, R. L. *The Shield of Nationality: When Governments Break Contracts with Foreign Firms*, Cambridge, Cambridge University Press, 2014.
4. UNCTAD. *World Investment Report: Investor Nationality: Policy Challenges*, Geneva, United Nations, 2016, xii.
5. Roy, T. "The Origins of Import Substituting Industrialization in India," *Economic History of Developing Regions*, 32, 1 (2017), 71–95.
6. Ufimtseva, A. "The Rise of Foreign Direct Investment Regulation in Investment-Recipient Countries," *Global Policy*, 11, 2 (2020), 222–232.
7. Jones, G. *Multinationals and Global Capitalism: From the Nineteenth to the Twenty-First Century*, Oxford, Oxford University Press, 2005, 254.
8. Jones, G. *Renewing Unilever: Transformation and Tradition*, Oxford, Oxford University Press, 2005, 45–46, 86.
9. Godelier, E. "The Corporate Nationality: A Question of Culture and Community?" *Journal of Modern European History*, 18, 1 (2020), 28–47.
10. Lubinski, C. *Navigating Nationalism in Global Enterprise: A Century of Indo-German Business Relations*, Cambridge, Cambridge University Press, 2022.
11. Jones, "The End of Nationality?" 153.
12. Becker, S. *Multinationalität hat verschiedene Gesichter*, Stuttgart, Franz Steiner, 2002.
13. Vandamme, T. *Beyond Belgium: The Business Empire of Edouard Empain in the First Global Economy (1880–1914)*, Ghent, Ghent University Press, 2019.
14. Wilkins, M. "The Free-Standing Company Revisited," in Wilkins, M. and Schröter, H. G. (eds.) *The Free-Standing Company in the World Economy*, Oxford, Oxford University Press, 1998.
15. Harvey, C. E. *The Rio Tinto Company: An Economic History of a Leading International Mining Concern, 1873–1954*, Penzance, Alison Hodge, 1981.
16. Fitzgerald, R. *The Rise of the Global Company: Multinationals and the Making of the Modern World*, Cambridge, Cambridge University Press, 2015, 29.
17. Wilkins, M. *The History of Foreign Investment in the United States to 1914*, Cambridge, MA, Harvard University Press, 1989.
18. Wilkins, M. "Japanese Multinational Enterprise before 1914," *Business History Review*, 60, 2 (1986), 199–231.
19. Jonker, J. and van Zanden, J. L. *A History of Royal Dutch Shell, vol. 1: From Challenger to Joint Industry Leader, 1890–1939*, Oxford, Oxford University Press, 2007, 82.

20. Bertrams, K., Coupain, N., and Homburg, E. *Solvay: History of a Multinational Family Firm*, New York, Cambridge University Press, 2013.
21. Hertner, P. "Financial Strategies and Adaptation to Foreign Markets: The German Electrotechnical Industry and Its Multinational Activities: 1890s to 1939," in Teichova, A., Lévy-Leboyer, M., and Nussbaum, H. (eds.) *Multinational Enterprise in Historical Perspective*, Cambridge, Cambridge University Press, 1986.
22. Bonin, H. "First American Firms coming to France (from the 1900s to the 1930s)," in Bonin, H. and De Goey, F. (eds.) *American Firms in Europe: Strategy, Identity, Perception and Performance (1880-1980)* Geneva, Librairie Droz, 2009, 71-103, citation 85.
23. Lubinski, C. "Local Responsiveness in Distant Markets: Western Gramophone Companies in India before World War I," *Management & Organizational History*, 10, 2 (2015), 170-188.
24. Jones, *Multinationals and Global Capitalism*, 8, 12, 244.
25. Reckendrees, A. *Beiersdorf: The Company behind the Brands NIVEA, tesa, Hansaplast & Co*, Munich, CH Beck, 2018.
26. Jonker and van Zanden, *Royal Dutch Shell*, 251.
27. Wilkins, M. *The History of Foreign Investment in the United States, 1914-1945*, Cambridge MA, Harvard University Press, 2004.
28. Wilkins, M. "Japanese Multinationals in the United States: Continuity and Change, 1879-1990," *Business History Review*, 64, 4 (1990), 585-629.
29. Thomes, P. "Searching for Identity: Ford Motor Company in the German Market (1903-2003)," in Bonin, H., Lung, Y., and Tolliday, S. (eds.) *Ford 1903-2003: The European History, Volume 2*, Paris, P.L.A.G.E., 2003, 151-232.
30. Álvaro-Moya, A. "Networking Capability Building in the Multinational Enterprise: ITT and the Spanish Adventure (1924-1945)," *Business History*, 57, 7 (2015), 1082-1111.
31. Sluyterman, K. "Decolonisation and the Organisation of the International Workforce: Dutch Multinationals in Indonesia, 1945-1967," *Business History* 62, 7 (2020), 1182-1201.
32. Tolliday, S. "The Origins of Ford of Europe: From Multidomestic to Transnational Corporation 1903-1976," in Bonin, H., Lung, Y., and Tolliday, S. (eds.) *Ford 1903-2003: The European History*, Volume 1, Paris, P.L.A.G.E., 2003, 153-241
33. Schröter, H. G. *Aufstieg der Kleinen: Multinationale Unternehmen aus fünf kleinen Staaten vor 1914*, Berlin, Duncker & Humblot, 1993.
34. Reckendrees, *Beiersdorf*.
35. Reckendrees, A. "Business as a Means of Foreign Policy or Politics as a Means of Production? The German Government and the Creation of Friedrich Flick's Upper Silesian Industrial Empire (1921-1935)," *Enterprise & Society*, 14, 1 (2013), 99-143.
36. Jones, *Multinationals and Global Capitalism*, 209.

37. Jonker and van Zanden, *Royal Dutch Shell*.
38. Lubinski, *Navigating Nationalism*, 114-165.
39. Wellhausen, *The Shield of Nationality*.
40. Bucheli, M. and Decker, S. "Expropriations of Foreign Property and Political Alliances: A Business Historical Approach," *Enterprise & Society*, 22, 1 (2021), 247-284.
41. Decker, S. *Postcolonial Transition and Global Business History: British Multinational Companies in Ghana and Nigeria*, London, Routledge, 2022.
42. Sluyterman, "Decolonisation and the Organisation of the International Workforce," 1194.
43. Lubinski, *Navigating Nationalism*, 228.
44. Bucheli, M. and Salvaj, E. "Political Connections, the Liability of Foreignness, and Legitimacy: A Business Historical Analysis of Multinationals' Strategies in Chile," *Global Strategy Journal*, 8, 3 (2018), 399-420.
45. Reckendrees, *Beiersdorf*.
46. Jones, *Renewing Unilever*, 141.
47. Braun GmbH (ed.) *90 Years of Braun (1921-2011)*, Cologne, Geschichtsbüro, 2011, 62-67.
48. Jones, *Renewing Unilever*, 239.
49. Dyer, D., Dalzell, F., and Olegario, R. *Rising Tide: Lessons from 165 Years of Brand Building at Procter & Gamble*, Boston, MA, Harvard Business School Press, 2004, 217-218, 233.
50. Tolliday, "The Origins of Ford of Europe."
51. Hodges, M. "The Japanese Industrial Presence in America: Same Bed, Different Dreams," *Millennium: Journal of International Studies*, 18, 3 (1989), 359-376.
52. Wellhausen, *The Shield of Nationality*.
53. Jones, *Multinationals and Global Capitalism*, 254.
54. Autor, D. H., Dorn, D., and Hanson, G. H. "The China Syndrome: Local Labor Market Effects of Import Competition in the United States," *American Economic Review*, 103, 6 (2013), 2121-2168.
55. Helleiner, E. and Pickel, A. *Economic Nationalism in a Globalizing World*, Ithaca, NY, Cornell University Press, 2018.
56. Kobrin, S. J. "Bricks and Mortar in a Borderless World: Globalization, the Backlash, and the Multinational Enterprise," *Global Strategy Journal*, 7, 2 (2017), 159-171.
57. de Jong, B. and Zwartkruis, W. "The EU Regulation on Screening of Foreign Direct Investment: A Game Changer?" *European Business Law Review*, 31, 3 (2020), 447-474.
58. Jones, G. and Da Silva Lopes, T. "International Business History and the Strategy of Multinational Enterprises: How History Matters," in Mellahi, K. et al. (eds.) *The Oxford Handbook of International Business Strategy*, Oxford, Oxford University Press, 2021, 45.

Further Reading

Bonin, H., Lung, Y., and Tolliday, S. (eds.) *Ford 1903–2003: The European History, 2 vols.* Paris, P.L.A.G.E., 2003.

Decker, S. *Postcolonial Transition and Global Business History: British Multinational Companies in Ghana and Nigeria,* London, Routledge, 2022.

Jones, G. *Renewing Unilever: Transformation and Tradition* Oxford, Oxford University Press, 2005.

Lubinski, C. *Navigating Nationalism in Global Enterprise: A Century of Indo-German Business Relations,* Cambridge, Cambridge University Press, 2022.

Reckendrees, A. *Beiersdorf: The Company behind the Brands NIVEA, tesa, Hansaplast & Co,* Munich, CH Beck, 2018.

ANDREA LLUCH AND
RORY M. MILLER

14

Multinationals, Latin America, and Dependency Theories

14.1 Introduction

The growth of foreign direct investment (FDI) in Latin America and antagonism toward it from nationalists proceeded hand in hand. In the late 1960s and early 1970s, two developments caused tensions to become particularly acute. First, the number of multinational enterprises (MNEs) operating in the region increased significantly, as governments pursued policies of import substitution industrialization (ISI), using tariffs, exchange controls, and subsidies. Much of the new investment focused on the three largest economies: Argentina, Brazil, and Mexico. However, the possibilities offered by smaller markets in Peru, Chile, Colombia, and Venezuela also attracted manufacturing MNEs to establish subsidiaries there. Second, long-standing criticisms of the behavior of foreign investors, which centered on accusations that they contributed little to economic and social development and caused considerable damage to Latin American interests, became encapsulated in the growing popularity of academic theories of dependency. This reflected broader discontent with the nature of the "progress" that the region had experienced since World War II, which had left large sections of the population marginalized.

After 1945, social scientists in several Latin American countries had begun to imagine a new global economy, challenging the economic orthodoxies of the developed world. Building upon the work of Raúl Prebisch, an Argentine economist who became the first director of the

United Nations Economic Commission for Latin America (ECLA, CEPAL in Spanish), they contended that global trading and financial systems actually constrained the development of countries in the region.[1] Prebisch had argued that commodity producers were suffering from a long-term decline in terms of trade, and that Latin American countries should focus on industrialization and structural reform to modernize successfully. However, a new wave of dependency writers in the 1960s went much further. Within the English-speaking world, André Gunder Frank quickly became the best known. Frank's analyses of the economic histories of Chile and Brazil led him to argue that Latin American countries had developed most successfully when their links with the developed economies had been weakest – for example, during the two world wars. For him, foreign trade and investment had produced underdevelopment.[2] Other authors offered more nuanced arguments, but had less influence on academics outside the region due to delays in translation. In a book published in Spanish in 1969, but in English not until 1979, Fernando Henrique Cardoso and Enzo Faletto, for example, argued that Latin America was engaged in "associated dependent development," in which local business elites became dependent on MNEs and on the state, with little autonomy of their own.[3] During the 1970s, dependency theories became the dominant paradigm among economists and social scientists working in and on Latin America.[4] The result, to quote the title of an influential book that Raymond Vernon of Harvard University published in 1977, was a "Storm over the Multinationals."[5]

What can business historians contribute to the analysis of the MNEs' impact in Latin America? First, their focus on continuity and change allows them to place developments in a long-term perspective. We thus see the growth of dependency theories and governments' attempts to control MNEs, especially in the late 1960s and early 1970s, as the outcome of a long history of economic nationalism and criticism of foreign investors. This perspective also allows us to see continuity in the antagonism toward new FDI, especially from China, which arose later, in the 1990s and early 2000s. The influence of dependency theories never went away. Second, business historians obtained access to the internal archives of many MNEs and governments that were not available to the dependency theorists, allowing us to verify or reject their arguments. It is clear, for example, that Frank's assumptions about the impact of the world wars are simply misleading. Third, the development of business history within Latin America allows us to see much more clearly how local business elites, on which there had been little previous research, interacted with and responded to FDI. Overall, business history now encompasses studies not just of the political economy of FDI, but also of social, cultural, and environmental issues. The body of research published since the 1970s allows us to identify and explain complexities in the experiences of different countries, and social groups within them, which the generalizations of dependency theorists overlooked.

The academic literature on international business normally distinguishes between resource-seeking MNEs and market-seeking MNEs. We employ that distinction here. Resource-seeking MNEs in oil, mining, and agriculture had a longer history and could be found throughout the region, wherever opportunities for commodity export production existed. Manufacturing MNEs developed later, especially from the 1930s, and were much more concentrated in the largest economies with the strongest states. Compared with resource-seeking MNEs, they faced and created very different problems and opportunities, and their impact on Latin American societies went much deeper.

14.2 Resource-Seeking MNEs

Foreign direct investment in Latin American mining really took off from the 1880s, when British capital poured into Chile's nitrate industry. Rising demand for copper for the new electrical industries then encouraged US investment in Mexico in the 1890s, initially by Phelps Dodge and the Guggenheims. A New York syndicate acquired the Cerro de Pasco mines in Peru in 1901–1902, before purchasing other concessions nearby from Peruvian entrepreneurs. United States investment in Chilean copper arrived slightly later, but by the mid 1920s two major MNEs, Anaconda and Kennecott, controlled the three largest mines.

Foreign companies also developed the petroleum industry. After 1889 two British firms began to produce oil in Peru, but output remained low. In contrast, new discoveries by British and US prospectors in Mexico immediately prior to the outbreak of revolution there in 1910–1911 led quickly to the development of a much larger industry, which Standard Oil of New Jersey and Royal Dutch Shell (Shell) came to dominate. Investments by these two firms, alongside Gulf Oil, then allowed Venezuela to replace Mexico as Latin America's leading oil producer in the 1920s, a position it retained for the remainder of the century.[6]

Foreign investors also moved into various agricultural exports. United Fruit Company was formed in 1899, initially to exploit concessions in Costa Rica. A second important firm operating in Central America, renamed Standard Fruit in 1924, was established the same year. These companies' activities became extremely controversial and for many Latin Americans epitomized the highly exploitative nature of MNEs. Liebig Company, founded in 1865, possessed livestock ranches in Argentina, Uruguay, and Brazil, but the US meatpacking companies, which established themselves in the River Plate after 1908, purchased livestock from local producers. Apart from these examples, and US sugar firms in Cuba, Latin American landowners, not MNEs, produced the majority of the region's agricultural exports: coffee in Brazil, Colombia, and Central America; henequen in Mexico; cacao in Ecuador; and sugar and cotton in Peru.

Most benefits to host economies from commodity exports would flow through three channels: employment, local purchases of inputs, and taxes. These varied according to the nature of each commodity, the structure of its global value chain, and individual governments' policies. Additional processing in the host country would clearly have a greater economic and social impact than simply shipping a commodity straight to a port or railhead.

With respect to employment, first, wages in the export sectors that MNEs controlled appear significantly higher than in agriculture. In the early 1900s unskilled laborers at the Cananea mine in Mexico earned about three times the wages that agricultural workers received.[7] The same was true of the Huasteca oil field, also in Mexico, although more abundant local supplies of labor there led to rather lower daily wages than in Cananea.[8] In the nitrate zone in northern Chile, higher nominal wages attracted so many migrants from the central region that landowners complained of seasonal labor shortages. Employees in these export sectors thus often became a working-class elite. They also – eventually – came to enjoy significant nonwage benefits, such as company housing, schools, and healthcare. While foreign observers frequently complained that workers dissipated their earnings on alcohol, gambling, and women, this did effectively recirculate money, spreading the benefits to others. Elsewhere, in the Mantaro valley in central Peru, migrant mine workers reinvested collectively in projects in their home communities.

Higher wages in the export sectors did not deflect nationalist criticism of the MNEs' attitudes and behavior: Governor De la Huerta, a provincial governor in Mexico, complained in 1918 that miners had become "veritable slaves of the capitalists."[9] Moreover, these activities offered only limited opportunities for employment. The fifty thousand employed in the Chilean nitrate industry in the 1920s compared with half a million working in agriculture (total population was around four million). The Mexican oil industry probably also employed around fifty thousand at its peak in 1921, against a national population of almost fifteen million.

Second, with regard to the procurement of supplies, resource-seeking MNEs like the mining and oil companies, or United Fruit in Central America, frequently enjoyed concessions that permitted duty-free imports. This reduced the potential benefits to local industry. Nonetheless, demand for provisions in mining and oil camps located in isolated areas of the country did benefit landowners, traders, and transport suppliers. Nitrate workers and copper miners in the Atacama Desert, for example, consumed large quantities of foodstuffs produced in the center and south of Chile.[10]

Third, critics of resource-seeking MNEs often complained about the low level of tax revenues that Latin American states received. Apart, perhaps, from Chile, whose global monopoly of nitrate fertilizer allowed the state to impose a relatively high export duty, taxation was rarely optimal. Governments lacked knowledge of new industries and frequently offered extensive concessions in order to attract investors. The Rothschilds' copper mining operation in Mexico enjoyed exemption from provincial and national taxes for twenty years and from customs duties for fifty.[11] Some of United Fruit's tax concessions lasted for ninety-nine years.[12] It was only after 1948, when Venezuela began to implement a fifty-fifty profit-sharing agreement with the petroleum companies, that the state's revenues from the industry there expanded significantly. Chile also succeeded in extracting more from the US copper companies after World War II, but this followed years of low taxation and provoked a reduction in new investment.

Governments' use of the revenues they obtained from commodity exports also stimulated criticism. Many politicians simply utilized them to buy support, like President Gómez in Venezuela (1908–1935) or several Central American dictators. Subsequent administrations in Venezuela, again in search of political advantages, ensured that more benefits flowed to the country's middle and working classes. In Chile, where the state received roughly a third of the total earnings from nitrate, the elite used them partly to avoid taxation on their own income and wealth, but successive governments did also invest significantly in public works and education.[13] Chile's exceptionalism stands out, yet, even there, nationalist attacks on the mining MNEs and what critics regarded as a *"vendepatria"* elite (this literally means "selling the homeland," but the Spanish term has connotations of treasonable behavior) increased in intensity in the 1950s and 1960s.

Alongside the limited nature of these backward linkages into national economies, a consequence of the pressure that MNEs could exert on relatively weak governments, other criticisms focused on expatriate managers' treatment of their local workforce. In the early stages, recruitment was often difficult. Several firms, lacking roots in the regions where they had invested, employed labor contractors who offered migrant workers advances on wages and transport to the workplace. This system, often referred to as *enganche* (meaning "a hook"), was used in Peruvian copper mining and Mexican oil and mining, and to attract Bolivian and Peruvian migrants to the Chilean nitrate zone. Some critics alleged that this constituted a form of exploitative debt peonage, but many such workers returned each year. Some MNEs in the Caribbean, including United Fruit and the Venezuelan oil firms, also recruited English-speaking migrant workers from the British West Indies. However, there is certainly evidence of other forms of labor coercion. The Pearson oil interests in Mexico called on local government officials to secure workers in the Huasteca. In Guatemala, President Estrada Cabrera (1898–1920) allowed a United Fruit subsidiary to draft Indigenous workers for railway construction, while President Úbico (1931–1944) later tightened vagrancy laws to facilitate labor recruitment.

These practices raise questions about the extent to which foreign managers displayed racist attitudes and exploited ethnic differences within their labor force. Multinational enterprises paid higher wages to their own nationals than to local workers from the beginning, a source of persistent complaint. Foreign miners at Cananea earned a daily wage more than double that of their Mexican counterparts in 1906.[14] Moreover, the managers and technical experts working in MNEs, like oil drillers, often enjoyed salaries denominated in US dollars or pounds sterling, which protected them against local currency depreciation, as in Mexico after 1890, or Chile through much of the twentieth century. Foreign managers complained continually about Latin American attitudes toward work and their lack of time discipline.

Apart from wage differentials, other forms of discrimination were widespread. Skilled Mexican workers in the mines could not advance beyond the apprentice level until much later. Housing was normally segregated. Foreign managers and technicians lived in fenced compounds with solidly built houses, gardens, and social facilities. In contrast, local workers frequently had to construct shacks on wasteland, often low-lying marshland in areas like the oil fields. This exposed them to insect-borne diseases like malaria and yellow fever, and to gastrointestinal problems due to contaminated drinking water and poor sanitation. In some instances, MNEs deliberately exploited national and ethnic differences within the workforce to hinder labor cohesion and organization. In Central America and Venezuela, security officers were frequently black West Indians. In the River Plate meatpacking houses, the US MNEs imported techniques of labor control that they had employed in Chicago, assigning immigrants of different nationalities to different tasks in order to hinder organization. Only after the shock of the Mexican oil nationalization in 1938, which arose from a prolonged labor dispute, did MNEs like Standard Oil of New Jersey and Shell begin to promote local recruits into more senior management roles in Venezuela, a defensive strategy adopted deliberately in order to align themselves with the political and business elite.

The MNEs' alienation of their workforce lay behind several notorious incidents of repression: killings of protestors at Cananea in 1906; Santa María de Iquique in the Chilean nitrate zone in 1907; the workers of a British-registered tanning company, La Forestal, in northern Argentina in 1921; and a strike among Colombian banana workers in 1928. In all these cases, army or police commanders sided with foreign MNEs. Apart from routinely making payments to such officials to buy their support, companies took numerous measures to hinder worker organization: preventing outsiders from entering mining and oil camps, closing highways and demanding that local people carry passes, employing watchmen and guards, paying informers to infiltrate workers' meetings, and firing and blacklisting those they regarded as agitators. Nonetheless, antagonism toward the MNEs' management also stimulated some of the earliest and most powerful trade union organizations in Latin America (along with workers in strategic industries like the railways and ports). In 1925, almost all seven thousand workers at the Chuquicamata copper mine in northern Chile went on strike, denouncing the "Yankee Company" and "the imperialistic domination of North America."[15] Labor nationalism was similarly apparent at critical junctures in the Mexican and Venezuelan oil fields and the Peruvian mining industry.

Washington's preoccupation with the threat of communism after 1945 provided US companies with further opportunities to weaken or co-opt labor. During a strike in Tocopilla, in northern Chile, the owners of Chuquicamata labeled the strikers as communists and Indians, thus using race to denigrate their employees. In Venezuela, the Acción Democrática party exploited its close links with the principal oil workers' union to present itself to the business elite and Washington as the alternative to communist infiltration. Most notoriously, United Fruit's labeling of the Arbenz government in Guatemala as communist, and its lobbying of sympathetic officials in the Eisenhower administration, led to a coup in 1954, inspired by the Central Intelligence Agency. In Chile, a US telecommunications company, ITT, made every effort to sabotage the election of a socialist president, Salvador Allende, in 1970 (see Chapter 6 for more detail).

Resource-seeking MNEs showed little concern for the environment, as Chapter 2 emphasizes. The oil companies and banana firms destroyed large expanses of tropical forest and avoided carrying out remedial activities when they reduced their operations. Almost from the beginning, the petroleum industry created problems of pollution, whether from sudden blowouts, or more subtly, through everyday leakages from pipes and tanks. The contamination of Lake Maracaibo in Venezuela, even in the 1920s, was such that local residents could not use the lake water, while wildlife and farm animals died. In Mexico, saltwater intrusion seriously damaged the MNEs' oil wells after 1921, leaving the inhabitants of northern Veracruz, in the words of environmental historian Myrna Santiago, with "large areas of deforested land blanketed in oil, polluted streams and river-beds, diminished oyster beds and shrimping areas, and irreparably damaged hunting grounds."[16]

Little research on accidents and health in the extractive industries has taken place, which is not surprising given the state's lack of concern and the MNEs' desire to conceal these problems. One must conclude, however, that mining and oil workers, especially, traded higher wages for poorer health and often an earlier death. Ordinary laborers in the Huasteca oil fields, according to Santiago, were "subject to high levels of occupational risk, toxic environments, tropical disease, and the vagaries of weather."[17] Accidents seem to have been frequent, often caused by workers' unfamiliarity with new machinery. The misuse of dynamite and rockfalls killed miners, while smelters slowly poisoned them. Compensation for death or serious injury did not exist, making it a common demand in labor disputes. Even when the state did legislate for companies to pay compensation for accidents or long-term health problems, in Mexico and Chile in the 1920s, workers had to negotiate tortuous bureaucratic processes to obtain anything.

Multinational enterprises therefore had little incentive to introduce measures to limit work-related injuries or deaths. As noted already, workers in the extractive industries and their families frequently suffered from tropical diseases and gastrointestinal ailments. More insidious were long-term problems resulting from prolonged exposure to atmospheric pollution and the respiratory diseases that miners across the world suffered following exposure to noxious dust. As one union leader commented in 1942: "Miners usually died before reaching retirement age."[18] Although Chilean doctors had undertaken extensive studies of silicosis in the 1930s, mine managers continually refused to recognize and screen for the disease. More recently, chemicals that Chiquita (as United Fruit was renamed in 1990) used in banana packing in Costa Rica appear to have caused an increase in infertility among workers.[19] Whole communities might be affected. In Chuquicamata in Chile, water supplies were contaminated with arsenic, while the prevailing wind blew chlorine and sulfur into homes. High levels of toxicity in the soil and atmosphere eventually caused the town to be abandoned in 1992. In the case of La Oroya in Peru, where Cerro de Pasco Corporation opened a smelter in 1922, a Peruvian human rights and environmental specialist, Areli Valencia, estimates that more than a hundred tons of effluents, including arsenic, sulfur dioxide, lead, and bismuth, were emitted every day.[20]

One can therefore see many reasons why left-wing politicians, trade unions, the media, and the popular mood turned against resource-seeking MNEs. However, a shift toward the local recruitment of professionals and managers after the 1950s altered the balance between government and business, since the state could now tap this expertise and knowledge. Several resource-seeking MNEs in mining and oil thus suffered expropriation and became state-owned enterprises, or else faced greater regulatory scrutiny. Plantation companies, in contrast, had rather greater flexibility and could relocate production if political problems became too burdensome. In Guatemala, for example, Chiquita moved its focus from the more heavily unionized and regulated north of the country to the south.[21]

The pro-market reforms of the 1990s, often summarized under the label of "Washington Consensus," led to renewed investment in the extractive industries.[22] As discussed in Chapter 3, Chinese interest in Latin America's natural resources, in particular, began to increase. In 1992, the state-owned Shougang Group acquired Hierro Perú, the Marcona iron and steel complex nationalized twenty years previously. Chinalco, a minerals producer, later moved an entire town in central Peru in order to access rich copper deposits.[23] Through the 2000s, the Chinese presence in Latin America expanded across various extractive sectors, including oil, mining (iron and copper), and agriculture (soybeans).

This resurgence of resource-seeking FDI rekindled debates about the MNEs' impact, and in particular their social and environmental consequences (see Chapter 2). Much of the earlier hostility reappeared. Doe Run, for example, a US corporation that acquired the La Oroya smelter in 1997, was eventually forced out of Peru in 2009. In 2012, a nationalist center-left government in Argentina forcibly acquired 51 percent of Repsol's interest in YPF, the state oil producer privatized in the 1990s, leading to prolonged legal conflicts. Other lengthy disputes arose in Ecuador, where the government clashed with Chevron; Venezuela, where the state restricted foreign oil companies' exploration activities; and Bolivia, which nationalized its hydrocarbons industry in 2006.

In contrast to earlier periods, the growth of local community opposition, often focusing on concerns about the MNEs' environmental impact, added a new voice to the debates. International nongovernmental organizations advocating for environmental protection and Indigenous rights now provided publicity and support to local activists: Incidents no longer went unreported. The Rio Blanco mine in Peru, a Chinese-financed megaproject, for example, was suspended in 2018 after a resistance network mobilized rural communities and urban youth, as well as lawyers and academics, and blended street protests with legal action. Resistance, however, especially when led by Indigenous and female activists, also became as dangerous as some worker protests had been a century before.[24] Debates over the environmental consequences of lithium extraction or foreign mining companies' acrimonious entanglements with local communities thus have a long backstory.

14.3 Market-Seeking Manufacturing MNEs

Although some industrial firms established subsidiaries in the largest Latin American markets before World War I, FDI in manufacturing really began to expand in the 1920s and 1930s, especially in consumer nondurables like household goods, toiletries, and foodstuffs. Ford and General Motors also invested in vehicle assembly plants in the 1920s, using imported components, in Argentina, Brazil, and Mexico. The imposition of high import duties and exchange controls during the Great Depression of the early 1930s further encouraged MNEs to invest rather than lose markets to rivals. More deliberate ISI policies followed World War II: Developmentalist governments now attempted to deepen the industrialization process by encouraging local production of intermediate and capital goods, using protective tariffs, exchange controls, and subsidies. This resulted in significant FDI in sectors like machinery, domestic appliances, chemicals, and pharmaceuticals.[25]

Before the 1990s MNEs' investment decisions depended on the size and potential of the target market and, given that most operated in sectors characterized by oligopoly, the actions of global competitors. Unilever, for example, carefully monitored the activities of Procter & Gamble, Colgate-Palmolive, and Nestlé. The most attractive markets possessed a growing urban middle class with the disposable income to purchase consumer products ranging from toiletries and household goods to automobiles. Moreover, Latin American elites and middle classes had a long-standing preference for foreign products, which symbolized modernity and provided markers of status. Indeed, some local manufacturers adopted English-language brand names to enhance their appeal.[26] Having invested initially in Argentina, Brazil, and Mexico, MNEs began to establish subsidiaries in the 1950s and 1960s in smaller markets like Chile, Peru, Venezuela, or Colombia, often as joint ventures and in response to individual governments' ISI measures. Nonetheless, the three largest economies remained the most attractive locations for FDI in sectors like motor vehicles, machinery, electrical appliances, chemicals, and pharmaceuticals.

This surge of investment quickly became a target for economic nationalists influenced by dependency theories. Several governments attempted to regulate FDI in order to boost national economies rather than open them completely to MNEs: Brazil, Argentina, and Mexico all imposed strict local content requirements on automobile manufacturers from the late 1950s. Argentina, for example, prohibited the importation of finished vehicles while offering tax and foreign exchange concessions for plants using locally produced components. The five Andean Pact countries (Peru, Colombia, Ecuador, Bolivia, Chile), which formed a common market in 1969, enacted their famous "Decision 24" in 1971. This placed strict limits on new FDI, including "fade-out" clauses, which aimed eventually to bring foreign enterprises under local control. In 1973 Mexico tried to confine new foreign investors to joint ventures with local capitalists.

Such controls did not last. The debt crisis of the early 1980s, caused by over-borrowing on Eurodollar markets, stimulated the introduction of austerity measures to overcome fiscal deficits and balance-of-payments difficulties. This initially resulted in a painful economic recession throughout the region, discouraging new investments in manufacturing. Market liberalization had already begun, particularly in Chile and, in less extreme form, Argentina and Uruguay. Elsewhere, after a period marked by uncontrollable inflation and the failure of alternatives, and with the encouragement of the World Bank and the International Monetary Fund, economic liberalization seemed to offer the best recipe to overcome the crisis. By 1990 dependency theories had lost much of their popularity.

This economic turmoil and policy uncertainty caused MNEs to reconsider their strategies. Inflation and exchange rate volatility encouraged short-term decision-making. Some withdrew from particular markets. Automobile companies closed factories in countries like Peru and Chile once governments reduced tariff protection and ended subsidies. However, new FDI began to arrive in the 1990s. Governments started to seek private capital to improve public utilities and services, and to provide incentives for MNEs to incorporate their Latin American facilities into global value chains. The North American Free Trade Agreement (NAFTA) of 1994 between the United States, Canada, and Mexico, discussed in Chapter 8, encouraged new FDI in the Mexican automobile industry, for example, to supply the US market. Many countries agreed to investment protection clauses in the bilateral and multilateral trade agreements that they signed with commercial partners: Chile provides a significant early example of such a strategy.[27]

Apart from their access to global resources of finance, legal expertise, and management, manufacturing MNEs depended on two intangible advantages to overcome the costs of doing business in Latin America: modern technology, protected by patents, and the power of their brands, protected by trademarks and supported by intensive marketing expenditure. Foreign advertising agencies quickly followed the manufacturing MNEs into the region: J. Walter Thompson (JWT) established offices in Brazil and Argentina in 1929, initially to support their General

Motors accounts, but soon expanding into other business. McCann Erickson followed in 1935. These firms introduced modern market research techniques, developing ways to segment markets and, in particular, to pitch to female consumers. Multinational enterprises in sectors like pharmaceuticals, toiletries and cosmetics, or food processing seem to have spent considerably more than local competitors on advertising and promotion, further increasing barriers to entry and disadvantaging domestic firms.

With thousands of MNEs investing in manufacturing in Latin America, generalizing about their social impact is difficult. The arguments here draw upon evidence from well-studied industries such as motor vehicles, chemicals and pharmaceuticals, household goods, toiletries and cosmetics, and tobacco. By examining the backward and forward linkages of the MNEs' activities, and in particular their social impact, this perspective differs from that of dependency writers in the 1970s and 1980s, who focused on economic and political issues: the threat that MNEs posed to political sovereignty, their frequently aggressive behavior, problems in regulating them, and their impact on the balance of payments.

The most important backward linkages were MNEs' procurement policies and employment. Foreign firms imported much of their equipment, especially in the early stages. Indeed, dependency writers often complained that companies used secondhand machinery to commence production in Latin America, which impeded efficiency and was inappropriate for labor-abundant economies. As with resource-seeking MNEs, host governments frequently offered concessions to encourage investment. In the 1920s, for example, Argentina charged lower tariffs on vehicles imported in kit form, and on the rubber that tire companies required. Later, in the 1950s, Volkswagen secured cheap credit from state agencies in Brazil to finance construction of a new factory in São Paulo.

Many governments regarded the motor industry as a cornerstone of industrialization and imposed local content requirements to stimulate the growth of suppliers. Brazil introduced such measures in 1956, followed by Argentina in 1959, Mexico, Venezuela, and Chile in 1962, and Peru in 1965. Their precise nature differed: 90 percent of sales revenue in Brazil in the 1980s, 80 percent in Argentina, and 60 percent in Mexico.[28] One consequence was that MNEs providing components invested alongside the final producers. Bosch, Lucas (auto-electrics), Perkins Diesels, Pilkington (safety glass), GKN (drive trains), Ferodo (brake pads), and tire manufacturers like Goodyear, Firestone, and Dunlop all had factories in Latin America by the end of the 1950s. Local content requirements added to the industry's employment effects. The most successful country at maximizing returns from MNE production of automobiles was probably Mexico, where domestically owned components firms expanded thanks to government restrictions, supplying not only producers in Mexico but eventually US manufacturers as well.[29] The NAFTA accord of 1994 facilitating access to the US market provided a further stimulus to both MNEs and domestic components suppliers.[30]

The motor industry thus became a major employer, especially in the largest economies. An estimate for Mexico in 1977 put those directly employed in the sector at thirty-nine thousand, with a further fifty-eight thousand working in supplier firms, as well as thousands working in sales and distribution.[31] There were around fourteen hundred local and foreign establishments manufacturing components, employing seventy-five thousand people, in Argentina in 1967.[32] Jobs in the industry were prized. Automobile workers in Brazil in the late 1950s enjoyed high wages and good additional benefits, at least before a military dictatorship after 1964 repressed trade union activity, and hence real wages.[33] Much the same happened in Argentina. Until the 1976 military coup, workers in the industry possessed strong trade unions which frequently headed broader antigovernment protests, most importantly the Cordobazo, an uprising in northwest Argentina that shook the country's military regime in 1969.[34] Ford workers were active in mobilizing others in the northern industrial belt of Buenos Aires during the Peronist governments of 1973–1976, before repression set in (see Chapter 6). At the end of the decade, automobile workers in São Paulo participated in a forty-one-day strike, led by a future president, Luiz Inácio Lula da Silva, a key step in the Brazilian military's eventual withdrawal from power.

Local workers in the MNEs' manufacturing plants would clearly benefit from acquiring mechanical skills that they could transfer to other occupations, including self-employment. But what of managers?

Generally, manufacturing MNEs imported not only the technical staff required to commence operations, but also their managers, unless, as in Argentina, they could draw upon a well-educated expatriate community, like the British or Germans. In many MNE subsidiaries foreigners continued to dominate upper levels of management. By the 1980s, however, some firms had begun to promote Latin American recruits to senior positions, especially in areas that required good understanding of local culture and institutions, like human resources, marketing, sales, and advertising. Nevertheless, expatriates often retained the leading financial and strategic roles. In essence, local managers seem to have faced an informal "glass ceiling" until late in the twentieth century.[35] Only rarely was one transferred to another subsidiary of the same firm or a permanent role at company headquarters.

As noted already, most resource-seeking MNEs in Latin America did not develop positive forward linkages. This was not true of manufacturing companies, whose products clearly altered consumption habits and opened opportunities for small-scale entrepreneurs and employees in local firms. The motor industry, for example, completely transformed transport and mobility. Official statistics show that in Argentina the number of vehicles increased from around 600,000 in 1955 to 3.3 million in 1975, a third of which were for commercial use; the figures for Mexico are very similar at 551,000 and 3.3 million. The most startling increase occurred in Brazil, though, where the number rose from 694,000 to almost 6 million over twenty years, with a much higher rate of growth in private cars.[36]

This industry had three major impacts on society. First, the growing use of cars and trucks required considerable support services: franchised dealerships, gas stations, repair shops, and spare parts. Almost all the employees in these establishments were local, and they were not just in "formal" enterprises. By the 1970s, a whole sector of the "informal economy" had sprung up to fabricate components and undertake cheap repairs to keep aging vehicles on the road. Second, ownership of a vehicle provided individuals with opportunities to develop income-generating activities: taxi services, minibuses (frequently organized into driver cooperatives), or trucks carrying goods and, in rural areas, people too. While long-distance bus services under local ownership, using vehicles produced by MNEs, developed as trunk roads improved, relatively few large logistics companies existed in Latin America: The trucking industry depended heavily on owner-drivers. Third, motor transport stimulated the expansion of cities and reordering of urban space. Although a few subways existed, in Buenos Aires for example, in most cities buses and collective taxis replaced tramways and suburban railways. Automobiles were essential both to the development of middle- and upper-class suburbs and to the growth of shantytowns, known as *favelas* in Brazil, or *pueblos jóvenes* in Peru, within and on the margins of major cities. The urban poor who settled there relied heavily on motor transport to get to work.

Multinational enterprises producing consumer nondurables also offered opportunities to local entrepreneurs in the distribution of branded goods. Traveling salesmen in early twentieth-century Mexico, for example, dealt in products as disparate as Bayer's aspirin and Singer sewing machines.[37] In Argentina, *turco* traders (Syrian and Lebanese immigrants) peddled J. & P. Coats' sewing thread around the interior, as well as Unilever's soaps. As a Unilever director visiting Brazil in 1941 noted, "a special feature is the Syrian trade in São Paulo and Rio, which supplies small retailers on a cut-price, cash-and-carry basis."[38] And as new methods of communication developed, the MNEs' advertising and promotional expenditure provided local radio and, later, television stations with a significant income, especially through the medium of the soap operas or *telenovelas* they sponsored.

At the upper end of the market, department stores, most famously Harrods in Buenos Aires or El Palacio de Hierro in Mexico City, attracted wealthy shoppers with displays of foreign brands. Women in particular became targets for marketing agencies. In Brazil, JWT regarded them as "a class that could afford to buy the goods and products of modern consumer society."[39] Several European and North American MNEs specializing in cosmetics opened factories in Latin America to appeal to this market: Revlon in Mexico in 1948; Wella in Chile, Brazil, Argentina, and Mexico between 1952 and 1961; and Avon in Brazil in 1958. The latter made extensive use of women in their sales activities, although they never reached senior management positions.[40]

The MNEs had an impact on women's lives in other ways. The introduction of appliances like refrigerators, washing machines, vacuum cleaners, and floor polishers freed up time. Alongside this came the development of household products such as detergents, cleaning fluids, and disinfectants. Hardly surprisingly, advertisements for all these products filled the pages of women's magazines, as well as commercial breaks on radio and television within programs directed at a female audience, reinforcing gender norms: The MNEs' marketing departments regarded women's role essentially as one of maintaining a clean and efficient household (as in North America), as emphasized in Chapter 10.[41]

As dependency-influenced writers argued in the 1970s, however, the rapid growth of manufacturing MNEs also had several negative consequences on Latin American societies. First, much of the growth in FDI, especially after 1950, came through acquisitions, displacing local entrepreneurs. Even before then, British consumer goods firms like J. & P. Coats and Reckitt & Sons had acquired local competitors simply with the intention of closing them down. However, the tobacco industry offers a particularly egregious case in which MNEs marginalized local producers. Except for British American Tobacco (BAT), which arrived in the early twentieth century, international cigarette firms paid little attention to Latin America until the 1960s. Stagnant sales in their developed world markets then forced firms like Philip Morris and RJ Reynolds to look for new opportunities. A combination of price competition via cheap contraband imports (often supplied through Paraguay) and the MNEs' heavy expenditures on marketing forced out local producers; BAT, for example, took over the long-established Nobleza Piccardo firm in Argentina, while Philip Morris acquired Massalín Particulares, effectively creating a duopoly.[42] A parallel process occurred in pharmaceuticals, where the technically advanced and branded drugs produced by MNEs and supported by heavy advertising undermined independent laboratories. However, many foreign pharmaceuticals firms confined themselves to secondary manufacture and packaging in Latin America, utilizing materials imported in bulk. This provided them with enormous potential to charge high prices, as evidenced by studies undertaken in the 1970s, as well as to engage in transfer pricing through over-invoicing.[43]

Second, critics argued that MNEs' products were more suited to the developed world than to poorer countries. Pharmaceuticals again provide a good example. International firms undertook very little research and development in Latin America. Their production and marketing focused on drugs intended to treat Western ailments such as cardiovascular disease, cancers, headaches, constipation, or diabetes, rather than the endemic and epidemic diseases that afflicted the poor. As in the developed world, their products targeted the middle-class "worried well" in cities, rather than the mass of the population. Poor regulation in many countries also meant that MNEs ignored requirements to inform users about side effects, as well as allowing them to continue to market drugs for which approval had been withdrawn in North America. The fact that many Latin Americans used pharmacies rather than doctors, even for drugs that were available elsewhere only by prescription, made matters worse.[44]

Over the longer term, other negative aspects of the MNE presence became clear. The tobacco companies' heavy expenditures on advertising and promotion stimulated a significant increase in consumption. Governments did little to regulate advertising of cigarettes or enforce health warnings on packs until much later. In Argentina the strength of the tobacco-growing lobby and its political influence obstructed more effective public health policies. Lung cancer became a leading cause of death, especially among men. The rate in Brazil, for example, peaked in 2008, reflecting an increase in smoking that had occurred in the 1970s.[45]

The consumption of carbonated soft drinks also became a significant public health problem. Coca-Cola established its first bottling plants in Central America, Mexico, and Colombia in 1927, again supported by intensive advertising and promotional campaigns. In Mexico, this contributed to one of the highest rates of obesity in the world, together with associated diabetes and kidney disease. The company made constant efforts to undermine public health campaigns, developing close links with politicians. President Vicente Fox (2000–2006) had, in fact, been responsible for Coca-Cola's Mexican operations prior to his political career.[46] Further public health problems arose from the atmospheric pollution caused by motor vehicles, especially those that were older and poorly maintained: Lima, Santiago, São Paulo, and Mexico City all became notorious on this score.

A final issue concerns human rights. Many MNEs blocked the formation of active trade unions. Military governments in Argentina

(1966–1973, but especially 1976–1983), Brazil (1964–1985), and Chile (1973–1990) provided them with an opportunity not only to clamp down heavily on workers' organization but even to collaborate with security authorities in identifying individuals for arrest and torture (see Chapter 6). Multinational enterprises like Volkswagen and BASF, faced with criticism from human rights activists at home, actively colluded to "whitewash" the Brazilian military regime in the German media.[47] In this, MNEs in manufacturing differed little from the international banks that issued loans for Latin American governments prior to the debt crisis. They too ignored the human rights abuses that military dictatorships were perpetrating against left-wing activists.[48]

14.4 Conclusion

Between the 1960s and early 1980s three processes occurred simultaneously: a rapid increase in FDI in Latin America, especially in manufacturing; the growth of academic interest in MNEs globally; and the evolution of popular economic nationalism in Latin America into academic theories of dependency. Latin American social scientists criticized the role of foreign investors, accusing them of hindering autonomous development and exacerbating underdevelopment. Initially, the resource-seeking MNEs present in the region since the end of the nineteenth century became the primary targets. However, the growth of dependency theories and the apparent failure of development policies in the 1960s also led to increasing questioning of the many market-seeking MNEs investing in manufacturing, which nationalist governments had previously encouraged in their efforts to stimulate industrial development.

In terms of an overall balance sheet, one can understand why economic nationalists and authors influenced by dependency theories were so critical of resource-seeking MNEs: Economically they had repatriated a high proportion of their earnings; politically they had frequently been associated with pliant dictatorships and the repression of worker organizations; and socially they left few benefits, given the relatively low proportion of the population they employed and the damage they caused to people's health and the environment. The evidence on manufacturing MNEs in Latin America is much more ambivalent. They employed many more people, and the forward linkages from their activities were much more significant, changing consumer habits and culture and providing many small entrepreneurs with business opportunities. Nonetheless, it required high levels of expertise and regulation from governments to stop them from playing the system to their advantage; they displaced many local producers when they expanded via acquisitions, and they too had negative effects on public health and the environment that became evident only over the longer term. In addition, little real technology transfer took place, in contrast to Asian economies.

Although they may have erred in detail, dependency theorists were essentially correct to point to the asymmetries of knowledge and power inherent in the relationship between MNEs and local governments and business elites. Latin American governments fell into the dilemma facing economic nationalists almost everywhere: Progress required foreign capital and technology, as well as extensive institutional reform, but it was the foreign investors who possessed the advantages.[49] A weakening of state capacity in the region after the 1980s debt crisis did not help, although market liberalization did encourage the growth of some new MNEs originating in Latin America (*multilatinas*), especially firms with their origins in Mexico, Brazil, and Chile.

Overall, while the impact of resource-seeking and market-seeking manufacturing MNEs differed across time and space, it was the wealthier groups within society in the largest countries who gained most. Poorer social groups seem to have benefited little, and indeed often suffered from the MNEs' activities. The controversies of the 1970s did not disappear with economic liberalization following the debt crisis. Deep differences remained, both in academic and popular opinion, over the evaluation of the MNEs' role: Those on the left of politics remained profoundly distrustful and critical, often still adhering to notions of "dependency," while business elites and politicians on the right generally welcomed FDI. In the early twenty-first century, the development of China and international concern over climate change brought increased pressure for the exploitation of natural resources, especially the minerals required for a "green" transition. The demand for foodstuffs to supply global markets stimulated the intensification of agribusiness, often encouraged by MNEs like Monsanto. These developments stimulated a new wave of activism, as well as further dependency-influenced analysis across the social sciences. The agenda widened, however, to incorporate the growing role of foreign financial interests in extractive activities like mining and agribusiness, and the impact of MNEs on Indigenous populations, local communities, water and land resources, and the environment.[50] The long-term productive, societal, and environmental impacts of MNEs in Latin America remained a matter of intense debate and research.

Notes

1. Fajardo Hernández, M. *The World That Latin America Created: The United Nations Economic Commission for Latin America in the Development Era*, Cambridge, MA, Harvard University Press, 2022.
2. Frank, A. G. *Capitalism and Underdevelopment in Latin America*, New York, Monthly Review Press, 1967.
3. Cardoso, F. H. and Faletto, E. *Dependency and Development in Latin America*, Berkeley, University of California Press, 1979.
4. Kay, C. *Latin American Theories of Development and Underdevelopment*, London, Routledge, 1989.
5. Vernon, R. *Storm over the Multinationals*, Cambridge, MA, Harvard University Press, 1977.
6. Brown, J. C. "Why Foreign Oil Companies Shifted Their Production from Mexico to Venezuela during the 1920s," *American Historical Review*, 90, 2 (1985), 362–385.
7. Gonzales, M. J. "United States Copper Companies, the State, and Labour Conflict," *Journal of Latin American Studies*, 26, 3 (1994), 651–681.
8. Santiago, M. "Rejecting Progress in Paradise: Huastecs, the Environment, and the Oil Industry in Veracruz, Mexico, 1900–1935," *Environmental History*, 3, 2 (1998), 169–188, at 181.
9. Gonzales, M. J. "US Copper Companies, the Mine Workers' Movement, and the Mexican Revolution, 1910–1920," *Hispanic American Historical Review*, 76, 3 (1996), 503–534, at 5295.
10. Cariola, C. and Sunkel, O. *Un siglo de historia económica de Chile 1830–1930: Dos ensayos y una bibliografía*, Madrid, Cultura Hispánica, 1982.
11. Gonzales, "United States Copper Companies," 654.
12. Bucheli, M. "Multinational Corporations, Totalitarian Regimes and Economic Nationalism: United Fruit Company in Central America, 1899–1975," *Business History*, 50, 4 (2008), 433–454, at 448.
13. Bowman, J. R. and Wallerstein, M. "The Fall of Balmaceda and Public Finance in Chile: New Data for an Old Debate," *Journal of Inter-American Studies and World Affairs*, 24, 4 (1982), 421–460.

14. Gonzales, "United States Copper Companies," 662.
15. O'Brien, T. F. *The Revolutionary Mission: American Enterprise in Latin America, 1900–1945*, Cambridge, Cambridge University Press, 1996, 181.
16. Santiago, "Rejecting Progress in Paradise," 182.
17. Santiago, M. "Extracting Histories: Mining, Workers, and Environment," *RCC Perspectives*, 7, (2013), 81–87.
18. Vergara, A. "The Recognition of Silicosis: Labour Unions and Physicians in the Chilean Copper Industry, 1930s–1960s," *Bulletin of the History of Medicine*, 79, 4 (2005), 723–748, at 742.
19. Anner, M. "The Contested Terrain of Global Production: Collective versus Private Labor Governance on Guatemalan Banana Plantations," *Review of International Political Economy*, 31, 1 (2023), 382–408, at 386.
20. Valencia, A. "Human Rights Trade-Offs in a Context of 'Systemic Lack of Freedom': The Case of La Oroya, Peru," *Journal of Human Rights*, 13, 4 (2014), 456–479, at 468.
21. Anner, "The Contested Terrain."
22. Babb, S. "The Washington Consensus as Transnational Policy Paradigm: Its Origins, Trajectory and Likely Successor," *Review of International Political Economy*, 20, 2 (2013), 268–297.
23. Gervase Poulden, "Morococha: The Peruvian Town the Chinese Relocated." https://dialogue.earth/en/business/5898-morococha-the-peruvian-town-the-chinese-relocated, accessed November 20, 2024.
24. Picq, M. L. "Resistance to Extractivism and Megaprojects in Latin America," in Vanden, H. E. and Prevost, G. (eds.) *Oxford Encyclopedia of Latin American Politics*, Oxford, Oxford University Press, 2020, 1–27.
25. Grosse, R. E. *Multinationals in Latin America*, New York, Routledge, 1989, 23–24.
26. Orlove, B. (ed.) *The Allure of the Foreign: Imported Goods in Postcolonial Latin America*, Ann Arbor, University of Michigan Press, 1997.
27. Perrone, N. M. *Investment Treaties and the Legal Imagination: How Foreign Investors Play by Their Own Rules*, Oxford, Oxford University Press, 2021.
28. Grosse, *Multinationals in Latin America*, 75.
29. Bennett, D. and Sharpe. K. *Transnational Corporations versus the State: The Political Economy of the Mexican Automobile Industry*, Princeton, NJ, Princeton University Press, 1985, 193–226.
30. Klier, T. H. and Rubenstein, J. "Mexico's Growing Role in the Auto Industry under NAFTA: Who Makes What and What Goes Where," *Economic Perspectives*, 41, 6 (2017). 29.
31. Bennett and Sharpe, "Transnational Corporations," 218.
32. Bil, D. "Un análisis en perspectiva histórica del comercio exterior de las autopartes argentinas," *Tiempo & economía*, 2 (2015), 111–135.

33. Wolfe, J. *Automobiles and Progress: The Brazilian Search for Modernity*, Oxford, Oxford University Press, 2010, 128.
34. Brennan, J. and Gordillo, M. "Working Class Protest, Popular Revolt, and Urban Insurrection in Argentina: The 1969 Cordobazo," *Journal of Social History*, 27, 3 (1994), 477–498.
35. Grosse, *Multinationals in Latin America*, 105.
36. Mitchell, B. R. *International Historical Statistics: The Americas and Australia*, Basingstoke, Macmillan, 1983, 716–720.
37. Bauer, A. *Goods, Power, History: Latin America's Material Culture*, Cambridge, Cambridge University Press, 2001, 165.
38. Arthur Hartog's visit to Brazil, 1941, Unilever archives, file OSF 3/10.
39. Woodard, J. P. "Marketing Modernity: The J. Walter Thompson Company and North American Advertising in Brazil, 1929–1939," *Hispanic American Historical Review*, 82, 2 (2002), 257–290, at 270.
40. Jones, G. "Globalizing Latin American Beauty: The Making of a Giant Business," *ReVista*, 16, 3 (2017), 10–14.
41. Pérez, I. *El hogar tecnificado: Familia, género y vida cotidiana (1940–1970)*, Buenos Aires, Biblos, 2013.
42. Shepherd. P. "Transnational Corporations and the International Cigarette Industry," in Newfarmer, R. (ed.) *Profits, Progress, and Poverty: Case Studies of International Industries in Latin America*, Notre Dame, IN, University of Notre Dame Press, 1985, 63–112.
43. Gereffi, G. "The Global Pharmaceutical Industry and Its Impact in Latin America," in Newfarmer, R. (ed.) *Profits, Progress, and Poverty: Case Studies of International Industries in Latin America*, Notre Dame, IN, University of Notre Dame Press, 1985, 227–298.
44. Gereffi, "The Global Pharmaceutical Industry."
45. Leiter, A., Rajwanth, V., and Wisnivesky, J. P. "The Global Burden of Lung Cancer: Current Status and Future Trends," *Nature Reviews. Clinical Oncology*, 20 (2023), 624–639.
46. Gómez, E. J. "Coca-Cola's Political and Policy Influence in Mexico: Understanding the Role of Institutions, Interests, and Divided Society," *Health Policy and Planning*, 34, 7 (2019), 520–528.
47. Gray, W. G. "Stabilizing the Global South: West Germany, Human Rights, and Brazil, 1960–1980," *German Yearbook of Contemporary History*, 2 (2017), 119–135.
48. Altamura, C. "Global Banks and Latin American Dictators, 1974–1982," *Business History Review*, 95, 2 (2021), 301–332.
49. Suesse, M. *The Nationalist Dilemma: A Global History of Economic Nationalism, 1776–Present*, Cambridge, Cambridge University Press, 2023.
50. Katz, C. *Dependency Theory after Fifty Years: The Continuing Relevance of Latin American Critical Thought*, Leiden, Brill, 2022.

Further Reading

Jenkins, R. *Transnational Corporations and Industrial Transformation in Latin America*, London, Macmillan, 1984.

Jones, G. and Lluch, A. (eds.) *The Impact of Globalization on Argentina and Chile: Business Enterprises and Entrepreneurship*, Aldershot, Edward Elgar, 2015.

Lluch, A., Monsalve Zanatti, M., and Bucheli, M. (eds.) *A Business History of Latin America*, New York, Routledge, 2025.

Miller, R. *Britain and Latin America in the Nineteenth and Twentieth Centuries*, London, Longman, 1993.

Newfarmer, R. (ed.) *Profits, Progress, and Poverty: Case Studies of International Industries in Latin America*, Notre Dame, IN, University of Notre Dame Press, 1985.

Index

Adani Group, 306
Adidas, 99, 270, 285, 286
Africa, 12, 21, 44, 48, 55, 57, 92, 103, 120, 130, 228, 245, 258
  Chinese MNEs in, 77–82, 222, 282
  corruption in, 276–283
  Indian pharmaceutical firms in, 303
  MNEs and imperialism, 294
African Continental Free Trade Area, 204
agreements, 97, 192, 235
  double taxation, 126, 137, 176, 182
  international, 97, 101
  preferential trade, 202, 204
  trade, 193, 201, 204, 350
air pollution
  automobiles, 49, 356
  respiratory diseases, 346
  smelting, 40, 41, 51–52
Airbus bribery scandal, 275
Akamatsu, K., 91
Alcatel-Lucent, 273–274
Allende, S., 129, 156, 345
Alstom, 53, 273
Amazon, 31, 167, 229
Americanization, 230, 322, 326
Amin, I., 306
Anglo-Iranian Oil Company (AIOC), 154

Angola, bribery, 272
anti-foreign sentiments, 24, 321, 330
apartheid (South Africa), 24, 160
Apple Inc., 27, 31, 102, 167
Arbenz, J., 154–156, 345
Argandoña, A., 267
Argentina
  British investments in, 123
  dictatorship, 157–159
  Ford, 157–159
  La Forestal, 345
  LAFTA, 200
  meatpacking industry, 252
  Mercosur free trade area, 26, 200
  motor industry, 348, 353
  Sarmiento (1868–1874), 148
Arzner, D., 247
ASEAN Industrial Cooperation (AICO) scheme, 203
Asian financial crisis (1997), 207
Associated Banks of Europe Corporation, 198
Association of Southeastern Asian Nations (ASEAN), 202–204, 206
Australia
  Adani Group in, 306
  Nestlé investments in, 16
automobile industry, 42
  CAA Amendment, 49
  gender dynamics, 249

automobile industry (cont.)
  global value chain, 96
  impacts on society, 353
  Latin American, 350–353
  pollution, 49, 356
  Sino-American JV, 70
Avon, 354
  female leadership, 255–256
  sales strategy, 243

BAE corruption scandal, 271
Bali Concord I (1976), 202
Banana Export Countries Union
  (UPEB), 160
Bangkok Declaration (1967), 202
Bank of England, 22, 178
banking sector, 22, 54, 178, 241, 318
Barbie dolls, 246, 254
Base Erosion and Profit Shifting
  (BEPS) initiative [OECD], 184
BASF, 159, 179, 357
Bata, 300–301
beauty industry, 16
  Avon, 255–257
  Brazilian, 55
  Chinese, 67, 257
  environmental impact of, 43–45
  Latin America, 354
Beiersdorf, 16, 152, 323, 327
Beijing Jeep Corporation, 70
Belgian taxation system, 23, 171, 175
Belt & Road Initiative, 77, 79
Berliet, 70
Bhopal disaster (1984, India), 51, 304
Biden, J., 29, 135
Bilderberg, 127
BMW, 76, 198
Body Shop, The, 226
Bolivarian Alliance for the Peoples of
  Our America (ALBA), 200
Bonsucro, 106
Botín, A., 257
Braden Copper Company, 251

Brazil, 200
  automobile workers in, 349
  beauty MNEs, 55
  dictatorship, 130, 159
  favelas in, 354
  Ford in, 248
  Fordlândia project, 16, 42
  JWT, 350, 354
  LAFTA, 200
  Mercosur free trade area, 26, 200
  motor industry, 351
  recycling, 57
Breemen, O. v., 277
Brexit, 29, 192, 207
bribery, 266
  A. G. Leventis, 278
  ABB, 272
  Airbus, 275
  Alcatel-Lucent, 273–274
  Alstom, 273
  anti-bribery measures, 283–285
  BAE, 271
  British Leyland, 277–278
  Chinese MNEs, 282
  Daimler, 273
  defense industry, 269
  Glencore, 280–282
  GSK, 273
  Heineken, 277, 278
  in Equatorial Guinea, 279
  in Switzerland, 271, 272, 284
  Lockheed, 269
  Lonrho, 278
  Odebrecht, 275
  Siemens, 269, 274–275, 284
  sportswear firms, 270
  Total, 273
  Walmart, 273
Bright Food Group, 73
British American Tobacco (BAT),
  68, 355
British Congress of Chambers of
  Commerce of the Empire, 131

Index 365

British Leyland and Africa, 276–278
British Petroleum (BP), 42, 49, 55, 177
British Virgin Islands, 81, 180, 182, 272
British/Britain
  "Buy British" initiatives, 320
  "vassal state," 26
  Anglo-Iranian Oil Company, 154
  anti-British sentiments, 120, 321
  banking sector, 22, 178
  Battle of Plassey (1757), 298
  Chamber of Commerce, 119, 123
  corruption, 266
  double taxation, 173, 177
  East India Company, 13, 65, 266, 296–299
  EU withdrawal, 29, 134
  FDI, 26
  imperialism, 296–299
  Indian Copper Corporation, 92
  investments in Argentina, 123
  inward FDI stock, 26
  Merchandise Marks Act (1887), 320
  Royal African Company, 13
  rubber production, 93
  tax havens, 176
  tax policy, 170
  Trading with the Enemy Act, 151, 315, 321
Brundtland Commission (1987), 52, 54
Bund der Industriellen (Germany), 121
business associations, 119–123
Business Roundtable, 131
Butterfly Brand, 67

Cadbury, 226, 304
Calderón, F., 206
Callaghan, J., 278
Canada
  Avon in, 255

Canada–United States Trade Agreement, 201
NAFTA, 26, 201, 205, 350
Canton Zug, 280
Cárdenas, L., 150, 250
Cardoso, F. H., 339
Cargill, 24
Castro, F., 200
Cayman Islands, 81, 180, 182
Central Intelligence Agency (CIA), 153–157, 327, *See also* coup d'état
chambers of commerce, 119–120, 127
Chanel, 254
Chávez, H., 200
Chile
  1973 coup d'état, 156
  Allende government, 129, 156, 345
  Chuquicamata mine, 40–41, 251, 345–347
  copper industry, 40–41, 51, 340
  debts, 158
  environmental regulation, 51
  Ibáñez (1927–1931), 148
  market liberalization, 350
  mining communities, 251
  occupational health issues, 346
  taxation, 343
China
  "debt traps," 78
  Cisco case, 106, 332
  CNOOC bid for Unocal, 331
  cosmetics industry, 257
  environmental regulation, 57
  expulsion of foreign MNEs, 325
  FDI, 31, 69–77, 99, 136
  global value chains, 102, 103, 107
  Nestlé, 305
  OFDI, 73, 76–77
  Opium Wars (1839–1842, 1856–1860), 64, 65, 318
  seaweed exports from Peru, 58
  tax policy, 183

China (cont.)
  Tiananmen Square (1989), 161
  WTO accession, 25, 73, 206
China's globalization, 64–83
  first wave, 65–69
  second wave, 69–76
  third wave, 76–82
Chinese Communist Party (CCP), 64, 69–73
Chinese MNEs, 31, 282
  ASEAN, 204
  beauty industry, 67, 256
  Belt & Road Initiative, 77, 79
  egg exports, 67
  environmental impact of, 57–59
  EV sector, 58, 76
  in Africa, 77–82, 282
  in Latin America, 347
  mergers and acquisitions, 74–75
  private MNEs, 74, 79
  resource extraction, 77
  restrictions, 135
  round-tripping, 99
  silk production, 68
  silver production, 66
  Sino-foreign JVs, 70
  smartphone sector, 80
  special economic zones, 70
  telecommunication, 80
  textile industry, 67
Chinese SOEs, 71–74, 77
Chrysler, 42, 229, 330
Chuquicamata mine (Chile), 40–41, 251, 345–347
cinema industry, 247–248
CIPLA, 303
Cisco, 106, 332
Clean Air Act (US), 49
climate change, 2, 48–49, 358, *See also concepts related to environment*
Clive, R., 298
cloaking, 308, 323–324

CO_2 emissions, 42, 56, *See also* air pollution
Cobden Chevalier Treaty (1860), 193
Coca-Cola, 44, 106, 302, 356
Cold War, 90, 97, 102, 107, 126, 153–160, 269, 270, 325
collective bargaining, 221, 229, 231–235
Committee of Common Market Automobile Constructors (CCMC), 198
company towns, 251–252
condoms, 246
Confederation of British Industry, 303
Congo, 55, 59, 77, 226, 269, 281, 324
  colonial exploitation, 17, 218, 276
  Gertler and corruption in, 282–283
Contemporary Amperex Technology Co Ltd (CATL), 76
copper mining
  Chile's, 40–41, 51, 340
  smelter emissions, 40, 41
corporate social responsibility (CSR), 54, 226–228
Corporate Sustainability Due Diligence Directive (EU), 30
corruption. *See also* bribery
  anti-corruption measures, 283–285
  armaments industry, 269
  as entrepreneurship, 267
  Foreign Corrupt Practices Act (US), 272, 273, 281, 283, 285
  grand, 267, 285–286
  in Africa, 276–283
  nepotism, 267
  petty, 267, 283, 284
cosmopolitan capitalism, 313, 317–320
cost-benefit approach, 295
Council for Mutual Economic Assistance (COMECON), 195, 224, 325

Council of Directors of European Industrial Federations, 122
coup d'état
  Allende (Chile, 1973), 156
  Arbenz (Guatemala, 1954), 154–156, 345
  Mossadegh (Iran, 1953), 153
COVID-19 pandemic, 30, 76, 107–108, 135
cultural imperialism, 249, 260, 304, 307
customs unions, 192, 195, 197, 203

Daimler AG, 159, 273, 330
Danone, 331
Dasheng Cotton Mill, 67
Dassler, H., 271
Davignon, E., 198
DDT (pesticide), 43, 45
debt crisis (1980s), 350, 358
Decision 24 (1971), 349
decolonization, 19, 90, 126, 153, 177, 179, 202, 220, 308, 315, 326
deforestation, 41, 42, 48, 94, 346
deglobalization, 11, 30, 173–176, 204, 220, 260, 301
Delaware General Corporation Law, 172
Delhi Cloth Mills (DCM), 304
Deng Xiaoping, 70
dependency theories, 5, 220, 338–340, 349, 350, 357
Desai, M., 302
DeSantis, R., 248
development assistance programs, 25
Dewang, C., 75
Díaz, P., 147
dictators(hip), 144–163
  Argentine, 157–159
  Brazilian, 130, 159
  Cold War, 153–160
  Díaz, 147
  first global economy, 146–151

Gómez, 148
Hitler, 150
Mussolini, 150
Pinochet, 156–160
World War II, 151–153
Diexian, C., 67
digitalization, 31
director's citizenship, 317–318
discrimination, 120, 122
  housing segregation, 342
  racial, 160, 218, 221
  workplace, 221
Disney, W., 248
division of labor, 26, 89, 107, 126, 201
Doe Run Company, 52, 348
Dole, 95
domesticity, 242
double taxation, 118, 124, 126, 137, 173–176, 182
dual nationality, 319, 325
Dunlop, 93, 177, 352
DuPont, 125, 152, 195

Earthrise, 45
East India Company (EIC), 13, 65, 266, 296–299
Economic and Monetary Union (EMU), 207
economic dislocation, 206, 207
economic integration, 15, 26, 194, 204, 329
economic nationalism, 220, 300–303, 313, 320–325
Egypt, 80, 126, 219, 273
Eisenhower, 155
electric vehicle (EV) industry, 29, 58, 76
Electrolux, 245
electronics industry
  Chinese, 73–74
  GVC, 98, 100
  Japanese, 329
embezzlement, 267

employee welfare programs, 226
employers' associations, 126
energy transition, 50
Enron scandal, 271, 284
environmental awareness, 38
environmental crisis
  acid rain, 49
  air pollution, 41, 48–53, 346, 356
  deforestation, 41, 42, 48, 94, 346
  industrial wastes, 42
  landfills, 57
  saltwater intrusion, 346
  soil erosion, 43, 94
  water pollution, 42–45, 48, 51, 346, 347
environmental degradation, 38
  automobile industry, 42
  beauty industry, 44
  copper mining, 40–41
  deforestation, 94
  oil companies, 42, 49, 345
  resource-seeking MNEs, 345, 347
  soil erosion, 43, 94
  textile industry, 43
  United Fruit, 43
environmental movement, 45–46
environmental NGOs, 46, 54, 56
environmental policy
  Shell, 49
  Unilever, 47
Environmental Protection Agency (US), 46
environmental regulation
  Brundtland Commission, 52, 54
  Chinese, 57
  Environmental Protection Agency, 46
  Global Climate Coalition, 49, 52
  Kyoto Protocol, 49, 52
  National Environmental Policy Act, 45
  Rio Conference, 53
  Stockholm Conference, 47, 52
  UN's attempts, 52
environmental scandals, 55
environmental, social, and governance (ESG), 54
Equatorial Guinea, bribery and corruption in, 279
Escorts Ltd., 304
Estrada Cabrera, M., 343
Eurodollar market, 22, 178, 350
European Coal and Steel Community, 195, 196, 202
European Common Market, 97, 329
European Economic Area (EEA),
European Economic Community (EEC), 125, 194–199, 202
European Free Trade Association (EFTA), 195
European League for Economic Cooperation (ELEC), 196
European Roundtable of Industrialists (ERT), 25, 132, 198
European Union (EU)
  Britain's withdrawal, 29, 134
  CO_2 regulations, 56
  Corporate Sustainability Due Diligence Directive, 30
  investment screening mechanism, 332
expatriate staffing, 17, 219–222, 323, 343, 352–353
export-processing zones (EPZs), 99
Exxon
  drivers of climate change, 48–49
  ICC membership, 52

Facebook, 167
Faletto, E., 339
fascism, 123
fashion industry, 44, 254
female (executive) leadership, 253–259
feminism, 255
Fiat, 195

Index   369

Firestone, 93, 352
first global economy (1840–1929), 12
    Chinese MNEs, 65–69
    dictatorship in, 146–151
    global business and, 13–17
    inequality, 103
    MNEs' collective political activism, 119–122
first wave of environmentalism, 40
Flick, F., 324
Flying Geese Paradigm (FGP), 91
Ford, 16, 151, 171, 225, 229–235, 248, 348
    European integration, 196
    Fordlândia project, 16, 42, 252
    global value chain, 97
    in Argentina, 157–159
    in Brazil, 248
    in Mexico, 202, 205
    independent trade unions, 229
    multi-domestic approach, 322–323, 328, 329
Ford, H., 151
Foreign Corrupt Practices Act (US), 272, 273, 281, 283, 285
foreign direct investment (FDI), 1, 11, 120, 332, 339, *See also FDI under specific countries*
    dictators and, 145
    first global economy, 14, 119
    hosts, 19
    restrictions on, 313, 315
    second global economy, 26
    substitution effects, 128
    World War I impact on, 15
Foreign Exchange Regulation Act (1973, India), 302
Fox, V., 356
Foxconn, 100, 102
France
    American challenge, 196
    bribery, 273–274
    Cobden Chevalier Treaty (1860), 193

Danone takeover, 331
    tax system, 171, 174
Frank, A. G., 339
Free Trade Area of the Americas (FTAA), 200
free trade areas, 26, 27, 192, 199–205, *See also* market integration
free-standing companies (FSCs), 15, 170, 174, 318
Friends of the Earth, 45

G7 Summit, 132, 134
Galbraith, J. K., 44
Gandhi, I., 302
Gandhi, M., 300
Gates, B., 135
gendered economies, 249–253
gendered international management, 253–259
gendered technologies, 241
    Durex, 246
    Ford automobiles, 249
    Mattel's strategy, 246
    movie industry, 247–248
    Singer, 242
    Tampax, 245
    Tupperware, 243–245
    Unilever, 245
General Agreement on Tariffs and Trade (GATT), 100, 125
General Association of Sugar Manufacturers (Spain), 194
General Electric (GE), 122, 125, 319
General Motors (GM), 16, 19, 42, 125, 151, 161, 171, 195, 205, 225, 231, 233, 234, 323, 328, 348
General Postal Union (1874), 194
geopolitical jockeying, 308
Gereffi, G., 89, 91
German MNEs
    Argentine dictatorship, 157, 159
    bribery, 273, 284
    cloaking, 308

German MNEs (cont.)
    environmentalism, 46
    in India, 301, 325, 326
    nationality, 153, 320, 323–327
    resilience, 16
    sportswear firms, 99, 270
Germany, 232
    Bund der Industriellen, 121
    Committee of British Industrial Interests, 124, 127
    dictatorship, 151–153
    FDI, 14, 15, 121
    invasion of Netherlands, 151–153
    invasion of Poland, 151, 152
    Ost-Ausschuss der Deutschen Wirtschaft, 127
    tax policy, 172, 175, 176
    US declaration of war (1917), 121
Gertler, D., 282
Ghana, 77, 220, 275, 279
GlaxoSmithKline (GSK), 174, 273
Glencore, 24, 55, 78, 280–282
global capitalism, 13, 22, 25, 27, 91, 108, 167, 170
Global Climate Coalition, 49, 52
global financial crisis (2008–2009), 29, 100, 107, 134, 167, 184, 204, 314, 331
global hopping," 98
global minimum tax (GMT), 184
global value chains (GVCs)
    antecedents of, 91–97
    automotive products, 96
    COVID-19 crisis, 107–108
    definition, 89
    electronics, 97, 100
    EPZs and SEZs, 99
    geographic and sectorial dimensions of, 101–103
    OEMs, 99–100
    participation, 100, 104, 106
    postwar period, 97–100
    semiconductor, 101, 108
    textiles, 95, 98
    watchmaking, 96, 98
globalist agenda, 118, 121, 128, 131, 134–135
globalization, 11
    backlash, 107
    Chinese, 64–83
    first global economy, 13–17, 65–69, 103, 119–123, 146–151
    great reversal, 18–22, 243
    reversal and divergence, 28–31
    second global economy, 22–28, 97–100, 221
Golden Shield Project, 106
Gómez, J. V., 148
Goodyear, 93, 352
Google, 2, 167, 184
Gou, T., 100
Great Depression, 23, 119, 123, 149, 300, 305
Great Reversal (1929–1979), 12, 18–22, 243
green initiatives, 47–50
Green, P., 280
greenhouse gas emissions, 42, 48, 49, 57, 58
greenwashing, 54
Guatemala
    1954 coup d'état, 154–156, 345
    Agrarian Reform Law, 155
    labor recruitment, 343
Guest Keen Nettlefolds (GKN), 304
Guggenheim Brothers, 41
Gulf of Mexico (America) oil extraction, 41
Guo, C., 68

Haas, E., 245
Handler, R., 254
Harriman, W. H., 324
Heineken, 48, 277–280, 326
Henkel, 47, 59
Hindustan Lever, 302, 303

Hindustan Thompson Associates (HTA), 302
Hitler, A., 150, 152
Hoffman, A. J., 46
Hoffmann-La Roche/Roche, 181
Hong Kong, 71, 98, 182, 271, 314
Hongsheng, L., 68
Hoover, 245
Hua, G., 70
Huajian Group, 79
Huawei, 80, 108, 135, 162
Hudson's Bay Company, 193
human rights violations, 29–30, 78, 91, 106, 157, 162, 356
Huntington, S., 146

Ibáñez, C., 148
IBM, 19, 74, 124, 125, 127, 161, 171, 302, 328
IG Farben, 152, 323, 325
Imperial Bank of India, 300, 302
Imperial Chemical Industries, 304
Imperial Continental Gas Association, 174
imperialism, 294
    Africa, 294
    cultural, 249, 260, 304, 307
    East India Company, 13
    in twentieth-century India, 299–305
    Indian MNEs and, 305–306
    Marxist theories of, 295
    United States, 327
import substitution industrialization (ISI), 338, 349
import tariffs, 321, 326
India, 43, 78, 90, 92, 97, 130, 178, 219
    Barbie's presence in, 247, 249
    Bata in, 300–301
    Bhopal disaster (1984), 51, 304
    British imperialism, 296–299
    Chamber of Commerce, 120
    colonial-era textile production, 43
    Dalmia Bharat Sugar, 106
    domestic sewing, 242
    FDI, 21, 293
    female executive leadership, 257
    Foreign Exchange Regulation Act, 22, 302
    German MNEs in, 120, 325, 326
    independence (1947), 293, 301
    iPhone production, 28
    IT sector, 303
    movie industry, 248
    nationalization, 301, 305, 307
    Patents Act (1970), 22, 303
    pharmaceutical sector, 303
    Rana Plaza collapse (2013), 29–30, 105, 221
    tax havens, 182
    Tupperware, 244
    twentieth-century imperialism, 299–305
India Pakistan Burma Association (1942), 303
Indian Copper Corporation, 92
Indian MNEs and imperialism, 296
    Adani Group, 306
    Chettiar business community, 305
    in East Africa, 306
    Tata's Corus Steel acquisition, 306
indigenization, 220, 326
Indonesia
    Lockheed, 270
    Sukarno regime, 157
    Tupperware in, 244
Industrial Revolution, 13, 39, 266
industrial wastes, 42, 57
inequality, 2
    corruption, 266
    gender, 259, 260
    GVC and, 91
    income, 17, 104, 106, 168, 170, 205
    social, 90, 177, 183
    spatial, 90, 219
    tax, 175

inequality (cont.)
   wage, 106
   wealth, 168, 170, 183, 206
Inflation Reduction Act (2022), 29
Inter-American Council for Trade and Production, 130
International Aluminum Cartel, 194
International Association for the Promotion and Protection of Private Foreign Investments, 21, 127
international business associations, 121, 122, 127, 130, 136
International Chamber of Commerce (ICC), 20, 52, 122, 123, 126–133, 285
International Code to Protect Foreign Investments, 127
International Copper Cartel, 194
International Court of Arbitration, 122
International Labor Organization (ILO), 20, 227, 233
   core international labor standards, 221
   creation of, 122
   guidelines for MNEs, 21
   Tripartite Declaration of Principles concerning Multinational Enterprises and Social Policy, 133
International Monetary Fund (IMF), 25, 30, 104, 133, 206, 302
International Organization of Industrial Employers (IOIE), 20, 122
International Telegraph and Telephone Corporation (ITT), 156
International Vienna Council (1978), 132
interwar period, 18, 90, 185
   international tax policy, 173–176

Swadeshi capitalism, 300
investment treaties, 21, 128, 134
iPhone (Apple), 28, 102
Iran, 24, 153, 273
Israel, bribery, 274

J&P Coats, 15, 319, 354, 355
J. Walter Thompson (JWT), 350, 354
Japan, 19
   attack on Pearl Harbor (1941), 152
   electronics industry, 97, 329
   FDI, 128
   female leadership, 258
   invasion of China, 69
   Keidanren, 128, 133
   Lockheed bribery, 269
   sewing machine, 242
   Starbucks, 26
   tax policy, 177
   trading companies, 22
Japanese MNEs
   anti-Japanese hostility, 322
   in ICC, 122
   in Southeast Asia, 203
   in US, 329
   restrictions, 135
Jardine Matheson, 65, 67
Jian, Y., 68
Jian, Z., 68
Jiangsu Sunshine Group, 79–80
John Swire & Sons, 65
Johnson & Johnson, 161, 316, 327
Johnson, L. B., 157
Joseph Nathan and Company, 174

Kabila, J., 282
Kan, Y.-S., 257
Kang, D., 266
Keidanren, 128, 133
Khashoggi, A., 270
Kilimall, 81
Kissinger, H., 156
Klubock, T. M., 251

Klynveld Peat Marwick Goerdeler (KPMG), 181
Kodama, Y., 270
Kohlberg Kravis Roberts & Company (KKR), 183
Kraayenhof, J., 181
Kyoto Protocol (1997), 49, 52

L'Oréal, 256
La Forestal, 345
La Oroya smelter (Peru), 52, 348
labor
　"alien" labor practices, 223
　cheap, 90, 203, 205, 225
　collective labor rights, 225, 230
　division of, 26, 89, 107, 126, 201
　expatriates, 17, 219–222, 323, 343, 352–353
　female, 242–247, 250
　gendered division of, 250, 252, 257
　internationalism, 232
　movement, 20, 121
　nationalism, 345
　organized, 228–235
　protests, 219
　recruitment, 344, 352–353
　wage differentials, 344
　wages, 341, 352
labor exploitation and abuse, 218
　child labor, 105, 106, 221
　forced labor, 105, 151, 162, 218, 221, 226
　hazardous working conditions, 218, 221
　racial discrimination, 218, 221
　sex work, 250
labor impact of MNEs
　in developed economies, 223–226
　in developing economies, 218–222
labor rights protection, 222
labor unions, 75, 98, 126, 149, 156–160, 197, 228

Latin America
　dependency theories, 339, 349
　economic nationalism, 339
　FDI, 338, 340, 348–350, 355
　market-seeking MNEs, 348–357
　MERCOSUR/L, 200, 206
　resource-seeking MNEs, 340–348
Latin American Free Trade Association (LAFTA), 200
Latin American Integration Association, 200
League of Nations, 20, 122, 169, 175, 176, 179, 194
Leguía, A., 148
Lenin, V., 294
Lenovo, 74
Lenz, R., 181
Lever Brothers, 15, 16, 44, 276, 302
Liebig Company, 341
List, F., 193
Lobato, M. Z., 252
Lockheed bribery, 269
London Rubber Company, 246
Lonrho, 278, 294
Louis Marx toy company, 98
Lubinski, C., 46, 254, 301, 316

"Magnificent Seven," 31
management education, 27, 326
Manko, K., 255
manufacturing MNEs, 16, 19, 203, 231, 319, 340, 348–357
Mao Zedong, 69
Marcos, F., 160
market integration, 191–193
　ASEAN, 202–204, 206
　cartels, 194
　European integration, 194–199
　free-trade zones, 199–205
　in the nineteenth century, 193
　MERCOSUR/L, 26, 200, 201, 206
　NAFTA, 201, 205–206
　social consequences, 205–207

market-seeking manufacturing
  MNEs, 348–357
Marshall Plan (US), 125, 195
Marubeni Corporation, 270
Mattel toy company, 98, 246
Mayar Silk Mills, Ltd., 67
Mazlish, B., 3
McCann Erickson, 351
McDonald's, 225
McKinsey, 22
meatpacking industry, 252, 341
Medici Bank, 12
Mehta, S., 296, 306
menstrual product development, 246
Mercedes Benz, 157
MERCOSUR/L, 26, 200, 201, 206
mergers and acquisitions (M&A), 74–75
Metal Box, 304
Mexican Revolution, 147
Mexico
  bribery, 273
  Cananea mine, 341
  Coca-Cola, 356
  Díaz's strategy, 147
  FDI, 147, 202, 206
  foreign vs. locally owned firms in, 57
  Huasteca oil field, 341, 346
  motor industry, 352, 353
  NAFTA, 201, 205, 206, 350
  oil sector, 41, 149, 231, 249, 341
  railroad industry, 250
  saltwater intrusion, 346
  tax exemption, 342
Mico World, 80
microchip GVC, 102
Microsoft, 31, 167
Midland Bank, 178
Minefee, I., 269
mining, 17, 40–41, 51, 251, 282, 340, 342
Mitsubishi, 203

Montenay, F., 255
Mont-Pèlerin Society, 131
Mooney, J., 150
Morarjee, S., 257
Mossack Fonseca, 183
Mossadegh, M., 153
Motion Picture Production Code, 247
movie industry, 247–248
multi-domestic approach, 322–323, 328
multiple nationalities, 68
Musk, E., 135
Mussolini, B., 150

Nanyang Brothers' Tobacco Company, 68
National Association of Manufacturers (NAM), 120, 125
national business associations, 120, 122, 125, 131
National Environmental Policy Act (US), 45
national interests, 125, 131, 331
nationality, 18, 124, 153, 230
  cloaking, 323–324
  cosmopolitan capitalism, 313, 317–320
  cultures, 316, 329
  director's citizenship, 317–318
  dual, 319, 325
  economic nationalism, 313, 320–325
  Flick's strategy, 324
  multi-domestic approach, 322–323, 328
  multiple, 68
  national management styles, 316, 330
  NIVEA, 327
  Shell, 319
nationalization, 126, 154, 301, 305, 307, 325, 330
nature conservation movement, 40

Nazi Germany, 19, 124, 150
Nehru, J., 301
nepotism, 267
Nestlé, 16, 44, 48, 127, 202, 259, 305, 307, 327
  baby formula scandal, 25
Net Zero Banking Alliance, 55
Netherlands
  Dutch-American tax treaty, 179
  Germany and, 127, 151, 176
  Heineken, 48, 277–280, 326
  Lockheed, 270
  Shell's dual nationality, 319, 325
  taxation, 173–176, 179
  Unilever, 151–152, 199, 302
New Deal coalition, 125
New International Economic Order (NIEO), 21, 52, 129
New Left, 226
Niarchos, S., 22
Nigeria, 80, 81, 220, 272, 277–278, 280–281, 283, 286, 294
nitrogen oxide (NO$_x$) emissions, 49
NIVEA, 327
Nixon, R., 132
North American Free Trade Agreement (NAFTA), 26, 201, 205–206, 350, 352
Norway, 257
  oil MNE, 272
  Unilever, 95
Nvidia, 1, 31, 102
Nye, J., 192

Obiang Nguema Mbasogo, T., 279, 280
Odebrecht bribery scandal, 275
offshore financial centers, 28, 30, 176, 177, 271, 280
offshoring, 98, 106, 177, 224, 229, *See also* avoidance industry
oil industry, 94
  bribery and corruption, 279–280

climate change, 48–49
  energy transition, 50
  environmental impact of, 41, 49, 345
  greenhouse gas emissions, 42, 48, 49
  Gulf of Mexico (America), 41
  Iranian, 24, 154
  Malaysia's palm oil production, 48
  Mexican, 41, 149, 231, 249, 342
  Norwegian, 272
  surge of oil prices, 129, 132
  Venezuelan, 148
Oldenziel, R., 241
Olympic Portland Cement, 174
Onassis, A., 22
opium trade, 65, 297
Organisation for Economic Cooperation and Development (OECD), 130, 227, 332
  Anti-Bribery Convention, 285
  guidelines for MNEs, 133, 233
  tax initiatives, 169, 179, 184
Organization of Petroleum – Exporting Countries (OPEC), 159
organized labor, 228–235
original equipment manufacturers (OEMs), 99–100

Pacific War (1941), 69
palm oil production
  Malaysia, 48
  Southeast Asia, 94
Paris climate change agreement (2015), 29
Patents Act (1970, India), 22, 303
Paul, S., 304
Pearl Harbor, 152
Pearson & Son, 41, 147, 343
Pearson, W., 147
PepsiCo, 106, 331

Peru
  export of seaweed, 58
  La Oroya smelter, 52, 348
  oil production, 340
  Rio Blanco mine, 348
Petróleos Mexicanos (PEMEX), 150
Pfizer, 178, 303
pharmaceutical MNEs
  GSK, 273
  India, 303
  Latin America, 355–356
  market integration, 199
  Pfizer, 178, 303
  Swiss, 181
  US, 130, 195
Philip Morris, 134, 355
Pinochet, A., 156–160
Pirelli, A., 123
pollution. *See also* air pollution; water pollution
  antipollution movements, 40
  petroleum industry, 346
  plastic, 44
pollution haven hypothesis, 39, 50
Prebisch, R., 338
Principles for Responsible Investment, 54
private advocacy forums, 127, 132
Procter & Gamble (P&G), 47, 53, 244, 259, 316, 328–329
pro-globalization dictatorial regimes, 147
progressive taxation, 174
proto-multinationals, 193
Puma, 99, 270
Putin, V., 162

racial discrimination, 160, 218, 221
racial hierarchy, 299, 302
Radio Corporation of America (RCA), 26, 98, 122, 225, 229, 321
Rana Plaza collapse (2013, India), 29–30, 105, 221

Reagan, R., 133
Reckitt & Sons, 355
Regional and Comprehensive Economic Partnership, 204
relocation, 99, 182, 225, 229
resilience, 16, 24
resource-seeking MNEs, 340–348
reversal and divergence (since 2008), 12, 28–31
Reza Pahlavi, M., 153
Rich, M., 24, 280
Riggs Bank and corruption, 279–280
Rio Conference (1992), 53
Rio Tinto Company, 318
Roche, 303
Rockefeller, D., 130, 132
Roosevelt, F. D., 124
Rousseff, D., 276
Rowland, W. ("Tiny"), 278
Royal African Company, 13
rubber production, 93
Russell & Company, 66
Russia's invasion of Ukraine (2014/2022), 135, 162, 332
Russian Revolution (1917), 16
Russia–West political tensions, 162
RWE, 135

Samsung, 102
Santiago, M., 250, 346
Sanyo, 98
Sarmiento, D., 148
Saudi Arabia, bribery, 270, 272
Schneider Rundfunkwerke, 73
seaweed exports, 58
second global economy (1979–2008), 12
  Chinese MNEs, 69–76
  global value chain, 97–100
  MNEs and, 25–28
  nationality and, 329–332
  origins of, 22–25
  tax system, 169

second industrial revolution, 39, 90, 193, 299
sectoral trade associations, 126
semiconductor GVC, 101, 108
semiconductor industry, 329
sewing machines, 240, 241
Shell, 41, 161, 173–176, 249, 341, 344
  anti-corruption measures, 283
  dual nationality, 319, 325
  environmental policy, 49
  ICC membership, 53
Sherwin-Williams, 66
Shiseido, 256
Siam Cement Group, 203
Siemens, 157, 193
  bribery scandal, 269, 274–275, 284
  in Argentina, 159
  in India, 301
  nationality strategy, 319, 325
Silicon Valley, 23, 27
silicosis, 347
silk production, 95
Silva, L. I. L. d., 352
Sinclair Oil, 151
Singer Sewing Machine Company, 15, 66, 241, 319
Single European Market, 25, 198, 199, 204–207, 224
Sklar, R., 294
slave trading, 13
Slobodian, Q., 118
smelting process, 40, 41, 51–52, 347
Smith, A., 297
Snowden, E., 332
soil erosion, 43, 94
solar industry, 50
Solvay, 319
Sony, 98
South Africa, 24, 160, 221, 229, 278–280, 300, 330
Southeast Asia, 91
  ASEAN, 202–204
  palm oil production, 94

rubber production, 93
Spain, 146, 229
  female leadership, 257
  General Association of Sugar Manufacturers, 194
special economic zones (SEZs), 70, 99
Sri Lanka, 78, 275
Staehelin, W., 181
Standard Fruit Company, 159, 341
Standard Oil, 41, 66, 93, 125, 127, 151, 152, 249, 269, 341, 344
Starbucks, 26, 167, 229
State Bank of India, 302
state-owned enterprises (SOEs), 71–74, 77, 195
Statoil, 272
Stockholm Conference (1972), 47, 52
submarine technology, 14
Suez Canal, Egyptian nationalization of, 126
Sukarno regime (Indonesia), 157
sustainability, 38, 54–55, 134
sustainable development, 52
Swadeshi capitalism, 300
Swiss MNEs
  bribery, 271, 272, 284
  cotton textile firms, 14
  offshoring, 98
  pharmaceuticals, 181
  tax competition, 172
  tax havens, 24, 175, 178
  watchmaking, 96
Switzerland, 2, 23, 24, 96, 98, 131, 172, 175, 178–184, 195, 253, 271, 272, 276, 277–280, 284, 323–325

Tampax, 245, 259
tampons, 245
Tandon, P., 302
Tanzania–Zambia Railway, 69
Tao, Y., 81
Tata, 300, 306
tax arbitrage, 169, 173, 179

tax avoidance, 168, 171, 176
tax competition, 168, 172, 180, 330
tax evasion, 168, 315
tax havens, 168–173, 175–181, 271
tax inequality, 175
tax planning, 168–171, 330
taxation
 British, 170
 China, 183
 decolonization, 177, 179
 Delaware, 172
 double, 118, 124, 126, 137, 173–176, 182
 French, 171, 174
 German, 172, 175, 176
 global minimum tax, 184
 interwar period, 173–176
 Japan, 177
 Latin America, 342
 low taxes, 23, 24, 178, 195, 343
 Model Double Tax Convention, 179
 OECD's initiatives, 169, 179, 184
 second global economy, 221
 subnational tax strategy, 172
 United States, 171
 until World War I, 170–173
TCL, 73–74
technological diffusion, 17
technology, 97
 first global economy, 14
 gendered, 240
 Silicon Valley, 23, 27
telecommunication MNEs, 99
 Chinese, 80, 108, 162
 US, 129, 156, 345
Tendrich, G., 245
Tesla, 1, 59
textile industry, 43, 95, 98
 Chinese, 67
Thatcher, M., 133
Tiananmen Square (1989), 161
tobacco industry, 355, 356

Tolliday, S., 96
Total, 273
Toyota, 203
Trading with the Enemy Act, 121, 151, 315, 321
Transsion, 80
Treaty of Paris (1763), 318
Treaty of Rome (1957). *See* European Economic Community (EEC)
Treaty of Westphalia (1648), 318
Trilateral Commission, 132
Tripartite Declaration of Principles concerning Multinational Enterprises and Social Policy, 133
Truman Committee, 152
Trump, D., 29, 134, 135, 206, 259, 284, 331
Tupperware, 243–245

Unilever, 23, 24, 127, 151–152, 161, 196, 199, 220, 302, 327, 349, 354
 anti-corruption measures, 283
 environmental policy, 47
 female leadership, 258–259
 ICC membership, 52
 menstrual product development, 245
 nationality, 316, 323, 325
 palm oil consumption, 48
 whale oil, 94
Union of Industrial and Employers' Confederations of Europe (UNICE), 131, 196, 197
United Africa Company (UAC), 48, 294
United Brands Company, 159
United Fruit Company (UFC), 43, 148, 269
 1954 Guatemalan coup d'état, 154–156
 and global value chains, 95
 corporate paternalism, 251

gendered labor, 250
labor exploitation, 219
occupational health issue, 346–347
tax concessions, 342
United Nations (UN), 52
  Code of Conduct, 133
  Model Double Tax Convention, 179
United Nations Centre on Transnational Corporations, 129, 133
United Nations Economic Commission for Latin America (ECLA), 339
United Nations Environment Programme (UNEP), 52
United Nations Global Compact, 54, 227, 285
United States (US), 102, 107, 153–157, 171, 178, 179, 345
  Agency for International Development, 25
  anti-foreign sentiments, 321
  as net creditor nation, 18
  banking sector, 22
  Canada–United States Trade Agreement, 201
  Central American dictators and, 149
  Chamber of Commerce, 119, 121, 125
  CNOOC bid for Unocal, 331
  corruption, 267, 269
  Department of Commerce, 121
  Dutch-American tax treaty, 179
  Foreign Corrupt Practices Act, 272, 273, 280, 283, 284
  hegemony, 134
  imperialism, 327
  Japan MNEs in, 329
  Marshall Plan, 125, 194
  McKinsey, 22
  NAFTA, 26, 201, 205–206, 350
  National Association of Manufacturers, 120, 125
  New Deal, 125, 151
  Sino-American JV, 70
  subnational tax strategy, 172
  toy manufacturers, 98
  Trading with the Enemy Act, 121, 315, 321
United States (US)
United States–China Business Council, 132
United States–China tensions, 30, 101, 107, 135, 162, 332

Valencia, A., 347
Venezuela
  50/50 profit-sharing agreement, 343
  Lake Maracaibo contamination, 346
  oil production, 341
Vergara, A., 251
Viard, V., 255
Vieille Montagne, 317
Vietnam, 97, 207
  bribery, 274
  GVC participation rate, 104
Vivendi, 134
Volkswagen (VW), 55, 158, 198, 351, 357
Vredeling Directive, 197, 199

wage premium, 224
Wallerstein, I., 91
Walmart, 201, 273, 285
Wanxiang, 75
Washington Consensus, 100, 133, 347
waste management, 57
watch industry, 96, 98
water pollution
  arsenic, 347
  beauty industry, 44
  Chuquicamata mine, 347

water pollution (cont.)
  copper mining operations, 41, 51
  eutrophication, 47
  Lake Maracaibo, 346
  oil spill, 41
  synthetic detergents industry, 45
  textile dyeing, 43
Watson, T. J., 123, 150, 152
Weisman, M., 284
Whole Foods, 226
wind energy, 53
Wise, B., 243
women
  and cars, 249
  domestic sewing, 242
  empowerment, 244–247
  female condoms, 246
  leadership roles, 253–259
  sex work, 250
  social exclusion, 258
  tampons, 245
  targets for marketing agencies, 354
  Tupperware parties, 244

workplace discrimination, 221
World Bank, 25, 133, 302
World Economic Forum (WEF), 133, 136
world systems theory, 91
World Trade Organization (WTO), 100, 134, 204, 303
  China's accession to, 25, 73, 206
  Seattle protests (1999), 191
World War I, 15, 18, 96, 122
  market integration, 194
  nationality-related issues, 320–324
  restrictions on FDI, 313
  taxation until, 170–173
World War II, 19–22, 38, 43, 97, 124, 126, 151–153, 245
  market integration, 194
  restrictions on FDI, 314

Xi Jinping, 77

Yellowstone National Park, 40

For EU product safety concerns, contact us at Calle de José Abascal, 56–1°, 28003 Madrid, Spain or eugpsr@cambridge.org.

www.ingramcontent.com/pod-product-compliance
Ingram Content Group UK Ltd.
Pitfield, Milton Keynes, MK11 3LW, UK
UKHW022137240226
468380UK00018B/351